IT TAKES A THIEF

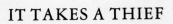

Cover: *The Beggar's Opera* by William Hogarth (detail)
Courtesy of the Tate Gallery

The true Effegies *of*

JONATHAN WILD.

In the Condemned Hold, Newgate. Probably based on a sketch from life

IT TAKES A THIEF

The Life and Times of Jonathan Wild

GERALD HOWSON

NEW PREFACE BY ANTHONY POWELL

THE CRESSET LIBRARY

London   Melbourne   Sydney   Auckland   Johannesburg

The Cresset Library

An imprint of Century Hutchinson Ltd

62–65 Chandos Place, London WC2N 4NW

Century Hutchinson Australia Pty Ltd
PO Box 496, 16–22 Church Street, Hawthorn,
Victoria 3122, Australia

Century Hutchinson New Zealand Ltd
PO Box 40–086, Glenfield, Auckland 10,
New Zealand

Century Hutchinson South Africa (Pty) Ltd
PO Box 337, Bergvlei 2012, South Africa

First published 1970 by Hutchinson as *Thief-Taker General*
This edition first published 1987
© Gerald Howson 1970, 1987
Preface © Anthony Powell

Made and printed in Great Britain by
Richard Clay Ltd, Bungay, Suffolk

British Library Cataloguing in Publication Data

Howson, Gerald
    [Thief-taker general]: It takes a thief: the
    life and times of Jonathan Wild.
    1. Wild, Jonathan   2. Crime and criminals—
    Great Britain—Biography
    I. [Thief-taker general]   II. Title
    364.1′092′4   HV6248.W48

ISBN 0 09 170861 3

To Vera

Contents

viii

Illustrations

Preface to the Cresset Library edition*

In spite of propaganda to the contrary, some of it rather half-baked, a close examination displays professional criminals – one would be inclined to include in that category professional traitors like Maclean or Philby – as neither very pleasant people, nor, in themselves, even particularly interesting. This does not mean that their actions may not have interesting repercussions.

It is one of the many merits of Gerald Howson's *It Takes a Thief* that he faces this fact squarely. 'Wild had no sensitivity', he writes, 'probably little creative imagination and, morally, was an oaf.' He possessed, on the other hand, ingenuity, cunning, resource, energy, and an undoubted taste for playing a double game. In fact Mr Howson shows that there is good reason to suppose Wild gave the language the useful phrase to 'double-cross'.

Starting in a modest way as a young buckle-maker from Wolverhampton, who became a ponce, then ran a brothel, Jonathan Wild (1683–1725) worked his way up to be not only an immensely successful racketeer, but also one of the best known public figures of his time. He did this by means that had been used for centuries – false witness, blackmail, protection, receiving – but brought to these methods improvements of his own, the most notable being his refusal to handle stolen goods himself.

---

* First published in the *Daily Telegraph*.

In the eighteenth century there were no regular police. At the same time, the Law was tough. It may come as a surprise to some, for example, that in 1721 a woman was burnt alive for coining. Thieves were hanged for stealing a small sum, but the penalty varied according to the circumstances in which the theft took place, so that the operation of the Law (administered in dog Latin, even doggier French) was open to much manipulation.

Wild became assistant to the Under-City-Marshal, a thoroughly disreputable person called Charles Hitchen. This was not in fact an official post, though Wild behaved as if it were, carrying a silver baton, and making arrests as and when it suited him. Hitchen, incidentally, was homosexual, and the book contains a lively account of an eighteenth-century homosexual brothel.

Mr Howson, whose research has been colossal, goes to the original documents, so that instead of having a lot of second-hand opinions, of little or no interest, so familiar in books about persons like Jonathan Wild, we are supplied with the real stuff; and fascinating it is. Much of Wild's labours were devoted to returning stolen goods to their owners for a price never less than half their value – a comparison can be made with modern art theft – then arranging for the execution of the thieves when they became idle or awkward.

For supplying evidence that led to an execution the informer got £40. The value of money in the past is always hard to compute and Mr Howson's workable but rough-and-ready system of multiplying by 20 can lead to apparent anomalies. At the same time it is on record, even if ironically, that a parson could be 'passing rich on forty pounds a year', so that it may be seen that informing could be a remunerative industry.

However, the most interesting aspect of Wild is certainly the manner in which he took hold of the imagination of contemporary writers. To supply a subject to Defoe, Fielding and Gay is not given to every criminal. The Fielding connection with the original is tenuous; 'The Beggar's Opera', on the other hand, very close to the mark.

Indeed, to re-read 'The Beggar's Opera' after Mr Howson's book is not only to appreciate the extraordinary brilliance of Gay's work, but also to learn a lesson about the transmutation of life into art. That is to say Gay deals (literally) lock, stock and barrel with the material of Jonathan Wild's life: the thieving, receiving, murdering, executing – and above all, the informing.

Gay is absolutely true to life. He is witty, satirical, tender, moving – but he is never *sentimental*. The love affair with Polly momentarily out of the way, Macheath disports himself with tarts, who immediately betray him, and quarrel about the reward in high-flown language. Lucy asks nothing better than to poison her rival; Peachum and Lockit love their daughters in their own manner, but do not wish to see them united – above all, not married – to friends of the family so precariously placed in the world of crime as highwaymen.

In comparison with this, one can well imagine what sickly stuff would be dished out in a musical about, say, the 'Train Robbers', Kray brothers or 'Torture Gang'. Indeed, in a recent revival of 'The Beggar's Opera', although gangsters' and prostitutes' choruses were convincing, some of the humour of personal relationships was lost in a present day inability to understand the amusement inherent in formal speech, and – what Gay so much appreciates – the enormous banality of the criminal mind. It was Wild's highest ambition to become a Freeman of the City of London, and he was genuinely surprised when he was himself arrested.

Mr Howson's careful tracing of the careers of minor characters suggests a large, but not boundless, criminal world. The related picture is valuable. The mystery remains about what happened to the very considerable fortune piled up by Jonathan Wild.

Anthony Powell

Acknowledgements

To the Right Hon. the Earl of Dartmouth, for permission to use the three letters by Jonathan Wild among the Dartmouth Papers in Staffordshire County Records Office, and to the County Records Office for supplying copies of the letters.

To Mr. P. E. Jones, O.B.E., Assistant Keeper of Records at the City of London Guildhall, and his Deputy, Miss Betty Masters. Their help has been invaluable and their unfailing courtesy transformed a most difficult task of research into a pleasure.

To Mr. James Howgego, Assistant Librarian in charge of maps and prints at the Guildhall Library, for the great trouble he has often gone to in hunting out rare prints, and for allowing me, without reservation, to draw on his enormous knowledge of old London topography.

To Miss E. D. Mercer, late Deputy Head Archivist at the Middlesex Records Office; to Miss P. S. King, Senior Assistant Archivist, for her help in clarifying intricacies of the eighteenth-century Sessions Records; to Mrs. Susan Avery and Miss Anne Crawford for their great patience in helping to decipher and translate some of the hardly legible documents.

To Miss Jessie Dobson, B.A., M.Sc., Recorder of the Hunterian Museum of the Royal College of Surgeons of England, for allowing me to quote from her pamphlet on Jonathan Wild, and to Mr. Eustace Cornelius, Sub-Librarian at the Royal College of Surgeons, for his help in research.

To Mr. L. C. Hector of the Public Records Office, for helping me in my research into eighteenth-century ink-erasers and forgery techniques. To Michael Corkery, Barrister and A.D.P.P., for explaining to me, a novice, the elements of our judicial system. To Peter Fryer, who kindly allowed me to use his card index of tracts, etc. To Professor Robert Halsband, Professor A. V. Judges Mr. Eric Partridge, Mr. Peter Quennell, and Navin Sullivan for answering my queries and giving encouragement and advice.

To the Staffs of the Print Room and Reading Room at the British Museum, the Guildhall Library and the London Library.

Finally, to Donald Rumbelow, for help so frequent that it is best acknowledged in the text—but especially for allowing me to draw on his researches into the history of the City of London Police, and for helping to establish the date of Wild's petition for the freedom of London.

Dating

Until September 1752 the legal year began on 25 March ('Lady Day'), although in general usage it began on 1 January. Thus a reader who may wish to look up the original documents of a trial held on, say, 19 January 1719 will find them under 19 January 1718, or '1718/19', in the Sessions Records and Sessions Papers.

City of London Records were dated by 'Mayoral Month', but these have likewise been converted into conventional dating.

Acts of Parliament and some legal records were dated by 'Regal Year'. Thus an Act entitled '*4 George I c. 11*' means it was passed on the 4th year of George I, and was the 11th Chapter of the Statutes of that year. George I's year began on 1 August and ended on 31 July, which means, since he ascended the throne in 1714, that the Act was passed between 1 August 1717 and 31 July 1718.

By the eighteenth century all the countries of Europe except Britain and Russia had converted from the Julian ('Old Style') to the Gregorian ('New Style') Calender, originally introduced in 1582 by Pope Gregory XIII. The New Style Calender, however, was in advance of the Old Style by 11 days, and when it was adopted in England in 1752, these 11 days were suppressed and Wednesday 2 September was followed by Thursday 14 September. Although many historians do so nowadays, I have *not* converted to New Style, for the subtraction of 11 days from every date in this book would needlessly complicate the task of the reader wishing to refer to the original sources.

'And it is certain, that the greatest Part of his dark Proceedings wou'd still have continu'd a Secret to the World, had it not been, that in his gay Hours, when his Heart was open, he took Pleasure in recounting his past Rogueries, and with a great Deal of Humour, bragg'd of his biting the World; often hinting, not without Vanity, at the poor Understandings of the greatest Part of Mankind, and his own superior Cunning.

And indeed, when we consider that it is not a Man's Grandeur, or high Station in the World, but the strange Adventures of his Life, and his Art and Conduct in the Management of Things, which give us a Curiosity of looking into his History—I say, when this is granted, we need make no Apology for collecting these Materials, and offering them to the Publick—for here they will meet with a System of Politicks unknown to *Machiavel*; they will see deeper Stratagems and Plots form'd by a Fellow without Learning or Education, than are to be met with in the Conduct of the greatest Statesmen, who have been at the heads of Governments.

And indeed, when Things are rightly compared, it will be found that he had a more difficult Game to play; for he was to blind the Eyes of the World, to find out Tricks to evade the Penalties of the Law; and on the other Side, to govern a body of People who were Enemies to all Government; and to bring those under Obedience to him, who, at the Hazard of their Lives, acted in Disobedience to the Laws of the Land—This was steering betwixt *Scylla* and *Charybdis*; and if he had not been a very skilful Pilot, he must long since have split upon a Rock, either on one Side, or the other.'

The Life of Jonathan Wild from his Birth to his Death
by 'H. D.', Clerk to Justice R—. 1725

Part I } *Rise to Power*

§ I § *Introduction*

On 15 February 1725, 'the renowned Jonathan Wild' was arrested and committed to Newgate. The news did not cause great surprise, for his reputation had become increasingly tarnished over the previous months by all kinds of unsavoury rumours.

Since about 1712, a great wave of crime had been gathering momentum in southern England, and had reached its climax in the 1720s, its din providing a sort of underworld chorus to the 'South Sea Bubble' and the other social and moral disorders at that time disturbing 'the King's Peace'. Renewed outbreaks of 'Mohocking' (upper-class hooliganism), riots by weavers and apprentices, scandalous rumours of secret 'Hell Fire Clubs', alarming rumours, rather better founded, of treasonable conspiracies and Jacobite invasions, accompanied by numerous arrests, an outbreak of farm-burning and cattle-stealing, culminating in the so-called 'Black Act', which raised the number of capital felonies to over 350 and constant attacks on the mails and stages, all added to the atmosphere of violence and insecurity created by the financial crash. Reports of robberies on the roads round the capital, complained the *London Journal* again and again, were coming in daily, 'nay, almost hourly', and the other newspapers observed that the highwaymen were behaving with a boldness and ferocity unknown before. They shot or hamstrung the horses, beat the passengers, sometimes murdered the coachmen, and on one occasion cut out the tongue of an old pedlar-woman nearby, who had rashly called out to the passengers that she recognized the villains. On another, at ten o'clock at night, two tough high-waymen called Spiggott and Cross had 'robbed a hundred Passengers, whom they took out of several Waggons, and, having bound them, set them all a-row in the Road'. According to the *Daily Journal*, mail robberies alone were costing the government more than £10,000 per annum (perhaps $500,000 in modern money). At night, bands of horsemen had ridden into the streets of the City itself, sometimes holding up three or four coaches in a single night. Gangs of armed robbers on foot (footpads), sometimes twenty strong, were so common that they had come to be accepted as a normal part of the nightly London scene. Every occasion and place where people gathered attracted pickpockets by the hundred. In 1712, Under City-Marshal Hitchen told the Court of Aldermen that he personally knew 2,000 people within the 'Bills of Mortality' (109 parishes covering parts of central and east London) who lived by thieving alone, and by the 1720s the number had almost doubled. In fact, the number of professional thieves in London and Westminster, full-time and part-time, was somewhere between 10 and 12,000. The Metropolis was being plundered wholesale.

The peace officers of the Crown, which is to say about a dozen independent bodies of men who rarely co-operated with and generally obstructed one another, were hopelessly inadequate, and many were deeply involved in crime themselves. As if this were not bad enough, such street lighting as there had been since 1680—convex-glassed lanterns, throwing out 'great Rays of Light', invented and financed by Edward Hemming and subsidized by a tax—had now fallen into disuse since Hemming lost his patent in 1717. Newspapers complained that while the streets were in almost total darkness, especially in summertime, the lighting tax had been increased. We were being robbed, as it were, both from above and below. No man's house was safe unless it was fortified by palisades and redoubts and defended by a small private army of servants; and no man might dine out unless armed to the teeth with swords, pistols, muskets and blunderbusses, as though he were 'going into a desperate Battle' in which, moreover, he must be prepared to fight against overwhelming odds.

Therefore, when Jonathan Wild (a native of Wolverhampton

who had settled in London *c.* 1709, only to be thrown immediately into a debtors' prison) began to provide a service by which those who had lost their possessions, through theft or even through mere carelessness, could get them back again for a fee at least appreciably less than their value, and when as an adjunct to this he showed himself to be an extremely skilful and courageous hunter-down of criminals and breaker of gangs, it is hardly surprising that the public first welcomed and then enthusiastically applauded him. Unlike the constables and such, Wild's men could move freely all over the country. He had agents in the ports and county towns of southern England, and they had arrested wanted men in places as far apart as Bristol, Portsmouth, Oxford, Gravesend, Maidstone and Dover. Between 1721 and 1723, he destroyed the four large gangs in London that comprised the hard core of the underworld, and for the next two years highwaymen gave the capital a wide berth—to the extent that there is not a single case in the records of a highwayman's being convicted or hanged at Tyburn from 1723 to Wild's death in 1725. The culmination of these events, which had involved him in countless affrays, street fights and riots, was reached when he captured the famous Jack Sheppard. He was now the first man in the kingdom to whom the public turned in all matters concerning the prevention of crime, and although he had no official status, the Privy Council had consulted him over the best means to combat the dangerous increase of lawlessness. His 'Office for the Recovery of Lost and Stolen Property' was by now almost a national institution—the 'Scotland Yard' of its day—and, as a matter of course, newspapers such as the *Universal Journal* put '*From Jonathan Wild's at the Old Bailey*' as a heading to their weekly crime reports.

However, during the Jack Sheppard affair, one of the gang, a poor rogue called 'Blueskin' Blake, seized Wild in front of the Sessions House and tried to cut his throat. The wound was not mortal, and Wild was patched up and sent home to rest for a few weeks. Blake, however, showed no remorse for his attempt at murder; on the contrary, with 'many bloody Oaths', he regretted only his failure, for he had intended to cut Wild's head off and throw it amongst the rabble in Sessions House Yard. Although the incident was not widely commented on at the time, people began to wonder if Blake, rogue though he was, might not have had some justification; and when a few days later Jack Sheppard, taking advantage of Wild's absence, made his last sensational escape from Newgate (certainly one of the most notable escapes in history) and became a national hero, the public quite suddenly turned against Wild. The celebrated catcher of thieves and master policeman became instead the incarnation of brutal, unjust, authority. Most accounts of Wild's life put this as the beginning of his fall, though it is my own belief that things began to go wrong for him about two years earlier. However, after a series of extremely complicated manœuvres and intrigues, which I shall set out in their proper place, Wild was arrested in February and brought to trial at last in May 1725, where he was condemned to death for taking £10 as a reward for returning some stolen lace to the owner. He himself had instigated the theft. During his imprisonment, articles appeared in the press complaining that for many years now it had seemed as if no one could be acquitted, condemned, reprieved or hanged, except at the pleasure of 'Honest Jonathan'.

Further disclosures revealed that far from combating the crime wave, Wild had been the principal driving force behind it; that he was himself virtual 'Regulator' of the underworld he was supposed to be suppressing; that the Lost Property Office was simply a clearing house for the huge quantities of stolen goods his own gangs (each allocated an area of London) supplied to him; and that the hundreds of criminals he had 'brought to Justice' were casualties, or 'fall guys' to use the best expression, in a dark and hidden gang-warfare waged against enemies, rivals, and rebels. He was besides involved in every kind of crime—coining, forging, smuggling, protection rackets on brothels and gambling houses and even, it would seem, a fairly sophisticated form of that 'Rachmanism' which caused such an outcry in London in 1963, as though it were something new. The head of the 'police' was the same man as the head of the underworld—in any novel such a situation would be considered far-fetched. As a fact of everyday reality, it was monstrous and absurd. The satirists, of course, were delighted. Jonathan Swift called Jonathan Wild 'the Great', and the Tory opposition journalist Nathaniel Mist hailed Wild as a 'great Genius' and model for future statesmen, especially Whig statesmen. It happened that that very week, the Lord Chancellor, Thomas Earl of Macclesfield, was on trial at Westminster Hall for taking bribes and embezzling public money to the value of £100,000 (about $5,000,000 in modern money), and the chance to point out the similarities between statesman and thief was too good to miss. While most of the pamphleteers enjoyed the comic, even farcical, side to Wild's story, a few, notably Defoe, dwelt on its moral and tragic side. London was an inferno and Jonathan its Prince of Darkness, who had ruthlessly sacrificed hundreds of lives, many of them innocent and by him brought up to crime from childhood, for mere worldly ambition. Nevertheless, all were agreed upon its novelty, for here was a man who had organized crime to a degree never dreamed of before, raised it, indeed, almost to the level of a national danger. 'The Life of Jonathan Wild', wrote Defoe, 'is a perfectly new Scene.'

This brings us to one of the many puzzles concerning Wild. It is possible to describe him as the 'first' modern gangster, a shadowy precursor of Al Capone, whose world, London in the 1720s, was not unlike Chicago in the 1920s. If the two were to be weighed by the cost in misery and human lives alone, then Wild's career was the greater disaster. Conversely, he can be regarded as the 'first' modern policeman, foreshadowing Vidocq* by a century; for the Bow Street Runners were modelled to some extent on his posse of thief-takers, and so it would not be facetious to call him the 'Father of the C.I.D.' But 'first' is a word belonging to journalism rather than history. Many criminal practices we might believe to be modern, such as the protection racket, the systematic use of blackmail, suborned witnesses, intimidated juries and corrupt law-officers, the supporting of criminals in prison, or the hiring of specialists for specialized robberies, are in fact very old and were well known to Wild and his circle. Jonathan had many precursors who did everything he did. Several of them, who were the foremost rivals he had to deal with when he began his career, were not even outsiders like himself, but respectable officials of the City of London, including a Head Turnkey of Newgate, a City Marshal and even, perhaps, a City Recorder. His contemporaries knew this, and Defoe had had bitter experience of it. Why, then, were they so

---

* François Vidocq (1775–1857). French army officer and criminal who was employed under Napoleon as a police spy. After a term in prison to gain greater knowledge of the underworld, he was made chief of the detective department of the Paris police, with a group of ex-convicts under his command. He was dismissed after staging a daring robbery and arresting the thieves, whom he had led, himself, and died in poverty. Several books have been written about him, and he has been described as the first modern detective and prototype of all those who act on both sides of the law.

astonished when the truth about Wild was revealed, and why, for that matter, were no reforms consequently brought in to ensure that the catastrophe could not be repeated?

So far, authentic biographical information about Wild has been hard to come by—almost impossible for the general reader. *Jonathan Wild, Prince of Robbers*, by Frederick J. Lyons, has long been out of print, and the best modern accounts are even older.[1] The fullest biography is still that in the 1735 edition of *Select Trials at the Old Bailey*, but it has never been reprinted in an unabridged form since. It is also a very rare book. Whatever their virtues, none of these have much to say about the structure and pattern of London's criminal underworld when Wild arrived on the scene, and unless we have some idea of this, his history seems to be little more than a series of anecdotes and intrigues. Certainly, the kind of questions asked above can hardly be touched on.

In this new biography of Wild, which is intended only as a general introduction to a large and complicated subject—the origins of modern organized gangsterdom—I have tried, as far as it is possible, to fill in the gaps left by previous accounts, especially those gaps concerning his early years in a debtors' prison, the detailed means he used to gain power and break up the gangs, his relations with the authorities and, above all, the true reasons for his fall. My sources have been the original parchment *Sessions Records*, which are written mostly in a frightful and very abbreviated dog Latin, repertories of the Court of Aldermen and other such records, the printed monthly *Sessions Papers* (trial reports), *Select Trials* (itself a reprint of the *Sessions Papers* in book form, with some added biographies of the criminals), the daily and weekly newspapers, and, of course, a multitude of pamphlets, tracts, 'Dying Speeches', ballads and broadsheets. As these materials will be unfamiliar to most readers, who should be warned what is and is not trustworthy, I have listed them fully, with descriptive notes, in the Bibliography—especially the pamphlets, for the list contains some new items unfamiliar, I think, even to scholars. Again, as many of these sources are remarkable in themselves, and illuminate so vividly almost every corner of the social life of that turbulent age, it is my hope to publish a wide selection from them in a future volume—the evidence, as it were, for my case.

The recent trials of Richardson and the Kray brothers have

brought the subject of organized crime in England very much back into the news. The gangs of the former are said to have controlled south London, and those of the latter, north London, while the affair has been described as the first major confrontation between the new 'big time' gangsters and the C.I.D. It is tempting to wonder if many of the parties involved are aware that they have a common forefather in Wild, whose gangs controlled north London *and* south London, and virtually the 'police' as well.

₴ II ₴ *In the Compter*

In the days of Charles II, Wolverhampton was the second market town (*pop. c.* 6,000) of Staffordshire, so favoured because the people had supported the Royalists in the Civil War. Its thatched and beamed houses were clustered on the sides of a hill, round the ancient and towering church of St. Peter. This high position made the air healthy, but occasional 'fumes' from neighbouring coal-mines, and a thriving colony of iron-workers and locksmiths (said to be the best in England) were early portents of the great industrialization that was to come, and of the 'Black Country' that was to darken the landscape to the south and east during the next century.

Jonathan Wild, the first of five children, was baptized at St. Peter's on 6 May 1683, though we do not know when he was born. His father, John Wyld, or 'Wyldy', was a joiner and his mother sold fruit and herbs in the market.

Several pamphlets written at the time of his hanging said that he was lame or in some way deformed. Most of these tales were intended to raise a laugh at the expense of their subject. It was hinted that his deformity was the result of a misapplied salivation (a dangerous and painful mercury-ointment cure for syphilis) or that it was merely the outward sign of his evil nature. Others said he had been born so. One, writing under the name of '*H. D., Clerk to Justice* R—', said that Wild could put his hip out of joint at will, and so was able not only to evade the Duke of Marlborough's recruiting officers, who at that time were drumming up 'volunteers' for the war against France, but to travel successfully for a time with a quack doctress who performed 'miraculous' cures on him. Such an ability is extremely rare and depends on the shape and depth of the hip-socket. There is nothing abnormal about the socket of the skeleton that is reputed to be Wild's in the Royal College of Surgeons, and so the story may well have been made up by 'H.D.' as a picaresque amusement, or by Wild himself to cover up the true nature of his misfortune. However, it was also said that in his youth Wild liked to spend his time with the groups of travelling actors who visited the town. It is possible that he learned from them how to limp in a convincing manner, and that later he elaborated the story with each retelling.

He was educated at the Free School in St. John's Lane, which has been rebuilt twice since then and is now called The Grammar School. There he acquired a fair skill at handwriting (though not, to judge by some letters that have survived, at grammar or spelling), and at the age of fifteen was apprenticed to a bucklemaker. He served out his apprenticeship, entered the trade about 1700, and not long after married—one pamphlet actually giving the date as 10 April 1701. By this wife he had a son.

So much is fairly certain, though some pamphleteers said that he had several children by her, and one author, Captain Alexander Smith, insists that Wild was not a buckle-maker but a trunkmaker. In the single pamphlet Wild wrote, or dictated, he referred to himself throughout as a buckle-maker, and I think we can leave it at that. A careful search of all the parish records of Wolverhampton and other towns might reveal more children, but certainty would be difficult because 'Wild' was quite a common name in Staffordshire at that time.

Wild had two younger brothers, John and Andrew, and two sisters. John became a bailiff and was made Town Crier of Wolverhampton, but disgraced himself during the riots of the 1715 rebellion, when it seemed that the Pretender was likely to arrive in the town. Apparently, he was the ringleader mentioned in the town records who climbed on to the roof of the Presbyterian Meeting House in St. John's Street (near the Free School), toasted 'James III!' and with a shout of 'Fall on, boys!' incited the mob to wreck the building. Under his leadership, they went on to West Bromwich and pulled down the Meeting House there as well. A contemporary source describes this 'Mob' as being a 'Gang of ragamuffins, pickpockets and Gaol-birds' though how so small a town could have contained so many 'Gaol-birds' is hard to see. For his misdemeanours, John was whipped at the cart's tail twice round Stafford Town Hall and imprisoned for two years. It is curious that the carpenter contracted to repair the chapels was another John Wyld, aged forty-four.[1] John died in 1720, within a month of the family's mother. Andrew became a small-time criminal, working in the shadow of his famous brother, As for the sisters, one married a buckle-maker and the other a comb-maker. They both lived out their lives in Staffordshire; though again, we cannot be sure that some of the 'Mary Wilds' and others who appear in the Sessions Records, and lived in the Old Bailey, were not relations who had followed Jonathan to London after his success.

Because of the complete lack of information about these early years, the first biographers filled the gaps with comic stories they either made up or borrowed from old chapbooks. Leaving these aside, we are still left with a credible story that Wild first travelled to London in 1704 as servant to a lawyer called Councillor Daniel, and that he absconded or was dismissed for some ill-conduct. After this he became a 'setter' to some bailiffs attached to the notorious Marshalsea Court, which stood not, as might be supposed, near the Marshalsea Prison in Southwark, but in Clifford's Inn, Fleet St. A 'setter's' job was to hunt out debtors so that his employers could arrest them, and was about as sordid and joylessly brutal as any that could be imagined. The bailiffs themselves usually had to borrow the money with which they had obtained their positions in the first place (hence their nickname of 'Bound' or 'Bum' Bailiffs) and were compelled to resort to every means—including armed robbery, murder, blackmail and the arresting of innocent people for wholly fictitious debts—if they were not to find themselves in goal with their victims. In the bailiffs' private prisons, called 'Spunging Houses', debtors were supposed to be kept overnight before going to court, so that they might have a last chance to raise some money. This interim period was often extended to a week or more, during which the unfortunate debtor was subjected to a primitive but effective form of softening up—that is, he was treated kindly one day and chained in a dark cellar and beaten the next. This

gave the bailiffs a chance to bleed him of any money he might
have hidden somewhere, and to think up a pretext for having him
sent to prison. It was common for debtors to be committed to
gaol from the Marshalsea Court for owing a farthing candle or a
pint of ale.[2] 'H.D.' remarks with heavy sarcasm that Wild possessed in abundance the qualifications for this 'Post of Honour',
namely 'Vigilance, Sagacity, Patience, Quicksightedness, *cum
multis aliis . . .*'

There is a story that, before leaving home, Wild borrowed a
horse, which he sold in London. When, after finding his new
employment both less profitable and more dangerous than
buckle-making, he returned to Wolverhampton, the owner of
the horse allowed him to pay back the value by instalments.
However, after the second instalment, Wild refused to pay any
more because, he said, by refusing to pay he broke the 'articles of
his Contract', and that articles once broken could not be said to
subsist, and so were no longer binding.

After another four years or so, he became convinced of the
futility of his humdrum life and set off for London once more,
leaving his wife and child to fend for themselves as best they
could. The next positive fact is that shortly after his arrival he
himself became a debtor and was thrown into Wood Street
Compter.

There exist some documents which tell exactly what happened,
and refute as well the different legends that surround this affair.
Wild himself, for instance, said that he spent 'above four Years'
in the Compter, and that it was only this misadventure which
first brought him into bad company. Another is that he took as
mistress a notorious 'buttock and file' (pickpocket-whore) called
Mary Milliner, wife of a Thames waterman, who initiated him
into the secrets of the underworld, and that by their combined
resourcefulness they bought their freedom.

In 1712, an Act of Parliament (*10 Anne c. 29*) was passed for
'The Relief of Insolvent Debtors', under which all prisoners,
who as a result of their imprisonment had now become 'utterly
disabled to satisfie and pay all their several Debts', should be
granted their freedom, so that they should not become 'burthon-
some to the Nation'. Each prisoner applying for this pardon had
to draw up schedules of his assets and remaining debts, and
creditors would have to be content with such payments as could
be made from the assets. A notice of every pardon was to be

published in the *London Gazette*. Finally, all documents were to be kept by the Clerk of the Peace (for the Act applied to London prisons only). Fortunately, they were never destroyed, and can still be examined in the Guildhall Records Office;[3] indeed, the string round them was so ancient and powdery when I first saw them, that I wondered if it had ever been undone since 1712.

The first action brought against Wild was on 11 March 1710. It was by William Smith of 'Blew ancor alley White Crosse Street', to whom Wild owed £2 (the Schedule says 39s., but 1s. was deducted by the court). Wild was arrested on 13 March on the actions of Smith and four others, to each of whom he owed £2, except one Robert Pearson, to whom he owed £4 (about $200 in modern money). Only one of these people was a woman, Eleanor Roberts, of Goswell Street, and unless her name turns up elsewhere, it is impossible to say whether or not she was the 'female Quack'.* However, Smith's is the interesting name, for he was a burglar who often appears on the Old Bailey records from 1710–20. Wild's charm and power to inspire confidence—in short, his personal magnetism—must have been as remarkable as contemporary reports suggest, for in 1711 or 1712 he persuaded Smith to lend him a further £3 ($150) and at the same time not to bring a second action of debt against him. Yet in 1719, when Wild was at the height of his prosperity and fame, he arrested Smith as an accessory to a petty burglary and had him transported for seven years. In 1720, Smith escaped back to London, where Wild found him and again 'brought him to Justice'. This time, Smith was transported for fourteen years, but died on the journey. The fact, however, that Wild knew Smith well enough in 1710 to borrow £2 shows that he was in bad company before he went to the Compter, and that his later picture of himself as an innocent led astray by fellow-prisoners was pure rubbish.

The Compters, or 'Counters', were two ancient prisons where people in the City of London were held to account for their debts. The older, in Poultry at the east end of Cheapside, had been there since 'time immemorial'. The second had been transferred from Bread Street in 1555. The building shown in the

---

* F. J. Lyons says that Wild and the doctress bilked the people of Warwick of £150. In London she became so jealous of the attentions he paid to other women that she took out an action of debt against him—a common revenge in those days and it was this that brought him to the Compter. The story comes from 'H.D.'.

print (*plate 1*) was put up in 1670 after the Great Fire. The front opened on to Clement's Court, a narrow alley leading off the east side of Wood Street, which runs between Cheapside and London Wall. The Compter was finally closed in 1791 (when the engraving was made) and the prisoners moved to Giltspur Street. The site is commemorated now by a concrete block of offices called 'Compter House' at the southern end of Wood Street, built after the area was burned down for the second time in its history during World War II. Behind Compter House is Mitre Court, beneath which are the three remaining dungeons of the old prison. They are used as wine cellars by the firm of Norton & Langridge, and the proprietors will hospitably show round anyone who wants to see them.

Like all prisons then, the Compter was divided into 'Sides' (sometimes called 'Wards') of varying conditions of discomfort, and a prisoner was put into the Side he could afford. The best was the 'Master's Side', where a prisoner had his own cell, with bed, chair, table and any possessions he could bring with him. Then, in descending order, came the 'Knight's Ward', 'Twopenny Ward', and 'Common Ward'. At the bottom, as a part of the Common Ward, was the 'Hole'.

Wood Street Compter was used also as a general prison. Most people arrested in the City were taken there for a night or two before going to Newgate, and there was a section reserved for 'Rats'—that is, drunks, street-walkers, vagabonds, stray children and other nuisances picked up in the night by the Marshals or the Watch. The gaolers were called 'Javelin Men'. They acted in addition as a 'private' police force under the Sheriff, who, as the officer responsible for seeing that all court sentences were actually carried out, was in charge not only of debt-collecting and the giving of punishments, but of all London prisons except Newgate. Thus the javelin men marched as an armed escort, along with the Marshals, Constables and Sergeants' Yeomen, to the Tyburn processions on execution days.

All accounts of prisons at this period speak of 'garnish'. This was the money gaolers demanded of new prisoners on arrival, if the prisoners wished to be treated with a minimum of humanity. A certain amount of 'garnish', under the name of 'Fees', was perfectly legal, and the rates were published from time to time on official broadsheets called *Fees of the Sheriff's Court*. One of these, dated 1709, shows that a prisoner entering the Master Side had to pay 22s. 6d. (or about $50 in modern money) and 13s. 6d. for the Common Ward.[4] Some idea of what this sum must have meant to the average poor prisoner can be gained from Henry Fielding's remark of twenty-five years later. As a magistrate, he had to clear out a house full of labourers and their families, mostly Irish immigrants. When he searched the thirty inhabitants of this house as they spilled into the street, he found that all the money between them came to one shilling.

It must be understood that these fees were the absolute legal minimum and bore no relation to what was actually extorted. The keepers and turnkeys charged what they could get. At every stage up or down the social scale you had to pay, and life in the Compter, unless you were very tough and cunning, was a nightmarish downward progress in which you watched yourself descend helplessly towards the dreaded 'Hole'. Worse still, you would find that all the older prisoners were allied with the turn-keys against you, and would demand 'garnish' for themselves. New arrivals who refused to give gratuities were tossed in blankets, thrown into the cesspits, or simply refused food or warmth until they changed their minds. According to a House of Commons Report,[5] this process was called 'Making the Black Dog Walk'.

In theory, prisoners were supposed to follow their trades, though how any could have done so is difficult to see. As an alternative, they were sometimes allowed out in chains to beg. However, the Repertories of the Court of Aldermen of 16 June 1724 show that the Aldermen felt that the sight of prisoners begging with boxes round the gaols and in the passages nearby was 'a Great Dishonour to the Good Government of this City' and that last recourse was forbidden. To obtain their freedom, prisoners had not only to pay their entrance fees, clear their debts and somehow keep alive, but to pay their discharge fees as well. These, like the entrance fees, were stipulated but in practice had no limit. Some prisoners were kept in the Compters for years simply because these could not be found, for a keeper would be tempted to hang on to a prisoner for as long as he appeared to be a source of income, and to raise the necessary discharge fees at every petition for release. Thus it was not uncommon for prisoners to remain there until they died, although there are recorded cases of a few who were permitted the desperate remedy of selling themselves into slavery on the plantations.

When he was arrested and taken to the Compter, Wild was

apparently without resources. 'Here', says Defoe, 'he suffered great hardship, having no Friends to help him out, or Money to maintain him within, so that he was on the Common-side, and far'd as other People in those Circumstances do fare, that is to say, very hard.' It is not known if one of the three existing cellars was once the 'Hole', but it is hard to see how it could have been worse than any of them. The curved brick roof of the largest is about 9 ft. high. Light and air come through an 18-in. funnel, like an upside-down drain, at the far end. The 'Hole' was said to be 33 ft. long, 15 ft. wide and 12 ft. high; otherwise it was probably identical to the existing cellar. The beds were shelves built up the wall very closely one above the other, each holding three or four prisoners, like those at Belsen and Auschwitz. Here about seventy people lived, men, women and children, dependent entirely on such charity as the gaolers allowed to filter down for their food, crowded together in more filth than would be permitted in any pigsty, in freezing cold and damp, and in total darkness, month after month, year after year. Only an intermittent, faint, grey glow down the funnel proclaimed the march of successive days. We have no figures for the death-rate in this place, for during the House of Commons enquiries into the state of gaols in 1719 and 1728, the Aldermen of the City of London stood on their rights and refused to allow the Parliamentary committees into any of their prisons. However, the 1719 Committee discovered that in the Marshalsea 300 people had died of starvation or gaol-fever in the previous three months alone, out of a total of under 1,500 prisoners. To judge by a return of 1725, the Wood Street Compter held about 400 debtors and an unregistered number of felons and 'Rats'. A proportionate figure of between four and eight deaths a week from these causes would not therefore be unreasonable.

Wild, nevertheless, did not die. On the contrary, he managed to gain the confidence of the gaolers. He must have been willing to undertake jobs which other prisoners looked on as degrading —cleaning refuse from cesspits and cells, running errands for wealthier prisoners—or perhaps the experience he had gained as a bailiffs' setter enabled him to work various semi-legal tricks and 'fiddles' which made him indispensable as an entrepreneur. Perhaps as well his acquaintance with criminals enabled him to mix more freely with the felons than other debtors could do, or would even wish to do. The turnkeys were naturally more afraid of the felons than of the debtors, many of whom were quiet and otherwise respectable citizens, and so they treated them with more respect and less brutality. The documents show, at any rate, that Wild was able to pay off three debts, but that he incurred eight more, and that he was yet secure enough to lend £33 to four other people, besides 'severall others wch I cant remember being Small'. One of these was a man called Obadiah Lemon, to whom he lent £10 (or $500 in modern money). Lemon was a well-known thief who specialized in 'The Rattling Lay', or stealing from coaches, and he remained a close associate of Wild's for several years, acting not only as a skilled thief but as an informer. When finally some of the gang turned on him and impeached him, he disappeared, perhaps under Wild's protection.

Wild extricated himself from the 'Hole' and even from the Common Side, and sometime in 1712 was given the 'Liberty of the Gate'—that is, he was made a senior trusty whose job was to check in prisoners ('Rats' and such) brought during the night and to take them to the house of the nearest magistrate next morning. The Gate was used as a convivial meeting-place by whores, strollers and other 'night characters', and it was here no doubt that he met Mary Milliner.

F. J. Lyons devotes several pages to their relationship, and describes how this 'beautiful' but amoral girl astonished Wild by her knowledge of the underworld and made him feel that in comparison to her experience in ways of getting money from its rightful owners he was but a child. The fact is that we know nothing of her at all. Defoe took the trouble to consult the Compter books and found that she 'was such a well-known Jade that she was never reckoned to be a Prisoner there . . .' While it is perhaps not surprising then that I have found no mention of her in the surviving Compter records, it is more curious that I have never found her name on any other Sessions records either. I have, however, come across a 'Mary Molyneux' from time to time. On the King's Bench Rolls for the Easter Term of 1719, for instance, she was indicted of receiving stolen goods and fined (though she should have been transported or even hanged). Defoe and *Select Trials* both say that Mary Milliner and Wild remained on good terms until the end, and occasionally did business together (like Peachum and Diana Trapes in *The Beggar's Opera*). 'Milliner', therefore, could have been a cockney mispronunciation of 'Molyneux', and the fact that Mary Molyneux never got into serious trouble could then be explained by Wild's protection.

Despite his position of privilege and relative comfort, Wild could have remained in the Compter for the rest of his life, for if his assets came to £33, his debts now stood at £61 6s. od. (or about $3,200), plus the discharge fees. In September 1712, however, the Act for the relief of debtors became law and Wild, along with most of his fellow-prisoners, applied for his 'Deliverance'. The schedules were drawn up (see *Appendix I*), notice of his petition was published in the *London Gazette* on 4–8 November 1712, and he was told to await the December Sessions of the Peace. Therefore, any impression he later gave of having obtained his freedom by energy and cunning was, to say the least, untruthful.

Meanwhile, two names occur on the records of this period that are of considerable importance in Wild's career. The first is William Field. In October 1712, the Court of Aldermen was enquiring into the disgraceful activities of their new Under City-Marshal, Charles Hitchen, who was trying to organize wholesale dealing in stolen goods as a side-line to his duties as a senior police officer. Two young thieves from his retinue (he was a homosexual), Christopher Plummer and William Field, were committed to the Compter in September on suspicion of picking pockets. On 8 October they were taken to the Guildhall, where they gave informations against their employer Hitchen, and were granted their freedom in exchange. Wild would almost certainly have been the man who escorted them to the Guildhall; but even if this were not so, there can be no doubt that this was when they became acquainted. Field ('Filch' in *The Beggar's Opera*) was to gain immortality of a sort as the man who betrayed Jack Sheppard to Wild and so appear as a villain in every story and play that has been written about Jack Sheppard from 1724 until today. In fact, as we shall see, he impeached in turn every one who was connected with him, hanging in the course of his remarkable career between fifteen and thirty people.

The second is Elizabeth Harris. She appears as one of Wild's creditors, for he owed her a £12 bond. The debt was presumably among those he did not have to pay, for by 1720 the enmity between them would seem to have been implacable. She must have known Field too, for in that year he turned evidence against her husband (whom Wild had arrested) and, as the expression went, 'hanged him'. The following year she tried to avenge her husband by implicating Field and others in a series of burglaries, and only failed when Wild appeared in court and defended him. The case has a more than fleeting interest, however, because one of the characters in the drama being enacted behind the scenes was Moll King, who, I strongly believe, was the chief model for Defoe's *Moll Flanders*.

It is odd that of the documents concerning Wild's release, the most important, his Discharge Sheet, is missing. Indeed, it seems to be the only Discharge Sheet missing from the whole collection. It is important because it would have contained a list of what debts he paid off and what he did not. I cannot help wondering, therefore, if its disappearance is merely accidental (and a coincidence), or if Wild in the days of his prosperity and influence bribed a Clerk of the Peace to return it to him or destroy it. Even if he was legally free of the debts listed on it, it might perhaps have been produced as evidence of malicious intent when it was revealed that Wild was trying to hang a person who had once lent him money, and that he had never honoured the debt.

Wild attended the Sessions of the Peace at 10 a.m. on 8 December at the Guildhall. The Sessions Book shows that he was 'proved a Prisoner by William Sweetland' and that Hannah Easely summoned the creditors. The documents would seem to show that prisoners were not actually discharged until the 16th. Then, along with a verminous swarm of ragged and starving fellow-debtors, Jonathan Wild was 'delivered' to the streets of London. The first thing he did was to set up house with Mary Milliner (or Molyneux) in a small brothel in Lewkenor's Lane, Covent Garden.

⧚ III ⧚ *'The System'*

It is natural for us now to think of organized crime as belonging to a plush world of penthouses, casinos, sleek cars and expensive women. The slums and squalor where the money is made may be the battlefield but, in fiction at least, they are kept decently in the background, where they can perform the humble duty of adding contrast and pathos to the story. The decidedly unglamorous appearance of Joe Valachi at the Senate investigating committee or of the Kray brothers and their circle at the Old Bailey have done nothing, and will do nothing, to dispel the myth, which after all has grown round a kernel of observed fact, for without it even the best-written thriller would soon become boring. In our present case, however, the opposite is true. The more we strip away from the story its encrustations of legend and exaggeration and the closer we get to the observed facts, the more extraordinary it becomes. Further, it takes place in a world so remote from our experience and so surprising and weird in its details that no romantic heightening is necessary. Of the city Wild knew virtually nothing remains beyond a parcel of street names and an occasional house, church or public building already likely to disappear. The administration, the laws, the police, the character of the underworld itself, have all changed beyond recognition; and without some acquaintance with these Wild's story can hardly be understood even in its general outline.

In this chapter, therefore, I shall try to explain as briefly as possible the system of which Wild was to take such ingenious advantage, seizing his opportunities with both hands; and in the next to enter what has been almost a *terra incognita*—the origins and early history of 'thief-taking' and the status it had acquired by the time Wild emerged from the Compter. His publicity was so successful that it dazzled his contemporaries as well as later generations, to the extent that he became known as the only and original 'thief-taker'. Unique he may have been, but not in the sense that he was an isolated phenomenon. He did not invent the profession he made so peculiarly his own; indeed, he did not 'invent' anything. Yet, when his history is seen in its proper context it becomes more credible, and his skill in penetrating and taking over the criminal establishment of his time appears the more remarkable.

By 1712, the Cities of London and Westminster were completely joined by streets and squares and, together with built-up parts of Middlesex and Surrey (e.g. Clerkenwell, Southwark), the whole was known for convenience as the 'Metropolis'. It extended east to west from Wapping to Bond Street (or St. James's Park), and, north to south, from Moorfields (or Sadler's Wells) to St. George's Fields, Southwark. The population was in the region of 660,000, but this included neighbouring villages such as Chelsea, Kensington, Hampstead, Islington, Bow, Stepney and Camberwell. It was, compared to a modern city, a rural place of cobbled mud-covered streets, with animals and animal scents and noises everywhere. Apart from the forest of church spires, the features most unfamiliar to ourselves would be the thousands upon thousands of painted signs hanging outside not only taverns and inns, but every shop, office or house where business was done, and, in Westminster, the brightness—red, ochre, glistening white—of the new architecture.

Yet if London was a unit geographically, politically and administratively it was not. The Lord Mayor of London, whose power (diminished beyond the city walls) extended as far as Temple Bar, and the High Burgess of Westminster, whose area included Holborn, Soho and Mayfair (then largely pasture ground), had little to do with each other and, as far as they were concerned, ruled separate kingdoms. 'London' was therefore a loose word. Accurately, it meant the City within the walls, and the 'Liberties' immediately surrounding them, and its use to mean the whole Metropolis was still not common. The growth of the Metropolis had been haphazard. Entire villages and hamlets had been swallowed without being cleared and new houses and tenements built round, or on top of, the crumbling cottages and barns. Plague laws had included stipulations against uncontrolled building but in their determination to get rents landlords had evaded the laws by extending their premises underground or by erecting jerry-built sheds in their courtyards. Thus the first 'rookeries', many of which were still standing in the days of Dickens and Mayhew, were created. The situation was at its worst in those anomalous areas immediately outside the City walls called the 'Liberties'. The name referred to the special privileges granted them, which in turn derived from the fact that the 'Liberties' had once contained the sites of monasteries. Some Liberties were exempt from certain taxes, others given a mon- opoly of certain trades; others again forbade entry to the Lord Mayor and yet others, like the 'Rolls' in Chancery Lane, were exempted from having soldiers billeted on them. The confusion was further complicated by the problem of the right of 'Sanc- tuary'. In the Middle Ages, any wanted person who took refuge in a church or other consecrated place was granted 'sanctuary'— that is, he could not be arrested even by the Crown—so long as he stayed there, and this right was protected by an elaborate structure of traditions and laws. After the closure of the mona- steries by Henry VIII, it was argued that the grounds where they had once stood were still consecrated and that the rights of sanctuary could not be taken away. This opinion was supported not only by lawyers, who found the existence of 'sanctuaries' useful in negotiating cases, but also by some monarchs—notably James I. As a result, the City became ringed with numerous little 'bastard Sanctuaries' (indeed there were some inside the City itself) where debtors, refugees, immigrants, adventurers and criminals lived out of reach of the law, and in time the larger places became veritable 'Kasbahs' where constables, marshals and even the militia, dared not enter except in great strength. However, during the seventeenth century they were 'closed' one by one. The climax was reached with a series of riots, murders and executions in 1691 in the famous 'Alsatia' in the district between Fleet Street and the Thames officially called Whitefriars. This was closed in 1697 and by 1712 only one 'bastard Sanctuary' remained, at the 'Mint' in Southwark. Nevertheless, the old sanctuaries continued to be criminal areas: Whitefriars, Shoe and Fetter Lanes, parts of Holborn (especially Saffron Hill), parts of Smithfields and Barbican, Whitechapel, Bankside and, in Westminster, the Savoy, Covent Garden (up to St. Giles) and a warren of tumbledown streets, of which the most famous was Thieving Lane, around Westminster Abbey. Here were concentrated the majority of the paupers who made up nearly a quarter of the population of the Metropolis, besides the poorer artisans, shopkeepers, porters and casual labourers, and a bewildering variety of vagabonds and criminals. The weird cant names of their professions give them a brilliance of colour that has no doubt intensified with the passage of time: Millkens (burglars), Rattling Lay (stealing from coaches), Hook-pole Lay (pulling travellers off horses by means of long poles with hooks attached), Anglers (thieves using rods and fishing-lines), Wild Rogues (thieves using lines to whip hats, etc., from coaches), Badgers (water-thieves and corpse-disposers), Vulcans (picklock experts), Flying the Basket (throwing a boy into the basket of a coach so that he may toss out the bags), Autem Divers (church pickpockets), Knowing Fellows (highwaymen's scouts and spies), Buffers (horse thieves, who killed the horses by means of sharp wires thrust up into the animals' hearts, so that they could be skinned), Rufflers (strong-arm men), Adam Tilers (lookouts), Sneaking Budges (sneak-thieves), Ripping Coves (burglars who broke in by ripping up the roofs), Stags (informers), Abraham Men, Dommerars, Confek Cranks (who pretended madness, dumbness and epilepsy respectively), Faytors (forgers of documents), Kinchin Morts (little girls), Palliards, Tatterdemalions and Clapperdogeons (various kinds of wanderers), to name only a few from the multitude published at the time of Wild's death.

The forces of law and order intended to keep this ungovernable population under control consisted, as I have said, of several assorted bodies of men with no central authority. In earlier times, some central authority had been supplied by the Privy Council, working through the Recorder in the City and the High Burgess in Westminster. By now the Privy Council's activities in this field had shrunk to discussing the 'Dead Warrants' which the City Recorder brought to them after each Old Bailey Sessions. These meetings always took place late at night. The practical policing of the Metropolis was done partly by the Justices of the Peace, using their constables as assistants and servants, partly by the High Constables (whose office was not always clearly defined), partly by the Beadles and the Watch, partly by the King's Messengers and Press Messengers and partly by the City Marshals, besides various bodies of men under the Sheriffs.

The constables, beadles and watch were greatly restricted in their powers of arrest. They could not leave the boundaries of their divisions except by permission of the neighbouring constables. The old story of the watchman who refused to stop a burglar breaking into a house across the street, because that side of the street was in the next ward, may well be based on more than one actual incident. Nevertheless, the watchmen were not all so useless and decrepit as Henry Fielding described them, although his caricature has now been accepted as the whole truth. The City records show that many watchmen honestly tried to carry out their duties under impossible conditions and for the miserable pay of 6d. a night, and that others who did not were constantly being reprimanded, fined, imprisoned or dismissed. Some research needs to be done, to set Fielding's unfair picture right.

Besides this sort of restriction, however, a constable had to be very careful when trying, for instance, to break up a street riot lest he be prosecuted afterwards for wrongful arrest. There was always the chance that the young hooligan was related to a magistrate or, worse, to someone who could damage the constable's private business after his tour of duty was over. Worse still, he stood to lose heavily, *all* his possessions in fact, if any prisoner in his temporary custody should escape. One can see what this meant when one remembers that constables were unpaid and elected annually from rotas of citizens, rather as juries are still elected today. The system was obviously unsatisfactory, for a tradesman compelled to keep law and order in his district (and to build a strong-room in his own house) for a whole year was hardly likely to carry out his duties efficiently and keep his business going at the same time. Therefore, by the eighteenth century in London it had become common for citizens, when their turn came round for constable duty, to pay deputies to do their service for them. Any deputy who showed ability was likely to be reappointed by successive citizens, and so become an unofficial 'regular' constable perhaps for the rest of his active life.

The King's Messengers ('Queen's Messengers' in 1712) were a 'police force' responsible directly to the Privy Council. Their province was treason and other political matters, and during this time of Jacobite conspiracies their presence was a very real one in London. Coining, however, came under the heading of 'treason' and so they were also active as ordinary police. A similar body was 'The Press Messengers', whose job was to hunt out authors and printers of treasonable and otherwise undesirable literature, and to confiscate their presses.

In addition to all these were the forces under the Sheriffs— the Sergeants, Javelin Men, bailiffs (and their 'setters'), prison officers and the *Posse Comitatus* ('Power of the County'), which was a body of men temporarily enrolled at an emergency such as a riot, a threatened invasion, or a raid by a band of cattle-thieves, or highwaymen. The Lord Lieutenant of each county had his own part-time soldiers-cum-police too, under the name of the 'Militia', whose functions exactly duplicated those of the Posse. In the city of London, these bodies were combined under the name of 'Trained Bands'. As for the gaol-keepers and turnkeys, they performed a function now reserved for the police in that they frequently drove forth in coaches, armed to the teeth, to recapture escaped prisoners.

Finally, the Court of Aldermen of the City had a small private police force of its own—the City Marshals and their men. They had been instituted in the 1570s, under the name of 'Provost Marshals', in order to deal with the enormous numbers of vagabonds that had recently flooded into the City, but during the seventeenth century they had come to be a regular, salaried, force in their own right, whose work more or less duplicated that of the constables, beadles and watch, except that they had power to execute warrants of arrest over the counties surrounding London. Later in the century this range was extended to include the whole of England and even America. There were two Marshals, an Upper and an Under, or 'Second', and they were in charge of six 'young men', paid a shilling a day. They had to buy their places, but were paid not ungenerous salaries for those days: £100 p.a. to the Upper-Marshal and £60 p.a. to the Under-Marshal, plus an allowance for clothes and horse, and an annual 'tip' of £5 for good service. In addition they were allowed to sell a Freedom of the City annually, which brought about £30. They were given 6*d*. each from the entrance 'fee' of every prisoner

committed to the City prisons and no doubt had means of bullying money from the inmates of the watch-houses as well. Finally
they were allowed to raise a levy of £1 per head from every
stall-keeper at Bartholomew Fair (a notorious place, incidentally,
for traffic in stolen goods).

The two chief theatres of Wild's activities were Newgate and
the Old Bailey Justice House, and so far as the Old Bailey was
concerned, 'theatre' is less a metaphor than a literal description.
It can be seen in plates 2 and 3. The most striking thing about it is
that it was *open to the air*, a feature which gave it a dramatic, not
to say theatrical, even Italianate, appearance—a bizarre oddity of
this peculiar age. It was situated a little further south from the
present Central Criminal Court and stood back, and hidden, from
the street, in a courtyard, reached through an alley, called Sessions
House Yard. The prisoners, chained, were kept out in front of
the court in the Bail Dock all day (from 6.30 a.m. to 8 or 9 p.m.)
during sessions, summer and winter, regardless of heat, rain,
cold or snow. This had been ordered in 1714, after a Head Turnkey called Spurling (whose niece married Wild) was shot by a
prisoner at the swing-gate leading into the court dock.* From
here the prisoners could see and to a certain extent hear all that
went on in the court—who was condemned, who acquitted, who
burnt in the hand, and add their rowdy comments to the occasion.
The purpose of the open-air court was presumably to minimize
the risk of infection and at the same time give the waiting prisoners
a lesson in the majesty of the law. Nevertheless, seen from Sessions
House Yard, a trial at the Old Bailey must have resembled
nothing so much as a giant Punch and Judy show. The court
was not closed in until 1737, after the judges had long complained
of the 'Inclemency of the Weather'. (*See Appendix IV.*)

Newgate stood at the north end of the same street, on the site
of the present Old Bailey, and its central feature was the 60-ft.
tower spanning Newgate Street (the city gate opening through
below). This contained a number of strong-rooms for dangerous
prisoners, which were considered escape-proof until Jack Sheppard escaped from the strongest of them. By the same mental
process that inspired the Germans to put *'Arbeit macht Frei'*
('Work makes us Free') over the gates of their concentration
camps, the Aldermen of London adorned the tower of England's
greatest and most hated prison with the statues of 'Liberty'

* *See page* 130.

(with Dick Whittington's cat at her feet), 'Peace', 'Plenty', 'Concord', 'Mercy' and 'Truth'.

The prison continued on both sides of the street, a huge warren of cells, dungeons, halls, tunnels, staircases, holds and passages with wooden cells packed along the sides like hen-coops. The best part of the gaol was the Press Yard (not to be confused with the Press Room, where prisoners who refused to plead in court were pressed beneath weights), which was a row of cells opening on to a narrow passage (54 ft. by 7 ft.) where the wealthier prisoners could 'take the air'. The sun was just visible for a few minutes at noon in midsummer, on fine days. A cell here cost up to £500 deposit, plus 22s. a week rent and furniture *excluding* garnish. It was thus the most expensive place to stay in London by far, for in modern money this might represent about $25,000 plus $55 a week for a small bare room. The Hold was like the 'Holes' of other prisons, but more crowded and, being deeper underground, colder. The stone floor was deep with dead cockroaches, whose shells crackled under the feet with every step, and fat white lice swarmed all over the prisoners' clothes.

Besides Newgate there were about 150 other prisons in the Metropolis—felons' prisons, debtors' prisons, 'Bridewells' (houses of correction), workhouses, watch-houses, roundhouses, prisons belonging to Messengers, officers of the Admiralty, College of Heralds, etc., 115 bailiffs' 'Spunging Houses' and an unrecorded number of private prisons belonging to thief-takers.

While allowing for the fact that this was the early eighteenth century, when prisons were barbaric and corruption generally tolerated, it is still possible to point to one prime cause of the exceptional horrors and almost total corruption of the prisons and 'police' of London, and that is the custom by which every permanent official, from the City Recorder downwards, had to buy his place. Since at least the early seventeenth century this had been regarded as a serious but unavoidable evil. In 1652 the Common Council had tried to restrict the practice by limiting the number of offices that could be bought and by insisting that the moneys be kept to meet the expenses of the officers concerned. The posts were to be sold by public auction because it was hoped that higher prices would be obtained and so the expenses adequately covered. The City's finances, as a result of the Civil War, were too shaky to sustain these honest measures, and when it came to meeting expenses the money had usually been spent elsewhere. After the Great Plague, the Fire and the reconstruction, the City was reduced to borrowing money from every existing fund. In 1694 the Orphan's Act declared the City bankrupt, for it was found that the City owed £700,000 to the Orphan's Fund alone (this was a well-endowed charity for the upkeep and education of the children of deceased Freemen). Any restriction of the sale of offices was now out of the question until the City's finances could be put back in order. On 24 February 1703 an Act of Common Council was passed by which the proceeds of the sale of offices was to be divided into three parts: one to the Lord Mayor, one-third to the Sheriffs and one-third to the City itself, but it was not until the nineteenth century that the sale of offices could be brought under control and dispensed with. Meanwhile, the price of the positions rose with every sale. We know, for instance, that in 1712 Hitchen bought his post as Under-Marshal for about £700, whereas the 'official' price in 1696 had been £300. The cost of being a Keeper of Newgate or the Fleet rose to £5,000, and while we have no figures for the prices of turnkeys, they presumably went up in proportion. Thus the officers felt they had every right to recover this money by any means—hence the grim stories of blackmail, torture and murder. Hitchen justified his crimes with the universal excuse that he had 'bought his Place', as though the act of buying carried with it the power of absolution of all future sins. This system had the final disadvantage of making it impossible for the Court of Aldermen to discipline their officers. If a Marshal, for instance, were summarily dismissed and punished for extortion and receiving stolen goods, before he had recouped his £700, it would be impossible to find a replacement; for who would pay such a sum if he were not allowed to make it up again professionally? And while there was no money available for the paying of 'adequate' salaries, what other system could be devised?*

The law was in a similar dilemma. The judicial machinery was ancient and creaking; delays of many months, even in criminal cases, were accepted as a matter of course; and many of the law officers (including Old Bailey judges) took bribes from defenders and prosecutors alike. The language of the law was Latin. Commissions, indictments, recognizances, Sessions Books, etc., were

* The material and references for this paragraph were very kindly given to me by Donald Rumbelow, before his *History of Police and Crime in the City of London* went to press.

written in Latin, though admittedly a very corrupt, anglicized and abbreviated Latin, and any attempt at changing this was still being strongly resisted. It would detract from the mystery of the law, the judges maintained, and open the profession to amateurs; besides, if it was to be changed to English, why not to Welsh, Scottish, Cornish and Gaelic?

The answer to the growth of crime was to increase the severity of punishments. Between about 1680 and 1722, successive statutes raised the number of offences punishable by death from about eighty to over 350, to so many, in fact, that no one was absolutely certain what you could or could not be hanged for.

Crime was of two main kinds, misdemeanour (trivial offences such as drunkenness and swearing) and felony (the rest). It has been written in some history books that by this time all felonies were capital, but this is not true. Besides capital felonies there were common felonies; that is, felonies adjudged to be so under (or 'at') Common Law, and so not incorporated into any statute, and they were not capital. It is true that by the eighteenth century there were not many of these left, for the process of converting common felonies into capital ones had been continuing, as I have said, since the early sixteenth century. A good example of the way in which crimes were further categorized is in the larceny laws. Larceny could be 'Petty' (Petit) or Grand, Simple or Compound. If, for instance, you picked up a hat in the road and ran off with it, and when you were caught the hat was found to be worth less than a shilling, you were guilty of Simple Petty Larceny, and so of Common Felony only, for which the punishment was a fine, a whipping, a spell in a Bridewell, or perhaps transportation for seven years, according to the circumstances. If you held up a coach and stole *two* shillings at gun-point, you were guilty of 'putting in Fear' and so of Compound Grand Larceny, which was capital. Grand larceny was to steal 1s. or more from a person, 5s. or more from a shop or warehouse, 40s. from a house, but smaller sums became 'capital' if the robberies were compounded by 'putting in Fear', 'breaking and entering', etc., and all burglary (larceny between sunset and dawn) was capital. However, the subtleties in all this were infinite, and doubtful points were always supposed to be (and sometimes were) interpreted in the prisoner's favour.

The usual mechanism of argument was 'Benefit of Clergy'. This originated in the medieval arrangement by which clerics

were tried by ecclesiastical and not lay courts. With time, lawyers
had extended these privileges to include not only themselves
(first of all) but everyone who could read and write. Thus when a
man was pronounced guilty of a capital felony, the judge asked
him 'Have you anything to say why the sentence of the Court
should not be passed upon you?'* at which the prisoner would
'seek the Book'—that is, plead Benefit of Clergy. He was then
given a Bible and told to read verse 1 of Psalm 51, which soon
came to be called 'The Neck Verse'. The judge asked *Legit aut
non legit?'* ('Does he read or not?'), the Chaplain (called 'the
Ordinary' from 'Chaplain-in-Ordinary') would reply *Legit ut
clericus'* ('He reads like a clerk'), and the prisoner was whipped or
fined instead of hanged. At the same time he was branded on the
ball of the left thumb (called 'burnt in the hand', or, in cant,
'glymmed in the paw') so that he could not plead Clergy again.
By 1700 the custom had become a farce, for illiterate rogues
bribed the Ordinaries to whisper the words to them, often with
comic results, and it was abandoned in 1705. However, Benefit
of Clergy without the 'Neck Verse' continued to be a valuable
loophole through impossible statutes and every trial became a
debate on whether or not a prisoner was entitled to 'his Clergy'.
Jonathan Wild's main activities were in the most debated territory of all—that of accessories before and after 'Facts' (crimes)
and of aiding and abetting—and he exploited the opportunities
for hair-splitting and tongue-twisting with a skill that amounted
to genius. Branding, too, had become a punishment in its own
right as an alternative to hanging, especially when it was desired
to keep the thief alive so that he might appear as an informer
against his accomplices. It was a noisy and distressing business,
for prisoners, especially women, would start to shriek at the tops
of their voices in the Old Bailey court as soon as the executioner
began to heat his iron. For a time under William III, culprits
were branded on the face instead, but this was dropped under
Queen Anne. The iron frames, however, for holding still the
convicts' heads, were taken by the prison keepers, and used as
instruments of torture to extract 'garnish' from new arrivals at
the Marshalsea, the Fleet and Newgate.

Clearly the forces of law and order left much to be desired.
The ancient trunk of the law was overgrown with dense

* This question, of course, though now meaningless is still asked at this point
in felony trials.

foliage which urgently needed pruning; the institutions of law-enforcement were those of the Middle Ages and incapable, without radical changes, of dealing with the vastly more complex world of the eighteenth century. Though in the country the J.P.s might have been benevolent squires peacefully running their communities, in London the majority were half-educated scoundrels who had bought their places with the single object of making as much money from them as they could. Among the criminal classes, their claim to be guardians of the law was a bad joke, for everyone 'knew' that they took protection-money from the better brothels and gaming houses, while harassing the poorer ones. The constables were merely magistrates' servants and so, as an old ballad[1] put it, 'looked at the World through their Fingers'. The permanent officers, Marshals, bailiffs, turnkeys, etc., were committed to getting back the money with which they had bought their places, and before this all other considerations were put aside. The prisons were hopelessly overcrowded, owing to the recent influx of people into London and to the capricious way in which they could be arrested, and had descended to a level of horror scarcely equalled before or since.

A great deal of the onus of police work, therefore, still lay upon the private citizen, who, if robbed, was expected to do his own detective work, obtain a warrant of arrest from the magistrate, arouse the constable and, together with as many friends as possible, find and 'take' the thief. If robbed in the country, he had to raise the alarm in the nearest town; and if the robbery was serious, the Sheriff, the J.P., or any other prominent citizen could proclaim a 'Hue and Cry', so that a *Posse Comitatus* could ride forth and chase the highwaymen, exactly as in a Western film. There were many snags in this. One lay in the persuading of friends to come with you. For while there were plenty of 'Captains' and such who needed no encouragement to get into a fight, they were not always around when needed; while the more staid and serious were not always willing to risk injury, or perhaps their lives, in a world where 'security' was a concept hardly dreamed of. The statutes (beginning with those of Westminster and Winchester passed under Edward I) which were supposed to compel citizens to go on a man-hunt and appear in court as witnesses were hedged round with so many qualifications as to be now unenforceable. Again, no man knocked down in the street could be expected to get up and chase his attacker through the maze of pitch dark and slippery alleys of St. Giles or Whitefriars. To free himself, the thief had only to disappear into an alehouse, escape through a back door, and leave his pursuer to the mercy of the armed and violent inhabitants of the neighbourhood. In short, the duty of a citizen to leave his job and hunt down thieves was impossible to fulfil. Inevitably, a class of unauthorized adventurers arose who offered to do this work professionally.

{ IV } *The Founding Fathers*

We first hear of the true prototypes of Jonathan Wild, and so of all modern gangsters, in a pamphlet published in the same year as *Romeo and Juliet*, 1597. It was entitled *The Black Dog of Newgate; or the Discovery of a London Monster*, and the author was Luke Hutton. He was said to be the son or nephew of the Archbishop of York, but he turned highwayman and was hanged in the following year for a robbery committed on, of all days, St. Luke's Day, 18 October. The tract was probably written either in Newgate or just after his release, and there seems to be no possible reason to doubt the truth of what he says.

A second edition in the British Museum, dated 1638, gives three explanations for Hutton's mysterious title: it was a black stone in the condemned cell (then called 'Limbo') against which a desperate prisoner had dashed out his brains; it was simply a black conscience dwelling in black-conditioned people. The third said that it was the ghost of a poor scholar who, in the shape of a Black Dog, glided through the streets near Newgate before execution days. The scholar had been imprisoned for conjuring during the reign of Henry III. It was a time of famine and the prisoners had been reduced to eating one another 'alive', especially newcomers and those who could make least resistance. They ate the scholar and 'deemed him passing good meate', but were soon troubled by apparitions of this dog 'ready with his

ravening Jawes to teare out their Bowels . . . whereupon such a
nightly feare grew amongst them, that it turned to a Frenzie,
and from a Frenzie to Desperation, in which Desperation they
killed the Keeper, and so many of them escaped forth, yet
whithersoever they came or went, they imagined the blacke Dog
to follow . . .'.

To Hutton, the Black Dog was a villain on the right side of
the law, a gaoler, informer, blackmailer or any one of those 'who,
in the Name of Service and Office, were, as it were, Servants of
Newgate', and on the frontispiece of his tract the animal stands
on its hind legs, holding the Keeper's hand in sinister complicity.
Through the mouth of 'Zawney', Hutton tells us how these
'Wise Men of Newgate' or 'Coney Catchers' ('Rabbit catchers'—
a common name for all rogues in Elizabethan times) had scouts
all over London to bring them news of robberies and the whereabouts of thieves. The best 'conies', that is people who had
been robbed and needed help, were those who had come to
London on a short visit, for they were always in a hurry to be off
again and so were easy to bargain with. Hearing of a likely victim,
the Black Dog would approach him informally and offer not only
to restore the stolen money or goods but, God willing, capture
the thief. Each Black Dog had touts to whisper abroad his reputation as an honest citizen compelled to take on this work by a
strong sense of public duty, and was well-stocked with warrants—
some forged, some genuine and some out of date which should
have been destroyed, but were useful to browbeat illiterate
rogues with. Especially dangerous in his hands was a General
Warrant which he could sometimes persuade a magistrate to
issue to him, for it enabled him to arrest all 'suspect Persons'.
Then, having taken a deposit proportional to the theft (£2 on
£10 was considered reasonable) and armed with his warrants,
the Black Dog arrested every thief he could find, except the guilty
one, and took from each a 'fee' in exchange for his release. A day
or so before the 'Coney' was due to leave again for the country,
the Black Dog would arrest the real thief and, because he knew
exactly how much had been stolen, strike a bargain with him
over the spoils. Then, finding the 'Coney' on the very day he was
leaving, he would be able to palm him off with a small fraction
of what had been stolen, apologize and disappear. Out of each
robbery to the value of £10, the Black Dog could expect to make
from various hands—the 'Coney', the cutpurses he had first taken

up and finally the actual thief—at least £25, a considerable sum in those days. Hutton ends by saying that at the time of writing some of these Black Dogs had been in business at least thirty years—an important point I shall return to later. The whole tract is included in *The Elizabethan Underworld* by Professor A. V. Judges,[1] and anyone who wishes to learn of these tricks in all their complicated detail should turn to that invaluable book.

Despite their growing importance, we hear no more of 'Thief-Takers', as the Black Dogs came to be called, until the beginning of the eighteenth century, by which time they had made themselves virtual masters of the London criminal underworld. In doing so they had been greatly assisted by two important changes in the law.

The first concerned the receiving of stolen goods. Until the reign of Dutch William (1688–1702), this trade had somehow escaped the attention of law-makers. Under Common Law it was a misdemeanour punished by a fine or whipping. For centuries, receivers traded almost openly. The fourteenth century poem *London Lickpenny* tells how the poet had his hood stolen at one end of Cheapside and found it up for sale at the other. From about 1605 until the Civil War, Mary Frith, nicknamed 'Moll Cutpurse' (the original 'Roaring Girl') ran a shop in Fleet Street which was nothing less than a reception centre for stolen goods of all kinds, and she only ceased business when, being a fanatical Royalist, she followed the King's Party out of London. By the 1680s, there were hundreds of warehouses and repositories where thieves could sell their booty, within minutes of stealing it, at a price not far below its full value.

Then in 1691 a statute was passed to consolidate all previous acts against larceny (*3 William & Mary c. 9*). *Section 4* drew special attention to receiving. It made the receiver an accessory *after* the fact, and so liable to branding, whipping and/or seven years' transportation (at that time, by the way, felons usually had to transport themselves). 'By this Act,' says Defoe in his pamphlet on Wild, 'the Receiving Trade was spoil'd all at once. And when the poor Adventurer had, at the Hazard of his Neck, gotten any Purchase, he must run that Hazard over again to turn it into Money.'

Two years later, in 1693, the government embarked on a new policy of offering rewards for the capture of thieves, a policy intended to reinforce the harsher punishments for robbery in general. The Highwaymen Act of that year (*4 & 5 William & Mary c. 8*) offered £40 to whoever took a highwayman and secured his conviction with evidence. If more than one person was involved, the reward was to be divided between them. *Section 6* added that whoever took the highwayman could claim his horse, money, guns or whatever, provided they had not been stolen in the first place. This was to discourage innkeepers and others from hiring horses to suspicious-looking strangers. *Section 7*, which had far-reaching effects, offered a pardon to anyone, provided he was not a felon convict at the time, who informed on any criminals and thereby secured their conviction. It should be explained that the word 'highwayman' was taken to mean any thief.

During the next few years these twin policies of offering rewards and clamping down on receivers were extended still further. The important Shoplifting Act, which made the stealing of 5*s.* or more from a shop a capital felony, was passed in 1699 (*10 & 11 William III c. 23*), and contained sections nicknamed 'the Tyburn Ticket Act'. This exempted from all parish and ward duties, including the irksome one of being constable or having to pay a deputy, anyone who had captured and convicted a thief and been duly rewarded £40. This was followed in 1706 by *5 Anne c. 31*, which again returned to the problems of receiving and of rewards for informers. A receiver, while remaining an accessory after the fact, was henceforth to suffer death as a capital felon. An informer who succeeded in convicting his accomplices was to be given not only a free pardon, but a reward of £40.

The effect of these acts was paradoxical. Certainly, the number of receivers dwindled to very few, for the risks were now very great, and those few paid but 'Trifles' for the goods thieves brought them. Again, the intention behind the paying of rewards was not so much to goad citizens into feats of heroism as to break up the knots and gangs of thieves by luring them to betray one another, and in this it was certainly successful. But those who drew up the Acts did not foresee that they would immediately create an army of professional informers who would soon become blackmailers, perjurers and false-witnesses. To the thief-takers, who had plenty of such people working for them already, these new measures must have come down like manna from heaven. The statutes gave them virtual power of life and death over the thieves, especially the young ones whose petty transgressions would previously have been punished by no more than a whipping. The rewards in cash enabled them to put their affairs in better financial order. They were able to take over a great deal of the receiving trade, for their position on both sides of the law provided them with excellent cover, while the new encouragement to informers made it easier for them to impeach old-fashioned receivers and put them out of business. Finally the connivance of law officers and judges and, above all, the active co-operation of Sir Salathiel Lovell, the City Recorder, enabled them to keep their gangs more or less intact. Important thieves who were caught could be saved from the gallows and lesser thieves, with a little legal jiggery-pokery, hanged in their place.

The *British Journal* of 24 April and 2 May 1725 published two remarkable letters from an anonymous correspondent[2] who, in order to show there had been 'Thief-Takers of note long before Jonathan', described a case of exactly this kind of corruption which he had witnessed at the turn of the century. Lovell,* as presiding judge at several of the trials over which the case extended, vigorously defended a thief who had been guilty of stealing a trunk from a friend of the correspondent's and tried to convict another thief, called Morris Evans, who was innocent of that particular crime. Evans had been in Newgate at the time and expected to be hanged because, having been ordered to transport himself to America a year before, he had failed to do so. A thief-taker called Connelly came to him in prison and paid him £3 to confess to an additional crime (i.e. the theft of the trunk) so that the real thief, who belonged to a gang working under Connelly's, and ultimately Sir Salathiel Lovell's, supervision, could be acquitted. If Evans was going to be hanged, another confession would make no difference and the money would ease his last days. A sinister part in this plan was played by a young scoundrel called Joseph Hatfield, who acted as the 'Affidavit Man' (professional false witness, perjurer and informer, but Hatfield was also a thief), and the receiver to the gang was a woman well-known in those days called Moll Raby.

The plan seems to have been fairly standard procedure in cases of that kind, and it misfired this once, and so was discovered, partly through the unusual persistence of the gentlemen prosecuting, who suspected some kind of corruption but were not

---

* City Recorder from 1691–1713. A 'hanging judge' noted for his bad memory, and originator of the famous saying 'I've forgotten more law than you'll ever remember!'

sure what it was, and partly through the lucky intervention of Chief Justice Holt (the same who stopped witchcraft trials in England). The guilty thief had died meanwhile in Newgate, but Hatfield was branded and Evans discharged without trial.* In his summing up, Holt expressed his contempt for the City Recorder in less than guarded terms and declared it was high time thief-taking was made illegal.

The ancient offices and institutions of the City of London are now held in great respect and clothed in hallowed ceremony. It seems rather hard to believe, therefore, that so dignified an official as a Recorder, who after all is the senior judge in London (taking precedence after the Lord Mayor) and the official 'Voice of the City', should engage in the sordid racket of hanging thieves in Newgate for crimes they did not commit in order that others under his management could carry on in business.

There is, however, some supporting evidence for the *British Journal* from two writers who, in their factual journalism at least, have not had the reputation of being downright liars: Tom Brown and Daniel Defoe. At about the same time as this case, Tom Brown wrote a stinging attack on Lovell, saying that the 'Shoals' of prisoners condemned by Lovell at each Sessions were 'mere Sacrifices to his Avarice or his Malice', that he took bribes, and that 'he never saved any Man for his Money but that he hanged another in his Room'.[3] Defoe was even fiercer. In a satire against the City 'establishment' entitled *Reformation of Manners* (after the Society of that name, of which Lovell was a member) he said of the Recorder that:

> He trades in Justice and the Souls of Men,
> And prostitutes them equally to Gain:
> He has his Publick Book of Rates to show,
> Where every Rogue the Price of Life may know:

. . . .

* Gaol Delivery Roll 1952 (July 1700) in the Middlesex Records Office corroborates the story in the *BJ* even down to small details, which at least attests the accuracy of the author's memory twenty-five years after the event. The prosecutors, identified by initials in the newspaper, are revealed as Francis Harewood and Arthur Pepys, of the parish of St. Anne's, Soho. The names of Hatfield, Raby, Rogers (the real thief), etc., can be found again and again on the records of these years. Despite Lovell's claim that Hatfield would never commit a dishonest act again, being merely a poor lad led astray, Hatfield continued in crime until 1724, when he died in Newgate at the height of the Jack Sheppard affair. (*See page* 218.)

> Fraternities of Villians he maintains,
> Protects their Robberies, and shares the Gains,
> Who thieve with Toleration as a Trade,
> And then restores according as they're paid:

Most authorities since have felt that this poem was just a typically scurrilous piece of that scurrilous age, and that Defoe's accusations were hysterical and exaggerated. A year later (1703) Defoe was tried at the Old Bailey for writing *The Shortest Way with Dissenters,* his famous satire on extreme Tory attitudes. Sir Salathiel Lovell and his fellow judges treated Defoe with extraordinary harshness for so small an offence, sentencing him to stand in the pillory three times and to stay in Newgate until he had paid a fine which was so large that, they hoped, it would keep him there for the rest of his life. It has been suggested that the true reason for their severity was that they wished to revenge themselves for the things Defoe had said about them in *Reformation of Manners*. [4] The Hatfield/Evans case, itself a mere tip of the iceberg, supports this idea, for it suggests that Lovell especially was stung to fury and revenge not because Defoe's accusations were hysterical and scurrilous but because they were true.

But perhaps the most important part of the letters in the *British Journal* is the uniquely authentic glimpse they give of how the underworld was organized shortly before the arrival of Jonathan Wild, for it explains a great deal about his own career.

When the case was over, the author of the letters went to see Morris Evans, whom he found to be a 'pretty sensible young Fellow', and asked him why, after his miraculous escape, he did not give up thieving. This, Evans replied, was impossible unless he could 'banish himself, as he hoped to do'.

'For, said he, the Thief-Catchers are our absolute Masters; and they have Intelligence from Tapsters, Ostlers, and Porters Etc., at Inns, and from People, that only for a Disguise (*i.e. for enough gin to get drunk on*), cry things about the Streets; and others, who draw in Servants to be accessory in robbing their Masters; and they send us into several Wards and Stations (as a Corporal sends Soldiers to stand Centinel); and if we refuse to go, they'll immediately have us committed for some former Crime; or (as in your Friend's Case) bring Evidence to swear away our Lives wrongfully.'

There were at that time six thief-takers that he knew, 'and

where they kept their nightly Clubs, to which if their Gangs did not repair, they were in Danger; and from thence they must go wherever they sent them'. The thief-takers went daily to all the prisons looking for new offenders. They found out their cases, taught them how to plead and, if any of these novices had money, 'would soon find some Contrivance to bring them off; and whichever Thief-Catcher came first to such new Offender, he must be his Slave for ever after, and rob when he bid him, or be hang'd for refusing'.

The thief-takers sent their scouts into Moorfields and other such places where people gathered in the evenings for sport, to look out for apprentices who, by staying out too long (a transgression which often resulted in a severe beating), were afraid to go home. It was not difficult to lure these into gin-shops and afterwards involve them in escapades. Then they could swear robberies against them and, if possible, get them committed for a spell in prison. Likewise, they posted scouts at the coaching inns, to look out for girls arriving from the country and lure them, in the time-honoured manner, into whoring or, if they were servants, browbeat them into stealing from their employers.

Evans admitted, however, that thieves now were generally better off under the thief-takers than on their own, because the thief-takers were better organized. For one thing, thieves could rarely make much of stolen goods because of their ignorance, whereas thief-takers, by corresponding together, soon learned the value of everything. They were able to rent warehouses in obscure places and employ men and women to alter stolen goods so that they could not be recognized. Although Evans did not mention the fact, this was an inestimable boon since the new laws against receiving. Again, the thief-takers did at least do what they could for the thieves who worked under them, and Evans said that Hatfield, for instance, always had a 'Purse of five or six-hundred Pounds to bribe the Recorder, and Court Officers, and their Servants, and had, by that Means, many times escap'd hanging.'

The gang to which Hatfield and Moll Raby belonged, and which Lovell protected, must have been a successful one, for £500 might represent £10,000 or $25,000 in modern money. From the parchment records, from the printed *Sessions Papers*, the *Newgate Calendar* and Captain Alexander Smith's *Lives of the Highwaymen*,[5] the membership of the gang can be reconstructed.

Smith's book is especially useful for, although most of his 'biographies' (e.g. Moll Raby's) are complete fiction stolen from old stories and plays, he always included a few authentic facts taken from *Sessions Papers* now lost. There is a list of the gang, with the others mentioned in this book, in Appendix III. Those familiar with the social history of the period may be interested to see Jack Hall as a member of it. He was the most famous burglar of the age, and his *Memoir* is still widely quoted because of its description of Newgate and vocabulary of thieves' cant. More significant, however, is that some of the names provide a link with Jonathan Wild himself. Moll Raby was eventually betrayed by Hatfield and Arthur Chambers after they had robbed the house of Lady Cavendish in Soho Square and blamed it on to her. Arthur Chambers was married to a 'buttock-and-file' called Moll Pines. After his death, Moll Pines married a thief-taker called Richard Yeomans. Now, in his life of Wild, Captain Smith says that the two most important thief-takers in London before Wild appeared on the scene to drive them out of business were Richard Yeomans and, curiously, a woman called 'Jewish Moll'. The Middlesex Gaol Delivery Rolls show that Yeomans was condemned to death in January 1717 for an armed robbery in Whitechapel, but was later reprieved under the new Transportation Act and sent to Annapolis with the first batch of prisoners. His wife Moll Pines, with two other women, Martha and Magdalene Yeomans, followed him there in 1722. Of 'Jewish Moll' there is, as yet, little trace, except that she was the wife of a ballad singer.

It is clear that when Wild embarked on thief-taking—that is, blackmail, bribery, informing, framing, receiving and theft compounded together by thieves, thief-catchers and the 'authorities'—he was entering an already well-developed, 'sophisticated', profession with a long and important history behind it. Like the selling of offices, it was regarded as an evil for which the cure (a regular police force) would be worse than the disease. Thus when Chief Justice Holt said that after Hatfield's trial he would allow no thief-takers in his courts, and some members of Parliament who were present said they would try to pass a Bill which would put a final stop to this 'complicated Mischief', nothing in fact was done. The 'complicated Mischief' had become the most effective and least expensive way of keeping crime under control, and so many law officers were involved in it that anything less than a complete reform of the whole judicial, police and penal systems would have been useless.

In May 1713, Sir Salathiel Lovell died. He was probably Wild's most important precursor and therefore deserving of a prominent place in the history of organized crime, and his system was ripe for taking over. A few weeks later, Under-Marshal Hitchen, who had been practising thief-taking openly and shamelessly for a year in competition with free-lancers and officials of all kinds, including the head Newgate turnkey, Spurling, employed as his new assistant Jonathan Wild, whom we left, it will be remembered, as a penniless discharged debtor settling in at Lewkenor's Lane with Mary Milliner, or Molyneux.

❧ V ❧ 'The Twang'

Lewkenor's Lane was in the middle of the Hundreds of Drury, a criss-cross labyrinth of streets and passages between the Strand and Holborn. It was in effect one large red-light district, a dangerous, rip-roaring place of which it was said that a man could not walk from the Piazza to the Rose tavern once without venturing his life twice (the distance was about fifty yards). Round Covent Garden square, beneath the arches of the Piazza, were the more expensive gaming houses such as 'Howells' and 'Pharoah's Tables' (named after the game of Faro) where government secretaries, rakehell lords, stock-market 'projectors', magistrates, highwaymen, footpads and even a few adventurous apprentices mixed together in a most democratic confusion. Among the 'regulars' were the ferocious Lord Mohun and (later) the Duke of Wharton (whose life could serve as a model for every *Rake's Progress* from Hogarth to *Brideshead Revisited*), the 'Mock Counts' such as Count Conyers and Count Viana, the clergyman turned highwayman, gambler and forger, the Rev. Joseph Lindsey, and, of course, the famous Colonel Charteris, who earned his fortune by taking his winnings in land rather than money, and used the income to finance high-class prostitution. Above such places were the brothels, nicknamed 'Vaulting Academies'. The most pricey was Mother Wisebourne's, whose girls cost £50 a night; though considering that in modern terms this might mean between £750 and £1,000, the fee seems incredibly high. Her brightest stars were Elizabeth Mann and Sally Salisbury. Elizabeth Mann, alias 'The Royal Sovereign', was a 'Posture Woman' who performed in front of an audience with a candle on a pewter dish. It is said the girl undressing in the foreground of Hogarth's well-known orgy-scene in *The Rake's Progress* is preparing for just such an act. Behind her, 'Leathersides' holds the dish in readiness. The room is supposed to be in 'The Rose' itself, which was on the corner of Russell Street and Drury Lane, but the time is the 1740s. Sally Salisbury, born Sarah Pridden, was in 1712 a girl of twenty-two whose affairs with important ministers of state provided pamphleteers (especially anti-Tory ones) with an endless fund of dirty jokes. It was said that Sally had gone with another girl and Viscount Bolingbroke, Secretary of State, one night down to Greenwich Park, where they had all thrown off their clothes and run about naked 'in Imitation of the Deer'. Sally had arranged with the park-keeper that their clothes should be taken away, and so Bolingbroke was forced to buy them new ones. On another occasion, she had been held upside-down while 'Mr. Secretary' and his friends threw gold coins between her legs. Her liaisons brought down no governments, however.

Lewkenor's Lane was renamed many times: Lutenor's Lane, Newtoner's Lane, Newtonhouse Lane, Charles Street and finally Macklin Street, after the actor. It had long had the reputation of an evil place. In Dryden's *Wild Gallant* there is a brothel there called *The Cat & the Fiddle*; in Pope and Swift's *Miscellanies* it is mentioned as the place of residence of a thief-taker called Summers, and it is mentioned as a place to hire girls from in *The Beggar's Opera*. However, in the *Sessions Papers* of February 1687 (in the British Museum) there is an account of four thief-takers who arrested a man on a General Warrant (of the kind used by the 'Black Dogs' a century earlier) and imprisoned him in 'Mr. Gilbert Thomas's Prison-House in Lukenor's Lane'. They chained him to the floor, beat him and left him to die of starvation. Now, the street is perfectly respectable and occupied by warehouses, shops and a few small flats. Then, it was narrower and surfaced with trodden mud which turned to slime in the rain. After dark the only light came from the doors and windows of the gimcrack dram-shops, brothels and night-cellars that packed the Lane from end to end. The houses were tiny and rat-infested, with twisting collapsing stairs, and in the day the street was festooned with tattered sheets and sodden mattresses hanging out to dry.

Here, Jonathan Wild began his extraordinary career in the most humble circumstances, that is, as a common prostitute's bully.

In his life of Moll Raby (who, it will be remembered, was betrayed by Joseph Hatfield), Captain Smith describes how she and her husband Humphrey Jackson went out on 'the *Buttock & Twang*': 'So whilst the decoy'd Fool is groping her with his Breeches down, she picks his Fob, or Pocket, of his Watch or Money. And giving a sort of *Hem!* as a Signal she has succeeded in her Design, then the Fellow with whom she keeps Company, blundering up in the dark, he knocks down the Gallent and carries off the Prize.'

When Hitchen came to write his pamphlet against Wild, which he called *The Regulator*, he adapted this passage; for although he knew more about the underworld than Smith, he was almost illiterate:

'When he was a Twang, alias followed the Tail of his wife (Mary Milliner) a common Night Walker, no sooner had she pick'd a Pocket, and given him the Signal, by a Him, or other wise, but he had the impudence, and Courage enough, to attack the Cull, until the Buttock had made her escape.'

Jonathan Wild was at this time thirty years old. He was rather on the small side (5 ft. 6½ in. tall) but, lame or not, stocky and with a squarish face. Popular opinion in that age found it hard to accept that a consummate twister should at the same time be physically brave, and when at his trial Wild was shown to be a veritable incarnation of Reynard the Fox, the pamphleteers assumed that he *must* be a coward. Before that occasion, however, his contemporaries thought of him as a brutally courageous man who would, without a thought, shoot his way into a den of thieves while the constables stood trembling at the end of the street. Of his character we must deduce what we can from his life, from his pamphlet (which was not actually written by him), and from his utterances in court. Captain Smith says 'It is admirable to me how Jonathan Wild came to be so bold, as to fight a single Man, for I have often seen him Kikt, Buffeted, and Pull'd by the Nose, without resenting it in the least. . . .' As for his appearance, the engravings are too clumsy to tell us much. The best possibly is the one in Defoe's pamphlet (*Frontispiece*) for it could belong to the skull in the Royal College of Surgeons. The author of *Lives of the Most Remarkable Criminals* (1735, but the life of Wild is identical, word for word, to that in Captain Charles Johnson's *Lives of the Highwaymen* published in 1734) says that he was 'homely' to the greatest Degree'. He saw Jonathan sitting by the fire in the kitchen of the Rose Street Spunging House off Wood Street after he had been arrested in 1725, and added, 'There was something remarkably villainous in his Face, which Nature had imprinted in stronger Terms than perhaps she ever did upon any other.' If that were so, it is difficult to see how the public, let alone the thieves, ever trusted him in the first place.

We may take it, however, that Wild had 'Courage enough' to knock down Culls and Gallants, especially in the dark with their breeches down. His main problem was to dispose safely of the objects Mary or he stole. Now that a receiver was as liable to hang as a thief, and therefore hard to find and dangerous to deal with, the best thing was to sell what one stole to a corrupt constable, gaoler, Marshal or thief-taker, but this too had its own dangers. From his acquaintenace with William Field and others in the Compter, Wild was well aware of the disadvantages of working through such middlemen. There was an alternative called 'The Trap', but it could be used only occasionally. It involved calling on one of Mary Milliner's clients and telling him that unfortunately she had been committed to gaol for picking pockets, and that among the objects found on her was a diary with the gentleman's name on it. The gentleman would be anxious to avoid the scandal that would arise if he had to go to court and explain how she got it, and 'means' would be found for the affair to be settled privately and the diary restored. So long as the amount of money was small and the gentleman's humane instincts tactfully appealed to, this kind of blackmail worked well enough, but there was always the risk that the gentleman might prosecute regardless, Mary be hanged and Wild himself transported for seven years, or at least whipped and branded. Nevertheless, the 'Trap' demonstrated that diaries, letters, pocket-books, scraps of paper even, which ordinary thieves regarded as worth no more than a few shillings, could become objects of much greater value if a method could be devised of exploiting them on a large scale and in an outwardly respectable manner. For this, some sort of semi-official status or, failing that, protection was required.

Sometime in the summer of 1713 Wild left Lewkenor's Lane and rented a small brandy shop in either Great or Little Cock Alley. These were two little passages opening on to Red Cross Street, opposite St. Giles's Church, Cripplegate, where Milton is buried. There were several reasons both for the move and choice of place. First, he had incurred the displeasure of some criminals, one of whom had shot at him from a window as he was returning home late at night.[1] Secondly, he was involved with a family of coiners in Old Street, where most of the gangs of coiners seemed to have lived at that time, and he wished to be in a better position to supervise them. Hitchen claimed that Wild had learned the elements of coining while he was a buckle-maker, and 'knew how to plate a Crown Piece as well as any that followed that Employment'.[2] Thirdly, according to Hitchen, he had acted, while 'King of the Gypsies . . . the dark and hidden Part of a Stroler* . . . until, by Order of the Magistrate, his Skittish and Baboonish Majesty was set in the Stocks for the same.'[3] Obviously, Covent Garden was becoming unhealthy as well as inconvenient. But the main reason for Wild's move was that the foremost dealer in stolen pocket-books, etc., at this time was Under-Marshal Hitchen himself, whose territory was that of the City and its Liberties. In June 1713 he was temporarily suspended, but this only increased his determination to take control of all the thieves of London. Cripplegate was one of the notorious thieves' quarters adjacent to the Wall, and its maze of alleys and dilapidated houses provided excellent hiding-places for receivers. In his chapter on Hitchen and Wild[4] Donald Rumbelow suggests that Wild moved there deliberately in order to attract Hitchen's attention by undercutting him, or rather, by paying the thieves too much for the return of stolen papers. That is very likely, though it is just possible that Wild did this simply through inexperience. In either case, he was now well within the orbit of the Under-Marshal, whose large, ungainly, and slightly comic figure deserves a closer look than it has been given in previous accounts of Jonathan Wild.

* A 'Stroler' (i.e. 'stroller') was one who, pretending to be a gentleman's servant, tricked innkeepers and such into lending him money on the pretext that the master would be coming to the inn shortly.

{ VI } *The Marshal*

I have found no record of the date of Hitchen's birth, but it was probably about 1675. He became a cabinet-maker, and in 1703 married Elizabeth, daughter of John Wells, of King's Waldon, Hertfordshire. As he refers in a document to his 'family', presumably he had at least one child by her, although he was an active homosexual. They lived on the north side of St. Paul's Churchyard. In 1711, John Wells died and left his property to be divided equally between his two daughters.

Shortly after this, the place of Under City-Marshal became vacant and went up for auction. Hitchen persuaded his wife to sell her moiety and with the proceeds bought the place for £700 on 8 January 1712.[1]

It is curious that as soon as he took office his acquaintance with thieves became almost universal. It must be suspected that he had in fact been dabbling in crime, such as receiving, for several years before, and that he recklessly spent all his wife's money because he had discovered how such an office could be exploited. Of his appearance, we know only that he was 'big and remarkable', a 'tall Man, with a long Peruke and Sword, calling himself the City Marshal'. Soon he became a familiar sight in every tavern, dram-shop, brothel and eating-house between Temple Bar and Aldgate, and in the evenings he could be seen ambling slowly across Moorfields, the gold-braid glinting on his tricorn hat, while a troop of ragged pickpocket boys capered round him in attendance.

Early in September, a number of complaints against the new Under-Marshal were made to the Court of Aldermen, and on the 12th a committee under the retiring Lord Mayor Sir Gilbert Heathcote was appointed to examine them. By 27 October, ten informations had been taken. The most serious of them, because it involved a member of the nobility, concerned the loss of a letter enclosing 200 guineas from Lord Barnard to a Mr. Lawrence. Lawrence had then received an anonymous letter saying that if he wished for the bills to be recovered, he should apply to City Marshal Hitchen. During the negotiations, Hitchen told Lawrence that he had made an arrangement with 2,000 thieves living in the Bills of Mortality that they should bring their stolen goods to him 'and make the best of them'. Mr. Lawrence had paid Hitchen two guineas for the bills, but Hitchen only complained that their recovery had already cost him a guinea and a half, plus 6s. charges.[2]

It took Hitchen nearly two months to prepare his 'Answer'. After many 'Put-offs', he laid it before the Committee at seven in the evening on 16 December, the very day that Wild had been released from the Compter. 'The Answer of Charles Hitchen to the Severall Informations . . .' covers nine pages of foolscap without a comma or stop. It is written in a semi-literate attempt at 'legalese' and is very difficult to read; yet it is sprinkled with all sorts of unexpected social details. We learn, for instance, that if you posted a letter after hours, you were liable to have it thrown out again into the street after you left, if you did not tip the porter sufficiently. This, according to Hitchen, was how two boys had come by Lord Barnard's bills. They had gone to the General Post Office at midnight to post a letter and had had to pay the porter 6d. to take it in. They had found another letter, whose sender had failed to tip the porter, 'thrust out the Post Office Door', had opened it, found another envelope inside with a forwarding address on it, had opened that, and found the bills inside. On page 6 he says that he and some people were at the Ring in Moorfields 'to see the Wrestling and Cudgell playing And on a sudden there was on the other Side of the Ring a Gentleman in a great Consternation having as he said Lost his Letter Case or pockett book. . . . And thereupon the person who is called the Vinager or Ring Keeper seeing this Respond^t. (i.e. Hitchen)

WOOD STREET, COMPTER.

On the east side of Wood Street stood this Prison, pertaining to the Sheriffs of London, built in the Mayoralty of Sir Samuel Strange Kⁿᵗ (Sir John Smith, & James Edwards, Esqʳ being Sheriffs) in the year 1670.

Publyh'd Janʳ 1 1793 by N Smith Gᵗ Mays Buildings, Sᵗ Martins Lane

1 Wood Street Compter debtors' prison, where Wild was held from
March 1710 to December 1712

2 & 3 *Above* A rare woodcut of a trial at the old Bailey in the early
18th-century. *Below* Another little-known view. Between the wall
and the court is the Bail Dock. These two views show the theatrical
appearance of the Sessions House in Wild's day. (See *Chapter III
& Appendix IV*)

advised the Said Gentleman to apply himself to this Respond^t. . . .' In this case the thief turned out to be a James Jones, whom we shall hear of in the next chapter.

Hitchen's defence is full of comings and goings, and of meetings with mysterious women at midnight in Cheapside, of unknown little boys coming up to him at Moorfields and inexplicably presenting him with Bills of Exchange, and of whispering rendezvous in the upper rooms of taverns. We learn the names of the pubs and coffee-houses which the Marshal used as bases for his police work: Masey's Coffee House in Old Change; Mear's, in St. Paul's House Court, near Hitchen's own house; Hatton's, in 'Basin Hall' (Basinghall) Street, where he spent mornings reading over the 'Dayly Currant' (*Daily Courant*) and other journals for news of property lost, stolen or strayed; the 'Woolpack' alehouse, Foster Lane, from where he wrote his blackmail letters; the 'Cross Keys' in Holborn; the 'King's Head', Ivy Lane, where he lunched and whose proprietor was suspected by the Aldermen to be a receiver of stolen goods; the 'Queen's Head' in Paternoster Row, whose proprietor was likewise suspected of receiving.

Most of the complaints were of the exorbitant sums demanded by Hitchen for the return of stolen goods. Dudley Downes lost four Exchequer Bills, value £200, and had to pay fifty-five guineas (in modern money about £1,100 or $2,750) to get them back. Nathaniel Smith had had his pocket-book stolen by a whore and Hitchen had demanded twenty guineas for it. He obstructed citizens in tracing thieves, saying *it was dangerous to exasperate the pickpockets by stopping bills etc.* . . .

The fullest information is by Constable Wise of Shoreditch, dated 2 October 1712. Hitchen, wrote the constable, was often in the 'Three Tuns' and 'Black Horse' taverns in Moorfields, in company with notorious thieves, gamesters and others; that since the Marshal had begun to frequent such places, it was difficult to disperse the thieves 'out of that Division'; that the Marshal had arrangements with well-known burglars to distribute their booty; that he used, besides the two above-named taverns, the 'Blue Boar' in the Barbican and the 'King's Head' in Ivy Lane as meeting-places with the thieves; and that he had a gang of young pickpocket boys whom he met regularly in the Clerkenwell Workhouse, calling them affectionately his 'Mathematicians'. When Constable Wise had taken up six pickpockets in the 'Three

Tuns', Hitchen had accused him of acting outside his jurisdiction. Hitchen then produced a paper with the City Arms on it and claimed that this gave him power in three counties. After that, he took the thieves with him back into the City of London, and presumably set them free there. Wise said that Hitchen took rewards of £50 and over for returning stolen goods, and that a Newgate turnkey, Mr. Spurling,* had likewise received a pocket book from a thief, and then got £40 reward for it by answering an advertisement in the *Gazette*.

When Wild came to write his pamphlet against Hitchen six years later, he claimed that the anonymous letter which Mr. Lawrence had received was in fact a circular letter that the Marshal frequently sent out to people who had been robbed, and he even went so far as to quote the text. It is probably quite close to the original, though I suspect Wild added the last sentence himself:

To Mr. A— Merchant,

SIR,
I am Inform'd that you have lately had the Misfortune to be Depriv'd of your Pocket-Book. It is not long since I labour'd under the same Calamity, and perhaps to a greater Degree than you, I having Notes for very considerable Sums enclos'd in the same; but upon applying my self to Mr. *C—s H—n*, in St. *Paul's* Church-Yard, whom I was inform'd was the greatest Proficient in the Business of *Thief-Taking* in *England*, he took care to serve me effectually. There is no doubt but he will serve you likewise to the Extent of his Abilities, and I can assure you he has universal Acquaintance with, and Influence over all Persons in the Town Employ'd in Thefts of this Nature. But I must give you this Caution, that you go to him with your Pockets well lin'd, or He'll have nothing to say to you.

I am, tho' unknown,
Your Friend Etc.
A.B.

Wild quotes another letter which he claims Hitchen sent to a Quaker, from whom he was trying to extort money. The curious thing about the letter is, that although it looks like a piece of nonsense, it catches a habit of speech which the Marshal had—he

* *See page* 130.

often said 'thee' when he should have said 'thou' (perhaps he was North Country). In his defence, for instance, Hitchen makes Nathaniel Smith say, when he asked the Marshal to get back his pocket-book, 'I shall take itt as a favour if thee wouldst use thy best endeavours to recover it . . .':

To Aminidab Prim. *

Aminidab,

THO' Thee hast been with mee, and made a tedious Preachment, pretending to be owner of a Pocket-Book in my Custody; 'tis not thy Cant or Claim to Inspiration, shall deter me from pursuing my Interest. Thou hast hitherto grossly Impos'd upon mee, and shewed that thou art a thorough-pac'd Deceiver; but Thee must not think, by thy plain Ways of Hypocrisy, thy untrimm'd Coat, Buttonless Hat, and extensive Band, to cast a Mist before mine Eyes; for Zounds Thee must tell the Truth, I am fully satisfied the Flesh has been powerful, that Thou has folded *Tabitha* in thine Arms, taken up the Veil of Iniquity, and jump'd into the Mouse-Trap of Sin. Thy Back deserves a Rod for thy Carnal Intrigues, And if Thee dost not speak to the Purpose, the Jest will be carried so far that I shall be oblig'd, to bring thee before a Magistrate, which will greatly expose Thee before the Righteous Congregation. O *Aminidab* remember thy Guilt, and fill up the Breach thou hast made in the Female's Reputation.

I am,

THY FRIEND,

C.H.

On receiving the letter, says Wild, the furious Quaker took it to a distinguished apothecary living in Poultry, who laid it before the Court of Aldermen. I found no such letter, or mention of one like it, among the papers; but as these are incomplete and may still be added to, the question of its existence must be left open.

Nevertheless, how did Wild come to know so many details about this affair? I have mentioned that two of the Marshal's 'Mathematicians', William Field and Christopher Plummer, were in the Compter at the end of September. Among the papers on

---

* 'Aminidab' was the popular name for Quakers at the time. It probably derived from the Quakers' predilection for Old Testament names, and 'Aminidab' was the most obscure and outrageous Old Testament name anyone could think of. 'Prim', of course, just means 'prim'.

Hitchen is a Warrant for the Keeper to bring them to the Guildhall, and a note saying that they were questioned and, on the
strength of their evidences, given their freedom by Sir Charles
Peters on 9 October. I have also remarked that Wild, who was
then petitioning for his own release, must have known Field if he
did not actually escort him to the Guildhall, and he certainly
knew Field for many years after. Another possible source was
Spurling, whom Wild may have met through Hitchen later. Add
to these the general gossip, and Wild's knowledge becomes
credible. It is only a pity that the statements of Field and Plummer
were not preserved.

To return to Hitchen, however, the core of his defence against
all charges was that he was being 'malitiously' persecuted 'by
Thefes & Robbers' and infamous persons 'of no Creditt', whose
informations were nothing but a parcel of lies, insinuations,
inferences, conjectures and hearsays.

The Court of Aldermen was in a dilemma. They could not, for
reasons I have tried to explain in Chapter III, dismiss him so
soon after he had taken office, for that would make it impossible
to find a replacement willing to pay £700 or even more. On the
other hand, they could not ignore him, for, as the Lord Mayor
reminded them when he appointed the committee, the Marshal's
behaviour was 'a great Indignity to the Honour of this City and
. . . in a more especial Manner it is a Reflection upon the Officers
in the Lord Mayor's House. . . .'3 They put the matter off, therefore, until after Christmas, and did not read Hitchen's defence
until 16 January 1713. Then they came to no decision. Meanwhile,
the embattled Marshal was doing his best to prop up his collapsing
fortunes. On 24 March 1713 he submitted a paper which proposed
methods of 'detecting Thiefes & other fellons' in London. Lists
should be made of brothels, disorderly houses, receivers and pawn-
brokers. Felons who intended to impeach their comrades should
be kept apart from them, and not thrown together among the
common crowd at Newgate. The government should instruct
the public, by means of broadsheets nailed-up on notice boards,
in the different methods used by footpads, burglars and pickpockets. A reward of a quarter-part of goods stolen should be
given to such as expose the receivers and pawnbrokers who deal
in them, 'which will be ye means and occasion of great diffidence
between ye Buyers and Sellers of Stolen goods'.

He ended by hinting that he was not paid enough:

As to that part of ye order which relates to ye detecting of Thieves If itt bee soo intended that I must prosecute & convict I must Say 'tis not in my power to charge them with any Pticulor Acts whereby to convict them, tho' they beare ye Generall Character of Thieves But I will endeavour as farr as in mee lyes to find out such Psons who may bee proper evidence having reasonable time allowed for that purpose & an allowance Suitable to the charges.

The paper was set aside and at last, on 24 June 1713, Hitchen was suspended in his office until he could prove that he was worthy of it once again. The Court said that those involved were free to prosecute if they thought fit. Curiously enough, none did.

Charles Hitchen was now thrown upon his own resources. He still retained power of arrest and could obtain warrants when needed. Without his three men, however, he lacked an assistant. Jonathan Wild had lately moved into Cock Alley and was running a small brandy-shop. He was also serving the public in his humble way by returning stolen letters and diaries to their owners, and paying too much for them. Wild himself tells us what happened next:

'After the *M—l's* Suspension in his Office, that he was forbid Attendance on the Lord Mayor, He on a time applied himself to the *Buckle Maker* near *Cripplegate*, Addressing himself to him in the following Manner:

I am very sensible that you (calling him by his Name) are let into the Knowledge of the Intrigues of the *Compter*, particularly, with Relation to the Securing of *Pocket Books*: But your Experience, says the *M—l*, is Inferior to mine, I can put you in a far better Method than you are Acquainted with, and which may be Facilitated with Safety: For tho' I am Suspended, I still retain the Power of Acting as a Constable; and notwithstanding, I can't be heard before my Lord Mayor as formerly, I have Interest amongst the *Al—n* upon any Complaint. But I must first tell you (the *Buckle Maker*) that you'll spoil the Trade of Thief-Taking, in Advancing greater Rewards than are necessary: I give but Half-a-Crown a Book; and when the Thieves and Pick Pockets see you and I Confederate, they'll submit to our Terms, and likewise continue their Thefts for fear of coming to the Gallows by our Means. Concluding, you shall take a

Turn with me as my Servant or Assistant, and we'll commence our Rambles this Night.

Thus began a partnership which lasted about a year. They quarrelled, as such people must, and when in 1718 Hitchen became alarmed by his old partner's astonishing rise to fame and wealth, he tried to discredit him by publishing an attack or a Discovery on him (*see page* 100), Wild countered with another and it is from these two pamphlets that most of our knowledge about Wild's early career and the world he lived in derives. Hitchen's pamphlet describes Wild as he was in his time of rising success, *c.* 1717; Wild's goes back to the time, 1713–14, when he was the Marshal's Deputy, or 'Man', and so comes in naturally here.

╬ VII ╬ *The Protection Racket*

The western limit of the Marshal's area of jurisdiction was the gate at Temple Bar, whose site is now commemorated by the statue of the gryphon outside the Law Courts.

Accordingly, therefore, the Marshal and his man began their tour at Temple Bar and called in at various brandy-shops along Fleet Street. 'Some of the Masters of these Houses, Complimented the *M—l* with *Punch*, others with *Brandy*, and some Presented him with their *Fine Ale*; offering their Service to their worthy Protector: the *M—l* made them little Answer, but gave 'em to understand, all the Service he expected from them, was to give him Information of Pocket-Books, or any Goods Stoll'n, as a *Pay-back* as he called it.'

The squalor and misery of these night scenes in Wild's pamphlet are given a deceptive glitter by the baroque formality of language and behaviour. The Marshal is again speaking:

. . . for you Women of the Town (Addressing himself to some Females in one of the Shops) make it a common Practice to Resign things of this Nature to the Bullies and Rogues of your Retinue, who upon Occasion, fill you with dreadful Apprehensions, under a Notion of their being Officers of the City. But this shall no longer be born with; I'll give you my Word, both they and you shall be Detected, unless you deliver all the

Pocket Books you from Time to Time meet with to me. What do ye think I bought my Place for, but to make the most of it? And you are to understand this is my Man (pointing to the *Buckle Maker*) to assist me; and if you at any Time for the Future, refuse to yield up the Watches, Books Etc. as you take or come into your Hands, either to me or my Servant, you may be assured of being all sent to *Bridewell*, and not One of you for the future shall be permitted to walk the Streets.

When the Marshal seizes some pickpocket boys and upbraids them for not meeting him earlier that day, they reply 'We have been Stroling over *Morefields*, and from thence to the *Blew Boar* in pursuit of you; but not finding you as usual, we were under some Fears that you were Indispos'd.' When he sends them packing, with instructions to bring everything they steal to Wild or himself, and a warning that if they do not they shall swing for it, for 'we are out in the City every Night to observe your Motions', they take their leave 'making their Master a very low *Congee*' (bow).

Wild's story is certainly substantiated in its incidental details, such as the name of the 'Blue Boar', by the documents in the Guildhall Records Office.

On another evening, the Marshal and his deputy seized a 'Buttock-and-file' in a brandy shop. She had stolen a watch and it was their plan to commit her to the Compter if she did not give it to them. As soon as they found her, they showed 'an enrag'd Countenance . . . becoming the Design' and 'the Company said that the Master and Man look'd as sour as two *Devils*. "Devils!" said the Marshal, "I'll make some of ye *Devils*, if ye don't immediately discover the Watch and Pocket-Book I am employ'd to Procure!" "We don't know your meaning Sir," answer'd some. "Who do you Discourse to?" said others. "We know nothing of it".'

Hitchen offered the woman a guinea for the watch. She complained to Wild that it was hard when he gained five or ten guineas for each theft and would not bestow five or ten shillings 'on us unfortunate Wretches'. The watch was in pawn for 40*s*., 'and if he did not advance that Sum, she would be oblig'd to Strip herself for the Redemption; tho' when her Furbelow-Scarf was laid aside, she had nothing underneath but Furniture for a Paper-Mill'. The Marshal gave her 30*s*., and, of course, the watch was never returned to the owner.

The Marshal extorted money from innocent and guilty alike.

'A File' who had stolen a watch was forced to confess that she had sold it to a watchmaker for 5os. The watchmaker was arrested and forced to surrender it without compensation, after which the Marshal returned it to the owner for a reward of three guineas. Another thief who had picked a pocket-book from a crowd watching a man in the pillory was 'persuaded' to exchange it for a watch the Marshal had taken from a whore. Hitchen explained that the watch was 'safe' because the owner would be ashamed to prosecute the woman (Nathaniel Smith's case in the documents of the Committee is similar to this). On another occasion Wild was led into a trap and drubbed with fire-irons. Instead of helping, the Marshal basely fled, but when the time came to collect 'smart money' (protection money) he kept most of it to himself. A clergyman who was in an alley 'pissing against the Wall' was jostled by a streetwalker. When he protested, the Marshal seized them both and forced the clergyman to pay a security to avoid being charged with indecent behaviour. The Marshal even tried to 'protect' some respectable taverns and eating-houses. This was a failure, for the enraged proprietors and their waiters seized him, beat him with cudgels and tossed him in a blanket.

A biscuit maker from Wapping lost a pocket-book containing a £100 Exchequer Bill and applied to Wild for its recovery. Wild advised the biscuit maker to advertise in the newspapers and stop payment of the bill. A few days later the Marshal called on the biscuit maker and began to cross-examine him, desiring to know above all if he had employed anyone else to look for it. 'To which the Bisket-maker answer'd, he had Employ'd one *Wild*: Upon which the *M—l* told him he was quite under a Mistake; he gave him to understand that he should have applied himself to Him, who was the only Person in *England* that could have serv'd him; being well assur'd it was entirely out of the Power of *Wild*, or any of those Fellows, to know where it was; (which was very certain, he having it at that time in his Custody) . . .' There followed a wrangle about the reward that should be paid, the biscuit maker having offered £10 and the Marshal demanding £50. After a few days, on Wild's advice the biscuit maker offered the Marshal £40, to which the Marshal replied 'Zounds Sir, you are too late!' Wild later discovered from the boy who had first stolen the bill that it had been sold to Hitchen for four or five guineas almost within the hour, and was later changed for its full value in such a way that it could never be traced back.

The Marshal being now ready for another Adventure, going up *Ludgate Hill*, he observ'd a Well-dress'd Woman walking before; which he told the Buckle-maker was a lewd Woman, for that he saw her Talking with a Man. This was no sooner spoke, but he seiz'd her, and asking her who she was, she made Answer that she was a *Bailiff's* Wife. 'You are more like to be a Whore', said the *M—l*, 'and as such you shall go to the *Compter.*' He forced her to go with him to the 'Nag's Head', Cheapside, and sit on the far side of the room shivering (it was winter) while he ate his supper by the fireside. When he had finished, he remarked that if he had been an informer or the like, she would willingly have treated him to a meal without his having to ask, continuing, 'You may do what you please; but tho' we that buy our Places seem to go for nothing: I can assure you it is in my Power, if I see a Woman in the Hands of *Informers,* to Discharge *her*, and Commit *them*: You are not so Ignorant, but you must guess my Meaning.'

She paid for his supper. Knowing what we do about bailiffs and their wives, perhaps we should not waste too much sympathy on her.

As the master of Jonathan Wild, Hitchen lacked his pupil's finesse. His approaches to the victims of robberies were crude, his manners coarse, his bargaining erratic and greedy. He antagonized the public because he lacked the patience so essential to his line of dealing and would often sell the stolen goods to receivers, or dispose of stolen bank notes at gaming-houses, before the owners had been brought to the proper pitch of paying the 'rewards' he wanted. He antagonized the young thieves because he never paid them more than half the promised price, saying that 'such Rascals are ignorant how to Dispose of their Moneys'.

One Night, not far from St. *Paul's*, the *M—l* and the *Buckle-maker* his Man, met with a Detachment of Pick Pocket Boys; who instantly at the sight of their Master, took to their Heels and ran away. The *Buckle-maker* ask'd the meaning of their surprize, to which the *M—l* answer'd 'I know their meaning, a Pack of Rogues; they were to have met me in the Fields this Morning with a Book, I am Inform'd they have taken from a Gentleman, and they are afraid of being secur'd for their Disobedience. There is *Jack Jones* among them—we'll catch the Whores Birds!'

Jack, or James, Jones we have already heard of as the boy who stole the wallet at Moorfields Ring. Hitchen and Wild caught Jones and accused him of burglary besides picking pockets. This happened to be true. Jones confessed and impeached his three companions. He was taken before a Justice next morning, and said that the others were hiding in a house in Beech Lane in the Barbican, between the north end of Red Cross Street and White Cross Street. Wild and Hitchen went 'privately in the Night' to seize them.

Listning at the Door, they overheard the Boys with several others in a mixt Company: They entred the House, where they met with 10 or 11 Persons, who were immediately in a great Rage: enquiring what Business the M—l had there, and salluting him with a few Damn ye's; which occasion'd the M—l to make a prudent Retreat, pulling the Door after him, and leaving his little Man to the Mercy of the Savage Company. In a short Space, the Marshal return'd with a Guard of Eight or Ten Watch-Men, and a Constable; at the Door the M—l out of his dastardly Disposition, tho' his pretence was a Ceremonious Respect, oblig'd the Constable to go in first but the Constable and the M—l were both so long in their Compliments, that the Man thought they neither of them would venture in); at last the Constable entring with his long Staff extended before him, the M—l Manfully follow'd, crying out 'Where are the Rebel Villains? Why don't ye secure them?' The M—l's Man answer'd that they were under the Table, upon which the Constable pull'd out the juvenile Offenders, neither of them being above 12 Years of Age.

As their robberies had been committed in Surrey (the 'Fields' being St. George's Fields, Southwark), the boys were tried at Kingston Assizes. '. . . . the Bill was found* the M—l Endorsing his Name on the Back . . . to have the Honour of being an Evidence against these Monstrous House Breakers.' The boys were acquitted, however, when their parents showed that the Marshal had been the occasion of their ruin by employing them to rob 'in the Fields'. The Marshal was reprimanded and the Court observed that his main interest in the boys seemed to be the chance

---

* That is, there was found to be a case against them. These matters were decided by the Grand Jury, which sat every month before each Sessions. In such a case, the indictment was marked *Billa Vera* (True Bill). *See also page* 248.

of claiming the £40 rewards on their heads. Hitchen returned to London enraged, leaving Jonathan Wild to pay the costs.

The Under-Marshal's interest in the boys, had the Judge known it, was not entirely confined to the money they might bring in, dead or alive.

One Night the *M—l* invited his Man the *Buckle-maker* to a House near the end of *Old Bayly*; telling him he would introduce him to a Company of *He-Whores*. The Man, not rightly apprehending his meaning, ask'd him if they were Hermaphrodites?

'No ye Fool!' said the Marshal, 'they are Sodomites and such as deal with their own Sex instead of Females.'

This being a Curiosity the *M—l*'s Man had not hitherto met with, he willingly accompanied his Master to the House; which they no sooner Enter'd, but the *M—l* was Complemented by the Company with the Titles of Madam, and Ladyship; the Man asking the Occasion of those uncommon Devoirs, the *M—l* said that it was a familiar Language peculiar to that House. The *M—l*'s Man was not long in the House before he was more surpriz'd than at first. The Men calling one another 'My Dear', hugging and kissing, tickling and feeling each other, as if they were a mixture of wanton Males and Females; and assuming effeminate Voices, Female Airs Etc., some telling others that they ought to be Whipp'd for not coming to School more frequently. The *M—l* was very merry in this Assembly, and Dallied with the young Sparks with a great deal of Pleasure, until some Persons came into the House that he little expected to meet with in that place; and then finding it out of his Power to secure the Lads to himself, he started up of a sudden in a prodigious Rage, asking the Frolicking Youth, if they were become so common as to use those Obnoxious Houses; and told them that he would spoil their Diversion; upon which he made his Exit, with his Man. Going out of the House, he said he suppos'd they would have the Impudence to make a Ball. The Man desiring him to explain what he meant by that, he answered that there was a noted House in *Holborn*, to which such sort of Persons used to repair, and Dress themselves in Women's Apparel for the Entertainment of others of the same Inclinations, in Dancing Etc. in imitation of the Fair Sex, telling him if he were to come into the Room where they were present upon such an Occasion, that he would take them for so many Cats a-Catterwawling. 'But', says he, 'I'll be reveng'd on these Smock fac'd young Dogs. I'll watch their Waters, and secure 'em, and send them to the Compter.'

Accordingly, the *M—l* knowing their usual Hours and customary Walks, placed himself with a Constable in *Fleet Street*, and dispatch'd his Man to the *Old Bayly*, with some likewise to his Assistance, to Apprehend them in their return Home. About the usual Hour of their Separation, several of the sporting Sodomites were seiz'd, by the *M—l* and his Man, and their Assistants, in Women's Apparel, and Convey'd to the *Compter*. Next Morning they were carried before the Lord Mayor in the same Dresses they were taken in. Some were compleatly Rigg'd in Gowns, Petticoats, Head cloths, fine lac'd Shoes, Furbelow Scarves, and Masks; some had Riding-hoods; some were dressed like Shepherdesses; others like Milk-Maids with fine Green Hatts, Wastcoats and Petticoats, and others had their Faces patched and painted, and wore very extensive Hoop-petticoats, which were then very lately introduced. His Lordship having examined them, committed them to the Workhouse, there to remain during pleasure, and, as part of their Punishment, order'd them to be publickly convey'd thro' the Streets in their Female Habits. Pursuant to which Order, the young Tribe was carried in Pomp to the Workhouse, and remain'd there a considerable Time, till at last one of them threaten'd the Marshal with the same Punishment for former Adventures; who thereupon apply'd to my Lord Mayor, and procured their Discharge. This Commitment was so mortifying to one of the young Gentlemen, that he died in a Few Days after his Release. Any Gentleman that wants to be Acquainted with the Sodomitish Academy may be inform'd where it is, and be graciously introduced by the accomplish'd Mr. *H—n*.

Wild's picture of the Academy is accurate, and almost certainly refers to a house in Field Lane, Holborn, kept by a woman with the remarkable name of Mother Clap.* In 1726–7, there was a

* The names of these 'Madames' of Augustan London are really extra-ordinary: Mother Wisebourne, Mother Needham, Mother Jolly, Betty Careless and Mother Clap. It would almost seem that they had been invented to describe their roles in life, like those of the characters in Restoration comedies —'Mr. Vainlove', 'Captain Brazen', 'Lord Foppington', etc.—but these were

drive against her 'Academy' and similar places, in which more than fifty men were taken to Newgate and later tried. It came out in evidence that 'marriages' were performed there, with ceremonies, wedding-veils, rings, and bridal chambers. A more genial picture of the 'Mollies' (as homosexuals were called then) can be found in the gossip column of Mrs. Crackenthorpe, *The Female Tatler*, where she describes a shopping visit to the fashion 'boutiques' of Ludgate Hill in 1709. The assistants were the 'sweetest, fairest, nicest, dish'd out Creatures; and by their Elegant Address and Soft Speeches, you would guess them to be Italians.'

> We went into a Shop which had three Partners: two of 'em were to Flourish out their Silks; and, after an obliging Smile, and a pretty Mouth made, Cicero-like, to expatiate on their Goodness; and the other's sole Business was to be Gentleman Usher to the Shop, to stand completely Dressed at the Door, bow to all the Coaches that pass by, and hand Ladies out and in. We saw Abundance of Gay Fancies, fit for Sea-Captains' Wives, Sheriffs' Feasts, and Taunton Dean Ladies.
>
> 'This, Madam, is wonderful Charming. This, Madam, is so diverting a Silk. This Madam—My Stars! How *Cool* it looks! But *this*, Madam—Ye Gods! Would I had 10,000 Yards of it!'
>
> Then gathers up a Sleeve, and places it on our Shoulders. 'It suits your Ladyship's Face wonderfully well.'
>
> When we had pleas'd ourselves, and bid him 10*s*. a Yard for what he had asked 15: 'Fan me ye Winds, your Ladyship Rallies me! Should I part with it at such a Price, the Weavers would Rise upon the very Shop! Was you at the *Park* last Night Madam? Your Ladyship shall abate me 6*d*. Have you read the *Tatler* today? Etc.'
>
> These Fellows are positively the greatest Fops in the Kingdom; they have their Toilets and their Fine Night-Gowns; their *Chocolate in the Morning,* and their *Green Tea two Hours after*; Turkey Polts for Dinner; and their Perfumes, Washes, and Clean Linen, equip 'em for the Parade.[1]

Finally Moorfields itself, where Hitchen was seen so frequently, was notorious for the homosexuals who solicited there in public, apparently the names they were born with. Mother Needham, the most famous, may be an exception, for a Sessions roll of August 1724 gives her name as 'Elizabeth Bird, alias Needham'. Hogarth used her name for satirical purpose ('Need 'em') in '*The Harlot's Progress*'; but then 'Moll Hackabout' was actually taken from a real person, Kate Hackabout, as well.

to the extent that the path along the wall dividing the two gardens was known as 'Sodomites' Walk'.

The events related by Wild presumably occurred in the winter and spring of 1714. In September 1713, Hitchen had petitioned to be reinstated, but the matter was deferred. In December he asked the Court of Aldermen to consider his proposals for the repression of thieving in the City, which he had made the previous March. They were read a second time in January. On 6 April 1714, Charles Hitchen was restored to his place as Under-Marshal, on his promise of a 'better Demeanour therein for the Future'.[2]

It is probable that the serious quarrels between Wild and Hitchen broke out shortly after this, although the two may have continued an uneasy partnership until the autumn. Now that he was reinstated and had his 'Men' to work for him once more, the Under-Marshal could have had little need of an assistant whose resourcefulness and independence must have been alarming. Jonathan Wild, for his part, must have found his semi-official status as the Marshal's Deputy useful, but the crude behaviour of the Marshal himself an increasing liability. Besides, thief-takers and officers like Hitchen, who were to some extent protected by their pretended or real authority, restricted their trade to articles that were easy to dispose of but hard to trace, such as bank bills and watches, or could be used for blackmail, such as pocket-books and diaries; but for larger things, such as clothes, elaborate jewellery, fabrics, silver plate and furniture, there was still no easy outlet at all. Wild had found the answer to this problem, but it could succeed only so long as no one was aware of what he was really doing.

⟨ VIII ⟩ *Cock Alley*

Seven weeks after Hitchen had been reinstated, the following advertisement appeared in the *Daily Courant* of 26 May 1714:

> Lost on Friday Evening 19th March last, out of a Compting House in Derham Court (*i.e. Durham Ct.*) in Great Trinity Lane, near Bread Street, a Wast Book and a Day Book; they are of no use to any one but the Owner, being posted into a Ledger to the Day they were lost. Whoever will bring them to Mr. Jonathan Wild over-against Cripplegate-Church, shall have a Guinea Reward and no Questions asked.*

It is the first I have been able to find of the many hundreds of similar advertisements Wild put in the newspapers during the next ten years. Apart from telling us his address, however, it contains several clues to his method at this early stage of his career. A 'Wast' or Waste Book was a rough account book in which entries of transactions were made at the time of business, to be posted into a proper account-book afterwards, and a Day Book was a list of the day's business in the order in which it was done. As Wild pointed out, they were of no use to anyone but the owner, and therefore would not interest a receiver. They had been stolen from a counting house and not a brothel, and so could not be used for blackmail. As blackmail was the best protection

* I.e., about £21 or $50 in modern money.

4 Wild's house in the Old Bailey, a little to the south of Prujean
Court. The shop-front was added at the end of the 18th-century,
the engraving being made just before the house was pulled down
in 1813

5 A caricature of Wild in his office

against the owner who might try to prosecute the dealer for compounding a felony, it was unlikely that such articles would interest a thief-taker either.

Jonathan Wild's solution to this problem was of the kind that might be called truly professional—that is, it was direct and deceptively simple. *Select Trials* says that shortly after leaving Hitchen, Wild called together a meeting of some of his chief 'Prigs' (thieves) and laid the matter before them:

You know, my Bloods (*quoth he*), that as *Trade* goes at present, you stand but a *queer* Chance; for, when you have *made* (taken) anything, if you carry it to the *Fencing-Culls* and *Flash Pawn-brokers*, these unconscionable Dealers in *contraband* Goods will hardly *tip* ye a quarter of what it is worth; and, if ye offer it to a Stranger, it's ten to one but you are *hobbled* (arrested). So that there's no such Thing as a Man's living by his Labour; for, if he don't like to be half-starved, he must run the Hazard of being *scragg'd* (hanged)—which, let me tell ye, is a damn'd hard Case! Now, if you'll take my Advice, I'll put ye in a Way to remedy all this. When you have been upon any *Lay*, and *spoke* to some Purpose (stolen something worth while), let me know all the Particulars; and I'll engage to *pay-back* the Goods to the *Cull* that owns them, and raise ye more *Cole* (cash) upon that Account, than you can expect from the rascally *Fencers*. And at the same Time take Care that you shall all be *Bowmen* (successful thieves).

Wild also 'took Care' that his thieves brought him only the particulars of stolen goods, not the goods themselves. He saw that the mistake made by receivers and thief-takers alike, including Hitchen, was to take possession of the goods for cash. If a man was never in possession, he could not come under the Receiving Acts. He therefore made it his business to discover the address of anyone whom his thieves had robbed and call at the house. There, hat in hand, he would explain how he had heard that My Lord had suffered this unfortunate loss, but that he had an idea where the goods might be found, or at least who it was that had possession of them; or, alternatively, that an honest pawnbroker had been offered some goods the day before, and had stopped them on suspicion of their being stolen—perhaps the gentleman's were among them. Jonathan Wild would then offer to arrange for the goods to be returned, adding that the affair must be handled with caution lest the thieves, or the broker, take

fright and the goods be lost forever. If the person questioned
Wild's integrity, or asked how he should know so much about
the theft, Wild answered 'that it was meerly Providential; being,
by meer Accident, at a Tavern, or at a Friend's House in the Neighbourhood, they heard that such a Gentleman had his House
broken open, and such and such Goods Stolen, and the like.'[1]

If the person continued doubtful, Wild would leave in a huff:
' "Sir (*says Jonathan*), I come only to serve you, and if you think
otherwise, I must let you know, that you are mistaken. I have told
you, that some Goods being offered to pawn by a suspected
Person, the Broker had the Honesty to stop them; and therefore,
Sir, if you question me about Thieves, I have nothing to say to
you; but that I can give you a good Account of myself, my
Name is Wild, and I live in *Cock-Alley* by *Cripplegate*, where you
may find me any Day of the Week; and so, Sir, your Humble
Servant." By this Affected Resentment, he seldom failed of
bringing the injured Person to treat with him upon his own
Terms, which on such Occasions he commonly advanced.'[2]

Defoe tells the same story, but maintains that Wild always sent
someone else, such as Mary Milliner. It is more likely, I think,
that in the early days Wild would have handled such a delicate
part of his business himself.

Finally, Wild established his good faith by offering to advertise
in the press for the goods on the client's behalf or, more deviously,
suggested that the client should advertise for them himself.
Thus it can be seen that the advertisement in the *Daily Courant*
served many purposes, and most of them hidden. It allayed the
suspicions of the public, the authorities and, of course, the owner
of the books; it proved that Wild did not have the books himself;
it served as a sign to the thieves that the owner was ready to
come to terms; if Wild genuinely did not know who had stolen
the books, it brought new thieves into his circle; and finally, it
made Wild's name familiar to the public in general. As for
pocket-books, money, watches, etc., an advertisement was a
more subtle and effective insinuation of blackmail than the old
personal approach employed by Hitchen and practitioners of the
'Trap'. The following example, in the *Daily Post* of 2 November
1724, comes from the time when the device had been perfected:

Lost, the 1st of October, a black shagreen Pocket-Book, edged
with Silver, with some Notes of Hand. The said Book was lost

in the Strand, near the Fountain Tavern, about 7 or 8 o'clock
at Night. If any Person will bring the aforesaid Book to Mr.
Jonathan Wild, in the Old Bailey, he shall have a Guinea
Reward.'

The 'Fountain Tavern' (commemorated now by a plaque) was
then a notorious brothel, and 'Notes of Hand' implies that Wild
knew the identity of the owner of the pocket-book—indeed, that
Wild had the book in his possession already. From this, it followed
that the owner could not afford to forget the book, but would
have to get in touch with Wild and retrieve it for a considerable
fee, or explain to his wife (or mother) what he was doing at the
'Fountain' at 8 o'clock at night on 1 October.

The last difficulty—that of actually returning the goods without compounding the felony—was the easiest to overcome.
While Jonathan kept to his 'poor peddling Trade', as 'H.D.' calls
it, of stolen account-books, diaries and letters, the danger was in
any case not very great. The financial value of such articles was
hard to assess, and for that reason no jury was likely to fix it above
the capital level (1s. if stolen from a person, 5s. from a shop and
40s. from a house, etc.) should an owner, by some mischance,
take Wild or the thief to court. In practice, most owners were
glad to get their books back as quickly as possible and with a
minimum of fuss:

> After he had bargain'd with the People, and they were come by
> his Appointment to pay the Money, and receive the writings,
> he led them into a Room contriv'd for that Purpose; where
> pushing back a small Pannel of the Wainscot, a Hand us'd to
> appear with the Writings in it, and the Parties were to take
> them out of that Hand, and put the Money into it, without their
> seeing the Body which belong'd to it; so that they could not
> say he had ever taken any of their Money or receiv'd the
> stolen Goods.[3]

When, becoming more familiar with the pitfalls in the law, he
extended his trade to more profitable goods, such as the clothes
and fabrics I mentioned, he arranged appointments between the
clients and the thieves at convenient places—street corners,
squares, bridges—where the goods could be returned and the
money paid. In these early months, Wild did not bother to take
rewards for his services, for he had a sufficient share of the money
paid to the pawnbroker and the thieves.

So long as he kept to these indirect methods, Jonathan Wild never ran more than the risk of a common law misdemeanour, and this risk was to a large extent covered by the gratitude of his clients. Some early accounts (and F. J. Lyons) say that one client, a quack called Dr. Cornelius Tilburn, did indeed prosecute Wild, and was so decisively defeated that Wild was thereafter hailed as a genius by the underworld. I have reason to believe, however, that Tilburn's case did not occur until 1719.* In trying to reconstruct this period of Wild's history it is safer to discount all previous biographies, including Lyons's, and start afresh.

It would appear that in the summer and autumn of 1714, Wild was engaged in quite a fierce struggle, both with rival thief-takers and with gangs of thieves over which at this stage he had no control. If his plan was to work, the thieves would have to recognize his 'authority', and authority could be acquired only by making unhappy examples of some of them. In this, it would seem that he did not scruple to claim that he was an agent, or 'Deputy' of the City Marshal, although his relations with Hitchen were now severed and had never been more than private and personal.

An examination of the *Sessions Papers* and of the 1735 edition of *Select Trials* (the relevant information having been cut from later editions) shows that in August and September 1714 there were a number of burglaries committed in and near Whitehall, and by the recurrence of names obviously they were the work of one gang. The first was on 18 August, when three burglars, Robert Parrot, Will Parker and John Chance, stole a quantity of valuable jewellery, silver and vestments from the house of the Bishop of Norwich in King Street (which was then at the southern end of Whitehall). Wild must have built up a good intelligence service outside the City of London, for he quickly arrested Chance, discovered that the goods had been sold to one William White of Holborn, and persuaded Chance to impeach his accomplices, Parker and Parrot. He arrested Parrot but apparently failed to catch Parker. At the same time, he approached the Bishop of Norwich and told him that he had taken the villains. The Middlesex SP (*Sessions of the Peace*) Roll for April 1715 shows that White was arrested on suspicion of receiving but released for lack of evidence. Robert Parrot was condemned on Chance's evidence, but later reprieved and transported.

At the beginning of September, the Royal Chapel, or Ban-

* See page 95.

queting House as it is now called, in Whitehall was broken into,
the thieves having cut their way in from a house built against the
back of it. They stole, among other things, a silver gilt candlestick, whose loss was advertised in the newspapers. On the 27th,
the *Post Boy* announced:

> An Advertisement was inserted in this Paper, the 7th Day of
> September last, That a Silver Gilt Candle-stick was stolen out
> of the Royal Chapell at Whitehall. The Persons concerned in
> that sacrilegious Fact are since apprehended, by the great
> Diligence of the Deputy-Marshal of the City of London, and
> several others; and upon Examination before Hon. the Officers
> of the Board of the Green Cloth, were committed to several
> Gaols. The Prisoners' Names are, William Rigglesdon, John
> Parsons, and Elizabeth Shirley, the first has been suspected of
> several notorious Offenses, viz. Counterfeiting Bank-bills, and
> Forging Assignment on the Exchequer, and other Deeds, and
> has crowned his Villainy by being Principal in the aforesaid
> Robbery: he is now in the Marshalsea, and may be seen by any
> such whom he has wronged; and for a further Discovery of
> his wicked Practice, this public Notice is given.

Who was this 'Deputy-Marshal'? Like many officials before and
since, Hitchen was extremely touchy about minor distinctions of
rank and the correct rendering of titles: in fact, in his 'Answer'
to the Court of Aldermen Committee, he self-righteously describes how he corrected a woman (in Cheapside on the stroke of
midnight) who called him the 'City Marshal'. His title was 'Under'
or 'Second' Marshal, and I have never seen it called otherwise in
City records. A 'Deputy' was a temporary or surrogate, and Hitchen was never that even under suspension. I strongly suspect,
therefore, that this 'Deputy' was Jonathan Wild pretending to a
title to which he had no right.

There is only one fragment of evidence in support of Hitchen:
on 14 October he was given two extra Freedoms of the City to
sell as a reward for his diligence. 4 The Repertories do not say
what his diligence had been, and they may refer his proposals for
eliminating robbery, or indeed anything. On the other hand, there
is quite a lot of evidence in support of Wild. First, Riddlesdon and
Shirley are on Wild's famous 'List' (see Appendix II), in which
he says he arrested them for robbing the Banqueting House,
and Riddlesdon's name is still misspelt 'Rigglesdon'. Secondly,

we do know that not long afterwards Riddlesdon became one of Wild's thief-takers, and that therefore he must have saved himself by impeaching his two companions (the Sessions Rolls are unfortunately missing). We shall see that when Mrs. Knap was murdered eighteen months later, the first person Wild arrested was William White, who had received the Bishop of Norwich's goods. The most likely person to have informed him of White's whereabouts was Riddlesdon, for by then all the rest of the gang were dead. This in turn suggests, if it does not prove, a connection between Riddlesdon and Chance. Elizabeth Shirley was hanged in January 1715, and thus has the honour of being the first of Wild's recorded victims to reach the gallows.

On 2 November, John Chance broke into a shop in Northumberland Court, using the same means as Riddlesdon at the Banqueting House. He and a William Hoskins entered a shop next door, and with a drill bored holes along the edges of the wall panels. They removed the panels easily and climbed through. (This method is still not obsolete and was used in the famous robbery of paintings from Dulwich Gallery in 1966.) Wild arrested Chance again, and Chance again saved his life by impeaching Hoskins (also on Wild's list). After this, Chance left Westminster and tried the villages round the Metropolis. His first robbery was at Hammersmith. Perhaps he was trying to get out of Wild's reach. If so, he failed, and the luckless Chance, with his friend John Allen, was arrested by Wild in April and they were both condemned on the evidence of a third accomplice.

Thus within three months Wild had arrested seven people and secured the conviction of at least five. The rewards totalled £200. or perhaps more, which in modern money might represent £4,000 or $10,000. In the middle of this affair he moved from Cripplegate and rented a tavern from Mrs. Seagoe in Little Old Bailey. An advertisement in the *Daily Courant* of 24 December 1714 reveals that her tavern was called the 'Blue Boar' and that he was there a year earlier than has previously been believed:

A Watch & an Exchequer Bill for £1,000, No. 84289, lost by a Gentleman in Lyon's Inn. Whoever will bring the said Bill and Watch to Mr. John Jeffrey at the 3 Tuns Tavern in the Old Bailey, or Mr. Jonathan Wild at the Blue-Boar in the Old Bailey, shall have 10 Guineas Reward, and be askt no Questions, payment of the Bill being stopt.

The importance of the Whitehall robberies is that they show how Wild had already evolved the method he was to rely on for the rest of his life: first, take one member of a gang and persuade him to impeach two colleagues; then get a fourth to impeach the first, who might become dangerous later on, and the rest will go down like ninepins. It may be wondered why, after this exercise of power, the thieves did not become alarmed, unite against Wild and murder him before it was too late. The fact is that Wild's manner, like that of all strong personalities, was so persuasive and straightforward that he deceived everybody, and the thieves most of all. They failed to grasp that he had transferred the burden of risk from his shoulders on to theirs. During negotiations with a client, they remained in possession of the stolen goods. At any moment, their 'Factor', as he called himself, could turn and betray them if things started to go wrong, whilst they had no evidence against him with which to counter-attack, for he had not committed a felony. His assurance that so long as he did not know where they hid their stolen goods, they were in no danger from him, could not have carried much weight among the more intelligent, for obviously as time went by he would learn all their haunts and hideouts. In fact, of course, Wild was gradually drawing the little gangs and knots of thieves he knew into a more manageable system by encouraging them to keep to their specialized methods and within particular 'beats'. This, he said, would make it easier to serve clients expeditiously and so give the thieves a quicker return. They did not see that at the same time it enabled him to keep a more reliable check on them, for he had only to compare the details of robberies given to him by the public with the stories the thieves told him to discover if they were holding anything back or dealing through ordinary receivers. Perhaps they were so occupied by the day-to-day problems of survival, or were so used to Sir Salathiel Lovell, the City Marshal, the Newgate turnkeys, and all the other corrupt officials, magistrates, constables, bailiffs, setters and thief-takers, that they did not notice that Wild was different. His success becomes even more understandable if he spoke to them from some real or pretended position of strength, which again reinforces the probability that it was he who called himself the 'Deputy-Marshal of the City of London'.

{ IX } *Lost Property Office*

The Old Bailey was as good a business address for one of Wild's profession as any that could be desired. The very words 'Jonathan Wild's in the Old Bailey', which were to grace so many advertisements and newspapers stories in the coming years, had about them a ring of authority and tradition which would almost compel the public to associate his name with 'Justice', 'the Law' and the government of the land. If he was to keep a proper check on his thieves, he needed to gain free access to both Newgate prison and, during Sessions (which were held nine or ten times a year, but at no fixed dates and never in November), to that most curious of London buildings, the Justice House, and here he was within a minute's walk from both.

'The Old Bailey' is a narrowish street running north from Ludgate Hill, below the great west front of St. Paul's Cathedral, up to the church of St. Sepulchre's, Newgate. Today, it is somewhat undistinguished, most of its west side having been destroyed in World War II. The Central Criminal Court, with the gilded figure of blind 'Justice' poised on the dome and holding her sword and scales, stands at the top right-hand corner on the site of old Newgate prison. In the early eighteenth century, 'Great Old Bailey', as it was called, was a street of mixed character. There were a number of fairly big houses here and there—one of which Jonathan Wild bought in 1719—and numerous taverns, the

most famous of which was the 'Baptist's Head'. At the northern
end, the street split in two, 'Little Old Bailey' being a narrow lane
branching off to the left. Mrs. Seagoe's 'Blue Boar' was on the
right, or east, side of the lane, near the fork. In the nineteenth
century, the lane was pulled down to widen the road, and a
plaque on the wall commemorates the fact. Recognizances in the
London Sessions Rolls show that a large number of very poor
people—pickpockets and such—lived in the Old Bailey as well,
probably at the northern end where rents were low because of the
stench emanating from the prison.

At the 'Blue Boar' Jonathan Wild converted one of the parlours
into an office, ceased to call on those who had been robbed, and
depended on his growing fame to bring the public to him. He
charged a 5s. deposit, or search fee, to each client and, after
writing all the details of the robbery or loss in a book, would
gravely ask the client to call again in a day or two. At the second
visit, he would tell the client that he did have some news of the
missing goods, but unfortunately the rogues were threatening
to sell to a pawnbroker unless they got the price they wanted.
If only he could get to parley with them, no doubt he could bring
them down to a reasonable sum, but meanwhile, would the client
be willing to raise his 'reward' a little? And so it went on until
the figure, usually between a half and three-quarters the full
value of the goods, was agreed, and Wild told the client to go to
such-and-such a place with the stipulated money so that the
exchange could be made. If the grateful client now pressed a few
pounds into his hand, in consideration of the trouble he had gone
to, Wild felt bold enough to accept; and if any should ask him
how he could carry on this trade without being in confederacy
with the thieves, he would reply that while he admittedly had a
large acquaintance among such people, he used it merely for
gathering intelligence. When he was given details of a robbery,
he left messages for the suspected persons in the most likely
places, with instructions where to leave the goods if they wanted
the reward money, and a promise that no questions would be
asked. 'And where,' he would point out, 'is the Harm of all this?
I neither see the Thief, nor receive the Goods.' 'This was his
Account of the Matter,' says *Select Trials*, 'and they could get no
other.

Early in 1715, while the memory of his services to the Bishop
of Norwich and, apparently, the Board of the Green Cloth, were

still in the public's mind, Wild was able to come to the rescue of 'the Quality' once more. Lady Henrietta Godolphin paid a visit to a 'Mrs. H—n's' in St. James's Street, Piccadilly. Her chairmen left her sedan chair, which had crimson velvet cushions and damask curtains, outside the house and went to a neighbouring alehouse to await her return. While they were drinking, the chair 'was carried entirely off'. The chairmen immediately applied to Wild in the Old Bailey. After taking their crown deposit, he told them to come back in a day or two. When they presented themselves accordingly, he insisted on a considerable reward (some accounts say it was ten guineas). As soon as they had paid it, he told them to be sure to attend prayers at Lincoln's Inn Chapel next morning. They did so, and on coming out of the chapel were surprised and pleased to find the chair waiting under the piazza of the chapel, its cushions and curtains undamaged. 'H.D.' maintains that the people who stole the chair were in fact two of Wild's own men, who used to go through the streets disguised as chairmen, looking for parked chairs to steal.

It was while he was at Mrs. Seagoe's 'Blue Boar' that Wild really established his reputation, not only by the efficiency and seeming punctiliousness with which he returned stolen goods to the public, but by his skill and daring as a thief-taker. The capture of the highwayman Goodman, the destruction of Obadiah Lemon's gang, the apprehending of about fifty street-robbers and burglars and, as a climax, the discovery and capture of the gang that murdered Mrs. Knap, were the actions which made him famous and put his office on to a secure foundation. If I have distinguished between these two main sides of his business, and dealt with them in separate chapters, it is mainly for the sake of the reader. In fact each was so dependent upon the other they they cannot really be separated if either is to be properly understood. Obviously, thief-taking was the most dramatic of his many activities, and he had besides to appear in court as a witness against his victims. By a lucky coincidence, it was from about 1716 onwards that the shorthand-writers at the Old Bailey, who were freelance journalists writing up saleable copy for the *Sessions Papers* and were allowed in the court only by paying a fee to the Lord Mayor, began to take down verbatim speeches from the evidence. As a result, it is of Wild's thief-taking that we have the most detailed records. His office simply continued to expand and make money, and, apart from a few anecdotes and the innumerable advertisements (whose principal value now is as a check against dates), we know little about it.

After the Mrs. Knap affair in the summer of 1716, so much business flooded in upon Jonathan that he moved to a larger premises across the street, next to 'The Cooper's Arms' tavern, though still in Little Old Bailey. He more or less formally declared the place to be an 'Office for the Recovery of Lost and Stolen Property', but, however much he may have desired it, he was not able to make himself into an incorporated City business because he was not a Freeman of London. He took on two head assistants, Quilt Arnold and Abraham Mendez Ceixes, and a bodyguard of roughs to escort him when he went out. Within two years his office became, if not yet a national, at least a London institution and, as Defoe wrote, 'He was now Master of his Trade, Poor and Rich flock'd to him: If any Thing was Lost (whether by Negligence in the Owner, or Vigilance and Dexterity in the Thief), away we went to *Jonathan Wild*.' And later the same writer asked, 'How Infatuate were the People of this Nation all this while?'

They were 'infatuate', of course, because people who had just been robbed were usually in a rather hysterical state and willing to do almost anything to get their property back, and it was this above all which prevented them from seeing that Wild was levying contribution on the city as a whole. A typical example was that of a silk-merchant of Covent Garden who lost a piece of damask bespoke for the birthday suit of a duke, which was to be collected that afternoon. Frantic at the harm this might do his trade, the merchant took a coach straight to Little Old Bailey and offered thirty guineas cash for the immediate return of the cloth. Wild always reacted to this sort of thing by telling his clients to calm down, by pointing out that he was neither thief nor receiver, and by explaining that finding stolen goods took time. On the other hand, he always left room for hope and was careful not to throw too much cold water over his clients lest they become embittered and so difficult to deal with. He had a fine instinct for judging the right moment to strike a bargain.

On this occasion, he left the room a moment and then returned to say that nothing could be done within a week. While the merchant was imploring Wild to try harder, an assistant came in and asked Wild to speak to a man waiting downstairs. If some of these mysterious exits and entrances were necessary to business, many were no doubt put on to bring clients up to the right pitch of suspense. Wild came back 'with a very smiling Countenance' saying 'I protest, Sir, you're the luckiest Man I ever knew!' He explained that he had earlier sent a messenger across to a house frequented by shoplifters to say that while his client had offered thirty guineas for the return of the damask, if he did not get it now he would pay the same reward for the discovery of the thief. Wild told the merchant to go home, and reminded him that the thirty guineas was entirely his own and not Wild's idea, and that he himself neither wanted nor expected a gratuity. The merchant got his cloth back for twenty guineas in Southampton Street, as he was on his way home. When he returned to Wild later to thank him, and pressed the Thief-Taker to accept the ten guineas saved, Wild said that if the thieves, who were now 'pretty safe' from prosecution, thought twenty enough, then nothing had been saved. In the end, Wild took ten guineas, saying this was too much: ''Tis Satisfaction enough, Sir, to an honest Man, that he is able to procure People their Goods again.'

Wild, so the same account tells us,[1] behaved even more grandly to a lady who lost a pocket-book containing bank-drafts for nearly £2,000, which her husband had sent her from abroad. Having nothing else to live on, she was forced to borrow fifty guineas from the merchant on whom the bank-drafts were drawn, and at Wild's office offered 100 guineas to get her drafts back. Wild suggested that she went to have lunch at 'The Baptist's Head' nearby while he saw what he could do. She insisted he lunched with her. At the tavern she ordered chicken and sausages. Three quarters of an hour later, Wild joined her and told her to lay ten guineas on the table 'just in case'. When the cook came to say lunch was ready, Wild asked the lady to look outside and see if any woman was waiting at his door. The lady, to her great excitement, saw a woman in a scarlet riding-hood pacing to and fro in front of Wild's house. She ran back to the table, snatched up the money and, without a word to Wild, ran down the street to the woman. The woman gave her the pocket-book and a note saying 'Ten Guineas'. The lady paid her, added a tip of one guinea, and rejoined Wild in high spirits. When she came to pay for the lunch, however, she saw to her horror that her green purse, with the remaining thirty-nine borrowed guineas in it, had disappeared. Wild, for once off his guard, promised the lady she would not lose a farthing, and returned to his house to send off some agents to find the woman. Within half an hour, Abraham Mendez 'bolted into the Room' and told him that the woman was taken, with the purse on her, and was off to the Poultry Compter. 'You shall see, Madam,' said Jonathan 'what exemplary Punishment I'll make of this infamous Woman!' The lady said she would be quite happy to have her purse back, but would not prosecute the poor wretch for all the world. 'Would you not so, Madam?' said Wild, 'well, then, we'll see what's to be done.'

There were more whisperings in corners, and eventually the lady took Wild to the Compter in a coach, and waited in yet another tavern while Mendez recovered the purse. ' "She says Sir," says the Fellow to Wild, "she has only broke a Guinea of the Money for Garnish and Wine, and here's all the rest of it".' To her astonishment, the lady found, instead of thirty-nine guineas, forty-nine. Wild had forced the woman to pay back the reward and the tip, as well as the money she had stolen. In vain, the lady tried to make him accept ten guineas for all his trouble. ' "No," replied he, "nor ten Farthings. I scorn all Actions of such a Sort as any Man of Quality in the Kingdom. All the Reward I desire, Madam, is that you will acknowledge I have acted like an honest Man, and a Man of Honour." He had scarce pronounced these Words, before he rose up, made her a Bow, and went immediately down Stairs.'

Defoe (or whoever wrote the pamphlet attributed to him) was treated in a much less considerate fashion; his account, however, is the only eyewitness one we have:

I remember I had occasion . . . to wait upon Mr. *Jonathan* with a Crown in my Hand . . . and having made a Deposit, I was ask'd, as above, where the Thing was lost? At first he smil'd, and turning to one, I suppose, of his Instruments, 'Who can this be?' says he, 'why, all our People are gone down to Sturbridge Fair'; the other answer'd, after some pause, 'I think I saw *Lynx* in the Street, Yesterday.'

'Did you!' says he, 'then 'tis that Dog, I warrant you. Well Sir,' says he, 'I believe we can find out your Man; you shall know more of it, if you let me see you again a-*Monday*,' this was on the *Friday*: When the *Monday* came, truly I was told, they could not see the young Rogue, and they believ'd he was gone after the rest to the Fair, it being about the beginning of *September*.

After the Fair, I came again and again, but was put off from time to time, and could not at last be serv'd in the Case, it being only a Silver-hilted Sword, which the Thief it seems had found means to turn into Money, and then there was no coming at it; the Time also having been laps'd by his Honour, having gone to the Fair.

This 'Lynx' was in fact a real thief called Samuel Linn alias Lynx and belonged to the same gang as Obadiah Lemon (who, it will be remembered, had borrowed £10 from Wild in the Compter). Linn was hanged in February 1719, on Friday the 13th, which was the same day that Wild, for some reason, chose for his fifth wedding.*

As for Stourbridge Fair, Wild visited it annually—indeed it was because he was there in September 1724 that he failed to recapture Jack Sheppard. It was notorious for the thieves that descended on it, and on 30 September 1721, when the crime wave was at its height, the *London Journal* observed:

We hear that the late Sturbitch Fair has been pretty good this Year, and had been much better had not the whole Community of Files, alias Pickpockets, from all Parts, put in for a Share: their Number was so great, that those that have us'd the Fair these thirty Years do not remember the like.

* *See page* 131.

{ X } *Disciplining 'Rebels'*

'And some tell us (how true it is, I will not affirm),' wrote Defoe, 'he was oblig'd to give up every now and then one or two of his Clients to the Gallows, to support his rising Reputation: In which Cases, he never fail'd to proclaim his own Credit in bringing Offenders to Justice, and in delivering his Country from such dangerous People. . . . And that in these Cases, they add, That he managed with such Dexterity, that he always obtained publick Applause, as a mighty Forward Man to detect such Villainies. . . .'

Over the years, the number of 'Clients' he gave up 'every now and then' came to quite a handsome total—indeed, the exact number can never be counted. There is Wild's own list, which can be seen in Appendix II. The reasons for its publication will explained when we come to his trial, but meanwhile it is, despite its failings, the most useful document we have for unravelling the other, more vicious, side of his system.

We must ignore the fact that Edward Spencer and Joseph Hutton are at the top of Wild's list. The London GD (Gaol Delivery) Rolls show that these two, who hardly come into our story, were hanged on 20 February and 12 March 1716 respectively and that Hutton was hanged for stealing a sword from Captain James Cox, a chemist in Garlickhithe. However, the indictment says that he disposed of the goods at a house in Chick Lane,

Smithfields. As we shall see, the 'Red Lion' in Chick Lane (later called West Street), was one of Wild's secret 'Locks', or repositories for stolen goods, and this is probably the clue to the connection between Hutton and Wild.

Wild's first success as a thief-taker would seem to have been the arrest of Parrot, Chance, etc., of the Whitehall gang, and his first recorded victim on the gallows was therefore Elizabeth Shirley, hanged in January 1715. We have no news of him after that for fourteen months, when he arrested his first highwayman, James Goodman, alias Footman. The story not only is interesting in itself, but provides several clues to Wild's status by then. For one thing, he was able to enlist the co-operation of the Newgate turnkeys. This may be partly explained by his connection with Spurling who had been shot in September 1714, but the story shows that Wild was sufficiently well known already for people to think of him at once when a dangerous convict had to be arrested. Another point is that Goodman seems to have had no previous connection with Wild, and Wild was therefore acting, so far as the public knew, as a disinterested and 'mighty forward' man doing his public duty. The truth is that every arrest he made increased his authority over the underworld, so that anyone who failed to take him seriously was to be regarded henceforth as a 'rebel'.

The highwayman James Goodman was aged thirty-two and was by trade a carpenter. When he was a boy he had spent a year and a day in prison for hunting a deer and holding a 'Venison Party' in the woods near Aylesbury, in Buckinghamshire. Two years after his discharge he married and followed his trade for about nine years, 'but, then falling into ill Company, he neglected his Trade, and became very loose and extravagant, by which he brought his Wife and Children to ruin.' Early in 1715 he took to robbing on the highway as a last resort and in October, with two others, robbed a Mr. White of his horse, spurs and 1s. in Epping Forest, between Stratford and Ilford. On 17 December Mr. White saw Goodman and another highwayman called Stevens riding through the village of Bow (now, of course, part of the East End of London). Goodman was on Mr. White's horse. Mr. White describes what happened next:

I sent my Servant to demand my Horse, and he going up to them, they both clapt Spurs to their Horses, and rode away.

We pursued them. *Goodman* flash'd a Pistol at me, but it did not go off. Then they quitted their Horses, and got over a Ditch into a Field, upon which, I gave my Servant a small Gun, and order'd him to pursue them, which he did. The Prisoners fir'd twice at him, but miss'd him; he fir'd at them, but miss'd likewise.

'Damn it!' says one of the Prisoners, 'we'll kill or be kill'd, we won't be taken alive! Let's turn upon 'em, and fire again, for our Lives are as good as theirs!'

Upon this, my Man recharged his Gun with some Pebble-stones and, firing, wounded *Goodman* behind the Head. He presently fell down, and was taken. Another Person, whose Name was *White,* coming by, leap'd the Ditch, and pursued *Stevens* with a drawn Hanger; *Stevens* perceiving himself hard put to it, presented two Pistols at him; *White* bid him fire, but told him, if he mist, he would cleave his Skull; and thereupon *Stevens* dropt his Pistols and surrendered. We took from them two Musquetoons, a screw Pistol, which was loaded with three Bullets, and each of the other Pistols was charg'd with two.[1]

A hanger was a short sword, so-called because it hung from the belt; a musquetoon was a short musket; and a 'screw-pistol', or 'turn-off pistol', was one whose barrel could be unscrewed so that it could be loaded from the breech. Because they were light, both these guns were favourites with highwaymen.

Goodman was tried at the Old Bailey, found guilty and condemned in January 1716. It will be remembered that since the murder of Spurling in 1714, prisoners were kept all day out in the Bail Dock. This was the 'Time of the Hard Frost', when the Thames froze over from January to March 1716.* Although nowhere mentioned in contemporary records, the sufferings of the prisoners in the open can be easily imagined. At about seven in the evening on the last day of Sessions, while he was waiting with the others to hear the sentences, Goodman managed to jump over the Bail Dock wall and 'drop on to the Leads, whence he got over the Spikes into Session-house Yard, and so made his Escape thro' the Mob with his Fetters on'.[2] Now it happened that while he had been in Newgate, Goodman had sent some money to his wife

* Frost Fairs were held on the frozen river, and presses carried out so that broadsheets commemorating the event could be 'printed on the Ice'.

by a porter. This porter, assuming that Goodman would be hanged, decided to keep the money for himself, although he knew that Goodman's wife and children were on the verge of starvation. After his escape, the indignant Goodman got in touch with an 'Attorney' and went with him, and four of his henchmen, to arrest the porter, who was drinking at 'Mackerel's Quaker Coffee House' in Bartlett's Buildings (the site is now covered by the *Daily Mirror* Building at Holborn Circus). The four henchmen stood at the door with loaded pistols, lest anyone tried to arrest Goodman while Goodman was arresting the porter. As soon as the party left, the wretched porter now being in the charge of the 'Attorney', a boy was sent to follow Goodman to his lodgings and then to inform Jonathan Wild. Jonathan and the keepers and turnkeys of Newgate joined forces and went to take Goodman. There was a stiff fight at the door and on the stairs, but eventually Goodman was overcome and sent to Newgate. He was hanged on 12 March with Joseph Hutton. At the gallows he begged pardon of God and those he had injured.

Three weeks after, on the night of Saturday 31 March, a gang of five footpads robbed and murdered a lady called Mrs. Knap, as she was returning to London with her son from Sadler's Wells. After a 'Diversion' at the music-house by the spring, they had bought a link and walked through the dark as far as the wall at Gray's Inn Gardens. A soldier passed them, and then 'in an Instant', as the son described it at the trial, 'some Fellows coming up, my Link was blown out, my Hat and Wig were taken off, and I was knock'd down, upon which my Mother scream'd out, and thereupon one of them fired a Pistol close by me, and immediately I heard my Mother cry "Lord help me! help me!" and then the Rogues fled. I went to the Houses for Help, and the Soldier came to my Assistance. Having lighted my Link, I went back and found my Mother upon the Ground.'

An hour or so later, the same gang attacked a Mr. Middlethwaite as he was driving in his coach by a public house called 'The Pindar of Wakefield' in Gray's Inn Road. When he fired his blunderbuss and wounded one of them, the others fled. Probably they had come from the well-known meeting-place of thieves and highwaymen nearby, the appropriately named alehouse 'The Fox At Bay' at 'Black Mary's Hole', where, in the previous century a black woman called Mary Woolaston used to sell spring water at her house.

The affair was widely reported and a large reward offered for the capture of the footpads. Probably because one of them was William White, who had been receiver for the gang that had robbed in Whitehall in 1714 and so was known by William Riddlesdon, Jonathan Wild discovered the identity of the gang almost within a day. Loftily proclaiming that he 'never forgave Murther', he announced that he would bring the rogues to justice. On the next Sunday night, he heard that Will White and others were merry-making at 'Jack Wetherly's *Case*' in Lewkenor's Lane. No sooner had he arrested White and brought him back to the Old Bailey in a coach than another of his men told him that one James Airs (for whom, though unconnected with this matter, he had been looking for some time) was with a whore at the 'Bell' inn in Smithfields. When they reached the 'Bell', they found not Airs but Tom Thurland, one of the murderers, standing under the gateway with two loaded pistols in his hands. Wild and his men (presumably Arnold, Mendez and Riddlesdon) rushed him and knocked his guns down before he could fire. The next night they arrested a third member of the gang, Jack Chapman alias Darvel, in a dram-shop in White Horse Alley off Drury Lane. He was the one who had been wounded by Mr. Middlethwaite's blunderbuss. Then, a few nights later, Wild caught another of the gang, Isaac Rag, who had been hiding in the maze of alleys round St. Giles. He persuaded Rag, whom he wanted for other robberies, to make a confession implicating twenty other housebreakers, footpads and receivers. Only the fifth member of the gang, Timothy Dun, was still at liberty, and he had not been found when the trial came on at the Old Bailey on 18 May 1716.

In court, Isaac Rag said, '*White* was the Man that killed the Gentlewoman, for each of us had a Pistol with a Brace of Bullets, and, after the Fact, we went to drink together, and we all pulled out our Pistols to see who had fired, and we found that *White* had discharged his; we asked him, why he did so? And he said, he did it to frighten the Woman, and make her hold her Tongue.'

It is interesting that in the confusion of the moment, none of them knew who had fired (perhaps not even White himself, who probably thought of his reasons afterwards), and to see the unselfconscious way these professional criminals used legal phrases like 'after the Fact'.

White, Chapman and Thurland were condemned. They were all old thieves, and Thurland was supposed to be in Maryland, for he had been sentenced to death for burglary in December 1714, but had been reprieved for transportation the following August. White and Chapman confessed to the murder of Mrs. Knap, but refused to admit to anything else. White had served on board several men-of-war for about ten years during the War of the Spanish Succession. Jonathan now laid a wager of ten guineas that he would have Timothy Dun before the next sessions. Dun was, in fact, hiding in Maid Lane, near Bankside, in Southwark, and had not left the house since March. Weary of his confinement, he sent his wife to try and find out if Wild was still looking for him. The silly woman went to the Old Bailey and hung about the 'Blue Boar' all afternoon. Wild kept a discreet watch on her, and when she left, sent a man called Horney to keep her in sight. She crossed from Blackfriars to the 'Falcon' tavern, but as she stepped ashore she noticed another boat pulling into the quay. She climbed back in and asked the boatman to take her to Whitefriars. Walking through the streets by Temple Bar she saw Horney not far behind. She therefore went to Westminster (a long walk) and took a boat across to Lambeth, and thence walked all the way back to Southwark and slipped indoors in Maid Lane, she hoped unperceived. Horney was no more than fifty yards behind, and went up and marked the door with a piece of chalk, so that they could find the house next day. Shortly after dawn, Wild, Abraham Mendez Ceixes, William Riddlesdon and Horney broke down the door and started to run upstairs to Dun's room on the second floor. Dun, hearing them, got out of his back window on to the slanting roof of a pantry, the lower end of which was no more than seven feet above the ground. Mendez, meanwhile, had run into the yard and, seeing Dun slithering down the tiles, shot him and wounded him in the shoulder. Dun rolled over into the yard. Riddlesdon came and shot him in the face with small-shot where he was lying. Timothy Dun lived to be tried and hanged, and Wild won his wager of ten guineas. Besides this, Wild won the usual £40 per head, plus a £100 Treasury Reward offered for the capture of these particular criminals,* so that altogether his earnings from this episode came to £270 (£5,400, or $13,500 in modern money).

* Among the Treasury Papers is a Warrant dated 22 July 1717 for a Money Order of £100 to be paid to Jonathan Wild in accordance with the terms of the reward advertised in the *London Gazette* on 3 April 1716. (*Index of Treasury Papers* vol 32 (2), p. 458.)

Isaac Rag was probably paid a tiny sum, if anything at all, for his service. He was sent to the Fleet Bridewell (the House of Correction belonging to the parish of St. Bride's Fleet Street, from which all other 'Bridewells' were named), where he remained until 1718. In the summer of that year, Rag and another of Wild's 'Weekly Pensioners' called John Filewood (of whom more later) tried to organize a mass-escape from the gaol. In the riot, Rag had his eye shot out. He and Filewood were sentenced to four-teen years' transportation and were returned to Newgate. They did not leave for America, however, until 1720.

Wild's touch in dealing with the court and with the thieves was not always so sure. Not long after his move to the house next to the 'Cooper's Arms' (paid for, of course, by the money for arrest-ing Rag's gang), a burglar called Arnold Powell, whose name can be found many times on the Sessions Rolls of London and Middle-sex between 1710 and 1716, was committed to Newgate for attempting to break into a house in Golden Square. Wild visited him in the prison, saying that he believed Powell to be 'pretty *Flash of the Cole* and would find ways and Means to have him *topp'd* if he didn't *come down*' (that is, that Powell had money hidden somewhere and Wild would have him hanged if he didn't share it). Powell defied Wild to do his worst.

Wild started enquiries and found a Mr. Eastlicke, a glass-grinder of Fleet Ditch, and two other witnesses, whom he per-suaded to bring a prosecution against Powell for a robbery committed the year before. Powell became frightened and, sending for Wild, agreed to make the matter up. Wild was now left with the problem of disengaging the prosecutor, Mr. East-licke, and his witnesses.

At the beginning of the Sessions at the Old Bailey, Wild arranged (probably by means of a bribe) to have Powell's trial brought on early. He then told Mr. Eastlicke that the trial would not be coming on for three days, and that he would let him know in good time. Another version of this story says that Wild, hear-ing that the trial was to come on during the first afternoon, took Mr. Eastlicke and his friends to the 'Baptist's Head' and got them drunk. At the trial, the prosecutor and witnesses were called, and when they did not appear, Wild stood up and said he had no idea what had become of them. After Powell had been called to the Bar three times, he was acquitted and the judge, Sir John Pratt, Chief Justice of the King's Bench, ordered the

prosecutor's recognizance to be estreated. Mr. Eastlicke, however, heard next morning how the affair had been managed and
immediately applied to the court. Wild was severely reprimanded
and Powell ordered to remain in Newgate until the next Sessions.
This time, Powell tried to evade a trial by putting himself into a
salivation, but was tried and convicted of a burglary none the
less. He was hanged on 20 March 1717.

There is a slightly similar story about one Jack Butler who had
stolen a gold watch, some lace and other things, and had hidden
them in his room instead of delivering them to Wild. Jonathan,
at the head of a posse, had gone to fetch him from his lodgings, but
Butler had escaped through a back window and disappeared
into a dyer's shop. After a long search, Wild discovered that the
women of the shop had hidden Butler under a tub ('So, Mr.
Son-of-a-Bitch! cries Wild, 'have I caught you at last!') The
thief-taker swore he would hang Butler if there was never another
rogue in England. 'But notwithstanding these Menaces, *Jack*
knew the Secret of calming *Jonathan's* Wrath, and therefore
calling him aside, "If you'll step into my Room again," says he,
"and look behind the Bed's Head, you may find something that
will make you amends for your Trouble." *Jonathan* went, and was
well satisfy'd with what he found: but as *Butler* was apprehended
in so publick a Manner, it was necessary to carry him before
a Justice, and the Justice committed him to *Newgate*: and by
good Management, instead of being hang'd, he was only
transported.'³

Among many such stories is a long one, told by 'H.D.', concerning a 'broken Cheese-monger' whom Wild found hiding
from his creditors in Southwark Mint and set up with a horse and
guns for the highway. Disconcerted by the fact that after each
successful robbery Wild claimed nearly all his earnings, the cheese-
monger went to Oxford and worked on his own. Wild, hearing
of a new outbreak of highway-robberies near Oxford, obtained
a warrant from Chief Justice Pratt and went to hunt down the
'rebel'. Jonathan, 'stuck round with Pistols, as thick as an Orange
with Cloves, or like the Man in an old Almanac with Darts',
met the cheese-monger in the road and, while pretending to
parley with him, shot him dead. He took the corpse to the local
J.P. However, as the cheese-monger had come from a family
well-known in the county, Wild was arrested and had to take bail.
In the end, the affair was hushed up. The story seems to be a

garbled version of a real incident, for on 13 June 1719, the
Weekly Journal or Saturday's Post reported:

> Jonathan Wild, the British Thief-Taker, going down last
> Week into Oxfordshire with a Warrant from the Lord Chief
> Justice to apprehend two notorious Highwaymen, who in-
> fested that Country, met them within a few Miles of Oxford
> on the Road. But they hearing of his Design met him, and one
> of them fired a Pistol at him: but Jonathan having on the old
> Proverb for Armour, received no Hurt, and then he discharged
> a Pistol at them, which wounded one of them so terribly
> that his Life is in great Danger: the other was pursued
> and taken and committed to Oxford Gaol, and Jonathan
> has given Security to appear the next Assizes to justify his
> Conduct.

Next week, the paper followed up the story:

> The Highwayman shot by Jonathan Wild, near Oxford, is
> since dead of his Wound, and Jonathan Wild is still continued
> on his Recognizances for that Fact, it having been thought
> not reasonable to imprison an Honest Man for killing a Rogue.

Of the many 'Blood-Money' certificates, that is, the receipts for
the rewards paid to Wild by the Treasury, only one seems to have
survived. At least, there is a photograph of it in a magazine-
cutting of *c.* 1900 (perhaps from *Harper's*) in the Guildhall
Library,[4] and the original, presumably, is now in a private collection. The receipt for £40, signed by 'Jonathan Wyld', concerned
the conviction of Samuel Cole in August 1718, who, curiously
enough is not on Wild's list.

Samuel Cole, alias Valentine Newell, was a butcher's apprentice
who had run away and drifted into crime. He had been committed to Newgate, tried and acquitted, but had been kept in
prison because he could not pay his discharge fees. During his
stay he met a woman who had told him how to rob a certain
house by first taking employment there as a servant. She then
paid his discharge fee, and in addition gave him 2*s.* 6*d.* 'to buy a
Hammer to beat what Plate he should get into a small Compass'.[5]
He obtained the employment and stole the silver, which he then
sold to the woman. Almost immediately afterwards he was

arrested by Jonathan Wild, for it seemed that the woman had put him up to the robbery with the deliberate intention of betraying him, so that the reward money might be shared between Wild and herself. She was a well-known dealer in stolen goods called Elizabeth Burton, alias Taylor, alias 'Mother Hussle'.

On 20 May 1718 the 'Transportation Act' (4 *George I c. 11*) became law. It was intended to regularize the rather haphazard system of transporting felons to 'Virginia', as North America was called then. The crime wave and the growing number of criminals who had escaped hanging had brought matters to a crisis. Henceforth, all people over fifteen years old convicted of clergyable offences were to be transported for seven years, and of non-clergyable (but non-capital) offences for fourteen years. In 'Virginia' (usually Maryland or the Carolinas) the prisoners were sold to planters at about £10 a head. Jonathan Forward, the agent who had bought the concession in London for contracting ships, etc., was paid £40 a head to meet his expenses. His relations with Wild seem to have been cordial, for the two co-operated with each other in arresting felons who returned to England before their sentences were completed. Quite a number of transportation orders and landing certificates have been preserved,[1] and not only have they been invaluable in tracing the history of Wild's gangs, but they provide a unique, if reluctantly acknowledged, record of the origins of some of the oldest American families of that region. Their sentences completed, the felons could either stay on as settlers or return to England, *provided* they could pay their discharge fees to their masters and two local magistrates. As they were paid no wages, such fees were hard to come by. Prisoners serving seven years who returned before their time were given another fourteen years, and those serving fourteen years who returned prematurely were hanged, unless means could be found to secure yet another reprieve. A second Transportation Act of 1719 (*6 George I c. 23*) offered a £40 reward to anyone who arrested and convicted a 'returned transport'.

This was a great help to Wild; for despite the dangers of the voyage, the difficulties of finding money, and the even greater dangers in London, many felons did return and, consequently, made ideal employees. If they became troublesome, he had no need to invent false evidence against them, which always cost money, for he had only to declare their identity and commit them to Newgate to become eligible for the £40 reward. Furthermore, with such power he could easily employ them as false witnesses, without cost, against other people he wished to deal with. Thus the Act created for him an entirely new group of criminals who could be brought under his authority as soon as he had notice of their arrival in England.

However, there were two sections of this Act (*5 & 6*) which dealt with other matters altogether, and had been included simply because the Transportation Act was the only one pending at the time which dealt with criminal affairs. They were so obviously pointed at Wild that they soon came to be called 'The Jonathan Wild Act' in their own right. It was widely believed that they were the work of Sir William Thomson, a lawyer from Durham who had succeeded Sir Salathiel Lovell as the City Recorder in 1713. Opinions about the new Recorder varied, though it would have been difficult for him not to have been an improvement on Lovell. Both Defoe, who perhaps did not wish to offend another Recorder, and the author of *Lives of the Most Remarkable Criminals* (who seems to have been a lawyer's clerk) wrote of his humanity and sense of justice. On the other hand, Foss's *Lives of the Judges* says that the only remarkable things abour Sir William Thomson were his jealous and grasping nature and his determination to hold as many offices, and so draw as many salaries and perquisites, at the same time as possible. Between 1717 and 1721 he was Recorder of London, Solicitor-General, Baron of the Exchequer and Member of Parliament for Ipswich all at once, though each of these positions, except that of M.P., was supposed to occupy a man's full time. In *Jonathan Wild*, F. J. Lyons describes how Sir

William's thin hard mouth curled into a cruel smile as he pronounced sentence of death; but a portrait in the Mansion House shows an oval face, beneath a full-bottomed wig, with aggressive, rather staring eyes, and thick lips.

His relations with Wild at the beginning are not recorded, but to judge by the tone rather than the substance of early pamphlets, an undeclared hostility seems soon to have broken out between them, and this probably explains why many people believed that it was the Recorder who drafted Sections 5 & 6 of the Transportation Act.

They said that any person who took a reward for returning stolen goods to their owner, without at the same time arresting the thief and giving evidence against him, was guilty of felony. The degree of felony was to be judged according to the degree of the theft, so that, for instance, if the thief was condemned to death, then the taker-of-the-reward should likewise be condemned to death. Unfortunately there were a number of loopholes in the statute, which can be discovered by examining the text:

And whereas, there are divers Persons, who have secret Acquaintance with Felons, and who make it their Business to help Persons to their stolen Goods, and by that Means gain Money from them, which is divided between them and the Felons, whereby they greatly encourage such Offenders.

Be it enacted, by the Authority aforesaid, that wherever any Person taketh Money or Reward, directly or indirectly, under Pretence, or upon Account, of helping any Person or Persons to any stolen Goods or Chattels, every such Person so taking Money or Reward as aforesaid (*unless such Person do apprehend, or cause to be apprehended, such Felon, who stole the same, and give Evidence against him*), shall be guilty of Felony, according to the Nature of the Felony committed in stealing such Goods, and in such and the same Manner, as if such Offender had stolen such Goods and Chattels, in the Manner, and with such Circumstances as the same were stolen.

It was hoped that the words 'directly or indirectly' would cover every conceivable trick Wild and his fellow thief-takers might employ in accepting rewards. In practice, they did not, for Wild discovered even before the Bill was passed that an indirect transaction of money was almost impossible to prove if everybody took sufficient pains to cover his tracks. More doubtful still was the intent to make the taker-of-the-reward equal in guilt with the thief, so that he could be punished according to the seriousness of the theft. Suppose, for instance, the thief had not yet been caught, or was never caught; could the taker-of-the-reward be punished if the fact of the theft was not proved? Again, suppose the thief turned informer and was pardoned; how could the taker-of-the-reward be 'punished' in the same way?

Despite such faults, the law was obviously necessary, and one might assume therefore that it was speedily put into effect. This, however, did not happen, and once passed the law was allowed to rest for several years. Here, a common mistake about Wild's history should be corrected, which is found in *The Newgate Calendar*, almost all short articles about Wild, and even in that standard work, Blackstone's *Commentary on the Laws*.[2] Put simply, it says that Wild followed his evil course until Parliament in its wisdom enacted this law, and that Wild, persisting in his folly, was soon thereafter caught and hanged. A quick glance at dates will show that this is not true. Again, most of the early pamphleteers say that as a result of this law Wild's lost property business was greatly reduced, to the extent, says 'H.D.', that he seriously thought of closing it down and starting an insurance business instead.* It is true that there were not a great number of Wild's advertisements in the newspapers of 1718, but there were not all that many in the previous years of 1716 and 1717 either, for they did not become commonplace (with his name on, that is) until about 1719–20. Advertisements without his name (which may or may not have been his) continued through 1718 as frequently as ever.

'H.D.'s' story is supported by a report, admittedly a satirical one, in Applebee's journal, but that is in 1721—over four years later. It is possible, therefore, that Wild's activities did not trouble the Recorder's conscience very much, and that he intended to keep his law in reserve and use it only when an opportune moment should arrive at which, with suitable publicity, its dutiful enforcement might further, or protect, his own career. Nevertheless, he did send for Wild and warn him of the new state of things, adding that if Wild wished to concentrate entirely on catching thieves, he would be the first to rejoice and to assist him. As a result, Wild took rather more elaborate precautions in re-

* *See pages* 126–8.

turning goods to their owners: but otherwise, things went on as before, the Lost Property Office expanded, and Sir William was content to let it do so.

About a year after the new law was passed, Wild was indeed prosecuted for receiving, for assault, and for interfering with the course of justice, but these were private suits and had nothing to do with the Recorder.

'H.D.' says that one of the first things that gave Wild any fame was a dispute he had with a noted quack doctor called Cornelius Tilburn. Tilburn had been robbed, and suspected that Wild had the goods hidden somewhere, for the two could not agree on the price for their restoration. He therefore arrested Wild on an Action of Trover (i.e. a suit for the recovery of property, from the French *trouver*, 'to find'). Wild gave bail to the action, and in the lawsuit that followed defended himself so well that the quack was 'non-suited' and had to pay costs. 'This', says 'H.D.', 'gave him a great Reputation among his Friends the Thieves, who thought *Jonathan* the best Factor or Agent they cou'd employ. . . .'

However, in *Applebee's Original Weekly Journal* of 14 May 1719, there is a report which surely refers to Tilburn:

> Mr. Jonathan Wild appeared on his Recognizances at the Guild-hall to take his Tryall, but the the Quack Doctor not appearing, nor any of his Evidences, he was dismiss'd of the Prosecution.*

Now, it happened that shortly before, at the Middlesex Sessions of *Nisi Prius*, Easter Term 1719, Wild had been tried for receiving stolen goods, and although I have been unable to find the original documents, it is not unlikely that the prosecutor was Tilburn. If so, then the report quoted above refers to the tail-end of the affair, when the doctor had given up hope of success. The trial is briefly summarized in an eighteenth-century law book called *A Collection of Select Cases Relating to Evidence*, compiled by Sir John Strange in 1754,[3] and it shows how ingeniously Jonathan Wild, either by himself or through counsel hired for the purpose, was able to turn the law inside out.

The circumstances were that the prosecutor had been robbed, and the thieves caught, convicted and hanged. The prosecutor now wished to charge Wild with receiving the goods stolen. As no reward had been paid yet (another clue pointing to Tilburn), he could not charge him under 'The Jonathan Wild Act'. There remained the Receiving Act (*5 Anne c. 31*) of 1706, which made

* *See Appendix V.*

the receiver an accessory to the felony and liable to suffer death as a capital felon. However, Section 6 of this Act had a proviso which said:

> Provided always, That if any such principal felon cannot be taken, so as to be prosecuted and convicted for any such Offence, yet nevertheless it shall and may be lawful to prosecute and punish every such Person and Persons buying or receiving any Goods stolen, by any such principal Felon, knowing the same to be stolen, as for a MISDEMEANOUR, to be punished by Fine and Imprisonment, or other such corporal Punishment as the Court shall think fit to inflict, although the principal Felon be not before convict of the said Felony, which shall exempt the Offender from being punished as Accessory, if such principal Felon shall be afterwards taken and convicted.

This was intended to mean that if a receiver was caught and convicted, and if the thieves were not yet taken, then he was guilty of a misdemeanour only, and would be punished accordingly: but if later the thief was caught and hanged, the receiver need not fear that he would be tried again and hanged as a felon convict, for he had been punished already according to the law.

The thieves in this case had been taken but were dead, and so could not give evidence in court. The only thing to do was to charge Wild under Section 6, as provided, with a misdemeanour, under the plea that the thieves could not now be taken.

The judge presiding over the Easter Sessions was Sir John Pratt (whom we have come across already on two occasions), Lord Chief Justice and a member of the Privy Council. He seems to have been a rather colourless, unsympathetic person fond of boring, owlish jokes. He it was who refused to let Christopher Layer have his chains taken off at a conspiracy trial in 1722, although Layer, suffering from a painful urinary disease called strangury (from which Sir John suffered too), was bent double beneath the weight of them.

As soon as the prosecutor mentioned that the thieves who had stolen his property had already been caught, condemned and executed, Wild, or his counsel, objected 'that the Indictment would not lie, being only given by 5 Anne c. 31 in a case where the Felon cannot be apprehended: for it begins "Provided that if Etc.," which is only a Jurisdiction given under those particular Circumstances. . . .' In other words, the indictment was wrong:

if he was to be prosecuted for a *misdemeanour*, he could only be so under *this* Act if the thieves were still at large. But the thieves *had* been taken, and so under this Act he ought to have been prosecuted for a capital felony: whereas if he was to be prosecuted for a misdemeanour, then it would have to be under an earlier Act which contained no such proviso.

Sir John Pratt agreed, noting 'A Person cannot be prosecuted for a Misdemeanour in receiving stolen Goods, if the Felon is to be found', and Wild was acquitted.

Had Wild been charged with a capital felony, no doubt he would have argued that the indictment was wrong because the thieves, being dead, could not be taken, still less brought to give evidence, and that he should have been prosecuted for a *misdemeanour*, as Section 6 of the Act provided. It was an age in which such legal wrangling was enormously admired so long as it was successful, and it was natural that 'his Friends the Thieves' should regard him 'with a Kind of Awe' as the best factor they could ever hope for: but when at his last trial he attempted a similar manœuvre—that is, pleading that he should be acquitted because he was more guilty than the court was aware—he failed and was loudly ridiculed, and the very fact that he had tried it on was held up as an example of 'his matchless Impudence and Hypocrisy'. Again, when the Jacobite Christopher Layer, on trial for treason at Westminster Hall, crouched festooned with chains for several days while counsel disputed whether a particular Latin verb should be in the perfect or praeter-imperfect tense and whether or not a certain gerundive could be found in reputable classical authors (and who was or was not a reputable classical author), the public was as fascinated by this as they were by the melodramatic disclosures of treason and armed rebellion that were made when the trial got under way. Only an occasional satire like *Gulliver's Travels* spoke out of turn: 'I ASSURED his Honour that *Law* was a Science wherein I was not much conversed, further than by employing some Advocates, in vain, upon some Injustices that had been done me . . . I SAID there was a Society of Men among us, bred up from their Youth in the Art of proving by Words multiplied for the Purpose, that *White* is *Black*, and *Black* is *White*, according as they are paid. To this Society all the rest of the People are Slaves.'

Thereafter, the Lost Property Office went from success to success. In 1720, Wild opened a second branch in the street where he had begun, Lewkenor's Lane, and placed Mendez in charge: and he closed it again after some six months only because he found that he needed Mendez back at the Old Bailey to deal with the mass of work there and could find no trustworthy replacement. During the South Sea Bubble, trade was roaring. Here is a list of stock receipts stolen in Exchange Alley in May and June of 1720 alone: 2,000 for Salter's Hall, £800 in Sword Blade bank-notes, 1,000 in Arthur Moore's Royal Fishery, 1,000 in Wyersdal's Turnpike, 2,000 in the Company for Insuring Seamen's Wages, 3,000 in Shale's Insurance, 6,000 in Baker's Annuities, and others in the Grand Fishery, Garraway's Fishery, and the Wortley and River Douglas Companies. 4

A man who played an important part in this financial crash and in the uproar that followed was Nicholas Lechmere. Early in 1721 he was made Attorney-General. At once, Sir William Thomson, who besides being Recorder, etc., was Solicitor-General, charged that Lechmere had used his privileged position in order to sell company charters during the Bubble, and had used his chambers in the Temple as veritable public auction rooms. Parliament appointed a Committee of Inquiry to look into the matter, and they found that Sir William's charges were utterly false, and that he had acted in a spirit, not of public duty, but of private malice and envy. He was therefore dismissed as Solicitor-General, and Lechmere was elevated to the peerage.

One month later (April 1721), the 'Jonathan Wild Act' was brought into action at last, but, although the Recorder was now trying to mend the damage to his career, we must assume that this was a coincidence. Certainly coincidences were that the victim was called Thomson and, like Sir William, came from Durham. Wild must have heard of the case, which should have served him as a warning cloud on the horizon: but, perhaps because John Thomson was such an insignificant fellow, lacking completely the smart-Aleck cynicism and gifts of organization he himself possessed in such repellent abundance, he would seem to have ignored it. These very failings of Thomson's, however, give his last confession a pathetic dignity.

He was a veteran of the War of the Spanish Succession and had been at the taking of Gibraltar. On his return he married the first women he picked up (a prostitute) and together they kept a number of disreputable alehouses, which were closed for one reason or another. Then he tried to make up his meagre earnings by returning to their owners handkerchiefs, watches, etc., stolen by pickpockets, but his constant wheedling for more money and useless attempts at blackmail soon brought him to Justice Hall. The first prosecutor said that Thomson threatened to get one Kate Lunn to swear a bastard child to him: the second that Thomson had snatched two guineas out of his hand while they were arguing over the return of a watch Thomson's wife had stolen. Thomson protested that he had never heard of any Act prohibiting the taking of a reward, but he was condemned to death.

In Newgate, his misfortunes were increased by his wife, who prevented 'his preparing for another World' by railing at him and blaming him for the ruin of herself and her children.

When he found himself included in the Dead Warrant, he said he had no Reason to desire Life, for he believ'd, that no Man ever past his Time in such a turbulent Hurry, without having Leisure to consider whether he was running to Happiness or Destruction: but the many vicious Women he had conversed with, the riotous Houses he had kept, the Intreagues he had pursued to injure honest People, and the clamourous Mirth which followed their Success, were so far from affording him that Happiness which he expected from them, that he found they were very painful, and gave him great Uneasiness: for they were frequently alarmed, many Times suddenly surpriz'd, always in Terror, and under Apprehensions of Danger, and commonly one or other of their Company was in Trouble.

He lamented grievously, that all his Friends had now forsaken him in his Distress, and that tho' he lately had such numerous Acquaintance, he knew not, that he had one left who would procure a Coffin for him, or take Care that he should be buried.[5]

⁂ XII ⁂ *A Paper War*

At the very time when the Transportation Act was about to become law (April 1718), Jonathan Wild found himself under attack from the rear. Provoked beyond endurance by the dazzling success of his old comrade, Under-Marshal Charles Hitchen appeared before the public in the new disguise of pamphleteer, social reformer and moralist. His tract was entitled:

A True Discovery of the Conduct of Receivers and Thief-Takers, In and About the City of LONDON: *To the Multiplication and Encouragement of Thieves, Housebreakers, and other loose and disorderly Persons.*

It was dedicated to the Lord Mayor, Sir William Lewen, the Aldermen and the Common Council of London. It was printed privately and 'Given away Gratis' to show the author's public spirit.

His intention was to point out the iniquities that were going on in the name of law and order, and his recommendation was that the Lord Mayor should imprison all the Thief-Takers, 'Regulators' and Receivers, especially the most notorious (whom he does not actually name): 'Knock but away those Pillars of Debauchery, and the whole Fabrick of Robbing and Thieving, with other disorderly Persons and Practices, will all of them immediately give way and fall of Course.'

'In the finding out of this Secret,' he goes on, 'I have spent my Hat full of Money, . . . I have not yet had so much as one single

Farthing allow'd me in the City, for this or any other Charges I have hitherto been at in the Execution of my Office, which I take to be hard Usage, and that for the Future you will be pleas'd to consider and relieve the same Etc., . . .' Hitchen complained that threats had been made against his life, that he had been jeered at in the street, and that he could hardly continue to execute his duties unless the City provided him with a bodyguard. Meanwhile, things were going from bad to worse. He had little faith in the new Bill pending in Parliament (the 'Jonathan Wild Act') 'for, if I am rightly informed also, the Thief-Takers have already found out a Way to set aside the good Effect of the said Bill, before the same shall appear amongst them Etc., . . .' At the Old Bailey, 'the Judges complain and say, that they are tir'd with the Thoughts of coming to the *Sessions-House*; for that instead of finding their (*i.e. the criminals*') numbers lessen'd thereby, to their great Grief and Surprise, the oftener they come, the more they find.'

Hitchen particularly attacks a mysterious person called 'The Regulator'. In some passages this is obviously Wild, just as in others 'the Thief-Taker' is obviously Wild; but elsewhere he refers to 'the Regulators' in the plural, and in one place speaks of 'those famous Comedians, the Thief-Taker and the Regulator' as if they were two different people. Finally, when he came to publish his second attack on Wild, he empahtically called it *The Regulator*.

I think the word, which obviously meant something like 'the Boss', had become a term of abuse after the notorious 'Committees of Regulators' appointed in 1687 by James II to influence the outcome of elections in his favour. They had done this by cross-examining town councils, dismissing those not of his party, and by high-handedly changing the constitutions of the boroughs. Thus by 1718 the word probably had the same meaning as 'pocket Himmler', 'McCarthyite', etc. have for us—that is, a petty tyrant who abused his office, and had gained power without legal sanction by bullying, bribery and corruption. If so, it fitted Jonathan Wild very well.

In the body of his pamphlet, the Marshal exposes a manœuvre by which 'The Regulator' recently saved a gang of dangerous thieves and hanged a couple of 'Shim Sham' ones instead, and he shows his readers the 'Humours' of the underworld by taking them into a 'Flash Case' near Smithfields. In the middle, with scant regard for the needs of layout, he inserts a *Thief-Taker's Proclamation*. This is a rather childish parody of Wild's advertisements, or perhaps of a proclamation, now lost, by which Wild advertised his business in general. It is printed in 'Black Letter' (Gothic type), and at the head is a crude woodcut of a man being hanged in front of a crowd dressed in the fashions of sixty years before. The printer took it from old stock to save the cost of a new illustration, for the same picture adorns a seventeenth century ballad now in the Pepysian Library at Magdalene College, Cambridge.[1] (*See plate 6.*)

In the *Proclamation*, 'His Skittish and Baboonish Majesty' demands that all thieves deal directly with him from now on, instead of with their old 'Locks, Fences, and flash Pawnbrokers', for he is better equipped than them with 'skittish and felonious Informations *Etc.*' with which to subvert the proper course of justice. There are, however, some 'Rebels' who will not 'come down' and pay him his dues, for they claim he is as deep in the dirt as they are. He warns that although he dare not arrest them at the moment 'for Fear of my precious and felonious Neck *Etc.*,' he will publish a list of their names and places of abode, and if that has no effect he will have nothing further to do with them. To those who have seen the light and abjured their former receivers, he offers better financial terms than ever before, plus excellent legal protection if any of them should be captured: for, whereas a receiver would pay but £9 for goods worth £20 'at prime Cost', he will pay £10, take £6 for himself, and sell the goods back to the owner for £16, thus saving the owner ('or Cull *alias* Fool') £4, 'and if this is not doing the Business, the Devil is in it *Etc.*'.

Hitchen ends with a sort of sermon to 'The Society for the Reformation of Manners', chiding them that they should not 'set up one Evil to put down another' or 'do Evil that Good may come of it . . .' and says that either the Society is misled by its agents, or the agents themselves are deeply involved in crime, for crime goes on increasing.

Although he was not named by Hitchen, Wild saw that he was the obvious target. As he knew the truth about Hitchen's past better than anyone, the comic possibilities of the situation proved irresistible. Sometime in May he published his reply, and although it was anonymous, everybody knew that Wild had either written it or had dictated the substance of it to a hack-writer for polishing at a fee of two guineas. In those days, titles contained, as it were, their own blurb, and so his title-page ran:

AN ANSVVER TO A late Insolent LIBEL, entituled, A Discovery of the Conduct of Receivers and Thief-Takers, in and about the City of *London*: presumptuously Dedicated to the Lord Mayor, Aldermen and Common Council. Written by *C—s H—n*. Wherein is prov'd in many particular Instances, who is Originally the GRAND *Thief-Taker*: that a certain Author is Guilty of more flagrant Crimes, than any *Theif-Taker* [*sic*] mention'd in his Nonsensical Treatise: and that he has highly Reflected on the Magistracy of the City, in the said Scandalous Pamphlet. Set forth in several Entertaining Stories, Comical Intrigues, merry Adventures, particularly of the *M—l* and his Man the *Buckle-Maker*. With a Diverting Scene of a *Sodomitish* Academy.

The publisher was Thomas Warner, whose shop was at 'The Black Boy' in Paternoster Row, St. Paul's Churchyard. Besides printing and selling innumerable pamphlets, he printed the *Daily Journal* for his more famous rival, John Applebee, and must therefore have known Defoe, who was a part-editor and chief correspondent of the newspaper. He published also 'H.D.'s' life of Wild, so that 'H.D.'s' claim to have had access to first-hand information may have been true.

After disposing of Hitchen's accusations one by one (sometimes unconvincingly), Wild proceeded to show up the Marshal for what he was, 'the Original Grand Thief-taker . . . and my Old Master in Iniquity', by recounting those disgraceful episodes in the Marshal's career that have been related above in Chapters VI and VII. Of the conflict that followed, 'H.D.' says that '*Jonathan* laying himself too open, *H—n* dropp'd the Pen, and took up the Cudgels of the Law, with which he bang'd *Jonathan*, so that he thought fit to buy his Peace at the Price of a Sum of Money . . .' but that later Wild found means to make Hitchen 'entirely to quit his Pretensions'.

Whatever the truth of that, Hitchen had promised in his first tract to bring out a fuller 'Treatise', dedicated to His Majesty, on the prevention of crime. Now it appeared. All it turned out to be was a reprint of parts of his *True Discovery*, except that here, throwing caution to the winds, he named all the villains—Wild, Obadiah Lemon, Tom Edwards (keeper of the 'flash Case') and several dozen others. To guard against possible libel action, he gave it a new title:

> The Regulator: or, a Discovery of the Thieves, Thief-Takers, and Locks, alias Receivers of Stolen Goods, in and about the City of London.

In addition, he adopted the flimsy pretence that it was written 'by a Prisoner in Newgate'. At the back, he added a list of 'Flash Words now in Vogue among Thieves', a list of 'Flash Cases' and their proprietors (including Jonathan's brother Andrew), a list of Jonathan Wild's 'Weekly Pensioners', and a list of the convicts now awaiting transportation under the Transportation Act (which enables us to date The Regulator between June and August, when the convicts embarked). This answer to Wild's was published likewise by Warner, and by W. Boreham, who lived a few doors away at 'The Angel' in Paternoster Row. The Regulator was certainly libellous, and it was perhaps this which gave Jonathan the means to make Hitchen quit his pretensions.

As literature, Wild's pamphlet is really not too bad, but Hitchen's are excruciating. The only thing that makes them just readable is their unintended humour, for which the Marshal had an unusual gift. However, it is not the quarrel between them that is interesting now, but the picture the quarrel reveals of life in the criminal underworld of London during this obscure and confusing period. As Wild says at the beginning of his Answer: 'It is a common Observation, that when two of a Profession are at Variance, the World is let into many important Discoveries: and whether it be amongst Thief-Takers, or Lawyers, Merchants or Ministers of State, Clergy or Laity: an Expectation naturally Arises of some Billingsgate Treatment.' Today, however, we learn as much from what the authors implied or took for granted as from what they actually told. The Regulator and Wild's Answer are the only 'exposés' of this underworld written by insiders, and for this reason Hitchen's vocabulary of canting words alone is uniquely valuable.

The events described in The Regulator took place in 1717 and early 1718. It begins with a description of how Wild rigged his evidence and framed innocent men so that his own thieves should go free, just as thief-takers had done since the 'Black Dogs of Newgate' (though Hitchen speaks as if it were all outrageously new). The method, however, is a little more complicated. Three rogues, Obadiah Lemon, and two brothers called William and

Christopher Matthews—all 'Rattling Lay' experts—had robbed a lady in her coach as she was passing along the south side of St. Paul's Churchyard. They had been identified, so they thought, and were now in hiding. Wild sought them out and told them that one would have to become an 'Evidence *Etc.*' The crux of the matter was in this '*Etc.*' and it is explained in the next paragraph:

> Well then, saith the Thief-Taker, in order to blind the Justice, and that he may take the Information, is to induce him to believe that we are doing something for the good of the Publick: Therefore, you must put into the Information, a numerous train of Offenders, which have been concern'd with you, either in Robberies, or buying or receiving your stolen Goods: and at the same time you must be sure to promise him, the said Justice, that you will convict them all: and that there may be a perfect Harmony between us, you shall hear me, your Councillor, your Friend, your *Thief-Taker* and Factor, promise as faithfully, that I will apprehend, take, and bring them to Justice for the same.

They were, of course, to omit any evidence that might implicate Wild himself. Such an instance was the '60 douzen of Handkerchiefs that was taken on Mr *Kidlay*, from a Dyer's Servant, who they sent on a sham arront (*errand*), for which Handkerchiefs I received 30 Guineas from the Owner; but gave *Oakley, Lemmon*, and Mr. *Johnson*,* but 10 Guineas . . .' If they were to include that sort of thing, said Wild, his own neck might be in jeopardy, 'and upon such Terms, who the Devil will be your Factor?'

* A thief called Joseph Johnson, and not, as F. J. Lyons supposed, the famous Roger Johnson, who at this time had not met Wild, but was still gigolo to Mother Jolly at the 'King's Arms' tavern in Drury Lane. The *Kidlay* was a form of theft by confidence trick, and needed at least two accomplices. The first would get into conversation with a servant carrying a parcel, and discover whom he worked for, where he was going and what the parcel contained. Taking his leave, he would give the details to his accomplice, who would then run round in front, and come to meet the servant in haste, saying he had a message from his employer, who wished the servant to return at once, while he would take the parcel on to the client. In evidence, the servant usually never mentioned the first conversation, for he never realized the two men were connected. There were, of course, innumerable variants of this trick.

To put the matter more clearly, Obadiah Lemon should give himself up and impeach not the two Matthews brothers who, though guilty, were good thieves working for Wild, but 'a couple of Shim Sham Thieves', Hew Oakley and Henry Chickley, who, though innocent of this particular crime, were not working for Wild, and that Lemon should bring as many 'Informations' against the two as possible to make sure of a conviction. The arresting of the two unfortunates was to be left to Wild himself, so that he could earn his fourscore pounds at £40 a head. Thus two petty thieves, 'whom the Justices got little or nothing by' were hanged and the gang remained more or less intact. The arrangement also gave the Thief-Taker 'an Opportunity to rob or extort a Sum of Money out of all the rest in the Information, by making up, and compounding the Felonies with them, which by a modest Computation, cannot amount to less than a Hundred Pounds or More, *Etc.*' The final touch was that the two thieves would never know that it was Wild and not Lemon who had engineered their ruin.

Hitchen's story is over-simplified and wrong on some minor points, but in its general idea it is true.

The *Sessions Papers*[2] show that in October 1717 and January 1718 Obadiah Lemon did impeach 'a numerous train of Offenders' including Hew Oakley with twenty 'Facts' and Henry Chickley and four others with an unrecorded number each. Wild certainly arrested Chickley (No. 9 on his list) and probably the rest as well.

Obadiah Lemon's gang contained about a dozen members (excluding the women) and they were mostly specialists in the 'Rattling Lay' (stealing from coaches), in which craft they inherited a high tradition of skill. During the reign of Queen Anne, a group of coach-thieves called 'Wild Rogues' had become extremely clever at flicking hats, wigs and scarves out through coach-windows by means of fishing-hooks and lines. To prevent this, London coaches were fitted with perforated tin sashes, though this meant that the passengers had to travel in darkness and heat, and be thrown about, as Ned Ward said, like *'Peas in a Cullender'*. Then, on 30 September 1717, the *Weekly Journal or British Gazetteer* reported that a new gang had appeared on the streets and, by jumping on to the backs of coaches, cutting the leathers and snatching hats, wigs and jewellery out through the holes, had become a serious menace. We can see now that this was Obadiah Lemon's gang and that it was probably working under

Wild's control. He had certainly known most of them for several years, and Lemon since his days in the Compter.

Hew Oakley, however, was condemned not for the 'Rattling Lay' but for robbing a woman after Lemon had thrown ashes in her face. As Lemon said, 'By throwing Ashes in People's Eyes we have stole above twenty Hats and Wigs . . .' yet he was not hanged. As the cart was taking the prisoners up Holborn Hill to Tyburn, the procession was stopped and the hangman himself arrested. 'The poor Fellows waited two Hours under the Gallows, till being almost starved with Cold, and no Body would be got to undertake the Jobb, they were brought back to Newgate, where the Sheriff's Officers found some Difficulty to get them re-admitted.'³ There is a famous engraving of this incident in the *Newgate Calendar*, illustrating the life of John Meffe, another of the prisoners. They were kept in Newgate for a year and transported to Charleston on the *Eagle* in May 1719.⁴ Meffe returned, was arrested by Wild's agents in Maidstone, and hanged, being No. 66 on the list.

Henry Chickley (or Checkley) was condemned for robbing a 'Cull' of his 'Scout' (victim of his watch), though Lemon included in his information several 'Rattling Lay' offences near Aldgate and in the City. In Newgate, however, Chickley 'positively deny'd his being concern'd in the Fact he stood convicted for'. This disgusted the Ordinary, the Rev. Paul Lorraine, who wished to publish his confession according to custom (such confessions being sold under the gallows at 1½*d* a copy). Lorraine was further outraged when, an hour or so before the cart left on execution morning, he visited Chickley and his fellow prisoners to administer the last rites. A convict called Stone 'took out of his Bosom *one of those Creeping Creatures,* with which I suppose he abounded, and put it on an open Book that lay before Chickley, and said, *See how he Gallops over the Prayers!*' At Tyburn, the pair complained loudly to the mob that the clergyman had refused to administer the Holy Sacrament of the Last Supper to them. 'But,' wrote Lorraine in self-defence, 'upon my telling the People that were about the Cart, of their wicked and unheard of Behaviour, I do believe every Man of Reason and Religion was satisfied that the sacred Ordinance ought not to be given to such prophane and impious Wretches as they were.'⁵

The subsequent history of this gang may be dealt with briefly. They continued robbing coaches for another eighteen months, sometimes slashing the coach-backs, and sometimes resorting to the 'Chiving Lay', which was to slash the leather straps supporting the coach and, when the coachmen got down to see what had happened, make off with the boxes under the driver's seat. There was some trouble when Wild retired to Dulwich for a holiday, probably in August 1718, leaving Mendez in charge at the Old Bailey. One morning a gentlewoman called at the office and said that a thief had stolen £7,000's worth of bank-notes from her as she had been going to South Sea House to invest in the Company. She was able to give Mendez a description of some of the men in the street who had been near her when she had first missed her money, and two days later he arrested Joseph Johnson and two others (unnamed) of the gang. When Mendez took them down to Dulwich to face their master, Wild made them deliver up the money and all their personal effects, and then released them. He returned the £7,000 to the gentlewoman, 'but Jonathan got £400 by the Bargain'.

Then, in October, Obadiah Lemon, who had betrayed so many of his companions, was himself betrayed, together with Joseph Johnson and Samuel Linn, by Will Matthews. Matthews gave graphic descriptions of the robberies he charged his friends with: ' . . . Lemon got up behind the Coach, and cut the back of it so, that he put his Hand in, and took off the Gentleman's Wig, which he gave to the Prisoner (*Linn*) and then we all ran different Ways to the *Three-Tuns* upon London Bridge, where we had beforehand appointed to meet. I desired them to let me have the Wig, which they agreed to. We valued it at 3 Guineas, and I gave them a Guinea a-piece for their Shares: and here the Wig is.'

Another victim, with the attractive name of Dionysius Hicky, deposed that his portmanteau 'was suddenly taken out of the Coach, but I cannot tell how'.

'But I can,' interposed Matthews, 'for the Prisoner (*Johnson*) and I were out together upon the *Rattling-Lay*, as we call it, and meeting this Coach, the Prisoner went and privately open'd one of the Doors, and while the Gentleman was endeavouring to shut it again, I stept up on the other Side, and lifted out the Portmanteau. Then the Prisoner and I went into *Lincoln's-Inn-Fields*, where we broke it open, and pull'd the Guts out, and threw the empty Carcase over the Wall into *Lincoln's-Inn-Walk*.'

Joseph Johnson was transported. However, since the affair of the £7,000, he had stolen another bank-note of £1,000, which he was able to keep hidden in his clothes. When he arrived in Maryland, he bought his freedom, travelled to New York, bought some property there and 'set up for a Gentleman'.

Linn was less fortunate. At first, the jury valued the £7 wig at a mere tenpence and he was sentenced to transportation. However, Will Matthews persisted in his impeachments, and Linn was eventually condemned for a burglary and hanged. *Select Trials* lays the blame for this directly on Jonathan Wild, saying that he brought it about in revenge for the *contretemps* over Defoe's sword. The records support this to some extent. If, for instance, Matthews paid three guineas for the wig, why did he keep it until it could be produced in court as evidence, instead of selling it in the normal way, if he had not intended to betray Linn all along? If, however, he involved Linn in this robbery with the intention of impeaching him afterwards, then it could only have been at the instigation of Wild, for he would hardly have offered himself as King's Evidence if he had not been sure that Wild would bring him off safely in the end. This in turn would explain the relentless way he pursued Linn with impeachments until he secured a capital conviction. Finally, Linn denied to the last that he had been in any way concerned with the robbery he was to die for, although he admitted several others.

Obadiah Lemon disappears from the records after February 1719, yet there is no mention that he was ever caught. Perhaps Wild hid him away somewhere, even sent him to Flanders to become the 'Superannuated Thief' who managed his smuggling business over there. As for Will Matthews, he met the same fate as the rest in April 1720, when he was hanged for two robberies, but by then the gang as such had ceased to exist.*

In *The Regulator*, Hitchen denounces Wild generally as a receiver, protector of coiners, pickpockets and whores, and as a 'Thief-Maker', thus coining a phrase that lasted until the nineteenth century (it was much used by Sir John Fielding). He now identifies the 'Flash Case' near Smithfields as the 'Goat' in Long Lane, saying of the proprietor: 'Tho. Edwards, *alias* Country Tom . . . his present Wife had one Husband Hang'd and him twice in Newgate.' We shall hear more of Thomas Edwards later, for he was an inveterate enemy of Wild's and was to play an important part in his fall.

Hitchen makes Edwards admit that his house is kept in business

* *See Appendix V.*

like a windmill by four sails: gaming houses, bawdy-houses, receivers and thief-takers, all regulated by 'The Regulator'. 'There are four Sails that belong to my Mill. You see, Sir, the Sails go round: they follow each other; that in short, Sir, My House could not stand without them, my whole Dependence being altogether upon them; it is these that bring Grist to the Mill.' To which Wild's sarcastic reply was, 'This Advice is 'greeable to the Man imposing it, who hath a Windmill in his Pate beyond the Rest of his Bretheren in Iniquity....'

Hitchen rather clumsily introduces a 'Countryman' into the 'Goat' and tells us what may be seen there by means of a sort of catechism. The place is crammed with gin-sodden wretches carousing, smoking, shouting, swearing, weeping, 'some sleeping, others staring as if their Eyes would drop out of their Heads.' We meet housebreakers just out of Newgate, the Turnkey having fleeced them of all their money before their release; 'dirty young Wenches that shout lusty *Young Fellow*! like a Sailor'; 'Bunters' recently taken up by the Regulators for the workhouse and escaped again.

> *Question:* What are all that Heap of Boys at that Table, that are playing at Dice, swearing, Cursing, and grinning at each other like so many Hell-Cats? And that Man in the Silver-button'd Coat and knotted Peruke, with a Sword by his Side, what does he do amongst them?
> *Answer:* Sir, those Boys are Clouters, *alias* Pickpockets, and that Man in the Silver-button'd Coat is their Thief-Taker, to help them to Money for Pocket-Books...'

We meet various old thieves who are now used only as 'pushing-Touts' (lookouts) and spies to give notice of coming assemblies and race-meetings. We are shown groups of 'Battalions' (whatever they are) and women like Blue Sue, the daughter of Dancing Doll, and old Sue Belcher and her mistress Sarah Hall alias Fox, who has had three husbands hanged and the fourth condemned four times. A pickpocket, 'all over wet with his Hat and Periwig hanging over his Ears,' comes running in from a coach and flies upstairs. He had been caught, ducked several times in a horse-pond, taken down to the Thames, thrown in, pulled out, and put into a coach with a roaring mob chasing it. Some thieves have been following the elections, others the circuit courts. The Regulator goes from table to table, threatening, cajoling, bantering. Another old thief, booted and spurred with a whip in his hand, has just lost his partner, with whom he had worked for thirty years and never a dishonest act between them. Obadiah Lemon sits in a corner by himself, uneasy at having become an Evidence. A group of thieves throw down their cards and rush out to rob the crowds gathering to watch the opening of Parliament.

Question: What are those five Women that are fighting and crying as if they would break their Hearts?
Answer: Sir, their Husbands or Fellow-Men lie cast for their Lives, and are to be executed To-morrow; But hang them or let them alone, they will get others in their Room in a Day or Two.

In his *Answer*, Wild had said that for Hitchen to call him a Thief-Taker by way of insult was merely the pot calling the kettle black: but that in fact if anyone merited the title as a mark of public esteem, then it was Wild himself, who had already 'brought to Justice many notorious Malefactors, above Sixty in Number, which have been executed, besides Transportations . . .' Wild therefore neatly turned the Marshal's attack by inserting a notice in one of the weekly journals in which he now seriously proclaimed himself 'THIEF-TAKER GENERAL OF GREAT BRITAIN AND IRELAND'.

The title was eye-catching, certainly, but had Jonathan Wild been a little more reflective, he might have seen that it was hardly auspicious, for it carried echoes of the infamous Matthew Hopkins, 'Witch-Finder General' under Cromwell, and of the well-deserved end that came to *him*.

With this proclamation, the paper war seems to have died down —at least, we know nothing of the legal buffetings the pair might have exchanged afterwards. Of Hitchen, we hear no more until 17 October 1720, when an entry in the *Repertories of the Court of Aldermen* shows that he was granted an additional Freedom of the City to sell. In his application for this, the Under Marshal pointed out that he had been 'at great Pains and Expences in his Attendances at divers Fires, which has happened, as also in suppressing Riots, Visiting Watches, keeping Constables to their Duty and taking up Beggars, Ballad-Singers, Wheelbarrow Drivers, and other Strollers, Nightwalkers and Vagabonds . . . all of which had cost him £15 last Year and again the Year before, for which he has had no recompense.' He added that the Marshals were usually given £5 p.a. as an encouragement to do their duty, which had not been paid to him, and requested that this oversight should likewise be remedied.

{ Part II } *The Regulator*

{ XIII } *The 'Double-Cross'*

It is not too much to claim that Jonathan Wild was the most formidable criminal to appear in the Western world before Al Capone: certainly he resembled the gangsters of the twentieth-century more closely than he did his famous contemporaries in Europe, such as 'Cartouche', who were simply robber-chieftains in the old tradition. He was the first criminal to become a 'celebrity' known to everyone in Town, a good neighbour, a prominent citizen who petitioned for the Freedom of London, and a donator to charitable causes: the first to keep books like an accountant and to understand that crime is a business, and that it needs the same care, attention and planning that all businesses need if they are not to fail: the first to employ respectable lawyers on permanent retainer in order to outwit the courts with their own jargon; and the first, a quality much admired at the time, to use 'science' in the art of detection. Like his successors today, he never dropped the mask of respectability, although, unlike many of them, he was humorous enough to wear it sometimes in a spirit of self-mockery.

Although no one since has so nearly succeeded in bringing the whole of London's criminal underworld into one system controlled by one man, this was not due to any great or original idea of his, as many early accounts would have us believe. Jonathan Wild's genius lay rather in this skill at improvisation

and in his flair for what we would now call 'public relations'.
Where his predecessors had fumbled along in danger and obscurity, he somehow created the impression that everything he
did was a spectacular, nay, a hilarious success: and if he did not
invent a single part of his system, as he clearly did not, no one
before had ever been able to fit the parts together so neatly or
explain the problem—of how to run the 'police' and the underworld at the same time—with such marvellous and seductive
clarity.

Each part of his system was dovetailed into the others and
depended on them for its proper functioning. The Lost Property
Office depended on regular supplies from his thieves on the one
hand and on the gratitude of the public on the other. The money
paid by the public financed further robberies, which in turn
brought in more public. The more he collected details about the
public and the thieves who robbed them, the more easily he could
both plan future robberies and control the thieves. Thief-taking
prevented his thieves from disposing of their booty through
other agents, increased yet further the goodwill of the public
and brought in more money. The money and the goodwill
increased Wild's own power over the thieves, raised his standing
with the courts and judges, provided entry into prisons and enabled him to bribe City officers and magistrates, to pay attorneys,
and to place advertisements and 'publicity items' regularly in the
newspapers. All this strengthened his hold on the thieves yet
more, which in turn enabled him to organize better the supplies
for his Lost Property Office.

There is a story, derived from the memory of his machiavellian
intrigues, that attributes to him the invention of one of the com-
monest expressions in the English language. It is said that when
the details of a robbery, as they had been given to him by the
thief, tallied with those given by the person whom the thief had
robbed (and so constituted evidence of capital felony), Jonathan
put a cross against the thief's name in his book of accounts.
Thus he had a quick-checklist always ready for the time when
another victim was needed to go in place of someone more
valuable, or to earn another £40. Then, after the thief had been
given over and hanged, Jonathan put a second cross against the
first. From this, it is said, comes our expression *double-cross*.

He was ahead of his generation in his understanding of the
proper exploitation of the newspapers, and the value of carefully

planted 'news-reports', in the creation of what we would now call his image. Items like the following were almost as frequent as his advertisements:

> Last Saturday Night, Mr. May, a 'Change Broker, was set upon by a single Highwayman against the Men hanging in Chains upon Holloway, who took his Watch, Rings and Money. But the Place being immediately alarm'd, it happened that Jonathan Wild and one of the Turnkeys of Newgate, were drinking on Horseback at the Three Foxes in Holloway. Jonathan took to the Road, and fir'd a Pistol at the Highwayman, who got clear off: but they track'd him beyond Highgate by the Blood, the Slugs having wounded either him or his Horse. (*Applebee's Original Weekly Journal, 28 January 1721.*)

Such a story reminded the educated public not only of Wild's intrepid courage, but of his friendship with the forces of law and order. It might be mentioned in passing that one of the bodies hanging in chains at Holloway belonged to William Johnson, who, seven years before, had murdered the turnkey Spurling, the uncle of Jonathan's wife.

He would have been joyously at home in our present world of interviews with celebrities, illustrated articles whose simple purpose is to lure the eye to the advertisements next to them, and panels of mountebank 'experts' on television. His own impositions on the public took a form appropriate to the credulity of the age. When a rumour was heard, for instance, that the famous deaf and dumb astrologer Duncan Campbell had claimed that much of the credit for Wild's success should be given to himself, because he had taught the Thief-Taker General the secrets of 'the Black Art', Wild was delighted and encouraged the rumour to spread, for he knew that this would frighten the superstitious country-folk, particularly the Irish, who had come to live in the poor districts where he recruited his thieves. When he went out thief-taking or to supervise a band of his own men robbing, he carried a staff, like the Upright Men of old, to impress his authority on 'the ignorant Multitude'; but whereas the staff of an Upright Man had been made of ash or hazel his was a short baton of silver, doubtless adopted in imitation of, and rivalry to, the maces of the City Marshals. As he claimed that it represented the power of the Government, his staff was especially useful when, at the head of his posse, he attended race-meetings, prize-fights, Exchange

Alley, the opening of Parliament, markets and country fairs.
As 'H.D.' says,

> For the common People, seeing *Jonathan* there, were the more
> careless: because he always gave out, that he came to take some
> Rogues whom he suspected to be there, and the People had a
> Notion that his Presence frighten'd away the Thieves, and to
> countenance this Belief, he went doubly and trebly arm'd, and
> often wore Armour under his Cloaths, which he took Care to
> shew in all Companies; being attended by three or four, and
> sometimes half-a-Dozen terrible-looking Fellows by way of
> *Garde du Corps*, as if all the Thieves in *England* had vow'd to
> sacrifice him.
>
> This Grimace took very well, for it gave him an Opportunity
> of protecting and carrying off the Booty which was to be made
> in these Fairs; and if any of his Party was in Danger of being
> taken, these Myrmidons of his, who pass'd for his Body Guard,
> were to run into the Crowd, and under pretence of assisting the
> People, who were about to seize such Rogues, were to try to
> shuffle off, and favour their Escape.

The same author tells the story of a tradesman who, at a country
fair, recognized Jonathan Wild on horseback in the crowd. He
went up and asked him how he did, at which '*Jonathan* damn'd
him and bid him not trouble him with impertinent Questions'.
Therefore, when the tradesman accidentally encountered Wild
a week later with some friends in a tavern, he was surprised that
the thief-taker greeted him warmly and insisted he had a drink.
The tradesman asked Wild why he had cut him dead so rudely the
week before. ' "Z—ds," says Jonathan, "you disturbed me at my
Business, for I had at that Time twenty Pair of Hands at Work" !'
In the light of this, the following report in the *Daily Journal*
of 19 August 1721, besides showing the extraordinary figure
Jonathan was cutting at the time, takes on an added interest:

> On Thursday last there was a small Plate ran for at Acton,
> upon which Occasion a vast concorse of People were assembled
> there, a Quarrel arose between the Townfolks and the Strangers,
> which last being chiefly on Horseback, and the famous Jonathan
> Wild the Thieftaker being at their Head, as General, obliged
> the Country People to retire.

To cope with the enormous increase of trade, Wild bought a large house in Great Old Bailey, two doors south of Ship Court (about 30 yards south of Prujean Court, which is still there) on the west side of the street. Above the door hung the sign of King Charles I's head. The engraving, shown in *plate 4*, was done just before it was pulled down in 1803, and the shop-front would seem to be a late eighteenth century addition.

The date of his move can be deduced from the newspapers as sometime in October or November 1719.[1] On 26 September, Applebee's journal had reported, 'Mr. Wild, the famous Thief-taker, lyes past all hopes of Recovery, at his House in the Little Old Bailey', and on 3 October, the *Saturday's Post*, 'We hear Jonathan Wild, the famous Thief-Taker, lies a dying.' This must have been the illness referred to in many of the early biographies.

It happened that the Newgate Ordinary, the Rev. Paul Lorraine, died on 7 October, and on the 10th, the *Saturday's Post* took the opportunity for a jibe at the thief-taker:

'On Wednesday Mr. Lorraine, Ordinary of Newgate, departed this Life at his House in Town-Ditch: and we hear the Rev. Mr. Jonathan Wild (who is recovered from his late Indisposition) offers to officiate till another is elected in his Room, being, as he says, thoroughly qualify'd for the Place by the late State of Mortification pass'd through.'

On 7 November it returned to this matter, saying that the most likely candidates now were the Rev. Mr. Purney* and Mr. Charles Long, 'Jonathan, in regard to their superior Merit, having resigned all his Pretensions'. Finally, on 10 December, the *Daily Courant* published an advertisement for the return of a watch stolen from the Bury coach, in which Wild gave his address as 'The King's Head' in the Old Bailey.

Once installed there, Jonathan Wild began to affect the opulence of a Man of Quality. He bought a coach-and-six, complete with

---

* It was given to Thomas Purney, whom the vitriolic Mrs. Elizabeth Powell dismissed in her weekly *The Orphan Revived* as 'a Young Sucking Divine of 24 Years of Age'. His private pleasure was to write sickly, pseudo-rustic verse, which earned him the nickname 'Pastoral Purney'; and the editor of *Select Trials,* who poked fun at him whenever he could, called him 'snivelling'. Yet he seems to have been a pious and abstemious, though rather stupid, young man, and not at all the hypocritical drunk and whoremonger some authors have described. A dozen or so of his biographies of condemned criminals are in the Bodleian Library, and all are headed by the same curious woodcut.

liveried footmen, and stabled his horses at 'The Duke's Head' in Red Cross Street, Southwark.[2] This was conveniently near the Mint, and almost next door to a spacious 'lock', or warehouse for stolen goods, kept by the notorious Richard Greatorex, whom he later had transported. He turned one of the rooms of his house into a little museum of relics and trophies—bits of hangman's rope, jemmies, trickars, trepans, 'Engines for the forcing of Doors Etc.,' knives, guns taken from highwaymen, and pieces of blood-stained cloth—where he would show clients round before a transaction. Sometimes he would give them dinner, mentioning casually that the venison they were eating came from his own estate in the country (at Dulwich, perhaps?). In the evenings he held *soirées* in honour of his newest wife, to which he invited aldermen, councillors, magistrates, clients from the public at large, and even some nobles, whom he treated, says Lord Chester-field,[3] with 'an awkward Familiarity'.

In the mornings, he held *levées* at his getting up, in imitation of Louis XIV. Every day at about seven, his bedroom was attended by a court of highwaymen, cut-throats, pickpockets, bailiffs, lawyers and supplicants of every kind. While his servant helped him into his callimanco dressing-gown, slippers, and a turban to cover the polished silver plates grafted on to his shaved head, and served him with his breakfast of a pint of sherry and a bowl of thick chocolate, which he ate with a spoon, he heard applications for bail, petitions for the use of his favour, proposals from attorneys on the handling of future cases, and pleadings from mothers of young thieves whose trials were coming on the next Sessions. After these people had been sent off, he gave his orders for the day to the thieves who remained behind. Then he put on his coat, wig, cocked hat and boots, picked up his silver staff, and went down to the 'Baptist's Head', where the proprietor Mr. Wild-goose kept a sort of bank for him in case of emergencies, to deal with private matters.

He began to display an 'extraordinary Intimacy with certain Justices of the Peace, and would sometimes intrude himself into their Company, and drink with them at Taverns, when he us'd to leave Word at Home that if any Body should enquire for him, he was gone to such a Tavern to meet Justice *V—n* or Justice *C—n*. The Use he made of insinuating this Notion into their Heads was, that if any Information should be given to these Justices, against any of his Friends, he should have timely Notice of it

from them or their Clerks . . .'[4] I do not know who 'Justice C—n
was, but 'Justice V—n' must have been Justice Captain Gwyn
Vaughan of Southampton Street, Covent Garden, who seems to
have served Wild in precisely this way, as we shall see, when
Roger Johnson was arrested.

Wild was also careful to protect such bailiffs as he could when
they got into trouble. In May 1722, for instance, two bailiffs,
Johns and Bradshaw, forced their way into a brothel in Denmark
Court, off the Strand, shouting that they had a warrant from the
Lord Chief Justice, and that they would break down all the doors
in the house if they were hindered from searching the place. It
was, as I have mentioned, a favourite trick of bailiffs who wanted
to make up their incomes. This pair went too far, for they ran
upstairs, attacked the 'Lodgers' (i.e. customers) and stripped
them of their clothes, while the girls watched through 'a great
Slit' in the kitchen door. When, during the trial, an 'officer' said
that he knew one of the girls, Mary Lloyd, to be a common
night-walker, Wild immediately called out in his loud Staffordshire accent:

Lloyd! Let me look at your sweet Face, my Dear! O! I thought
I knew you . . . I am very glad to see ye, Child . . . I have been
hunting after you all over the Town . . . I have got an Information against ye for picking a Gentleman's Pocket of a Watch.
I am sadly afraid you lie out a-nights; for he told me he has
often been at your Landlady's, but could never find ye at
Home. Here, you Sir! (To a Messenger) go to Mr. *W*— in
L— Court and desire him to wait upon this Lady (*exit Messenger*).[5]

Mother Howard, the madam, called some witnesses to her
character, who 'deposed that she was a very civil Neighbour, and
that they knew no Harm of her, but only (as it came out on their
being cross examin'd) that she kept a Baudy-house, and that now
and then some of her Lodgers and Visitors would cry out
Rogues! Whores! Thieves! and *Murder!*' As Mr. W— was not at home,
Mary Lloyd was allowed to go free, but was arrested again the
following month. The bailiffs were acquitted.

With suitable fanfare, Jonathan Wild led sorties into the slums
of Whitefriars, St. Giles and the Mint, announcing in the papers
on one occasion that he and his posse had taken up a hundred
thieves in Southwark on a single morning.[6] Such expeditions

served also as recruiting drives to fill the vacancies left by older hands he had lately *double-crossed*. Besides fugitive debtors (like the 'broken Cheese-monger') and immigrants from the country and Ireland, he scoured the streets for waifs and abandoned children, 'strolling about in Misery and Poverty, . . . cover'd with Dirt and Rags', and, under the pretence of taking them into care and protection, set them to robbing. Suitable material too were the bootblacks and link-boys, and the children who slept in the ash-pits of the Glass House, near Wapping, to keep warm. 'Nay,' 'H.D.' wrote, 'it is said that nothing pleas'd him more than to see a Child or Youth of a promising Genius, and that such never wanted his Encouragement: insomuch that a Little Boy in a Crowd having at a certain Time stole a Pair of Silver Buckles out of a Man's Shoes, without being felt, his Mother, not a little proud of the Child's Ingenuity, presented him to *Jonathan*, who gave him half a Crown, with this prophetick Saying, *My Life on't, he'll prove a great Man*—But I must observe, that Jonathan's Prophecy never was fulfill'd, the Youth dying before he came to the Age of Manhood, for he was hang'd before he arriv'd at sixteen.'

Another author tells of one Stephen Barnham, who ran away from school to join Wild and was employed by Blueskin Blake. While Blake and a companion were buying a pair of gloves in a shop, the boy would crawl under the counter and take away what he could carry.[7] 'But, alas, he was not the youngest of Mr. *Wild's* Scholars. I myself have seen a Boy of six Years old, tried at the Old Bailey for stealing the Rings of an Oyster Woman's Fingers, as she sat asleep by her Tub, and after his being acquitted by the Compassion of the Jury, *Jonathan* took him from the Bar, and carrying him back upon the Leads, lifted him up in his Arms, and turning to the Spectators, said, *Here's a Cock o'the Game for you, of my Own breeding up!'*

In *Select Trials* there is a case of three boys, John 'The Grinder', Tom Picket and Henry Avery, who were impeached by their comrade Tom Eaves and arrested by Wild. They lived in a tenement in Crown Court, St. Giles—in fact, in the very heart of Hogarth's *Gin Lane*. The alley adjoined the poor burial-ground (near the present Tottenham Court Road underground station), where the dead were laid on top of one another in a large open pit, with only wooden slats between them, so that the stench pervaded the whole neighbourhood.[8] The boys were all about

sixteen years old, and it is obvious that Wild knew them very well.
They had, among many petty robberies, stolen a gold watch and a
snuff-box from a lady in Long Lane, Smithfields. In court, Eaves
said he had sent for Wild, and knew nothing of any snuff-box,
which he supposed the others had 'sunk' to cheat him out of his
share. Wild, however, said that he had arrested them all on his
own initiative: possibly he wanted to prevent Eaves from
claiming the reward. The transcript of his speech shows the
bantering, rather cruel, manner he used towards his young
protegés:

Upon — Worrel's Information I got a Warrant against *the
Grinder* for another Robbery. I went to a House he frequented in
Crown-Court in *St. Giles's*. Tom Eaves happening to see me
before I could get in, he thrust the Door to, and stood against
it, I swore, if they would not open it I'd fire thro' and clear the
Way directly. Upon that I was let in, and, searching the House,
I found *the Grinder* under the Bed, and so secured him and
Eaves.

Says Eaves, 'I hope, Mr. Wild, you have not me in your
Information?'

'No Matter what I have in my Information.'

'Why, Mr. Wild, I was never guilty of any Thing but snatching a Pocket.'

'Where?'

'In Long Lane.'

'Was there a Watch in it?'

'Yes, and a Snuff-Box.'

'And who was with you?'

'Why *the Grinder*, and Picket and Avery: and I can make
myself an Evidence—'

'Can you so? Very well!'

So I took Care of my two Chaps, and the next Day I went in
Quest of the other two, Picket and Avery, whom I knew to be
old Snatch-Pockets, and it was not long before I met 'em in the
Street.

'So,' says I, 'where are you two Gentlemen a-going?'

They said, they had heard *the Grinder* was taken, and they
were going to enquire how he came off.

'Come off!' says I, 'he is not *come on* yet, but you shall go and
see—I'll carry you to him.'

No, they said, they were satisfied with what I had told them.

'But,' says I, 'he'll take it an ill if you don't go, and why should you be against it?'

'Because,' says Picket, 'as we have sometimes been in his Company, and drank with him, may be he may swear some Robbery upon us.'

'May be so too,' says I, 'and for that very Reason I must take you with me.'

They afterwards own'd, that they were going to enquire if *Eaves* or *the Grinder* had impeached them, and, if they had found that neither of 'em had, they design'd to turn Evidences themselves.

Picket and 'the Grinder' were hanged, and in his account of 'John the Grinder', the Ordinary, Thomas Purney, wrote 'that he greatly regretted his being oblig'd to leave the World so soon ... and that he thought it the greatest Addition to his Misfortunes, that his Parents and Sisters were so overwhelm'd with Grief, that they could not bear to visit him in Prison.'

It was this use of children—taking them off the streets under the pretence of charity, putting them to robbery (and paying for their food only out of what they earned), and then sacrificing them to the gallows when they had served their turn—which aroused Defoe's greatest indignation. Yet he was almost alone in his opinion, and the other pamphleteers either ignored the matter or treated it with irony. The employment of children as pickpockets was as old and as universal as theft itself, and Wild was simply following an ancient tradition. Under-Marshal Hitchen was just as bad, and, to go back to the time of the 'Black Dogs of Newgate' if no further, there is a famous letter from Recorder Fleetwood to Lord Treasurer Burleigh, in which he describes how Wooten, an impoverished gentleman, had set up a school for young thieves behind his alehouse in Smart's Key, near Billingsgate. He had two 'Devices', by which a pocket and a purse were each hung from a figure festooned with hunting-bells, etc. The children had to empty the pocket and cut the purse without ringing the bells. The best pupils were awarded the titles of *Judicious Nipper* (cutpurse) and *Public Foister* (pickpocket).[9]

The attitude of the educated public towards Wild was equivocal. On the one hand, from 1719 until about 1724 they regarded him as the man above all others able and always ready to deal with crime wherever, and in whatever form, it might occur, and treated his comings and goings as 'news':

'They write from Bath and Bristol, that their Roads are much infected with Robbers, and that application having been made to Jonathan Wild, that Gentleman has resolved to take a Tour of those Cities, as soon as his Equipages can be got ready.'[10]

'Yesterday, Jonathan Wild Esq; set out for Bramber in Sussex, with a splendid Equipage, which has given Room for various Speculation.'[11]

In 1720, the Privy Council consulted him about ways and means to check the growing number of highway robberies.

'Wild, the cunning Artist, told them, Increase the Reward,'[12] and proposed £100 as a more tempting sum. Accordingly in May 1720 a Royal Proclamation announced that the reward was to be increased to £100 for anyone who captured a highwayman within five miles of Temple Bar. However, there was a delay of sixteen months, and it was not until 26 September 1721 that the Daily Journal reported that the Proclamation was now to be carried into effect. Then there was doubt as to whether the reward included the original £40 or should be added to it. In January 1722, therefore, a second Proclamation confirmed that the £100 should be added to the £40.

Meanwhile, Jonathan Wild had set up agents in many of the ports and county towns of southern England, who sent him information about the movements of criminals. Thus, in 1721, through these agents he arrested James Dalton in Bristol, John Meffe in Maidstone, Robert Perkins in Gravesend and William William in Dover (these were all returned transportees). When a highwayman called William Colthurst of Spiggot's gang (mentioned in the Introduction) was caught in Oxford under an alias, Wild was informed almost immediately and had him brought to London, where he was condemned. In this case, however, he had not used an agent as such, but had saved himself expense by persuading a gentleman, whom Colthurst had robbed some years before, to write to every town from where there was a report that a thief, who might answer to Colthurst's description, had been arrested. Therefore, when the newspapers reported that 'Jonathan Wild' had arrested this man in Portsmouth or that man in Southampton, we have no means of knowing whether they meant Wild himself, a paid agent, or merely an interested party doing his civic duty; for Wild, needless to say, always took the credit.

All the people above are on his list, and, as the claimant for the rewards, his name is on the backs of their indictments in the GD Rolls. Thus his claim to be 'Thief-Taker General of Great Britain and Ireland', although rather insolent in the educated public's view considering that he was a private citizen, really seemed to have substance to it. His agents were everywhere; his posse could move freely all over the country and had a greater range even than the City Marshals. This, the first thing that in any way resembled a C.I.D. or 'crime squad' in English history, was something unheard-of before.

On the other hand, they knew that Wild's men were all rogues and gaol-birds, that he himself, though colourful and energetic, was a coarse and ill-bred fellow, and that the results he undeniably got were achieved by means it were better not to examine too closely. As a result, he became a figure of fun.

The most familiar portrait, in this vein, of Wild is Peachum (*Impeach 'em* or *Peach on 'em*) in *The Beggar's Opera*, which was written in 1726-7, after Wild's death. In the first scene, Peachum sits in his parlour with 'a large Book of Accounts before him'. Running his finger down the 'Register of the Gang' in search of 'a decent Execution against next Sessions', he chooses who is worth protecting and who better hanged for £40. Women should be kept because they do not fetch rewards and, anyway, 'the Breed of the Game depends upon them'. *Crooked-finger'd Jack*, who has brought in five gold and seven silver watches, sixteen snuff-boxes, six-dozen handkerchiefs, four silver-hilted swords, half a dozen shirts, three tye-wigs and a piece of broad-cloth, all stolen in his leisure hours, must certainly be protected. *Wat Dreary* alias *Brown Will*, who has 'an underhand Way of disposing of his Goods', will be kept for no more than a Sessions or two if he does not mend his ways. '*Slippery Sam*: he goes off the next Sessions, for the Villian hath the Impudence to have Views of following his Trade as a Taylor, which he calls an honest Employment.' As for *Tom Tipple*, 'a guzzling, soaking Sot . . . a Cart is absolutely necessary for him'. When *Filch* comes in and announces that *Tom Gagg* has been condemned, Peachum says: 'This is Death without Reprieve. I may venture to book him. (*Writes*) For Tom Gagg, Forty Pounds.'

Here is an example of a satire which was outstripped by reality. A more telling example, because it was written when Wild was at the height of his fame and prosperity, concerned his scheme for insurance against theft, which he first proposed, apparently, in the autumn of 1721. While I have impugned Wild's reputation for originality in some fields, perhaps he should be given credit in this, as a pioneer in, if not the inventor of, what is now one of the most universal kinds of insurance in existence. 'H.D.' says that he even went so far as to pretend 'to settle a sufficient Fund, and give good Security for the Performance of Articles: sometimes shewing a manuscript Paper of Proposals, and consulting People whom he supposed to have any Understanding in those Affairs, extolling the great Use and Advantage this Project wou'd be to the Publick: not doubting, he said, but that all Trading People, as well as Gentlemen and Noblemen, who kept great Quantities of Plate in their Houses, wou'd for their own sakes encourage so useful an Undertaking....'

'H.D.' did not know whether Wild gave out this report 'only to amuse People, and to hinder them from enquiring any farther into his Affairs', or whether he was in earnest: 'but the Thing was generally receiv'd as a Banter, or as a Piece of Mr. *Wild's* Wit....'

It happened that in December 1721 there were a number of trials at the Old Bailey involving people who had been robbed during visits to brothels, to the diversion of the spectators, and shorthand-writers who were able to exercise themselves transcribing the regional accents of the gentlemen concerned for the *Sessions Papers.* One was a Scotsman, who explained what had happened:

> ... but a Murrain an her, for a wheedling Jead as she was, while she pretended to be so woundy loving, she picked the Bag of Money out of my Pockut. I dudent see the Baggage taok it, but I see her give it to *Mary Bun*, and *Bun* put it up her cooats, and thear I thuot to find it: but while I was feeling about *Bun, Bun* was too cunning for me, and handed it back to *Mab*. A Devil an 'em! (thuot I). If these be their Tricks, and so I began to maok a plaguy Upruor in the House....'[13]

Another was an elderly French Huguenot called Cassell, who had been robbed by 'Squinting Abigail' and the notorious Moll Harvey* at a house in Petty France, Moorfields. While he and Moll

---

* She appeared many times in the *Sessions Papers* 1720–30, was referred to as a 'Queen of the Underworld' by Defoe in his last pamphlet (*Street Robberies*), has been suggested as an original of *Moll Flanders*, makes a brief appearance

were tumbling on the bed together, she took his watch from his pocket, gave it to her partner, and they both ran away.

COURT: And did you run after them?
Cassell: No.
COURT: How so?
Cassell: Ah begare! Dare was de Raisong for dat . . . mine Breeshes ware down about mine Foots. (*Laughter.*) Vell! den anoder Voman come in and ask-a me . . .'

A day or two after these trials were published, the *Weekly Journal or Saturday's Post* (6 January 1722) had this to say:

We hear that Jonathan W—d, Gentleman, has projected a Scheme for raising a great Sum of Money by an Insurance on Robberies: this Policy is calculated for the Advantage of Insurers as well as the Projector: and seems to carry with it more Fairness and Demonstration than any modern Scheme either of our own or our Neighbours' Countries: it differs from other Policies in this remarkable Instance, that whereas in those the Adventurers were robb'd, and none escaped but such as had no Dealings with them: in this the Projector can demonstrate that no Persons shall be robb'd, except such as do not insure: which must raise the Value of this Stock above any Other, because it will put all People under a Necessity of insuring in their own Defence.

N.B. Insurances will be taken in for small Persons as well as for Houses, by which super-annuated Lovers, who walk the Streets late, drunk or sober, may preserve their Watches, Rings, or Handkerchiefs, from Contingencies, which will prevent a great many bawdy Trials, and Depositions, *De usu Flagrorum, in Re Venera.*

in A. P. Herbert's *Mr. Gay's London* (a selection of *Sessions Papers* of 1731–2) and even gained a mention in those standard digests of the period, *The Historical Register* and *The Political State of Great Britain*, in 1731. At the time of Wild's trial, she was arrested as a possible accomplice.

❧ XIV ❧ *Jonathan's Circle*

'H.D.' writes that during the later years Jonathan Wild was under continual financial strain, 'having three Wives living, and always a Seraglio of Mistresses, no less than half a dozen at a time, to maintain, according to his Rank.'

There was his first legal wife in Wolverhampton and their son, who was still a schoolboy. Then there was Mary Milliner. Some accounts say that in the days of his early prosperity he bought himself a diamond-hilted sword, with which to swagger through the streets like a 'Captain', and that the first thing he did with it was to cut off Mary Milliner's ear 'to mark her for a Bitch'. Defoe, as I have mentioned above, denied this and said that they continued to do business together until his death, and that she outlived him. Captain Alexander Smith calls her 'Jane Sprackle alias Sprackling'. Another pamphlet¹ says that an early wife was Mary Read, 'a Gentlewoman of a very good Family and Account, being one of the Daughters and Co-heiresses of Jerry Read, late of *Paddington*, in the County of *Middlesex*, Gent. *deceased*, and who had an Acquirement in *America*, whither she was in all Haste going, but was prevented by her Marriage with Mr. Wild'. The topical jokes here were, apparently, that a Jeremiah Read was hanged at Tyburn (Paddington) in 1715, and that a Mary Read was condemned to death in January 1719. She was reprieved for transportation on Friday 13, the very day she should have died, and on which Wild married his last wife. Possibly Wild interceded for her—but in any case, the author seems to have been muddled over the names of the women, confusing Mary Read with Mary Dean, although he was writing when Wild was still alive and untried.

After this, or after Mary Milliner/Molyneux(?), came Sarah Perrin, alias Graystone, Gregstone, Gregson, etc. (probably a thief), and then Judith Nunn, by whom he had a daughter *c.* 1716. It would be interesting if some parish register in the City should turn up her name, for this would be the original 'Polly Peachum'.

Next came the woman whom, according to Defoe, Jonathan loved above all the rest, and with whom he lived 'publickly', as he did not with any of the others. Her name was Elizabeth Mann. She had been a prostitute, but had been converted to Catholicism by a priest, confessed, granted absolution, and had turned penitent. Defoe described her as a 'very sensible and agreeable Person' and she made Wild an excellent wife for the short time they were together. When she died, *c.* 1718, she was buried in the churchyard of St. Pancras-in-the-Fields, now called St. Pancras Old Church. Defoe adds rather quaintly: '*Jonathan* retain'd such an impression of the Sanctity and goodness of this Wife, that he never forgot it as long as he liv'd: and order'd himself to be Buried close to her when he Died, which his Friends took Care to see perform'd, about Two of the Clock in the Morning.'

The other Elizabeth Mann, the 'Posture Woman' of Mother Wisebourne's house in Covent Garden, also turned Catholic and penitent: but as her 'biography' says that she died in 1724,[2] a possible confusion between these two can be avoided.

His next and last was Mary Dean, *née* Brown. Her uncle was the Newgate turnkey Spurling, whom Wild may have met through Hitchen. He seems to have been a unpleasant man, for not only was he a dealer in stolen goods, as the papers on Hitchen showed, but among the Aldermen Papers of 1708 there is a complaint by some prisoners against his brutality. At the Old Bailey sessions in September 1714, a woman called Jane Housden, a veteran coiner, was brought to trial. As Spurling ushered her through the half-gate into the court dock, another prisoner, called William Johnson, tried to follow her. When Spurling pushed him back, Johnson drew a pistol and killed him, 'Mrs. Housden at the same Time encouraging him in the perpetration of this singular

6 A primitive woodcut at the head of the 'Proclamation by his
Skittish & Baboonish Majesty' (i.e. Wild), in *A True Discovery of
Receivers, Thief-Takers etc.* by Charles Hitchen, the City Marshal.
To save cost, the printer used an old block from a 17th-century
ballad now in the Pepysian Collection. In his next pamphlet,
Hitchen became more daring and named all the villains. The
printer erased the houses, put the letters 'I–n W–d' in the sky,
and added a balloon from Wild's mouth saying 'I'm the Grand
Thief'. (*See Chapter XII*)

7 In the foreground, the Hawkins gang rob two ladies at Knightsbridge, while the watchman runs away; behind, they rob Lords
Bruce and Burlington at Richmond. (*See Chapter XVII*)

Murder'. The court immediately sentenced them both to death. In Newgate they behaved, according to the Ordinary Lorraine, 'as if they were wholly Insensible to the Enormity of their Crime . . .', a detail which suggests they had had reason to hate Spurling for some time. They were hanged in Sessions House Yard on 19 September 1714, and Johnson's body was hung in chains at Holloway, where it remained, with an increasing number of companions, for years. Mrs. Spurling stayed on at Newgate as the tap-woman in the Lodge. A pamphlet called *A History of the Press Yard,* written by a Jacobite officer in 1715, describes her as fat and as round as a barrel, but, despite her uncouthness, a good-natured old creature on the whole. Her niece Mary Brown married a thief called John, alias 'Skull', Dean. He was the son of a cabinet-maker and lived with him in the house in Little Old Bailey, next to the 'Cooper's Arms', which Wild rented after leaving Mrs. Seagoe's in 1716. This, it was said, was how he met Mary. It seems equally likely that he moved there because he already knew Mary through her uncle.

In May 1717 'Skull' Dean was arrested for burglary, but escaped from Newgate on pretence of going to the 'Necessary House'. He was caught again in Giltspur Street, Smithfields, when his fetters caused him to fall, and was hanged on 26 June.[3] Inevitably, rumour had it that he was put out of the way only because he objected to the attentions Wild was paying to his wife. Wild, naturally, denied this vehemently to the last, and, considering that Elizabeth Mann was probably still alive, perhaps he should be given the benefit of the doubt.

Several of the early pamphlets maintain that Wild married Mary Dean, according to the rites of the Church of England, at St. Pancras on Friday, 13 February 1719. There is no record in the Parish Register in County Hall, but that may be because he did not wish to be charged with bigamy and simply paid the vicar to leave it out; another reason may be that Mary was a Catholic and that such a mixed marriage was not recorded in the general register. Nevertheless, if he did, then it was not only an exceptionally bold choice of date, considering the superstitiousness of the age (even now, I think many would have qualms), but an exceptionally ghoulish one as well. For it was a hanging day at Tyburn, and several of the victims were Wild's, including Sam Linn and a man from Spiggott's gang called Sinnamond. Mary Read was reprieved, as I have said, at the last moment. If she had indeed been one of his mistresses, then the whole affair becomes incredible, for he was not to know she would be saved when he made the arrangements for the wedding. Even if he had brought off her reprieve himself, it is still peculiar, for it was at this time that he was being prosecuted with several felonies and misdemeanours, and was trying to put as good a public face on things as possible by 'bringing to Justice' an unprecedented number of thieves, petty, amateur and professional—no less than eleven in two Sessions.

On this wedding day, Wild gave gloves and favours (ribbons traditionally given at weddings since the days of jousting) to all the officers who attended at the gallows—including a King's Messenger, the Ordinary (Paul Lorraine) and the hangman, Richard Arnet, who later was to hang Wild himself (which will support the opinion that Wild chose a very bad day indeed). Gloves and favours were given to all the Newgate turnkeys, and ankers of brandy were issued to the prisoners for making a punch. The festivities lasted for several days.

Mrs. Spurling, notwithstanding such largesse, was firmly against the marriage. Her reasons are unknown, though some said at the time that she felt Wild was unsuitable because, as a result of that misapplied salivation, he could never have any more children. Whatever her reason, she became increasingly hostile to Wild—assisting prisoners to destroy written informations against his victims, etc.—until, at the end, she played a small but significant part in his downfall.

Of Wild's assistants—clerks, servants, thief-takers and 'Instruments'—we know a few scanty details. The most important was Abraham Mendez. A recognizance in the London GD Roll of April 1725 shows that his full name was Abraham Mendez Ceixes, of 'Berry Street' in the parish of St. Katherine Cree-Church. The sureties were stood by Isaac Mendez Ceixes and Jacob Chaves.

Bury Street was, and is, a narrow L-shaped street between Leadenhall Street and Houndsditch at the eastern end of the City. In the early eighteenth century, the neighbourhood was inhabited by a colony of Portuguese Jews, whose wealth and good taste at that time is attested by the large and elegant red-brick synagogue that they built for themselves in 1701. It is still standing and in use (in a little courtyard off Bevis Marks) and its interior, so I am told, has not changed since the days Abraham Mendez worshipped there with his family and friends. *Lives of the Most Remarkable Criminals* mentions him as 'a little Jew (called Abraham) that Wild kept'. Small or not, he was brave enough to go on thief-taking expeditions, and competent enough to run the office when Wild was away. He was also clever enough in this dangerous game to be arrested only once, in 1725 during the general collapse of Wild's empire, and then he was soon discharged.

The second assistant of note was Quilt Arnold, who, had he not worked for Wild, would have made a typical bailiff. A petition among the Sessions documents for April 1725 shows that he was illiterate, being signed '*Quilt M. Arnold, his Mark*'. He appears a little more distinctly during a fracas over a thief called Martin Bellamy.4 This person had achieved some distinction in the underworld by inventing a device (not described) by which sash windows could be thrown up suddenly and objects quickly removed from parlour window-sills. In the summer of 1723, Bellamy had the idea of forging a bank-bill in Wild's name, signing it 'Jonathan Wylde' and presenting it to Mr. Wildgoose at the 'Baptist's Head', who kept Wild's unofficial bank in the Old Bailey. It was cashed without question. Wild thereupon sent Arnold in pursuit. Arnold discovered that Martin Bellamy was hiding in the rooms of his brother Jonathan, for the boy of the house told him that Martin had gone upstairs a day or two before and had never come down. Arnold and his assistant Daniel Soames forced the door, but were unable to find Martin, who in fact was climbing down a rope he had lowered out of the window. For want of something better, they took his shoes, which the boy showed them standing by the door. The next day, Jonathan Bellamy went to Arnold's house and demanded the buckles from the shoes back, for they were his. Besides, by what authority had Arnold and his creature Soames entered his house? Arnold said that he had the 'Authority of *Jonathan Wild*, and this was such that they could have broken all the Doors in the House had they wished'. The matter ended in the Old Bailey in October 1723, and Wild had to defend his man against a charge of housebreaking and robbery. He said that he had given no orders to search the house, only to take Bellamy. 'And therefore, as to their entering the House in the manner they did, and rashly taking away the Buckles, I cannot pretend to justify 'em; but this I can say for *Quilt Arnold*, he has assisted me in apprehending one hundred and fifty Persons, the greater Number of whom have been prosecuted according to Law. He has been with me in several Houses, where there were Things of great value, but I never knew him guilty of taking any Thing.'

Quilt Arnold was acquitted, but Wild was sharply reprimanded by the court for not keeping a better control over his strong-men. To make matters worse, Arnold's wife Ruth was charged at the same Sessions with stealing four yards of ticking from a shoe-shop in the City. She had gone with another woman to buy a pair of shoes. As they left, the shop assistant noticed that the ticking had gone, and, running down the street, saw it poking out from under Ruth Arnold's red riding-hood. Some of it fell on to the roadway. She was transported.

As for Bellamy, he was caught by some of Wild's men in Chancery Lane, and taken in a locked coach to the 'Elephant & Castle' in Fleet Street, to await the pleasure of the Thief-Taker General. Wild, however, had gone to bed, and sent a message to say that if Bellamy gave his promise to attend the *levée* at Wild's house next morning, he could go free that night. Bellamy duly attended, and gave Wild five guineas as a token of repentance, with a promissory note for the remaining five. Wild then took him down to the 'Baptist's Head', spoke to Wildgoose, and said the affair was now forgotten.

Mendez and Arnold were honoured with a brief period of posthumous fame as the chiefs of Wild's retinue of villains in the Victorian melodramas about Jack Sheppard, though their names have since been forgotten with the plays. In the recent film *Where's Jack?* Wild's henchman was called, for some incomprehensible reason, 'Deely'.

The Life of Martin Bellamy names Wild's brother Andrew as being among the posse of thief-takers, though this seems rather doubtful. In *The Regulator*, Hitchen describes him, among the keepers of thieves' dens, as follows:

Andrew Wild, Brother to *Jonathan*, keeps a Case at the *Black Boy* in *Newtonhouse-Lane*, where his Wife Locks (receives) to a Parcel of young Lads that goes upon the Sneake: that is, to creep into a House in the Evening and taking what they can find. And when they have a good Booty he, the said *Andrew Wild*, tells them that his Brother hath bin their and that they are described by the Owner that they robbed, and that his Brother must have the paying them back, or his Wife must

have them at a low Price because they are to be returned by
him to his Brother.

Newtonhouse Lane was Lewkenor's Lane, where Jonathan himself first began. Andrew appears from time to time on the Sessions
rolls for petty offences. In April 1718 he was acquitted of receiving
and in July 1721 he was whipped for riot and assault. Two months
previously, he had been the 'Evidence' against the unfortunate
coiner Barbara Spencer. As this coincided with the prosecution
of another gang of coiners—that of Robert Harpham and the
blind watchmaker Cooper—it is possible that Jonathan had some
hand in it. Barbara Spencer was sentenced to be burned alive, a
punishment that shocked even that unshockable age. With his
customary lack of feeling, the author of *Lives of the Most Remarkable Criminals* says that when it became clear that the Privy
Council were determined to carry out the sentence, 'she seemed
excessivly surprized and concern'd at the Apprehension of the
Flames'. Terrible scenes took place at the stake, erected opposite
the gallows at Tyburn where the other prisoners were being
hanged. 'She was very desirous of Praying, and complain'd of the
Dirt and Stones thrown by the Mob behind her, which prevented her thinking sedately on Futurity. One Time she was beat
quite down by them.'[5] Applebee's journal of 15 July reported
that in the crush to see her 'several Persons lost the use of their
Limbs, others had their Arms and Legs broke, and two their
Eyes cut out'.

At the time of Jonathan's arrest, Andrew was in the Wood
Street Compter for debt. Perhaps he died there, for he thereafter
disappears from history.

'H.D.' relates that two of Wild's assistants, 'one *Felt-n*, a
superannuated Thief, and *Riddlesd-n*, an Attorney and Thief',
tried to set up against Wild at about the same time as Hitchen.
However, besides defeating Hitchen, Wild found means to get
Riddlesdon transported and to make Felton 'run mad'. The
London rolls of April 1719 show that an Edward Felton, a thief-
taker, was charged with assault, having cut out the eye of a
waterman, John Jones, with a sword. Wild was one of the
witnesses. In May Felton charged Wild with assault, but Wild was
exonerated. That is all the documents show. The most curious
detail, however, is that in the Sessions Book Wild is described
as a *Silversmith*. Perhaps Wild, in his desire to obtain a Freedom,

was trying to enroll himself into one of the City Companies.

Riddlesdon is more interesting. He appears first as the thief who broke into the Banqueting House and obtained his pardon by impeaching his accomplices in December 1714. Presumably he became one of Wild's thief-takers after that, although he was ordered to transport himself. In July 1716, he assisted in the arrest of Timothy Dun, during the Mrs. Knap affair, shooting him in the face after he had surrendered. In August, he was transported, owing, according to *Select Trials*, to Wild's impeachment. He returned in 1720 and was arrested in October, perhaps by Wild again. He was ordered to be transported again; and the saving of his life would appear to be due to the intervention of Charles Delafaye, Secretary to the Regency, who at this time was dealing with Secret Service and anti-Jacobite matters. It was through Delafaye, for instance, that Defoe relayed information about such seditious talk as he heard while editing the Tory and in fact pro-Jacobite *Weekly Journal or Saturday's Post*. Why Delafaye should have intervened on behalf of so humble a prisoner is a mystery, unless Riddlesdon had rendered the government some service as an informer against Jacobites.[6]

While in Newgate awaiting transportation, he taught some prisoners how to forge banknotes, which in those days had to be made out to individual persons, like modern cheques. The technique was to buy a note, payable to so-and-so, for £11 and with a chemical preparation, bought from a chemist in Snow Hill, erase all the letters except the first 'E', and write in '-ighty' instead, making the sum £80. The only difficulty was to change the note into coins, and this was how the prisoners were caught. At the Old Bailey, one of them said that it was not Riddlesdon who had taught them this formula, but the Rev. Joseph Lindsey, a clergyman who, after becoming a professional gambler, had turned highwayman, but secured his pardon by impeaching his accomplices in Spiggot's gang.[7]

At the same time, Riddlesdon became the lover of Mrs. Richard Revel, widow of one of the Newgate turnkeys, and she decided to go to America with him. Perhaps, like Moll Flanders and her Lancashire husband, they travelled as private passengers. They arrived at Annapolis on 18 May 1721, after a journey in which 22 out of the 129 prisoners had died. The Landing Certificate describes Riddlesdon as an 'Attorney-at-Law', about forty years old, and of 'a black Complexion'. Mrs Revel must have bribed his purchaser to give him his liberty, for they went to Pennsylvania. However, they soon quarrelled, and she returned to London where she bought a public house in Golden Lane.[8]

On 22 September, the *Daily Journal* reported that 'Riddlesdon & Hogg, two Felons, being lately return'd from Transportation, diligent Search is being made for them, to the end that they may be transported more effectually.' He was in fact in Newcastle-on-Tyne, courting a lady of 'good Family'. He promised to settle on her a jointure of £500 p.a. which he claimed to have in America. He was living under the name of 'Cornwallis', and was exposed when he solicited a local gentleman to obtain a pardon for 'one *William Riddlesdon*, who had been transported to America'. He fled to London, but was caught on the road and committed to Cambridge gaol.[9]

The girl, with commendable loyalty, followed him to Newgate and was delivered of their baby there. Meanwhile, he applied for bail on the grounds that he was an attorney due to be brought to the Bar as a Counsellor, but on 11 February, the King's Bench Court 'order'd him to the Bar in another Capacity to take his Tryal'.[10] He managed to procure yet another reprieve (through Delafaye or Wild?) and in May 1723 was permitted to transport himself again. *Select Trials* says he married the girl and that after his desertion her family, who had disowned her, relented and took her away. The Middlesex GD Book of July 1723, however, shows that he did *not* marry her, for it has an order to the effect that *Henrietta Maria Stanihurst* was to be held liable for all accounts owed by William Riddlesdon in Newgate.

Various sources tell us the names, but no more, of some of Wild's less important assistants: Isaac Illey (*Life of Martin Bellamy*), Horney (who tracked Timothy Dun), John Parry (who arrested Moll King) and, of course, Obadiah Lemon. Here, however, assistants merge into thieves who worked for Wild on a 'Weekly Pension', such as those Hitchen listed at the back of *The Regulator*.

Hitchen's list also contains a collection of short anecdotes which he felt ought to be made public: how Lemon and Will Matthews 'bit a Lob from a Ratler' (took a deal-box from a coach), for which Wild received a reward of seventeen guineas, but the owner, an old lady, had sewn sixty guineas into the sleeves of a gown, in place of the lead weights, and '*Wild* was cursed mad that he should lose so good a Booty'; how Wild protected Lemon and Edward Merrit (a 'Milken' or burglar) over and again from prosecution; how James Filewood was committed to Newgate by Justice Sanders for kidlaying, 'but *Filewood* being a great Favourite of Mr. *Wild's*, *Wild* went himself to the Justice and got his Discharge—but he gained Displeasure by it from one of the Turn-Keys, for the Turnkey ought to have a Feeling as well as *Wild*'.*

James Filewood is honoured by a 'biography' in Captain Smith's *Lives of the Highwaymen*, but it is nearly all fiction. The real Filewood, alias Violet, Villette, etc., was hanged on 31 October 1718 and is No. 57 on Wild's list, among the returned transportees. However, among the Treasury Papers[11] is a money warrant, dated 14 October 1718, ordering the reward of £40 for the conviction of James Filewood to be paid to 'Francis Bull *et al.*', and he was in any case hanged for burglary.

There were three Filewood brothers, and the one Wild arrested for returning from transportation was John, not James. He had been transported, as I have mentioned, for leading an abortive break-out from the Fleet Bridewell with Isaac Rag, and he returned late in 1720. He then continued stealing under Wild's supervision until he was unlucky enough to take a diamond-hilted sword from a captain at the Opera House in Lincoln's Inn Fields. Wild, wanting it for himself, offered a ridiculously low price for it, and Filewood sold it to a receiver. Accordingly, on 21 January 1721, the *Weekly Journal or Saturday's Post* reported that John Filewood had been arrested by Jonathan Wild on the rainy night of Tuesday, 17th, in Gracechurch Street, taken before the Lord Mayor, and committed to Newgate for returning from transportation. He was hanged in March.

This was the first returned transportee Wild impeached, and his action caused a shiver of alarm among the thieves. At the time of Wild's downfall, Filewood's name was remembered when others were forgotten, so that it was commonly believed that it was this incident which spurred the thieves on to conspire together and impeach their master.

Among the eighteen on Wild's list is the William Smith at

---

* Later, Wild and Justice Sanders fell out, for on the Calender of Middx. GD Roll 2360 (Jan 1721) it says: 'Jonathan Wyld, alias Bowyer, committed (*to Newgate*) by S. Sanders for insulting and abusing him in the execution of his Office as Justice of the Peace, 26th December.' I have found no clue to the cause or outcome of this affair, or why on earth Wild should have called himself 'Bowyer'.

whose suit, among others, Wild was committed to the Compter in 1710. In March 1720 Wild impeached him for a burglary in which he had used a small boy to climb in through a window[12] and he was transported. He returned from Annapolis in 1721, was immediately arrested by Wild and transported again— reprieved perhaps because of his age.

Another was the famous James Dalton. His life had already been a series of barely credible adventures. At the age of five he had watched his father hanged—indeed, his father had carried the boy between his knees in the cart to Tyburn so that he *could* watch. For a time he worked in one of Wild's gangs with William Field, who had also known Wild in the old days. Field impeached him in 1720, and he was transported on the *Honour* in May.[13] However, during a storm he led a mutiny of the prisoners and took control of the ship, landing himself, and fifteen others, at Vigo. The Governor of the town gave them passes, but when they discovered he had marked them '*Ladrones Ingleses*' ('*English Thieves*') they were forced to avoid the towns and trek across the mountains to the north coast. Here they eventually hailed a Dutch packet and, via Holland, made their way back to England. Dalton landed at Bristol and was caught in a burglary. Wild received immediate intelligence of this and had Dalton brought to London. His indictment, in Middlesex GD Roll 2362, is for returning from transportation and is endorsed by Jonathan Wild. He was never charged with the burglary, and it would seem therefore that Wild, by some means, managed to get that charge either mislaid or quashed. On the other hand, Wild seems to have done something to protect his life for, having originally been transported for fourteen years, Dalton was guilty of a capital felony. Instead, he was given another fourteen years. After this he disappears from Wild's history, but not from history altogether. On 19 August 1721, the *Saturday's Post* reported:

When the Convicts were lately carried on board a Ship at Limehouse-hole, in order to be transported to Virginia, a Ginger-bread Cake belonging to one Dalton (who was before transported and whose Father was hanged) was accidentally broke up, with which there was a File so conveniently bak'd up, that we may easily believe the Handcuffs could not long have withstood it. Upon which the said Dalton was tyed to the beers and dealt with according to his Deserts.

In America he terrified his master into giving him his freedom, and spent a year or two kidnapping negro slaves and selling them. He and his partners travelled between the mainland and various Caribbean islands, and such slaves as they could not sell they tied up and threw into the sea. When he returned to England, he was pressed into a man-of-war and sent to the siege of Gibraltar. Eventually he settled down to robbing again with William Field, but, learning no doubt from experience, saved himself by impeaching fourteen of his accomplices. He in turn, after robbing the celebrated Dr. Mead, was impeached by a professional false witness called John Waller and hanged. He became famous and was alluded to in several ballads and plays. In Plate 3 of Hogarth's *The Harlot's Progress*, which shows the magistrate Sir John Gonson coming to take Moll Hackabout to Bridewell, there can be seen over her bed a large case, which has printed on it: *James Dalton his Wigg Box*. John Waller was later set in the pillory, where the mob tore him to pieces.

Of all the thieves and informers who worked more or less permanently for Wild, William Field has left the most odious reputation, for he was cast as the sneaking Judas in the plays about Jack Sheppard. His reputation was deserved. He had begun as one of Hitchen's 'Mathematicians' and had informed against his employer to the Court of Aldermen. Then he impeached Dalton and several others in 1720, and again impeached Dalton's colleague, Wilson, when that person returned with the rest to London. At about the same time he impeached John Harris, husband of the Elizabeth Harris who had lent Wild the £12 bond in the Compter, although Harris had in fact been 'going straight' for a year. He was hanged, and in revenge, Elizabeth, hiding her feelings, tried to implicate Field and his wife (also Elizabeth) in a series of burglaries. They were saved by Wild, who in court declared, 'I heard *Elizabeth Harris* say, when her Husband was condemn'd, that she would stick the Prisoner, or Poison him, if she could get into his Company'.[14]

It would seem, however, that the struggle between Wild and Elizabeth Harris was more complicated than that. The indictments and the names of the informers on the backs[15] appear to reveal a pattern of conflict too intricate to unravel here, except to say that Wild counter-attacked by hiring (or forcing) several thieves, awaiting trial in Newgate, to impeach various people in Elizabeth Harris's party. One of these hirelings was Moll King

(her history is related in Chapter XVI) who impeached one
Richard Grantham. Ruth Grantham, his wife, in turn impeached
Elizabeth Smith, a friend of Moll King's and of Wild's party, etc.
Another clue is that Field's accomplice was called Anne Merritt.
According to Hitchen, Wild had a 'Weekly Pensioner' called
Edward Merritt; there were also two brothers of the same name
who were thief-takers (they organized the arrest of Spiggot's
gang in January 1721); and the recurrence of this not very com-
mon name in the same place (Wapping) and trade suggests a
family relationship. Anne was condemned and then for no apparent
reason reprieved and transported—which again suggests that
Wild held all the strings.

Another curious character who can be seen deep in this tangle
is Charles Strickland, by trade a 'Journeyman Soap-cask Cooper'
(soap-barrel maker). His sideline was to hire 'Persons, who
would swear any Thing that was required of 'em', on behalf of
prisoners who needed alibis. He served Wild on one provable
occasion at least (and several suspected ones), but it would appear
that he was not very conscientious in his work after he had taken
his fee, for several of the witnesses he procured had obviously
not been drilled in their stories, and the prisoners they were
supposed to get off were hanged. One wonders why Wild bothered
with him—he was eventually caught out at the trial of one of
Wild's men called Burridge, and committed to Newgate 'at
Pleasure' for perjury. These false witnesses, by the way, were
sometimes called 'Straw Men', for they identified themselves by
wearing straws in the buckles of their shoes, while they hung about
the Sessions House Yard.

After this affair, Field seems to have settled down to manage a
'lock', or warehouse for stolen goods, in Rosemary Lane, Wapping,
still under the supervision of Wild, and we shall return to him
when we come to Sheppard.

Something should be said here about these warehouses where
Wild stored his stolen goods until they could be returned to their
owners or sold abroad. One, apparently, was at Newington
Butts, in Southwark. Another was discovered in 1844, during
the demolition for the building of Holborn Viaduct. The building
was an ancient and dilapidated pub called the 'Red Lion' in
West Street (in Wild's day, Chick Lane) north of Smithfield.
The earliest recorded tenant was a gypsy called M'Waullen, who
had been a receiver in the 1680s. Next to the pub was a chandler's

shop, almost hidden beneath deep encrustations of filth, and the two buildings together were a Chinese puzzle of passages, trick staircases and doors concealed behind piles of rubbish. There were many trap-doors, secret cupboards and a staircase leading up to a sliding landing. This, when pulled in, left anyone running up the stairs teetering at the top. There were flip-doors at the side of another staircase, into which a fugitive could disappear, and doors which led pursuers round and back into the rooms they had just left. There was a coiner's furnace in the basement, a prison cell, and a trap-door which opened on to the Fleet Ditch running below the house. No doubt many of these features had been added during the century after Wild's death, for the place was used as a thieves' hideout until the last. A number of pamphlets were published about this original of 'Peachum's Lock', but unfortunately most of them, both in the British Museum and the Guildhall collections, were destroyed in World War II. According to some of them, quoted by F. J. Lyons, among the relics found in the ruins were two skeletons of men who had died violently, some instruments of torture, and a knife with *J. Wild* engraved on the handle. In the one pamphlet that has survived,[16] the only knife mentioned is a butcher's steel with '*Benj. Turtle July 19, 1787*' studded in silver on the haft. Turtle was a criminal who was hanged in the 1790s. Even though the connection with Wild seems to have depended more on legend, oral tradition and wishful thinking than on concrete evidence, the discovery of the 'Red Lion' gave a powerful fillip to the nineteenth century writers of romances and thrillers. It was precisely at the height of the craze for Jack Sheppard, caused by the success of Harrison Ainsworth's novel and the plays that followed it. The cobwebs, the clutter, and the atmosphere of villainy conjured up by those secret passages and panels fitted perfectly into the Victorian vision of a master criminal mind lurking at the dark centre of a sinister labyrinth. The literary tradition lasted long after its origin had been forgotten and buried beneath the accretions of melodrama and fantasy—through 'Moriarty' (whom Sherlock Holmes compared directly to Wild) and 'Dr. Fu Manchu', right down to the arch villains of Ian Fleming: 'Dr. No', 'Mr. Big', or 'Blofeld' and his 'S.P.E.C.T.R.E.', deep in their hideouts beneath the sea or under mountains.

Goods that were too 'hot' to keep in England were sent abroad, to be disposed of by the mysterious 'superannuated Thief'

(Lemon?) who managed Wild's affairs on the Continent. For the first few years, Wild presumably used the regular Channel smugglers; but in 1720 or early 1721, for greater security, he bought his own sloop and installed the famous Roger Johnson as captain.

Of all the rogues in Wild's circle, this Johnson seems to have had the most dependable instinct for survival, and after his death in 1740 (for he outlived all the others even though he was only forty-five when he died), his biographer[17] regretted that he had spent his life as a thief, 'for what a Politician was lost here'! He appears under his own name in Fielding's satire, *Jonathan Wild*, as the leader of the entrenched party (i.e. the Tory Party) of the prisoners in Newgate, whom Wild (i.e. Walpole) deposed through trickery, but in Harrison Ainsworth's *Jack Sheppard* he is called 'Van Galgebrok'.

The real Roger Johnson was born *c.* 1695 in the parish of St. Clement Danes in the Strand, where his father was a tailor who did a little pawnbroking on the side, and his mother kept a stall in Clare Market (there remains a street of that name at the bottom of Kingsway, behind the present Television House). When he was still a youth he took for his mistress Mother Jolly, proprietress of the 'King's Arms Tavern' in Drury Lane This was a standard Hundreds of Drury brothel, and as soon as he became familiar with the trade, Johnson ran it for her. He left her in about 1717. As she grew older Mother Jolly found the complexities of running such an establishment more and more difficult, and on 18 November 1721, the *Saturday's Post* reported that she was sentenced to three months' hard labour for running a disorderly house.

For a time, Johnson took to 'Preaching the Parson', disguising himself as a clergyman. He would knock at a house door, saying that he was about to visit his daughter and wanted to give her a present. However, he was short of change—at which he produced some Broad Pieces (20s. pieces from the reigns of James I and Charles I) and asked for something smaller. While the actual changing took place, he would palm false coins for the real ones, and leave the district. On 17 October 1718 he was condemned to death,[18] but later pardoned. Captain Alexander Smith, in his second biography of Parquot, says that Johnson saved his life by impeaching his own mother for coining; that she was committed to Newgate but died before coming to trial; and that his father then absconded and was never heard of again in London.

On 12 November 1720, the *London Journal* reported:

> This Week one Roger Johnson, who had formerly been con-
> demned, was committed to Newgate by the Bench of Justices,
> for what is called in Jonathan Wild's Dictionary the 'Kidlay';
> in our own Tongue, Shoplifting. He is likewise reckoned the
> most dexterous and polite Pick Pocket in Town, and by his
> Industry in that Way, has acquired too great a Fortune (as his
> Friends say) to be hanged.

Kidlay, of course, was not shoplifting but a form of confidence
trick.* As a result of this affair, Johnson was variously reported
as condemned to death or transportation, but the newspapers
and the records seem to have confused him with another called
Robert Johnson. At any rate, shortly after, he appeared publicly
at the Exchange as the newly-appointed captain of Wild's ship
(although he had no experience as a sailor), where he set up bills
of lading, etc., took on passengers for Flanders and Holland, and
advertised that he was 'to be spoken with' at the 'Graecian
Coffee House'. Within a year, Wild and Johnson had made so
much money that they were able to buy a larger ship for £500,
in which Johnson carried on a regular smuggling business, taking
cargoes of stolen goods to Flushing and Ostend, and bringing
back Flanders lace, Holland linen, spirits, and every kind of
contraband goods. There is an allusion to this in *The Life of
Elizabeth Wisebourne* by 'Anodyne Tanner',[19] which was published
in commemoration of the famous Covent Garden Madam, about
two years after her death in 1720. Among the clauses of what
pretends to be her will is the following:

'To his Grace the Duke of —, a Gross of right Dutch Condoms,
newly imported from Holland, by Mr. *Mendez*, the Jew.'

Besides this, Roger Johnson sometimes sailed his ship round
to the Irish Sea, and ran immigrants, and people evading the law,
to and fro from Ireland.

* *See page* 105.

{ XV } *Dividing the Map*

'But as *Jonathan* was a deep Studier of Nature, he knew that Men's Talents were different, and that he who had not Courage enough to bid a Man stand, upon the Road, might nevertheless make an excellent Pickpocket; and he took Care to see that no Man's parts should be mis-apply'd.' As a corollary he encouraged those who had found their vocations to remain in them and to confine themselves to their particular areas. This was not difficult as his thieves were, for the most part, conservative by nature and preferred to stick to the methods and territories they knew best. Thus 'Nature' assisted him, as I have said earlier, in keeping a check on them and in facilitating a quicker turnover at the Lost Property Office. His real problem was to keep the underworld divided for easier control without permitting it to fall apart. He achieved this by means of a working method, a 'system', rather than by means of an 'organization' in the modern sense, and in this respect his underworld was almost a microcosm of the nation as a whole.

Yet there must have been *some* organization, and we can gain an idea of what kind it was from a seventeenth century tract called *The Devil's Cabinet Broke Open*.[1] All sorts of rules are laid down governing the movements and dress of thieves: the minimum permitted interval between appearing in the same tavern twice; the routes to be followed when returning from robberies; the avoidance of recognition; which buttons are to be left undone to signify success or failure; highwaymen living in south London to rob on the northern roads, etc.; and it is safe to assume that by Wild's day these precautions had been improved. Moreover, Wild himself must have taken trouble to keep each gang in ignorance, as far as that was possible, of what the others were doing.

Therefore, when he was accused, after his arrest, of running a 'Corporation' of thieves (and 'H.D.' says he sometimes used the word himself), it apparently meant not a gang as such, but all the gangs for whom he acted as agent, adviser and director.

He gave grandiloquent titles to his two chief assistants, calling Quilt Arnold 'Clerk of the Northern Roads' and Mendez Ceixes 'Clerk of the Western Roads'. The titles were ambiguous, it being understood that these gentlemen were supposed to keep their respective 'Roads' clear of highwaymen; but equally, of course, it meant that these were the roads assigned to them for plunder. Of the various brands of thief infesting these roads, the most profitable were those who 'went upon the *Waggon-Lay*', and among them the most notable for many years was Thomas Edwards. We have come across him already as the proprietor of the 'Goat', the 'flash-Case' in Long Lane, Smithfields, described by Hitchen in *The Regulator*. Hitchen says nothing about his skill on the roads, but *Select Trials* says that he 'was indefatigable in his Calling, for he would sometimes follow a Waggon for 100 Miles together: he always lay at the same Inn where the Waggon put up, and when every Body else was a-Bed, he would creep down from his Room, and take a Box or Portmantua out of a Waggon, unbar the Inn Gates, carry his Booty into some private Field, and plant it under a Hedge, and so return privately to his own Bed again. . . .'[2]

In the *Daily Courant* of 18 March 1721 there is also this report of him:

'The Lord Mayor hath lately committed to the Wood-street Compter, one Thomas Edwards, who is suspected to be one of the Gang that used to rob the Waggons and Pack-Horses: At which Place, any Waggoner, or Pack-Horse Driver, that have been robbed, may have a View of him.'

Edwards, through his enmity with Roger Johnson, was to play an important part in the fall of Wild.

The waggons and coaches that escaped Edwards and his gang on the roads came under a fresh hazard as soon as they arrived at

8 Blueskin Blake tries unsuccessfully to cut Wild's throat in front
of the Old Bailey court. The costumes are rather out of period,
and the windows and wall behind were not added until twelve years
years later. We should have seen the clerks and judges staring
out, horrified at Blueskin's temerity. (*See Chapter XIX*)

Walk in Gentlemen

9 A satirical broadsheet done shortly before Sheppard's last escape.
The ostrich perhaps refers to Wild, or Walpole (as a man who
would swallow anything to stay in power), though one was on
show at Ludgate Hill at the time. Wild can be seen on the left of
the gate, receiving clients, and Sheppard in the middle window

their destinations in London, for Wild employed other gangs of men disguised as porters, whose job was to hang about inn-yards and collect baggages under the pretence of delivering them to their owners. Among these was Jeremiah Rand, of whom *Select Trials* tells an illuminating story:

> *Jonathan* one Day, going to an Inn in Smithfield, observed a large Trunk in the Yard, and imagining there might be something of considerable Value in it, he goes Home and orders *Jerry Rann* . . . to go and *speak with it*; *Rann* dresses himself like a Porter, and brings it off. It belong'd to Mr. *Jarvis*, a Whip-maker in that Neighbourhood, and he had sent it to the Inn, to be carry'd down into the Country; but, hearing that somebody had stole it, he apply'd to *Wild*, who, after a great many Delays, helped him to most of the Goods again for ten Guineas. *Wild* and *Rann* quarreling soon afterwards, *Wild* found Means to have him hang'd; but, the Day before his Execution he sent for Mr. *Jarvis*, and discovered the whole Affair to him.
>
> Mr. *Jarvis* was the more inclinable to believe this Account, because his own Servant informed him, that *Wild* was at the Inn, when the Trunk was laid down there. It was reported that *Wild* was threatened with a Prosecution for this; but Mr. *Jarvis* dying soon after, the Design dy'd with him.

Rann, whose real name was Rand, is No. 23 on Wild's list, 'for robbing and assaulting a Clockmaker's Servant of a Clock, who lives in *Lombard Street*'. The *London Journal* of 28 April 1722 shows that Wild arrested him that week, and Middlesex GD Roll 2387 shows that Rand (thus spelt) was convicted on the evidence of David Bewley, William Tomlinson ('*A Prisonar*') and 'Jonathan Wyld'. He was hanged in May, on the same day as Hawkins and Simpson, the then famous highwaymen who had robbed over fifty coaches and mail-trains (pack-ponies) in the previous year.

As such waggon- and coach-thieves stood in relation to the highwaymen, so various kinds of sneak-thieves stood in relation to housebreakers. There is a story of a shopkeeper whose account-books were taken by one of these. After a dispute with Wild over the price for their return, he paid £15 and found the books back in his shop. However, a week later they had gone again, for Wild had sent a thief to take them. Wild thereupon advised the shop-keeper to remove his safe into the back parlour, where the only entrance from outside was through a skylight. Wild then sent another thief, who, under the pretext of wanting to speak with the shopkeeper privately, went into the parlour, snatched up the books, which happened to be lying on a desk, and locked the unfortunate shopkeeper in 'his Counting-House'.

In order to gain access to the houses of the great, Wild formed coteries of what he called 'Spruce Prigs' to go to Court 'on Birthnights, to Balls, Operas, Plays, and Assemblies, for which Purpose they were furnished with laced Coats, brocade Wastcoats, fine Perriwigs, and sometimes equipp'd with handsome Equipages, such as Chariots, with Footmen in Liveries, and also *Valets-de-Chambres*, the Servants being all Thieves, like the Master'. It may seem unlikely that a common thief could pass himself off, no matter how well dressed, among the 'Quality' without soon betraying himself by some *faux pas*, but in fact there were always a few young men of good family who, hiding in the Mint from creditors or in some other disgrace, were only too willing to let Wild set them up for such ventures, There was, besides, considerable mixing of classes, especially in London; masquerades and balls were often crowded and boisterous occasions; and accents were not yet the infallible indicators of class they have since become in England. We have already encountered Riddlesdon as an authentic 'Spruce Prig'; Roger Johnson actually gained admission to Court on at least two occasions; and 'H.D.' tells of a young fop whom he saw Wild bullying at Southwark Fair for not reporting to him for two months. This youth was the son of a chairman, and he had come up in the world by playing gigolo and then pimp to his father's employer, a fast-living lady of Quality. Once he had nearly succeeded in picking King George I's pocket during the King's Birthday celebrations at Court, but had been frustrated by a woman who had pushed herself in front of him in her 'Fondness of shewing herself to his M—ty'. He picked her pocket instead. Finally, we have record of John Follard, one of Wild's inner circle of thieves, who was able to go about Lincoln under the name of 'Sir John Pollyard' without arousing suspicion —at least for several days.

'*Jonathan* sometimes paid a Dancing-master, to teach them to dance; that is, after he lost his own Dancing-master, the celebrated Mr. *Lun*, who died in his own Profession, *viz*: Dancing; being hang'd at Kingston for a Robbery on the Highway; who he sometimes said was a great Loss to the Corporation.'[3] The servants of these 'Spruce Prigs' were trained by ex-footmen and valets, like James 'Hell and Fury' Sykes, who, until 1720 was a running-footman in service with that most notorious of rakes, Philip, Duke of Wharton. As for domestics, in his treatise on servants[4] written in 1724, Defoe says, 'I have been told, our famous Thief-taker (as they call him) has a List of *seven thousand* Newgate-Birds, now in Services in this City, and Parts adjacent, all with Intent to rob the Houses they are in.'

Wild's men were the first, so it was charged later, to penetrate the Houses of Parliament, a fact which lends added interest to the following report in the *Daily Journal* (30 January 1722). The occasion was the debate on the project to build Westminster Bridge, which was being opposed, on the grounds that it was just another 'Bubble', by some who wanted the concession themselves:

> The Public Gallery was pack'd with Strangers of various Sentiments . . . among them a grave sort of Person who seem'd very strenuous for the Bridge (and who by his Habit appear'd to be a Projector) was taken in picking the Pocket of Mr. Hambleton, a Gentleman belonging to the House of Lords, at the very Door of the House of Commons: the Footmen immediately claim'd him as their Property, and conducting him to the Waterside, obliged him to fathom the River, according to an antient Privilidge belonging to those Gentlemen.

Indeed, it must have seemed to Londoners that year with the South Sea Bubble fresh in their memories, the crime wave at its height and Wild in the fullness of his prosperity, that 'all Mankind were turn'd Thieves' and that every public occasion was merely the signal for a new scandal. Nothing was sacrosanct:

'We hear that the Pall used at the Duke of Marlborough's Funeral, was the Perquisite of the Dean of Westminster; and that the same was taken away by Persons unknown.'

Finally there is a tale in which some of Wild's specialists, dressed as 'Beaux', laid a wager against a club of bell-ringers that their team could ring better peals; then, when the rival team had taken off their coats and hats at the country church to set to work, Jonathan's men made off with all their clothes, money (including the £500 for the wager), horses and the food they had brought for lunch.

Related to these 'Spruce Prigs' were those who went on 'the Lodging Lay'. The most notorious experts in London at this period were Mary Davis, alias 'Lady Smith', and Elizabeth Askew, alias 'Lady Green'. They went from house to house, one dressed in the height of fashion and the other as her servant (they alternated their rôles), rented apartments and then left with everything they could carry. Sometimes Mary Davis would hire herself as a chambermaid, using references from 'Lady Green', and then, in the middle of the night, pass all the valuables in the house out to her accomplice.[5] Elizabeth's nickname was 'Tawney Bess' and Mary Davis was called 'Wapping Moll' ('Fucking Moll') and 'H.D.' says that they were under the management of Jonathan Wild. In 1721 Mary Davis was transported and Elizabeth Askew stood in the pillory and fined ten marks (£8 7s. 8d.). We do know that Wild was involved with, and probably ran, a gang of Lodging Lay specialists in Southwark, led by Humphrey Jones and Joseph Allen, and that the wives of these two, who were sisters, ran a 'Lock' in the neighbourhood. But, if 'H.D.'s' story is in any way true, it would seem that the masterpiece of all Lodging Lay enterprises was carried out by Wild himself, and in the account, he is supposed to be telling the story:

A Gentleman had fitted up a House in *Queen's Square*, in a very handsome Manner, expecting to let it to some foreign Minister, or *English* Person of Quality; which as soon as 'twas ready, I equipt a Fellow, who had prov'd himself a Man fit for Business, in a plain neat Suit, gold-headed Cane, Snuff Box, Etc., a good Chariot, with two other Rogues for Footmen: This suppos'd Gentleman calls upon the Landlord, and offers to treat with him for the Hire of his House, which he said, if he lik'd his Terms, he would take a Lease of for Twenty-one Years; whereupon the Bargain was struck, and in a few Days the Leases were drawn, the Rent to be paid at half-yearly payments; and the Furniture was promis'd by the Squire to be brought in the *Wednesday* following.

The Week after, the Landlord calls at the House, to see his new Tenant, in order to promote a more intimate Acquaintance, but finds nobody there but a shabby old Man, and not one Piece of Furniture; but on the contrary, two or three Marble Chimney Pieces and Slabs taken down; He enquires of the old man the Meaning of it, who told him his Master order'd it, for he did not like the Fashion of 'em, and was pleas'd to have 'em altered.

The furious landlord was only pacified when the old man assured him that his master would come next day to make what satisfaction was required. But when the landlord returned next day at noon, he met 'some Men at the Door, carrying out two Chimney-Glasses, and several Pictures that had been fix'd to the Panels over the Chimney-Pieces . . .' He tried to stop these from being removed, and the tenant then appeared and demanded to know by what authority the landlord thought he was acting. The landlord claimed they were his own proprty, and demanded to know, in any case, why the tenant had been so long moving in.

'Sir,' says the Tenant, 'I have had two Children sick of the Small Pox, which hinder'd me from moving so soon as I expected, but tomorrow some of my Goods will be here.'

'But what are you doing with those you send away?'

'Why, I am for fitting up Things according to my own Fancy, and I don't matter the Expence of it; for, as I alter the Chimney-Pieces to another Form, the Glasses must be made to answer them, and the Frames of the Pictures I shall have made wider, to square with the Glasses.'

'When I fitted up this House,' says the Landlord, 'I thought it might have serv'd any Man of Quality in the Kingdom.'

'That might be,' says the Squire again, 'I'll have Things done aggreeable to my own Humour, for all that: When your Rent's due, I'll pay it; and when my Lease is expired, I shall leave the House in as good a Condition as I have found it.'

The landlord was too bewildered to carry on the argument and decided to wait until the next day, by which time the tenant would certainly have brought in some of his goods, which would be at least a minimum security against the alterations that had been made. When he returned, however, he was 'still more provoked, to see that all the Furniture that was brought, consisted of two old Chairs and a Table, not worth half-a-Crown; and they had in the mean Time been so expert in making the Alterations (as they call'd it) that they had took down a very fine new Staircase, and the Wainscot of the best Room . . .'.

The landlord arrested the tenant in an action of £500. Wild got his man bailed and ordered his attorney to summon the plaintiff before a judge, to show cause of action, 'which he failing to do, was oblig'd to take common Bail: But this not answering his Purpose (for in reality the Defendant ow'd him nothing), the

Landlord files a Bill in the *Exchequer Court*; upon which the Tenant prefers a cross Bill, obliging him to answer several Points, particularly the Letting the House to him; which as he could not deny, the Landlord's Bill was dismiss'd with Costs of Suit; and the Suit at Common Law went against him also, by Default: And the Tenant *going to work again upon the Premises*, the Landlord thought fit to make Overtures of Agreement; *viz*: that upon a surrender of his Lease, and giving up possession of the House, in the Condition it was then in, he would pay all his Charges, and release him (the Tenant) from all Damages whatsoever: Which, upon my Consent, since there was no more to be got, The Terms were accepted of; and so the Landlord, besides a Year-and-a-half's Rent, sate down at £400 Loss. Which, I suppose, will make him take a little Care how he lets his Houses.'

Queen Square, in Holborn, was begun in 1710 and completed *c.* 1716. Leases were granted to private and speculative builders, and the Middlesex Land Register shows that almost any of them would have answered very well to Wild's victim. They were plumbers, glaziers, carpenters and masons, men with little education or legal acumen who had become fairly rich through hard work and now wished to become property owners. They most of them intended to let their houses to foreign ambassadors. Perhaps, therefore, the story was based on a true incident (as most of 'H.D.'s' were), and embellished with a few sneers at the *nouveaux riches*.

The Lodging Lay still goes on, though no longer under that name. Readers of the James Bond story *The Spy Who Loved Me* will remember the description there of young married couples, or pretended married couples, who sign into American motels and, in the dead of night, load all the furnishings and fixtures of their cabins into station-waggons and drive away.

In his supervision of areas and functions, it was important for Wild to keep small-time receivers under a restraining hand, and for this a friendly Justice or two was always helpful. Humphrey Jones, Allen, and their wives at the 'Lock' in Southwark, for instance, were all transported in 1723 after Wild discovered that they had tried to dispose of a stolen watch for 'Blueskin' Blake. There is another case, too, which occurred when Wild and Mendez, walking down Holborn, saw a 'Gentlewoman' pass by in a coach. They knew that she kept a silversmith's shop on the corner of Calender Court in Drury Lane.

' "That's a Fencing Mort," says Abraham, "and I dare swear, that she has got a Mause of Wedge—let's Bone her"!' (*'That's a receiving woman, and I dare swear, that she's got a bundle of silver— let's search her!'*)[6]

They stopped the coach (perhaps Wild had some kind of warrant in reserve for such emergencies) and found indeed a large quantity of silver wrapped in a long pillow-case. They packed her off to the Compter and took the silver back to Wild's office. Almost immediately, Wild was told that a Jewish merchant from St. Mary Axe (near where Mendez lived off Leadenhall Street) was waiting in 'The Fountain' tavern opposite Newgate. The Jew said he had been robbed of some silver and offered Wild 2*s.* 6*d.* an ounce for its recovery. Wild replied that, assuming the plate now in his possession was the client's, he could have it, *provided a legal method was taken.* The Jew identified the plate, went before a magistrate and swore to it, but added that he did not wish to prosecute the woman. Legality justified, the woman was discharged and Wild was paid the sum that had been agreed.

Amateurs, of course, had to be excluded from the business altogether, except insofar as they could be made examples of at convenient moments. Early in 1719, for instance, when Wild was defending himself against several simultaneous attacks, three amateurs were misguided enough to try to interest him in their affairs.

The first was Joseph Holliday, who, on Christmas morning 1718, had pilfered a silver tankard from a Holborn alehouse and taken it, wrapped in his apron, to Jonathan Wild.

'I asked him whose it was?' (said Wild in court), 'He said it was his own. "But," says I, "why do you bring it to me? I am no Pawnbroker." He said he had been directed to me. "Well, and what will you have for it?" says I, and he reply'd that sure it was worth £3. "Aye," says I, "so it is, and I'll give ye the Money provided you can make me a good Title to it, and satisfy me that your Wife shall not come and break my Windows for buying it." By such Discourse as this, I amused him, 'till an Officer that I had sent for came and secured him.'

As *Select Trials* comments, Jonathan 'knew what Use to make of detecting this poor Fellow, who was a Stranger to him. "The World may see," says he, "that I am so far from encouraging Felons, that I take the first Opportunity of bringing them to Justice".'

Barely a week later, 'two ancient Women', who had apparently learned nothing from this object lesson, came to Wild's office with their proposal for armed robbery with murder.

Their names were Margaret Dowdell and Alice Wright, and, in fact, they could not have been as ancient as all that because one had a young child and was pregnant with a second. At the February 1719 sessions Wild recounted what happened:

On the 23rd or 24th of last Month the Prisoners came to my House, and said they wanted to speak with me in private; upon which I look'd at 'em very earnestly, and perceiving one of them to be with Child, I did not know but she might want a Father to it; However, I took them aside, and desired them to tell me their Business.

'Why,' says Dowdell, 'I have lost nothing, but yet I want something—I believe I can help ye to a thousand Pounds. Nay, I don't doubt of making it many thousands, if you'll be ruled by me.'

'Oh, by all Means,' says I, 'and I shall think myself much obliged to ye for putting me in the Way: Pray what's to be done?'

'Why you must procure me,' says she, 'two or three stout Fellows.'

'Very well,' says I, 'and how then?'

'Why then,' says she, 'the Business is to break open the House and take the Money. 'Tis the House of *John Wood*, a *Cane Chair-maker* in *Wormwood-street*, near *Bishopsgate*; and he has a Lodger, an ancient maiden Gentlewoman, that has got some Thousand Pounds in her Boxes under the Bed where she lies. Now, there is a Sawpit in the Shop, and the only way will be for one of the Fellows, in the Evening, to take an Opportunity of hiding himself in this Saw-pit, which he may do very easily, and so in the dead of Night he may let in his Companions; and then they must take care to secure two sturdy 'Prentices and a Boy that lodges in the Garret, for they will be apt to be very Refractory. But I beg that this may be done, if possible, without committing Murder—'

'Phoo!' says Alice Wright, 'People that go upon such Matters, must do as well as they can; they must take Care of themselves, and act as they shall see best for their own Security. Now, when these Boys are secured, it's the easiest Thing in the

World to come at the old Gentlewoman's Money; for she is gone into the Country to fetch more, and hers is underneath where the Boys lie. Then opposite to her Room is the Room where Mr. *Cook* and his Wife lie, but you must take particular Care of him, for he's a devilish resolute Man, and it might not be much amiss if he were knock'd o' the Head. And when that's done you may find Money in his Drawers, for he never is without. Right under his Room lies a Gentlewoman and a small Child; but I must desire of ye that neither she nor the Child may be hurt . . .'

'And so must I too,' says Dowdell, 'for I would not have them come to any Harm for the World!'

And when I had heard all this, I thought it was proper to take Care of my Chaps.

{ XVI } *The Fortunes of Moll Flanders*

Of the countless 'Bunters', 'Shoplifts', 'Buttocks', 'Files' and 'Autem Divers' who, infesting the markets, brothels and churches of the Metropolis, supplied Jonathan Wild with the greater part of his daily business, one of the most interesting is Moll King. No life of her was ever written, nor have we a record of any of her numerous trials;* in fact, even discovering her identity was a considerable task, for, like 'Moll Flanders', who would seem to have been partly based on her, she hid behind at least a dozen aliases. 'Moll Flanders' had nothing to say about thief-takers, but did emphasize that although the officers in the Old Bailey, and the thieves in Newgate, all knew her name and reputation, none knew what she looked like. Whether or not the Old Bailey officers and Newgate thieves were baffled by Moll King is less certain, for, although she would appear at the court several times at the same Sessions to face different charges under as many different names, Wild at least knew all about her and employed her for more than three years. Her story can be reconstructed from fragments of evidence and anecdote in contemporary pamphlets, newspapers, and the parchment Sessions Records, and it tells us a great deal about the intrigues and methods Wild employed in managing women of her kind.

Nothing is known, as yet, of her birth or background. In 1687

* See *Times Lit. Supp.*, 18 January 1968, p. 63.

she was whipped for stealing clothes. In 1691 she was twice indicted (once with Tom King—husband? brother?) of theft, but acquitted. In October 1693 she was accused of stealing an Alkareen petticoat (dyed alcanet, or scarlet), a hair fringe and 3 yards of white Flanders lace from a house in Cripplegate, but as none could prove she had actually broken in, she was found guilty of common felony only and burnt in the hand.[1]

Between 1697 and 1713, eleven women called Mary King were indicted of various offences at Middlesex Sessions alone,[2] but there is no means of knowing how many of these, if any, were our Moll King, and the lack of indexes of indictments in the City of London records makes it almost impossible to trace her history there either.

There is therefore a gap until 1718, when she turns up in *The Life of John Stanley* (pub. 1723, and almost certainly written by Purney, the Newgate Ordinary), in Defoe's life of Wild, and in the records once again.

John Stanley was a good-looking young man who, until his death in 1723, lived as a roistering 'Captain' on the generosity of infatuated women.* In 1718 he was seventeen years old, but, lodging near Soho Square, he frequently went to prayers at St. Anne's church because it was always full of young ladies who 'pray in their Paint and see their Heaven in Man'. Moll King (who, says Purney, was by then the wife of a 'City Officer') 'had a Humour of going thither too', attracted by the same bait; for she was 'well known for her Dexterity in borrowing Gold Watches, or Snuff Boxes, from Ladies (with whom she sat in a Pew at Church) by means of false Hands which lay demurely before her, while her true ones were busy elsewhere....'

The invention of this device has sometimes been attributed to the famous 'Jenny Diver' (real name, Mary Young, hanged, March 1741), who added verismilitude by folding these hands over a 'pregnant' belly, but here, at least fifteen years earlier, was Moll King already a skilled practitioner.

Smitten by the handsome young 'Captain', she got acquainted with him by stealing his gold watch and putting a gold box, of

---

* Any young man with money enough to buy himself a good pair of gloves, some lace, and a sword, could call himself 'Captain' and assume this gave him a licence to riot round the town. Thus the title was adopted by authors of picaresque books: 'Capt. Alexander Smith', 'Capt. Charles Johnson', 'Capt. Charles Walker', etc. It probably came from the boasting, swearing, duelling *Capitano* of the Italian Comedy.

twice the watch's value, into his pocket instead. When he saw, after prayers, that his watch was gone, she said she could take him to the woman that stole it. Over a bottle of wine, which he bought her while they were waiting, she put the watch back into his other pocket undetected, and then swore in front of everyone in the tavern that he had robbed her of the box. She described the box and the marks on it, and when he was searched and the box discovered, 'he being found guilty lay at her Mercy; but she desiring all to withdraw, threw herself about his neck, and embracing him declar'd how long how much she lov'd; and instead of his being made a Prisoner, own'd herself a Captive to his Beauty'. She gave him the gold box as a present, adding two diamond rings, and offered 'much more for the Continuation of his Friendship'.

In short, she completely lost her heart, and they went everywhere together, despite the fact that he was not yet eighteen years old and she must have been nearly fifty (a point the romantic Purney fails to mention).

Now, in his life of Wild, Defoe included a transaction, clearly based on a true incident, between Wild and a lady whose watch had been stolen in St. Anne's, Soho, and his purpose was to show how Wild handled the 'Quality' by appealing to their humane instincts, and at the same time ruled the thieves by terror.

Another Person applying in another and more material Affair, was treated with Respect by Mr. *Wild*, and a Pot of Tea brought out in Form: (N.B. The Crown being first deposited as usual). The Case related to a Gold Watch, with Trinkits and some Diamonds about either the Watch, and the Lady offer'd very considerably, for the restoring it, as I remember, £30, but no Advertisements had been publish'd. Mr. *Wild*, after the usual Enquiries of when it was lost? and where? And being told it was at St. *Ann*'s Church, *Westminster*, paused a while, and calls up a Servant, and asks aloud, 'Where was *M—ll K—g* last Sunday?'

'About *Westminster*,' says the Man, but the *Bi—h* would not tell where.'

'Was she Crank?' says Mr. *Wild*.*

* In cant, 'crank' usually meant one who counterfeited sickness to arouse compassion ('Confek Crank'), and no other is given in any canting dictionary, or Partridge's *Dictionary of the Underworld*. Here, however, it would seem to mean 'Had she any money or goods hidden on her?'

'I don't know,' says the Fellow.

However, turning to the Lady, says he (*Wild*), 'Madam, I fancy I shall be able to serve you, and perhaps for less Money than your Ladyship speaks of. If it be *M—ll K—g*, that Woman, I have in my Thoughts, as I believe 'tis, for she is a dextrous Jade at the Work, I'll have her safe before Morning.'

The Lady, full of Compassion, returns, 'Oh Sir! don't take her up. I assure you, I won't prosecute, I'll rather lose my Watch, than have any poor Wretch Hang'd for it.'

'Why? Madam,' says Mr. *Wild*, 'We can't talk with her, but by Threatening: We must not make a Bargain with her, that would be to compound a Felony. If I can perswade her to come and bring your Watch, and ask your Pardon, will that satisfy you?'

'Nay,' says the Lady, 'I don't know whether that would be safe, neither: If she will send it me, I had rather; and I'll forgive her, without asking Pardon.'

'Well, Madam, will you take it, and give the Porter that brings it 20 Guineas, if you please, but not to oblige you to it.'

'Whatever you say, Mr. *Wild*', says the Lady.

'Well, Madam,' says Mr. *Wild*, 'if I may have the Honour to see your Ladyship again.'

Lady Will it not do if I send any Body?

Wild Why, truly, no Madam: People that deal in these Things, do not care for Witnesses.

Lady Well, well, that's true: I'll come my self. What Day would you have me come?

Wild On *Thursday*, Madam.

Lady Well, Mr. *Wild*, what must I do? What will satisfy you for your Trouble?

Wild It is time enough, Madam, to speak of that when I am sure I can do you any Service. These Creatures are very loose, and I can't tell you how it may be.

Lady Well, Mr. *Wild*, I'll come furnish'd to pay my Respects to you.

Wild Madam, Your most obedient Servant.

(*Waits on her to her Coach.*)

Accordingly, *Thursday* coming, the Lady appears. Mr. *Wild*, in his Callimancoe* Night-gown (*the same he was hang'd in*),

---

* Callimanco—a woollen material. At this period, men commonly wore dressing-gowns for daily business indoors, and turbans or head-cloths on their heads.

receives her; and with a pleasant Look, tells her, he is very glad, to be able to say, that he believes he shall serve her. That it was the same Woman he suspected, and that the Jade had already pawn'd the Watch for some Money, but that it was but a little, and he was glad she had.

Lady Why? Mr. *Wild*.

Wild Because, Madam, if she had kept it all this while, it would have been ten to one but she had Broke something about it, or done it some Mischief.

Lady That's true, indeed. Pray, what has she Pawn'd it for?

Wild Not much, Madam, she has got but seven Guineas upon it yet.

Lady Well, Mr. Wild, what must be done?

Wild Why, Madam, if the People that have it, bring it safe and sound to your Ladyship, will you give me your Honour that you will ask no Questions, or stop the Person that comes with it?

Lady I promise you, on my Word, I will not.

Wild The Man that brings it may be a poor Innocent Fellow, that knows nothing of it.

Lady Well, well, he shall have no Harm or Interruption from me.

Wild Then I believe your Ladyship may hear something of it to Night.

Lady And what must I give him?

Wild I don't yet know, Madam, but I'll bring them as low as I can. Not above 20 Guineas, to be sure, Madam.

Lady That is very kind, indeed. Well, Mr. *Wild*, then I'll make it up to you. (*So the Lady Pulls out her Purse in order to give him some Money.*)

Wild No, Madam, not a Farthing. Besides, you have not got your Watch yet: Pray stay till you see whether the Jade will Perform; tho' I think, indeed, I am pretty sure of her.

Lady Well, I'll take your Word, Mr. *Wild*. (*Offers him Money again.*)

Wild By no Means, Madam; let me see if I can serve you.

Lady Well, Mr. *Wild*, if it must be so, I suppose I must come again then.

Wild It may be not. Will your Ladyship be pleas'd to stay about half an Hour.

Lady Ay, with all my Heart.

In about half an Hour, *Jonathan* having been call'd hastily out, comes in again immediately. 'Madam,' says he, 'if your Ladyship pleases to go into your Coach, and drive gently up .... *Street*, perhaps a Messenger may desire to speak with you as you go along.

'Very well, Mr *Wild*, I understand you.'

Upon the Lady's going along .... *Street*, a *Ticket-Porter*, with his Hat in his Hand, shows himself by the Coach-side, and the Lady taking the Hint, stops her Coach, and lets down the Glass, and speaking to the Fellow, says, 'Would you speak with me, Friend?'

The Fellow speaks not a Word, but delivers into her Hand the Watch with all the Trinkits and Diamonds perfectly safe; and when she had look'd upon it a little, gives her a Note, wherein was written nothing but thus in Words at length.

'Eighteen Guineas.'

The Lady immediately tells out the Money to the *Porter*, and he was going away: 'Hold! Honest Friend,' says the Lady, 'there's somewhat for yourself'; and gives him half-a-Guinea, and so dismiss'd him.

A Day or two after she makes Mr. *Wild* a Visit, and presents him with fifteen Guineas more: But with great Difficulty made him accept of it; telling her it was a great deal too much; and that he would not take it by any means, but at last accepts it, with the Ceremony of saying, he would not take it on account of the Watch, but for having been at some Trouble in serving her Ladyship, in which she was pleas'd to Reward him much more than he deserv'd; when at the same time 'twas very likely had part of the 18 Guineas too from *M—ll K—g*, who he frighted out of the Watch with threatening to have her put into *Newgate* for stealing of it.

On 19 October 1718 Moll King stole two watches in St. Anne's Soho, was arrested shortly after and, in December, tried under the name of 'Mary Golstone' and sentenced to death.[3] She 'pleaded her Belly', a 'Panel of Matrons' found that she was pregnant, and her sentence was reduced to fourteen years transportation.[4] Could the father, perhaps, have been Captain Stanley? Or, more prosaically, her husband, or one of the Newgate 'Wags' that hired themselves out as studs to impregnate women prisoners who were in danger of capital sentences? She remained in Newgate until February 1720—until, that is, her baby had been born and she had been allowed a few months to nurse it. During her last three weeks, one of her fellow-prisoners was Sarah Wells, alias 'Callico Sarah', who had likewise been sentenced to death (and reprieved) for picking a pocket in Whitechapel. 'Callico Sarah's' bully was a man called Everett,[5] and it is almost certain that this was John Everett, at that time a bailiff in Whitechapel High Street, who later achieved some fame as a highwayman.[6] His partner, according to his biographer, was Dick Bird. A year later, Moll King, on her return to England, used 'Bird' as an alias, and her partner was Richard Bird, whose recognizance shows that he was a butcher in Whitechapel High Street.[7] Therefore, although Moll King and 'Callico Sarah' may not have known each other before 1720, it is certain that they did from then on.

'Mary Gilstone', as Moll King now called herself, arrived at Annapolis on 23 April 1720,[8] and returned straight to England. On 2 July, the *Weekly Journal or Saturday's Post* (of which Defoe was part-editor under Nathaniel Mist) reported:

'One Mrs. King, an old Pick-Pocket and Shop-lifter, who about a twelve month ago was transported to the English Plantations in America, for seven Years, has found means to come back again, after whom diligent Search is made by them that prosecuted her, that she may be apprehended and brought to Justice.'

Actually, she had been transported for fourteen years. However, two weeks later, on the 16th, *Applebee's Original Weekly Journal* printed a letter pretending to come from 'Moll' of Rag Fair, but generally agreed to have been written by Defoe. In it, 'Moll' complained that, having returned from transportation, she was being blackmailed by a man who threatened to impeach her if she did not return to thieving and, what was worse, give him most of her money. Although Defoe did not mention it, the man was obviously Jonathan Wild.

Moll King continued thieving under Wild's 'protection' for a whole year until, by some mishap, she was caught on 14 June 1721 while robbing the house of Joseph and Mary Kinsallaugh in Little Russell Street, Covent Garden,[9] and committed first to Wood Street Compter and then to Newgate.[10] Charged with her were Richard Bird and Humphrey Burton (husband of the Elizabeth Burton alias Taylor alias 'Mother Hustle' who had betrayed

Samuel Cole to Wild in 1718), neither of whom were yet caught. On 17 June, the *Daily Journal* (the third paper Defoe was connected with at this time—for it often carried in the week stories reprinted verbatim on Saturdays by the other two) reported the incident without giving details:

'On Friday, Moll King, one of the most notorious Pickpockets of the Town, and eminently famous for assisting in stealing Watches at Ladies' Sides at Chrch, was again committed to her old Mansion House, Newgate.'

On her indictment she is called 'Mary Godson alias Bird alias King', and it says that she stole 'Divers Goods val. £50' (the goods being dress-materials, the property of John Farrell and Martha Kelley). The nature of the goods, the fact that they belonged to two different people, and the fact that the indictment says 'House' and not 'Shop', etc., suggest that Kinsallaugh's was the same sort of place as that where 'Moll Flanders' herself was arrested—'not a Mercer's Shop, nor a Warehouse, of a Mercer, but looked like a private Dwelling-house, and was, it seems, inhabited by a Man that sold Goods for a Weaver to the Mercers, like a Broker or Factor.'

After this, however, the plot thickens. Among the same documents (*Middx. GD Roll 2370*) there is a second indictment against 'Mary Golstone', late of the parish of St. Anne's Soho, for returning from the plantations and 'being at large in the parish of St. Paul's Covent Garden *on and as from 1 April*'. The Newgate Calendar* of July 1721 shows that 'Mary Godson alias Golstone' was committed to Newgate by Justice Gwynn Vaughan of Southampton Street, Covent Garden, both for the robbery of Kinsallaugh and for returning from transportation. This gentleman had the reputation of being one of Wild's 'tame' magistrates, and it is admittedly odd that his name occurs twice in mysterious connection with Wild.

The man who found Moll King 'at large' in Covent Garden was John Parry, who must have been one of Wild's men. For one thing, it was Wild and not Parry who claimed the reward for her

---

* The large sheet of parchment, up to 3 ft. long, on which the Deputy Keeper drew up a list of all admissions during the previous month, a day or two before the Sessions. At the bottom was a list of prisoners 'upon Orders'— i.e. who had been remanded for transportation, branding, further trial, etc. Being the largest skin, it was usually *rolled* round the other documents, which is why the records are called '*Rolls*'. The famous book, *The Newgate Calendar*, was obviously named after it.

capture (she is No. 74 on his list, and he specifically mentioned her when he petitioned for the Freedom of London); for another, Parry came from Wild's parish (St. Sepulchre's, Newgate) and so, had he been a City officer, would have been outside his area.

However, if Parry, acting for Wild, arrested her on 1 April, why did she not reach Newgate until June, and then only after being caught in a robbery? Why, in any case, put '1 April' when it was well known, having been published in the newspapers, that she had been in England since July the year before?

Wild must have had some arrangement with Justice Vaughan. To return from fourteen years' transportation was a capital felony, and so not bailable. On the other hand, there was a possible loophole in that there was no statute which *obliged* a private citizen (such as Wild) to arrest a returned transportee, and Wild might have argued that there was no reason to commit Moll King to gaol unless an interested party (such as the Transportation Agent, Jonathan Forward) was willing to prosecute, and that an affidavit swearing that he had 'seen her at large' would be sufficient. Then, if she was caught, all he needed to do was to get Simon Harcourt, Clerk of the Peace, to draw up the indictment, rather vaguely worded and back-dated to 1 April, to ensure that the reward would be paid to him and not to whoever caught her—in the event, the Kinsallaughs and their servants. But why wait until April? One possible explanation is that in April Moll King became troublesome, and that Wild did his deal with Justice Vaughan to frighten her into submission. If that, or something like it, is what happened, then the cases of John Filewood, James Dalton, William Burridge and several others become more intelligible.

At this time, however, Wild was engaged in putting down a rebellion in one of his gangs. It had started when William Field had impeached John Harris on Wild's behalf in 1720, and in revenge Elizabeth Harris was trying to implicate Field and some others in a number of burglaries.[11] Wild defended Field, as I have described earlier, by showing that the prosecution was malicious, and the others by recruiting prisoners to impeach those members of the gang who had taken Elizabeth Harris's side. The result was a period of complicated gang-warfare fought with false depositions, impeachments and bribes instead of tommy-guns (but none the less deadly for that). A curious part was played by a knot of women in Wild's faction: Elizabeth Smith, Elizabeth

Johnson, Elizabeth Smith alias Johnson, and Elizabeth Bird alias Smith. Could these names refer to the same person performing different rôles for Wild? If so, the spectacle of the same old crone turning up in the dock under one name in the morning, in the witness box for the defence in another case, under another name, in the afternoon, and for the prosecution, in yet another case and under yet another name next day, must have given the court some light relief. Elizabeth Bird, for one, had known Moll King at least since that lady's branding in 1693.

It would appear from the records therefore that when Wild heard of Moll King's arrest in Little Russell Street (perhaps she sent a messenger to him), he made sure that instead of being taken to the Gatehouse (the place for Westminster crimes) she was taken to the Compter, where he had friends; then got Vaughan to commit her to Newgate on the transportation charge as well, back-dated so that he, and not Kinsallaugh, could claim the reward; then told Moll King that he could save her life if she would impeach a certain person who was being fractious. If she refused, or if her evidence misfired, it would not matter too much because, although she would be hanged, he could at least claim the reward of £40. To do all this, however, he would have to ensure that she was acquitted of the robbery, and he would have to arrange that the trials came up in the right order, for after she had been convicted of returning from transportation, she would not be able to impeach anyone. At the July Sessions, that is what happened. She was tried first for the robbery (indictment No. 11) and acquitted. The clue as to how he managed it is the identity of the witnesses against her—Elizabeth Johnson and Jane Awbery ('Moll Flanders' was caught by two women). Surely it is more than a coincidence that in October this same pair of women were hired by William Strickland, who procured false witnesses for Wild, to defend two thieves involved in another Covent Garden robbery.[12] Probably, therefore, Wild ordered Strickland to search out the women appearing on Kinsallaugh's behalf and bribe them to give their evidence in such a way as to ensure an acquittal: to say that they could not swear to her identity, or that she was really stealing, etc. Then, after this success, Strickland decided to use them again for the two thieves (whom he assured that the women would swear anything that was required of them); but unfortunately he failed to teach them their stories properly and they were exposed.

Having been cleared of the robbery, Moll King was now free to be King's Evidence against Richard Grantham, whom she impeached of robbery and murder (indictment No. 24). Her co-witnesses were Elizabeth Smith (described as a 'Prisoner'), Samuel Bird, and Mary Taylor, besides some others. Mary Taylor was a member of the William Field/Elizabeth Harris gang, now torn by civil war, and may have been a sister of Elizabeth Taylor, alias Burton, alias 'Mother Hustle'—in short, Humphrey Burton's sister-in-law. (Humphrey, by the way, had been found and brought to trial, but acquitted after Moll King, and Richard Bird was freed on £200 bail—he was never charged). Richard Grantham was transported, but in October his wife Ruth impeached Elizabeth Smith, who was then transported in her turn.

The last case (No. 40—and the order of the trials does seem to have been wonderfully convenient for Wild) was for returning from transportation, and this time 'Mary Golstone' was condemned to death. On 28 July, however, she was reprieved and ordered to remain in Newgate 'at Pleasure'.[13] No reason was given, though it is unlikely that her impeaching of Grantham alone would have saved her, for she was only one of several witnesses and she was a very old offender. Either Wild interceded for her, or the government at this period were lenient towards women (though not men) who returned from transportation—one cannot be sure because the Privy Council did not keep minutes of its meetings, and cases such as Moll King's were decided as they came up.

The battle with Elizabeth Harris *et al.* ended with Wild victorious by December 1721, though he lost a few people, including Anne Merritt, Elizabeth Smith (or Johnson, etc.) and Mary Taylor, and gained some undying enemies. One of these was Kathleen Mackaine, alias Cook, who was to be one of the two women who hid Jack Sheppard from Wild after the great escape from Newgate in 1724.

The affair becomes more extraordinary when one remembers that Wild was doing this sort of thing all the time, and not just with Moll King but with a score of people simultaneously, besides running his office, attending fairs, supervising smuggling and organizing wholesale robbery. During all this summer and autumn, for instance, his main attention was directed to breaking up the two most important gangs of highwaymen in London—Shaw's gang and the Hawkins gang, as will be related in the next chapter.

If Defoe visited Moll King in Newgate, it was certainly during the next six months. Perhaps, before her reprieve, he intended to write a pamphlet about her as a contribution to Applebee's new line in 'True Confessions' of condemned criminals. After her reprieve, the pamphlet would have been useless, but her more cheerful outlook perhaps encouraged him to expand his notes into the novel. That she told him (or at least that he wrote) nothing about Wild or her impeaching a colleague is not surprising, for neither did any of the other criminals who worked for Wild and later left biographies (James Dalton, Roger Johnson, William Hawkins and John Dyer). Such things were shameful and best forgotten, besides being dangerous professional secrets, and her life depended on Wild's good will. I am not suggesting that *Moll Flanders* was simply a fictionalized biography of Moll King, only that she gave him the kernel of the idea, and many of the details of life among London thieves. Defoe certainly changed things a little, perhaps deliberately to hide Moll King's identity, and in the passage, for instance, that most closely resembles the newspaper reports, it is not Moll Flanders but her 'Instructress' who is described:

> The Comrade she helped me to, dealt in three Sorts of Craft; viz. Shoplifting, stealing of Shop-books, and Pockett-books, and Taking-off Gold Watches from Ladies' Sides; and this last, she did so dextrously that no Woman ever arrived to the Perfection of that Art, like her.

There is, besides, a considerable difference between Defoe's worldly-wise, rather demure, heroine and the poor wretch, the classic 'Autem Diver' (church-pickpocket), who was so ignorant that she could not be trusted with a watch lest she broke it, and was frighted out of her money by the formidable Jonathan Wild. The real Moll King was doubtless somewhere between these two extremes, with Stanley's reckless lover as a third; perhaps her authentic voice can be heard in those pages of the novel where a dry, hard-bitten Newgate woman, colder and less imaginative than Moll Flanders has elsewhere shown herself to be, catalogues one thieving trick after another to a listener who seems to be taking it all down in shorthand.

The name of 'Moll Flanders' was possibly suggested to Defoe by stories Moll King told him about 'Callico Sarah'. This was the kind of name Defoe wanted. 'Callico' was contraband silk;

'Holland' (linen, often contraband) would not do because it would have been confused with Susan Holland, whose famous seventeenth century brothel, 'Holland's Leaguer', was still remembered in ballads, broadsheets and a play. 'Flanders' was lace, usually contraband. Throughout January 1722, the *Post Boy* carried an advertisement for *The History of Flanders, with Moll's Map*[14] and that probably gave Defoe his inspiration. Herman Moll was a map-maker whom Defoe himself employed to illustrate his *Tour Thro' Great Britain* in 1725, and 'Moll' was not only a diminutive of Mary, but slang for 'whore'. Whatever the truth, it is known that Defoe visited Newgate regularly that autumn to see his editor Nathaniel Mist, who was confined there from 10 June until September. On 27 January, *Moll Flanders* was published by W. Chetwood, at 'Cato's Head', in Russell Street, a few doors away from the house where Moll King had been arrested. Two days later, Moll King herself was put on board the *Gilbert* at Tilbury and arrived at Annapolis on 16 July. Again she returned straight to London:

'Moll King, a most notorious offender, famous for stealing Gold Watches from Ladies' Sides in the Churches, for which she has been several Times convicted, being lately returned from Transportation, has been taken and is committed to Newgate' (*Daily Journal*, 20 Sep 1722 and *Saturday's Post* 22 Sep).

The London Sessions Roll for October 1722 shows that she was committed this time on the oath of the Transportation Agent, Jonathan Forward. Nevertheless, he delayed and she remained in prison for months. On 26 January 1723, Applebee's journal published a long article by Defoe, in which he wondered at the stupidity of thieves who left the safety of America for the hazards of London, and made matters worse by returning to the very places they were best known, to the same lines of stealing as before, and to the same gangs of rogues, 'as if they resolved to come to the same Jayl they went out of'.

Meanwhile, 'Callico Sarah' too had returned from America and, after a long search reported daily in the newspapers, was caught by Jonathan Wild.

This indeed was a vintage year in London gaols for women who inspired literature and art. The famous Sally Salisbury was in Newgate, having stabbed Mr. Finch, son of the Countess of Winchelsea, and she died there a few months later. Episodes from her life were incorporated into *The Harlot's Progress* and, later,

Fanny Hill. Kate Hackabout, whose name Hogarth immortalized in the same *Harlot's Progress*, was in the New Prison. Another Moll King (unrelated to ours), proprietress of the notorious 'Tom King's Coffee House' in Covent Garden, celebrated by Hogarth, Fielding and many others, was in the Gatehouse. Finally, it is a curious coincidence that Sally Salisbury's abortionist, who ran a home for unmarried mothers very like the one described in *Moll Flanders*, and 'Callico Sarah' both used the same alias—'Mary Davis'.

On 16 March the *British Journal* reported:

'The Gentleman who is bound to prosecute Moll King, the famous Robber of the Ladies of their Gold Watches at Churches, for returning from Transportation, received a Reprimand the last Sessions for ommitting Prosecution for several Sessions past; and the Court ordered her Tryal the next Sesssions.'

The next Sessions, however, Mr. Forward still did not appear and, considering that his recognizance was now estreated and he himself fined, his motives are mysterious. Perhaps Wild, or perhaps Defoe, prevailed on him to withhold his charge and offered to make up his expense; however, no explanation is recorded. In June, Moll King and 'Callico Sarah' were once again ordered for transportation for fourteen years, and once again were returned to that huge, cavernous ward on the top floor of Newgate where women awaiting transportation were kept, which 'B.L. of Twickenham, Gent.'[15] described as more horrible for its filth, stench, shrieking and foul language than anywhere else in the gaol, certainly than any of the men's quarters. They were put on board the *Alexander* galley (Capt. King) on 4 July (with nearly a dozen others of Wild's people) and arrived at Annapolis on 14 September. That is the last certain news of Mary King, alias Godman, alias Golston, alias Golstone, alias Gilstone, alias Goulston, alias Gouldstone, alias Gouldston, alias Godfrey(?), alias Godson, alias Bird; though if the Mary Goldham transported in 1725, the Mary Guliston in 1726, and the 'Mary King, Wife of Tom King' in 1734 (who by the date could not have been the proprietress of the Covent Garden coffee house), were our Moll King, still plying back and forth across the Atlantic Ocean, then she crossed it eleven times after 1720.

Shortly after being cleared of the Kinsallaugh robbery, Dick Bird set off on the highway with John Everett. They remained partners until Bird, impeached by Everett, was hanged. Everett himself was hanged after robbing 'Mrs. Manley'. Because of the fame he enjoyed as a result, it has usually been said that she was the celebrated Mary de la Rivière Manley, the novelist, friend of Swift, etc.; however, as that lady was dead, this must have been her cousin, a child's coat-maker from the Barbadoes, whose black servant, 'William Coffee', caused a stir at the trial.

As for 'Captain' John Stanley, whom Moll King had loved so passionately in 1718, is it possible to discern in him the shadowy, imperfect, original—idealized and sentimentalized by Moll in fond reminiscence, and simplified by Defoe for the purposes of his story—of Moll Flanders's 'Lancashire Husband'? In December 1723, three months after Moll King arrived at Annapolis with 'Callico Sarah', the real 'Captain' John Stanley was hanged at Tyburn for murdering his mistress, Hannah Maycock, in a fit of jealousy. He still had his looks, though heavy drinking, gambling and the hard work of spending several fortunes belonging to other people had coarsened him and made his arrogance and temper insufferable. He was constantly in duels over nothing and shortly before killing Hannah had knocked down a man and kicked a woman in the street simply because they didn't get out of his way quickly enough. Yet he had an attractive side, a certain impulsive, boyish charm and innocence that no doubt made women long to protect him from himself. When he killed the girl, in the parlour of a house in Old Bailey, he alternately protested she could not be dead, hoped that her soul was already among the damned in Hell, and threatened to kill all the other women in the house too; but when the surgeon came and told him that Hannah really was dead, he cried, 'I have had a Child by her, and it is now three Years and a half old, and if she dies, I must die, and the Child shall die too, and there will be an end of us all!'

Having neglected this son since his birth, he now lavished affection on him, and in Newgate 'he said, he hoped Christ would receive his Soul, *because* he had been so good a Father to his dear Child; Upon which Remembrance he would even shed Tears, and call the Deceased (*Hannah*) cruel, barbarous Etc.—He appearing to be very tender and indulging to the Boy, who lay with him till his Death.'

⸗ XVII ⸗ *The Science of Gang-Breaking*

In the early 1720s Jonathan Wild was engaged in a prolonged struggle to bring the remaining large gangs in the Metropolis under his control or, failing that, to destroy them. By the end of 1723 he had all but achieved his purpose; for, if the records are reliable evidence, there seem to have been no large gangs in London from then until after his death.

In January 1721, Spiggott's gang of highwaymen had been cornered in 'The Blue Boar' tavern, Westminster Broadway (frequented by Dick Turpin twenty-five years later), by a posse of volunteers under the direction of the Merritt brothers, and had been captured when the Rev. Joseph Lindsey (mentioned above) surrendered and offered to impeach the rest. At the trial Spiggott refused to plead and was pressed beneath 400 lb. of weights until he changed his mind—the scene is illustrated in a famous engraving in *The Newgate Calendar*. Spiggott, who could not remember 'that he had ever shed a Tear in his Life but once, and that was since his Condemnation at his final parting with his little Son', and Phillips alias Cross, 'the most audacious Rogue that ever stretched a Halter', were hanged, though Spiggott's body was carried off by the mob in the Strand and hidden.

Wild had already taken one of this gang, Sinnamond, who was hanged on Wild's wedding-day, Friday 13 February 1719, and was to capture the last, William Colthurst, in Oxford in December

1721. I have already suggested a possible connection between Wild and the Merritt brothers, who were thief-takers.

There remained the Hawkins gang, Shaw's gang, and Carrick's gang.

The Hawkins gang were highwaymen of the classic type, like Spiggott and Cross, and consequently the gang itself was small, about six strong. Shaw's gang contained thirteen known members and presumably several unknown ones. They were footpads, though a few robbed on horse when the occasion offered. Carrick's gang consisted entirely of footpads (many of them Irish immigrants) and contained thirty-two known members, with six more probables, and perhaps a dozen more still whose names have not come down to us. The inner circle of this gang were generally regarded as 'the most villainous Set in London'.

These gangs were not rigidly defined societies. Members drifted from one to another and back again; new branches grew out, separated from the main body, flourished and withered as the result of feuds, betrayals and hangings, and this natural process was during these years greatly accelerated, indeed raised almost to the level of a coherent drama, by the intrigues of Jonathan Wild.

John Hawkins had started as a footman and butler in various houses, but the debts he incurred through gambling 'forced' him to take to the highway. A physical description of him in a G.P.O. advertisement for his capture[1] hardly tallies with the conventional idea of what a brave highwayman should look like: '. . . a very fat Man, of a fair complexion, pretty Handsome, but somewhat Chub Fac'd about five Foot ten Inches high, wears most commonly a Cinnamon colour'd Cloth Coat, or a Dark Frock, . . .'.

His first gang broke up when one of them, Captain Leonard (an Irish Jacobite whose real purpose in England was to collect money and recruits for the Pretender) was captured by the King's Messengers. Leonard escaped, and Hawkins boasted afterwards that he had led the attack on the private gaol to 'spring' him; but as Applebee's journal of 5 July 1718 has a story in which one John Hawkins was instrumental in Leonard's recapture, it seems that this was a lie. Further, as Hawkins was imprisoned about this time, such a bretrayal would explain why he was released.

Hawkins was now joined by his brother William, who had

been captain of a smuggling vessel for some years, but the second gang scattered when one Pocock impeached them all. William Hawkins was thrown into the Compter and the others fled to Wales and Ireland. The man they left in charge of their booty, guns, swords, harness, etc., absconded to Holland with everything and was never heard of again.

On his return, Hawkins formed a third gang, consisting of James Wright, a barber from Ludgate Hill, and Ralph Wilson, a young lawyer's clerk from Yorkshire. In 1720, during the fevered summer of the South Sea Bubble, these three went out on forays two or three nights every week, sometimes riding into the City and attacking the coaches and sedan-chairs of speculators even as they were leaving Exchange Alley, where business continued long after sunset. On some occasions, such as when they robbed Lord Westmoreland, they were surprised by the Watch, who poured in upon them 'from all Sides', but a pistol-shot over their heads was usually sufficient to disperse them.

Jonathan Wild's attention was first drawn to this gang when the Lords Bruce and Burlington were robbed at Richmond of money, two gold watches and a sapphire ring. Lord Bruce went to Wild and offered £100 for the ring alone. Shortly afterwards, the gang robbed Sir David Dalrymple, Crown Advocate of Scotland, of £3 and a pocket-book. For the pocket-book Sir David offered Wild £60. Because they had no dealings with Wild, 'neither did he know any of us', the gang sent the pocket-book back to Sir David gratis, and if that is true, Wild must have been angered indeed.

In September 1720, the gang decided to go to Holland to sell their accumulated booty, not daring to approach Wild with it. On the day of departure Wright, wanting to recover Lord Bruce's watch (which he had pawned), arranged to meet them in the 'Queen's Head' tavern on Tower Hill. As they approached the tavern they sent a boy to see how the land lay, and were told that Wright had been taken by Jonathan Wild. Other accounts say that Wild had already given notice to barmen and such that he wanted the Hawkins gang, and someone knowing Wright had sent a message to the Old Bailey. As Wild entered, Wright drew his guns. Wild jumped on him and gripped Wright's chin between his teeth, hanging on until Quilt Arnold and the two bodyguards took Wright's pistols. Wild found the watch but, instead of returning it to Lord Bruce, gave it as a present to his wife Mary.

Hawkins and Wilson took horse to Oxford, where their only exploit was to deface a picture in the Bodleian Library.

Meanwhile, Will Hawkins had somehow turned the tables on Pocock, who was hanged, and got himself released. Wright was taken to the Marshalsea for the Kingston Assizes, the robbery of Lords Bruce and Burlington having been done in Surrey.

Jack Hawkins rode up from Oxford, leaving Wilson behind, and with William sailed for Holland. There they sold Lord Bruce's ring for £40, disposed of the rest of their booty for several hundred pounds, considered joining Cartouche, 'the most famous Robber in the World', but decided against it (luckily, for Cartouche was caught not long after, and 800 of his men were broken on the wheel, hanged by the armpits until dead, or sent to the galleys for life), and rejoined Wilson in London. Here, they met with a series of misfortunes. Jack Hawkins was wounded by two men, who unexpectedly leaned out of their coach and shot him with blunderbusses; then heavy rain kept them indoors, and when good weather returned their horses' heads were so swelled that they could not get them out of the stable. 'In this Disaster every Man's Wits were at work how to proceed for a Livelihood', and they were forced to rob on foot at Hyde Park Corner. Being unused to this, Wilson accidentally shot himself through the hand. Then James Wright sent a letter from the Marshalsea, asking for money and saying that Jonathan Wild was around daily offering large bribes for him to impeach the gang, but he'd be damned if he'd do it, Jack Hawkins having a wife and children. Wilson wrote of him later that 'he was a Man of the best Temper and greatest Fidelity to his Companions I ever knew in an Highwayman'. Nevertheless, the reappearance of Jonathan Wild threw the brave highwaymen 'into a Pannick Fear', and they all fled London, Wilson returning to his mother in York. Hawkins sent Wright a note before they left, saying that all he had earned from Lord Bruce's ring was £6, that the other booty had gone for almost nothing, and that he was sorry he could not give him more than this £3. In February, however, Wright was acquitted for lack of evidence, and reopened his barbershop on Ludgate Hill, vowing never to go back upon the highway. Thus, the Hawkins gang was temporarily broken up by Wild, and there we may leave them until the autumn of 1721.

On the night of Saturday, 24 June 1721, Mr. Philip Potts, a Surveyor of the Window Lights (i.e. assessor for the window-tax that had been instituted by Charles II), was riding home past the Tile Kilns at St. Pancras, north of London, when he saw three men barring his way across the track. One was tall and thin, two were short and stocky, and one of these carried a long staff. They were, in fact, James Shaw and two of his gang, James Reading and 'Long Isaac' Drew, a waggon-drover who lived in Southwark. Swinging his staff without a word, Shaw knocked Mr. Potts off his horse. Then the three footpads fell on him as he tried to get up, and the scuffle lasted until Reading picked up the staff and struck Mr. Potts across the head with all his strength. They emptied his pockets, took his sword, and left him lying in the road. He was found, staggering along, holding his hat over his wounded head, by two servants, whose masters had sent them to discover what the noise had been; but at Battle Bridge he cried, '*Lord have Mercy on my Soul! I can go no farther*'; and he fell down and spoke no more'. When his hat was removed, it was seen that the brain was exposed.

Mr. Potts's son, who succeeded to his father's post, offered £140 reward over and above the usual £40 (the increase to £140 having not yet come into effect), which meant a total of £260 to whoever found the murderers. The scent of so much money attracted the attention of Jonathan Wild.

It is not clear how long it took him to discover who the murderers were. He certainly knew Shaw, Reading, Drew and the rest of the gang very well. In May, Reading had been arrested for some offence, and, swearing 'that rather than be hang'd himself he'd hang half the-Nation, nay, he'd hang the Devil', he impeached as many of his accomplices as he could. One was a boy who, out of a romantic admiration for highwaymen, had been pestering Reading to let him join Shaw's gang. The boy had an unpleasant introduction to a highwayman's life, therefore, when he was arrested and told that Reading had sworn a robbery against him. Another was William Wade, nicknamed 'Shuffle', who was servant to the most famous highwayman then on the roads, Benjamin Child. 'Shuffle' was acquitted when Reading's various hired witnesses (supplied, I suppose, by Strickland) contradicted one another; but his nerve was broken and shortly after he stupidly let himself be caught by the Comptroller of the General Post Office. In a panic, he impeached his master Child, who was caught in Salisbury and hanged at Aylesbury. Benjamin Child seems to have been one of the few real highwaymen

who possessed at least some of the characteristics of the legen-
dary highwaymen of folklore. He never impeached his colleagues,
he was handsome and courteous, and he made the attractive
gesture of freeing all the debtors in Salisbury gaol by paying off
their debts. He was hanged in chains on Hounslow Heath, near
the scene of his major robberies, and it was believed that Wild had
played some part in the betrayal. This greatly enraged the highwaymen, especially Jack Hawkins, who swore ('God damn my
Blood and 'Ouns!') that he'd be revenged on somebody for poor
Child's sake. A third to be impeached by Reading was William
Barton, for robbing Lord Lisbon, a Treasury Officer. Barton, a
veteran of Marlborough's wars, was innocent of this, as he had
not been in England at the time of the robbery. However,
Reading had originally impeached Shaw, but when 'someone'
paid him £10 to change his mind, he impeached Barton instead,
who was hanged.

At the end of July, a Mr. Brownsworth went to Wild's office
with a story of highway robbery, and from the description Wild
was able to arrest, first, William Burridge (a fourth member of the
gang) and then, on Burridge's information, James Reading.
On 5 August the *Saturday's Post* reported that Reading 'designed to
be an Evidence again', and the information he was staking his
survival on was obviously the identity of the murderers of Mr.
Potts. Wild took Reading's statement but refused to help him
now that he had what he wanted; for, obviously, if he could pin
the murder on to Shaw, and delay Shaw's arrest until the end,
the more reward-money he could pick up (for other robberies)
on the way. However, he managed to get Burridge out on bail;
and this policy brought in its appreciation when Burridge, with
Shaw and a man called Wigley, robbed a Mr. Symbol Conyers
at Islington on 7 August. The next day, Burridge informed Wild,
who immediately had him committed to New Prison. Wild then
arrested Wigley and went in hunt of the rest of Shaw's gang,
now, reasonably, in hiding. On 19 August the *Daily Journal*,
after reporting the riot at Acton where Wild had played general
to the Londoners on horseback, continued its story:

'On Wednesday last, the murderers of the late Mr. Phillip
Potts, Collector of the Window-Lights, were beset by the above-
said Jonathan Wild, and several Officers; but notwithstanding
great Diligence was used to apprehend them, they found Means to
escape.'

Reading was condemned on Burridge's evidence; and at Wigley's trial on the same day, Burridge had the effrontery to say, 'I have known the Prisoner three years. He was the first Man who took me out Robbing.' A sheet of uncatalogued *Sessions Papers* in the British Museum proves that Burridge had in fact been a thief since 1712;[2] moreover, a Landing Certificate proves that 'William Burage' had been transported to Charleston in May 1719.[3] Yet no one brought this up at Wigley's trial, and Burridge was never charged with returning from transportation—an almost certain sign of Wild's protection. Even if he had demanded this protection from Wild in return for revealing that Reading knew who had murdered Philip Potts, the fact is still remarkable for showing what pressure Wild could bring to bear on the judges at the Old Bailey, who were, it must be remembered, the prisoners' only counsel for defence.

Wigley had the usual supply of false witnesses, but, as often happened with such people, they contradicted one another's evidence. Even his sister, who lived in Poppin's Court (which is still there) off Fleet Street, made a mess of things because she could not write and did not know where her brother lived, although she said she had often been there. Neither Wigley nor Reading were communicative men, and Wigley's life especially seems to have been secretive and sordid. He lived for some years 'unlawfully' with an old woman who kept a shed on Finchley Common, where she sold brandy, and it was rumoured that he had murdered her husband. He claimed that the old man was a brandy addict and had drunk himself to death in a barn at Hornsey. Reading and Wigley are Nos. 12 and 13 on Wild's list.

Burridge was returned to New Prison. Here, two more members of the gang enter the story: Nathaniel Hawes and John James. These two had been robbing on Hanwell Heath, Ealing. Hawes, who was nineteen, wanted to be admired as the most daring and chivalrous young highwayman on the road, although he had damaged his reputation a year before by impeaching a receiver. However, a branding in April had slightly restored his confidence, until, distrusting James over the distribution of their booty, he went to Wild and impeached James before James could impeach *him*. Wild put him into New Prison with Burridge, because he feared Hawes might be murdered in Newgate after being an evidence this second time—especially during the present epidemic of impeachments by all and sundry. He then arrested

James, who was in bed with two of his mistresses, in Monmouth Street.

'Long Isaac' Drew, the third of the murderers, had meanwhile taken a new partner, a youth called John Dykes. Such men as Drew preferred the young and innocent for partners because it was easier to keep them ignorant of underworld gossip. Therefore, if Drew were arrested, he not only had someone to impeach (an argument against working alone), but he could impeach him secure in the knowledge that his partners would not know enough to impeach back—a practice called 'Squeazing the Chats' (*squeezing the lice*). And so when Wild arrested them both at Drew's 'Lodgings' in Southwark on the night of 24 September (*Daily Journal*, 26 September), he found that whereas Dykes had little to offer but 'Trifles', Drew was able to impeach not only Dykes but to give evidence against Shaw for the murder of Mr. Potts.

John James and John Dykes were convicted in October. James had spent much of his life at sea and been captured by Spaniards and, later, by pirates. A hardened character, he said that, although he had often behaved brutally to people he robbed, he believed hanging was no deterrent to malefactors, for he had often watched executions without the least concern. He travelled to Tyburn in a coach paid for by his friends. Dykes, on the other hand, being a boy and condemned for stealing a penknife (value 5s.), while in the Condemned Hold 'would, at particular Times in the Night, start up, tear his Hair, and cry out in a very odd Manner; and at other Times would sing Psalms, and pray for several Hours together.'[4] With his usual fatuity, the author of *Lives of the Most Remarkable Criminals* describes Dykes's behaviour 'under these unhappy Circumstances' as 'very Mean, and such as fully show'd what Difference there is between Courage and that Resolution which is necessary to support the Spirits and calm our Apprehensions at the certain Approach of a violent Death'.

Of Shaw's gang, only Shaw himself was still at liberty. Meanwhile, Hawkins's gang reappeared in the suburbs of the Metropolis. Wilson had been brought back (rather unwillingly) from Yorkshire, and Wright replaced by a 'stout, brisk Man' from Lincolnshire called George Simpson. A strong hatred had grown between Will Hawkins and Ralph Wilson. Hawkins described Wilson as too ignorant of highwaymanship to be anything but 'first Porter to the Gang' and, despite 'his mighty Itch to Gaming', quite ignorant of 'the Levant at Dice, the difference betwixt loaded and Mathematical ones; the Slip at Cards, the Palm & other Bites'; and declared that far from being troubled by his conscience he had as 'great an Affection for anything that is r—sh as a Welshman has for Toasted Cheese, a Scotchman for Bonnyclabber, a Spaniard for a patched Cloak, an Italian for Buggery, a Dutchman for Butter, a Frenchman for the Pox'.[5] Wilson for his part said of Hawkins, 'This Fellow in Company is one of the most flustering Rascals I ever heard, no Man is so forward to strike another, because he confides in his Strength, yet no Man was so backward upon the Road.'

The gang established their headquarters in a dram shop in London Wall—in those days the City wall ran the length of the north side of the street, the south side being a line of tumble-down houses, stables and taverns. The proprietor was Edward Carter, a receiver of stolen goods in an area thick with competitors.

Will Hawkins recruited into the gang a ticket-porter called Butler Fox, on the same principle as Drew employed Dykes; and on the night of 2 September[6] the pair followed the 'Cissiter' (*Cirencester*) coach through Hyde Park Turnpike and held it up in Knightsbridge—then a row of houses to the west of the Knights' Bridge. Hawkins covered while Fox rode up to the window shouting 'God damn ye, deliver quickly or I'll fire among ye!'. Taking only 25s. and a corkscrew, they rode in a wide circle back to the Strand, whence Hawkins went to spy on the Huntingdon coach. This they intercepted on Mount Hill, and, finding Sir Edward Lawrence among the passengers, took from him 1½ guineas, 6 lb. of chocolate, 16 yards of fustian, 3 yards of blue cloth, ½ lb. of tea, a nightgown, a periwig, a blue coat, two turnovers (*headscarves*), two handkerchiefs, two Holland-linen shirts, Risby's *Miscellanies* and the last two volumes of Pope's *Homer*, besides a set of pewter buttons.

It was unlucky for Will Hawkins that the person he tried to sell the shirts to was a friend of Sir Edward Lawrence, whose footmen then came and arrested him. A year previously, James Wright, starving in prison, had refused to accept bribes and to betray Will Hawkins or anyone else to Wild, and when after his release he discovered that they had bilked him of the profits of their robberies, he had refrained from taking any revenge. Hawkins repaid Wright's magnanimity by impeaching him and by making sure that it was Wild who arrested him again. For good measure, he impeached everybody else he could think of, including Wilson, Simpson, Fox and even his own brother. Wild caught Simpson first, but as they arrived at the Justice's house the coachman inadvertently opened the door on Simpson's side, and Simpson jumped out and escaped.[7] Wild then took Butler Fox:

Upon the Information of Hawkins, I went o'Sunday to the Prisoner's House, and found him at Home with his two Brothers, and two other Men. I knew him by his Black Eye, and by the Buttons on his Breeches, which *Hawkins* had described to me, and told me, that they were the same they took from Sir *Edward Lawrence*. The Prisoner at first was very *obstropulus*, and swore that he would not go with me; but I pulled out a Pistol, and swore as fast as he, that if they made any more Resistance, I'd fire among them; and with that, he grew as quiet as a Lamb.

'For God's Sake Mr. *Wild*,' says he, 'Tell me how the Case is—'

'Aye, you Rogue,' says his Wife, 'This is your Friend *Hawkin's* doing—'

' 'Tis even so,' says I, 'Your Friend *Hawkins* has impeached ye.'

Then I carried him to Sir *Edward*, who took him before the Justice, where some of the Goods, which he had pawn'd, being produc'd, he owned that he had them of *Hawkins*.

In Newgate, Will Hawkins was bragging that everything had worked out as planned, that he had only drawn Fox into these two robberies to guard against just such a situation as this, that he had no further occasion for him, and that now was the time to make use of him.

By now, of Shaw's gang, Barton, Reading, Wigley, James and Dykes had been hanged, while 'Shuffle' Wade, Drew, Hawes and Burridge were in prison—all, directly or indirectly, through Wild's management. Of the Hawkins gang, Wright and Fox were in Newgate on capital charges and Will Hawkins had impeached the rest, and again this was due to Wild's management.

A small setback occurred on 21 November, when a woman was

put into the same cell in New Prison as Hawes and Burridge. Persuading the turnkey to let them light a fire, and shaking a length of rope and some tools out of her skirts, she engineered their escape. Hawes was caught almost immediately, trying to be a highwayman on a blind horse he had stolen; Burridge joined with Shaw again, with a surly and brutal prize-fighter called Robert Wilkinson, and with Thomas Milksop, who had been transported with Burridge in 1719 and had been making a long roundabout return journey ever since. The four began robbing on the roads between Islington, Highgate and Hampstead.

In December, James Wright, Butler Fox and Nathaniel Hawes were tried at Justice Hall. Will Hawkins claimed that Wright, John Hawkins and himself had robbed a coach in Marlborough Street, in *January* 1720.* In support, Wild stood up and said:

> I was at the *Fountain-Tavern* by Newgate, in Company with the Prisoner and *Will Hawkins*, when the Prisoner asked me to let him have his working Tools again (meaning his Pistols) which I had formerly taken from him, when he was committed to the Marshalsea. I told him I had none but a Pair that was in my Pocket. He then desired me to lend him any other Pair to go on the Road with; for, says he, 'I must take up the old Sport again.'

The point here is that Wright was not taken to the Marshalsea until *September* 1720 and was not released until February 1721: that is, a year *after* the robbery had taken place. Yet Wild's evidence was allowed and even included in the *Sessions Papers* report without comment. It almost passes belief that Wild was allowed to get away with such irrelevance and blatant perjury, in what was meant to be our foremost court of criminal justice, before a distinguished Bench which included Lord Chief Justice King, Baron Montague, Lord Mayor Sir William Stewart, three ex-Lord-Mayors and Sir William Thomson.[8] Yet, if anyone did dispute Wild's testimony, the shorthand-writers did not bother to note the fact down. The incident does show, however, that Will Hawkins had established a liaison with Wild long before his brother Jack or any of the gang suspected it.

* In the *Sessions Papers* written as '1719/20', which was the 'Old Style' method of writing dates (see note at front of this book). The detail is important here, as '1720' by itself would have meant '1721'.

Wild was not quite so successful with Butler Fox. Hawkins had made a bargain with Sir Edward Lawrence's footmen that if Fox was convicted they would have a share of the £140 reward, for as Hawkins himself had now become an Evidence, they would lose the reward for capturing him. Wild went round to all Fox's previous employers, asking them not to appear on Fox's behalf because he feared the case was not a strong one. Some of this came out in court, and in addition, although Wild said in evidence that he could prove Fox had been on the highway for three or four years, he was overheard to admit that this was Fox's first offence and that Hawkins was the greater rogue. Butler Fox was acquitted, but remanded until January to answer the charge of robbing the Cirencester coach, which Hawkins had also sworn against him.

At his trial, Nathaniel Hawes decided to emulate Spiggott and refused to plead. Sir William Thomson made a solemn speech pointing out that 'the Equity of the Law of *England* more tender of the Lives of its Subjects than any other in the World' allowed no one to be put to death without positive proof of his guilt; and as according to the humane constitution of the court the judges acted as counsel for the defence, what reason could Hawes have for his 'Brutish Obstinacy' in drawing upon himself 'the heavy Judgement which the Law has appointed for those who seem to have lost the rational Faculties of Men'?

Hawes was pressed under 250 lb. for seven minutes and then consented to plead. After his condemnation, when other prisoners 'said jestingly, that he chose Pressing because the Court would not let him have a good Suit to be hang'd in, he replied, with a great Deal of Warmth, that it was no such Thing, but that as he had liv'd with the character of the boldest Fellow of his Profession, he was resolv'd to Dye with it, and leave his Memory to be admired by all the Gentlemen of the Road in succeeding Ages.'

James Wright went to Tyburn dressed in his burial shroud. This started a fashion which grew throughout the century until it became more the rule than the exception.

The January Sessions had already begun when James Shaw himself was unexpectedly captured. The creaking machinery of the law was speeded up to such a pitch that he was brought to trial two days later. At the trial, against a background of snow falling outside the cavernous proscenium of the court on to the thieves and robbers chained and huddled together beneath their hats and cloaks in the Bail Dock, Wild gave what was in effect a concise diagram of the method he had employed in breaking gangs since 1714:

After Mr. *Pott's* Death, on *William Burridge's* Information, I took *James Reading*, and he impeach'd *Isaac Drew*, the Drover, and the Prisoner *Shaw*, for this Robbery and Murder, In Hopes of being admitted an Evidence against them; but he was disappointed by *Burridge's* being made an Evidence against him, for robbing Mr. *Brownsworth*. However, I took *Isaac* and *John Dykes*, together in *Holborn*, and each of these offered to be an Evidence against the other, but *Drew* succeeded, and *Dykes* was convicted on his Evidence. The Prisoner Shaw, being apprehended for robbing Mr. *Hungate* (of his Horse), he thought likewise to save himself by impeaching *Drew*; but Drew, going first before the Justice, impeach'd *Shaw*; *For*, says he, *there's no other Remedy, and if I don't leave off this Trade, I shall come to be hang'd*.

James Shaw had been a considerable villain and the driving force behind his gang. He had murdered several of the people he had robbed, but among those he had not killed were a few celebrities. One was the Covent Garden 'Mock Count', Count Viana, whom Shaw had met returning from a gambling house at Hampstead Wells with a magistrate (who was officially supposed to be suppressing gambling houses). They had £400 winnings hidden under the seat of their coach. In the Condemned Hold Shaw said therefore that he was not so great a villain as the world supposed because it had always been his firm opinion that it was a much greater sin to rob the poor, or the Church of God, 'than those who would have spent the Money he took from them in Gaiety and Luxury, or those who perhaps unjustly acquired it by Gaming'. 'And yet it does not appear', adds *Select Trials*, 'that in any of his Robberies, he gave himself the Trouble of enquiring into these Particulars. Did he take it for granted, that Providence would suffer none but the Rich and the Wicked to fall into his Hands?'

Shaw's body was gibbeted by the roadside between St. Pancras Church and Kentish Town, but his friends took it down and buried it in a ditch, where it was not discovered until April.[9]

At Butler Fox's trial for robbing the Cirencester coach at Knightsbridge, which took place after Shaw's, Wild and Will Hawkins repeated their evidence; but, perhaps because their stories had been shown to be so dubious before, Fox was again acquitted.

After his first acquittal, however, Sir Edward Lawrence's footmen, nervous that they might after all not get a share of the reward, had gone to Will Hawkins in the Gatehouse (where he had been transferred after turning Evidence) and between them they concocted a story by which they hoped to hang Fox once and for all. In September, John Hawkins and George Simpson had held up and robbed Colonel Archibald Hamilton in his coach on Wimbledon Common. John Hawkins gave all the details of the incident to his brother William; Wild (so it was alleged) bribed the coachman to swear to Fox's identity; and Fox, having been acquitted of two robberies of which he had been guilty, was now condemned at Kingston Assizes in March of a robbery of which he was innocent.[10]

This story is supported by three curious details. First, Wild's name is *not* on the back of either of Fox's indictments or in the GD Book among the witnesses bound to appear,[11] yet appear he did, twice. Secondly, he seemed to have it so fixed in his mind that he was the man responsible for bringing Fox to 'justice' that he put him as No. 22 on his list—for, of all things, robbing Sir Edward Lawrence! Thirdly, when the court asked Will Hawkins what had happened to Colonel Hamilton's rifled barrel gun they had stolen, Hawkins said he had thrown it over a wall; whereas Wilson wrote that he had seen this gun in Jack Hawkins's hands after the robbery. Therefore, Wilson knew Hawkins was lying. Now, in 1723-4, Wild gave a musketoon to 'Blueskin' Blake. It passed into the hands of Sir John Fielding and a century later appeared on exhibition at the Society of Antiquaries in 1866.[12] It was of Scottish make, and the Colonel came from a distinguished Scottish military family. It is unlikely that Wild would have given Blueskin a gun he had bought rather than one from his 'Lock'— which would have been stolen or given to him by one of his thieves in return for some service or favour—and if Will Hawkins was the thief, he would hardly have given Wild a present of that kind for nothing. Therefore, if this musketoon, wherever it is now, should turn out to have a rifled barrel, it is just possible that it is the same that Jack Hawkins took from Colonel Hamilton

—a fact which, considering its history of intrigue and treachery, should increase its interest and value.

In March also William Burridge was taken for horse-stealing. For his false witnesses he contracted the inevitable Strickland, and the fact that Strickland appeared in court himself suggests that Wild was making at least a pretence of saving Burridge's life. Strickland and a woman he hired (who claimed to be a maid at the 'Royal Oak', Leicester, where Burridge said he was at the time of the robbery) became so confused with their evidence, being out in their dates by nearly a month, that as they were taken away to be charged with perjury, the constable said 'Do ye hear Mr. *Soap-Cask-maker*, and you, Mrs. Maid of the *Royal Oak*? There's a new Lodging provided for ye! You have made a fine Kettle of Fish on't efaith! Come along. . . .'

During all this time, the remainder of the Hawkins gang committed about fifty highway robberies. Because they never went far from London they were able to criss-cross the city several times in a single foray: on three successive nights they held up the Worcester, Bristol, Gloucester, Cirencester, Oxford, Chichester, Ipswich and Portsmouth stage-coaches, and 'touched' the Bury coach every day for ten days. Eventually, they robbed the Bristol Mail, and the 'Hue & Cry' and proclaimed rewards were so great that the gang broke up in a chaos of mutual impeachments. Wild joined the hunt and kept himself in the newspapers as much as he could: 'Through the Means of Jonathan Wild, we hear that the Gentleman whose Lodgings were lately broken open in Philpot Lane, and who lost over £6,000, has recovered some part of his Money . . .'; '. . . in the Midst of this Plenty of Villainy, Jonathan Wild makes a good trade of it. For on Tuesday last, he took no less than three Highwaymen. . . .'[13] It must therefore have been extremely galling when Hawkins and Simpson were found in a tavern in the Old Bailey only a few yards from his house. After a long and dramatic trial they were condemned and their bodies hung in chains on Hounslow Heath, within sight of Benjamin Child.

The remains of Shaw's gang drifted over to join Carrick. One of these was Thomas Milksop, lately back from Virginia. Another was Robert Wilkinson, a thick-set man 'of low Stature' and 'surly and brutish Temper' whose main ambition was to be a prize-fighter and a promoter of bear- and bull-baiting. He spent most of his time at Hockley-in-the-Hole arena, Clerkenwell, where he competed in fist and cudgel fights of all kinds, and 'no Man could be more elevated than he, with the horse Acclamations of Carmen and Butchers, though he shared their Compliments but in Common with his Fellow Brutes, the Bull-Dogs'.

❦ XVIII ❦ *A Crack in the Ice*

In May 1722, six regiments pitched camp in Hyde Park. The reason, after many rumours, turned out to be another Jacobite conspiracy to set up the Pretender. It had been betrayed by the Pretender's allies, the French, who at that time wished for more friendly relations with England. London was now troubled by the King's Messengers, who arrested not only Jacobites but 'objectionable' people of all kinds, and by informers who saw in their patriotic duty a chance to settle old scores with private enemies. Although the danger was over before the regiments arrived, the camp remained until the end of the year, and became a place to go to on warm summer evenings.

On the night of 4 June, one of the visitors was Peter Martin, a Chelsea Pensioner of between sixty and seventy years old. He left about midnight with two ladies and a gentleman. They offered to see him across the meadows to Chelsea Hospital because it was now raining hard, but he cheerfully told them he was quite able to look after himself. He set off into the night, using his fusil (light musket) as a walking-stick. When he reached the corner of Buckingham Wall (now Lower Grosvenor Place), which in day-time was a broad gravel way pleasantly shaded by tall trees, but on that night was dark and full of large and dangerous puddles, he was surrounded by what must have seemed an army of footpads.

James Valentine Carrick, a short, fair-haired man, son of a

wealthy Irish jeweller, had been drinking in a tavern with five of his gang: Robert Wilkinson, Daniel Carrol and Robert Lincoln (both Irish), Will Lock and Joseph 'Blueskin' Blake. Will Lock, who turned Evidence, described what happened then, although Blueskin's name was deliberately left out of the story: '. . . about ten at Night, we all went out upon the Street Robberies, and, seeing this Chair, says *Carrick*, "let's follow it".'

The chair was carrying a Mr. Fleetwood Clark to his home in Conduit Street, and the thieves stopped it in a court near Golden Square. 'I staid at the lower End of the Court to watch: *Lincoln* went to the upper End for the same Purpose; *Wilkinson* stood with a Pistol over one Chairman, and *Carrol* over the other, and *Carrick* robb'd the Gentleman.' Wilkinson then gave one of the chairmen a 'Plaguy Knock o' the Pate with his Pistol', and 'a Woman at the same Time looking out at Window, and asking, What was the Matter?, *Wilkinson* damn'd her for a Bitch, and fired his Pistol at her: the Bullets broke the Glass and just missed the Woman. It was a rainy Night.'

After that they went along Piccadilly to Hyde Park Corner and then turned down the lane called 'Pimlico' (now Grosvenor Place). 'We saw the Pensioner coming up with a Fusee in his Hand: which at first I thought had been a Stick. *Wilkinson, Carrol* and *Lincoln* jump'd over the Ditch first, and Carrick and I follow'd. Then *Wilkinson* stopp'd the Pensioner, and seized his Gun. The Pensioner cry'd out "Thieves!", upon which *Lincoln* punch'd him in the Face with a Pistol, and knock'd him down. A Door being open'd at a House just by, they sent me to watch who came out. When I returned, I found the Pensioner lolling between *Carrick* and *Wilkinson*. As they led him he rattled in the Throat, and he not going fast enough, *Wilkinson* took a Sword, and said "Damn ye, go along!" and thrust it several Times into his Back. The Pensioner sunk down: Lincoln rifled his Pockets, but finding nothing but a Key and a Knife, he threw them away, and said "Damn him! He has got no Money", and so we went off. A Hackney Coach coming along we stopped it: but finding it was empty, we let it pass.'

As they approached Hyde Park Corner again, they met an officer from the camp, Captain Langley, driving in through the gate in another hackney coach. Wilkinson went up to it and pointed the Pensioner's fusil at the Captain, demanding his money. Captain Langley drew his sword and Wilkinson pulled the trigger, but the gun would not go off. Daniel Carrol stepped up and fired his pistol, Carrick fired another and Wilkinson pulled out his pistol and fired too. Lock believed they all missed, but in fact one of the slugs went through the Captain's shoulder. Unimpressed, the Captain bade the coachman drive on. The footpads all shouted at once that if he 'offer'd to move' they'd shoot him down off the box. They then rushed the Captain with drawn swords, and in the fight the gallant Captain was wounded seven times. The turnpike men, who could not have been more than fifty yards away (and who, since the robbery at Knightsbridge by Hawkins and Fox, had been equipped with speaking-trumpets), did nothing. However, says Lock, 'the Noise alarming the Centry, two Soldiers came towards us, which I observing, I flapt my Hat (*uncocked it and pulled the brim down*) and crossed the Road. The Soldiers coming up first to me, and asking what was the Matter?, I answered, "I believe there's some Rogues a-robbing a Gentleman: for God's Sake go and help him!" With that, they went towards the Coach, and one of them cock'd his Piece at *Carrol*, but it only flash'd. "God damn ye!" says *Carrol*, "down with your Pieces!" and, as he spoke, he presented his Pistol, but that only flash'd, as well as the Soldier's Musket. At seeing this, *Wilkinson* stept up, and struck one of them on the Head with the Pensioner's Gun, which broke with the Blow: and more Company coming up, the Coach got off and our Party retreated. *Wilkinson* was for returning: "God damn 'em," says he, "let's go back and kill 'em all!" but we would not agree to it. Then he threw away the broken Gun at the End of Tyburn Lane.'

The public was shocked that a brave veteran should have been stabbed to death in the back. The murder seemed absolutely pointless, for everyone knew that a Pensioner would never carry more than a shilling or two about him. Besides, the facts that three of the footpads were known by their voices to be Irish (and so potential Jacobites and traitors) and that both the victims were soldiers attacked within sight of the camp did nothing to calm the already tense mood in London. Therefore, the King ordered the Privy Council to offer £100 reward for the capture of each of the murderers, over and above the rewards already payable under the Highwayman Act and the Proclamations of 1719 and 1722. Thus, whoever caught and convicted all six would earn £1,400 (*c.* £28,000, or $72,000 in modern money).

Jonathan Wild came forward as the man to bring these rogues to justice. Yet, to turn against these six would inevitably lead to turning against the whole gang, which must have promised to be a hazardous adventure: for if his system had a flaw, it was that once the chain-reaction of impeachments was set in motion, it was apt to run out of control when everyone became intent on impeaching everyone else in the effort to save himself. So long as numbers could be kept within limits, Wild managed effectively enough, as was seen with Shaw's gang: but Carrick's gang was so large that it comprised the greater part of the hard core of London's underworld. In fact, it was four gangs loosely bound together. One, centred round Carrick, was about fifteen strong and contained ten Irishmen. The second, containing Blueskin Blake (and Nathaniel Hawes for a time), was about six strong. The third, about a dozen strong, was led by a fierce youth of eighteen called Edward Burnworth. The fourth, again about six strong, revolved round an Irishman called Humphrey Angier, who with his wife Elizabeth kept a brothel first at Charing Cross and, after 1721, at St. Giles. Elizabeth and her brother William Duce came from Wolverhampton, and had been under Wild's friendly eye since their arrival in London *c.* 1715. In this group was John Dyer, an informer almost as venomous as William Field.

Among the Irishmen was a striking figure called John Malhoney, of whom *Select Trials* says, 'he was a tall, big-boned, swarthy, grim Fellow, had an uncommon Fierceness in his Looks, and he swore with a Voice like Thunder'. He usually wore 'a large Silver lac'd Hat, a black Cravat, and his Wig tyed up in a Bag', and had for a certain period been friendly with Wild's wife, to the extent that she toyed with the idea of bedding with him when she discovered that Jonathan could have no more children. Wild, however, tried to charge him with coining, at the very time when Andrew Wild impeached the coiner Barbara Spencer. Malhoney had married a rich old woman, only to find that she had given all her money and furniture to her daughter and son-in-law the day before the wedding.

Joseph 'Blueskin' Blake deserves special mention, if only on account of his later fame as Jack Sheppard's companion. He was twenty-four years old, and if early stage representations of him are anything to go by, he was a large, fat, lazy young man of coarse sensibilities. He was by now an incurable gaol-bird, having been in and out of every prison, workhouse and House of Correction in the Metropolis since the age of twelve, and it was generally believed that he owed his continued survival to Jonathan Wild. Nevertheless, he was not the stupid oaf Sheppard described. Once, when he and a thief with the memorable *alias* of John 'Junks' (real name, Levee) held up a coach on Blackheath, the gentleman inside begged them not to frighten the lady, who was pregnant. Blueskin considerately held his hat at the door, saying they would be content with whatever the passengers gave them. 'Junks', holding the horses, heard a lot of money drop in, but when he came to look found only a little copper. Henceforth, he suspected Blueskin was too sharp for him. Blueskin has been oddly represented in plays and stories—from Edward Viles's blood-and-thunder *Blueskin* (perhaps the longest novel ever written) down to the recent film *Where's Jack?*. In an item of a TV series of 1968 called *Rogue's Gallery*, Blueskin was a 'goodie' of about forty years old, with an inexplicable German accent: and in *Where's Jack?* he was again middle-aged, tough, dependable and honest. In that film, however, is given an interesting explanation of his nickname: as an old artilleryman, his face was stained blue by burning powder. Unfortunately, the real Blake was not a soldier at any time in his short life. The nickname was fairly common, and in his case may have referred to a port-wine mark on his face, or to some joke between himself and another thief in his group who had been at school with him, William Blewit ('Blew Skin' and 'Blew It').

Wild had known all these people for years. They had been regular suppliers to his Lost Property Office, and some of them he had 'protected' since they were boys (notably Blueskin, Blewit and Burnworth). The disadvantage of this was that if he knew them, they knew *him*. His motives in destroying Carrick's gang, therefore, were probably as complicated as everything else in his life. Plain greed was doubtless one, the itch to empire-building a second and the necessity to maintain his system a third; but it would seem from his behaviour at the time of his trial that he had fallen victim to a form of 'double-think', so that even now he had come to see himself as the honest servant of King and Country he had always pretended to be. Thus, in his view, the ambiguous nature of his Lost Property Office was merely something forced on him by the chaotic conditions of the age, and the cold-blooded ruthlessness with which he surrendered his old drinking-companions and protégés to the hangman was no more than his stern sense of duty.

At any event, he did nothing for two months. Meanwhile, in

early July, Carrick and Malhoney were captured after robbing Mr. William Yonge, the new M.P. for Honiton (and later Secretary-at-War, playwright, and authority on correct pronunciation), of his gold watch and some papers. At a farcical trial, Carrick tried to outwit Mr. Yonge by arguing over details of dress and guns, and so further and further implicated himself. They were condemned, and at the gallows (18 July) Carrick, who had adopted his middle name 'Valentine' as a mark of his prowess with the ladies, 'instead of praying with the rest of the Criminals, he employ'd that Time in Giggling, taking Snuff, making Apish Motions to divert himself and the Mob . . . and then, giving himself some pretty and genteel Airs (as he seem'd to think 'em) in adjusting the Halter about his Neck, the Cart was drawn away.'

Owing to Mr. Yonge's importance, a 'Hue and Cry' was proclaimed, and magistrates led their posses into the alleys of Covent Garden to hunt down the whole gang. On 7 July, the *Weekly Journal or Saturday's Post* stated that 'a List is given of 15 Persons whose sole Business is to rob about the Streets of London; the Chief stiles himself *Major*, and has already been try'd in Surrey and Middlesex'. On the same day the *Weekly Journal or British Gazetteer* said that 'William Yonge, son of Sir Walter Yonge Bart. and Member for Honiton, has given a most particular charge to the Peace Officers of London & Westminster and Parts adjacent, to make the most diligent Search for a Gang of Street Robbers, being about 50 in Number.'

A few days later, some constables went to 'The Cherry Tree' in Wild Lane, Drury Lane, where Burnworth and his crew ejected them again violently. They returned with a posse of armed men under a Justice, and in the fracas took a few of the gang (some were hanged and the others, including Blewit, were transported),[1] but the majority escaped. Burnworth himself disappeared for several months. The same thing happened when three or four Justices went 'with Peace Officers etc. to a Night House in the Strand'. The *London Journal* of 14 July said that the place was in great disorder and most of their quarry escaped 'through out-of-the-Way Back and Trap-Doors. . . . The said Justices have received several undeniable Testimonies, which they will make use of very speedily: that a certain Person receives Hush-Money to a vast Sum from several People in the City of Westminster, and it's suggested, that he illegally gains about £1,200 a Year from the Brandy-Shops alone in that Liberty. They have likewise receiv'd Information,

that even one of the O— (*officers*) connives the same Way at a Knot
of Rogues, who have taken a House of his (which was ordinarily
rent at £40 a Year) at a Rate of £100 a Year, in which Place their
Villainies are concerted by Assemblies that are held there once or
twice a Week.'

Then Wild, after so long a silence, suddenly became active and
between 23 July and 4 August tracked down and apprehended
twenty-one of the gang, including Robert Wilkinson, Will Lock,
Lincoln, John Dyer and Blueskin Blake.[2] First, he took Wilkinson
before Justice Hewit and persuaded him to save himself by
impeaching Carrick, Carrol, Lincoln, Milksop, Richard Oakey,
Lock, and a man called Ping. The next day he took Will Lock
before Justice Nathaniel Blackerby and persuaded him to make an
'Information' containing *seventy* robberies by almost everyone in
the gang, as well as the murder of the Chelsea Pensioner. The
conventional procedure was that whoever impeached first, won. On
this occasion, however, Wilkinson's 'Information' was set aside,
and Lock's accepted because of its greater value. Blackerby gave
Wild a warrant to transfer Wilkinson, Milksop, Lincoln, Dyer and
the others from New Prison to Newgate on 17 August.[3] There,
Wild's plans were slightly upset when someone stole Lock's
'Information' from his pocket while he was asleep and gave it to
Mrs. Spurling, the Tap Woman (and Wild's wife's aunt). She,
determined to frustrate the Thief-Taker General at every opportunity, read it aloud to all the accused, and Wild and Lock had to
invent a new 'Information'. This must have been a pretty flimsy
affair, for, apart from Wilkinson, Lincoln and Milksop (who were
condemned), all the gang were released some time in September.
Only one of Lock's charges were brought to the Old Bailey, and
then it turned out that the prosecutor, a Frenchman, could
remember neither the day nor even the month he was robbed, and
all the thieves were in any case dead.[4]

Daniel Carrol, who had been present both at the murder of the
Pensioner and the robbery of Mr. Yonge, was nearly caught in
Russell Street, Covent Garden; but as he was being chased he
turned, pointed behind him and shouted 'An Arrest!' In the confusion he got into a house, locked the door, and escaped through a
back window.[5] He made his way to Ireland, where he was betrayed
by his mistress.[6] *Select Trials* says he was eventually shot by a
thief-taker, though whether or not this was one of Wild's thief-
takers is not recorded.

Nevertheless, in comparison to the feeble efforts of the magistrates (we hear no more of their lists and 'undeniable Testimonies'), Wild had achieved a remarkable success; and this probably did more than anything else to cause some magistrates to look on him with increasing ill favour.

The next events, although crucial to Wild's career, are unfortunately puzzling, and their clarification is not helped by various mistakes in the records. To begin with, the gang were obviously outraged that Wild had so treacherously turned on them, which they believed he had done for the sake of the rewards. In fact, such a wholesale round-up had probably been forced on him by the copious informations of Will Lock, but that was not the kind of subtlety to interest them. Accordingly, when they came out of Newgate in November and returned to robbing on Blackheath, Hampstead and Islington commons, they swore to murder Wild at the first chance.

In 1726 Defoe wrote a history of Burnworth's gang,[7] which in 1722 had been part of Carrick's gang, and he was probably thinking of this affair when he said that their numbers were reduced from thirty-two to eleven (the numbers tally with the records) 'by the particular Malice of *Jonathan Wild*, because they would not come into his Government'. Later in the same text he wrote that when Blewit returned from America with two comrades, one of them 'got at last into the Hands of *Jonathan Wild*, and being upon ill Terms with *Jonathan* on former Accounts, was left to the Law, and though he had not done any considerable Exploits since his Return, was hang'd upon the single point of returning. This was one of the Articles which the Gang never forgave *Jonathan* for, but vowed his Destruction: which one of them, that is *Blueskin*, attempted afterwards in the boldest Manner, and which showed what desperate People they (i.e. *Wild and his posse*) now had to deal with.'

Blewit did not return from America until January 1723, when he was immediately rearrested, though not apparently by Wild. It had happened that there had been another mutiny on ship and Blewit had informed the captain before it had become serious. Therefore, on his return he was treated leniently and, instead of being hanged, was allowed to transport himself back to America. However, he disappeared, and, like Burnworth, whose gang he later joined, he may have been kept by Wild. Thus there is no record of who was hanged, for he is not on Wild's list. As for the gang's refusal to come into Wild's 'Government', it would seem that they were already in his government before the quarrel began, and that Wild's problem was to keep them there.

Another confusion concerns Richard Oakey, whom Nathaniel Hawes sneered at as 'a Size too little for a Hero, and fit for nothing but to clean Pistols and sell the Goods they stole'.[8] Oakey had once been a pickpocket, but when his partner, a prostitute, had been beaten to death by a client, he joined two burglars, John Harvey and 'Cock Eye'd Jack'. Jonathan Wild caught them all in 1720 after a burglary in Southwark, and Oakey saved himself by impeaching the other two. After a year with Carrick's gang, he was caught by Wild again in the general round-up. *Select Trials* says he was acquitted, but the GD roll shows he was sentenced to transportation.[9] Yet he was back with the gang, having been released, in November, and all went well for them until the evening of 10 December, when they encountered none other than William Yonge, and took from him the same gold watch that Carrick had taken in July. With Mr. Yonge was Colonel Cope, who was later to lose the Battle of Prestonpans, most of his men being asleep, and so become the object of a ribald Scottish ballad, '*Hey, Johnny Cope, are ye waukin yet?*'.

Blueskin sold the watches to a receiver called Richard Greatorex, who lived at the 'Helmet' in Red Cross Street, Southwark,[10] near where Wild stabled his horses, and other goods to Allen and Jones, the Lodging Lay experts who also lived nearby.

' Wild began by arresting Blueskin. There was a stiff fight, which ended when Blueskin received a sabre-cut across the head. This is curious, for Blueskin had been left out of Lock's Information and, it would seem, had promised to Wild to impeach the gang again at the first opportunity after their release. Yet he had been loud in his denunciations of the Thief-Taker General, and now swore to die rather than be taken. Yet, again, no sooner was he wounded than he offered to impeach the gang, as previously arranged. This might be explained by the inconsistencies of human nature, Blueskin's unstable character, or by the fact that he had denounced Wild with the rest because he did not wish to be suspected of being implicated in any of Wild's intrigues. By 16 January, the whole gang (or at least the dozen or so of whom we have records) were back in gaol, besides Greatorex, Allen, Jones and their sister-wives, all taken by Wild. It seems from Wild's account, however, that it was not Blueskin's but John Dyer's treachery which led to the taking of the gang in the first place:

Some coming (I suppose from the Prosecutors) to me about the Robbery, I made it my Business to search after the Prisoners; for I had heard they used to rob about *Hampstead*; and I went about it the more willingly, because I had heard that they threaten'd to shoot me thro' the Head. I offer'd ten Pounds a Head for any Person who could discover them; upon which a Woman (*John Dyer's* Wife) came and told me that the Prisoners had been with her Husband, to entice him to *turn out* with them, and if I should promise he should come and go safely, he would give me some Intelligence. I gave her my Promise, and her Husband came accordingly, and told me that *Levee* (*John 'Junks'*) and *Blake* were at that Time cleaning their Pistols at a House in Fleet Lane. I went thither, and seized them both. I heard the same day that *Flood** was apprehended in Southwark for another Fact, and sent to Bridewell, where I found him safe. The Person, who gave me Intelligence where to find *Blake* and *Levee*, told me, that he had two Rings to sell, and I supposing that they might be of use in detecting the Prisoners, lent him 12*s.* upon them, and here is one of them.

Oakey, Matthew Flood, and John Levee alias 'Junks' were condemned on Blueskin's evidence (although again there is confusion about Oakey in the records), and *Select Trials* says that they had nothing to offer in their defence, but 'they all vehemently exclaimed against *Jonathan Wild*'.[11]

Blueskin now expected to be not only released but to be given some part of the £420 reward money. However, the court told him he was entitled to neither, for he had put up a violent resistance at his arrest and was lucky to have been accepted as an Evidence at all. As he was not willing to transport himself, he was ordered to be remanded in the Wood Street Compter until he could find adequate surety for his good behaviour. Nevertheless, Wild paid for the cure of his wound, and gave him an allowance of 3*s.* 6*d.* a week 'for a considerable Time'.[12]

Of the survivors of the gang, some were transported, including the receivers, sailing with Moll King in July 1723, and a few were released. The full reward was paid to Wild, who had now earned

---

* Matthew Flood, another member of this gang, was the son of the Keeper of the Clink Prison in Southwark and worked on the river. With what is perhaps a touch of deliberate humour, the Middlesex Sessions Book for May 1721 lists him as 'Mattheus Flood—Waterman'.

£900 from the gang, besides perhaps half that much in addition from sums extorted from the prisoners during negotiations. He also gained a new informer in John Dyer.

It was Humphrey Angier who first noticed this person at the Old Bailey house of William Strickland, the procurer of false witnesses. Angier had been curious that Dyer 'was always muffled up in a great Coat and looking very shy', and when Strickland told him that Dyer came from Salisbury and was in hiding because he had shot a footman, Angier invited Dyer to join the gang.

At the trial of Levee and Flood, he said that these two and Blueskin had forced him to rob with them by swearing to include him in an Information if he refused. 'So I went with them to Hide Park, where they stopt a Coach, and then I ran away from them.'

In April 1723, free again, he led a number of robberies in Chelsea Fields (the area between what is now Victoria Station and Eaton Square) with Angier, Duce and some others. Their first victim was a Mr. Holms. Dyer took the money, but, as his companions moved off, he spoke to Mr. Holms a moment and kissed his hand. The gang was dispersed next day after a disastrous attack on the coach of Lady Chudleigh,* in which an armed patrol had appeared and killed one of their number called Rice.

Eventually, and after many vicissitudes (during which Dyer committed two murders, Duce one, and Angier, terrified, took refuge in his old regiment at Henley) Dyer impeached the gang to Wild. What really occurred is impossible to say because the various accounts given by Dyer, Duce, Mr. Holms and Wild were all obviously false.

It happened that that month a gang of horse-and-cattle stealers in Hampshire called 'the Waltham Blacks' (because they blacked their faces), who had been creating a tremendous stir, were on trial at Reading and Wild went out to attend. He told the *British Journal* (22 June 1723) that he 'accidentally' met Humphrey Angier on the road and arrested him for murdering Captain Brett in the Strand in 1722 and for murdering a woman in St. James's Park in 1721. In fact, Angier had already been acquitted of both these crimes. Moreover, Wild had arrested Angier's wife Elizabeth the

---

* Mother of Elizabeth Chudleigh, Duchess of Kingston, who achieved fame and a place in most books on eighteenth century social life in England, by dancing naked as 'Iphigenia' at a masquerade in 1748.

day before, and the day before that both Duce and Dyer had been arrested at the Angier's brothel in St. Giles. This had been done not by Wild but by the High Constable of Holborn, Jones (who was to arrest Wild himself). Jones had gone to Angier's brothel to find the two men, whom he suspected of attacking Lady Chudleigh, and had taken them to Justice Blackerby. Wild was at the Justice's house within the hour and, for no reason that was explained, Dyer was admitted as the Evidence. At the trial Wild had the face to pretend that this was the first time he was aware that Duce and Dyer were acquainted, although he had known both for years and Duce, specially favoured because he came from Wolverhampton, since he had been a boy.

The affair has the look of one of Wild's typical intrigues. At the trial of Oakey, Levee and Flood, Wild must have promised Dyer protection if he undertook to betray the gang when need arose in the future—just as he had promised Blake protection at the trial of Wilkinson and Lincoln. Therefore, when the gang robbed Mr. Holms in April, Dyer tarried behind and kissed the gentleman's hand. Holms said in court that Dyer had merely apologized for the robbery, and explained that they were poor men stealing out of necessity. However, Dyer kept the money and the gang accused him of cheating them. What he really said, it would seem, was that his name was Dyer and that Holms should go to Jonathan Wild, who would ensure the return of the money. Then he kissed Mr. Holms's hand as a sign of his good intentions and kept the money so that Wild could pay it back, together with two letters of Holms's as evidence. Now, in his list, Wild wrote against Duce's name 'The Prosecutor (Mr. *Holms*) found out by me.' This means that *he went to Holms* (not that Holms came to the office) after he heard about the robbery, and this he could only have heard from Dyer. Having made sure that Holms was properly drilled in what to say at the trial, Wild now had only to pretend that he went to Justice Blackerby's as soon as he heard of the arrest, for he already had a cast-iron case against Duce, with Dyer 'signed up' as the Evidence. This would explain how he had arrested Angier at Henley (and not 'accidentally' on the road to Reading, as he told the newspapers), for only Dyer knew where Angier was.

At the Old Bailey, William Duce and another of the gang, James Butler, were tried on the evidence of Dyer and Wild. Wild said:

I was with them before the Justice. I found that Duce and Dyer
were acquainted, for they both had got Pumps on their Feet,
and the Pumps were of the same *make*; whereupon I asked them,
if they did not *make* (i.e. *steal*) them at such a House. I have
known Will Duce from a Boy. His Mother came to me since he
was apprehended, and said, that her Son could make the
greatest Discoveries: and therefore, she hoped I would get him
to be an Evidence. I went to see him in Newgate, and there he
himself desired to be made an Evidence, and was going to
confess to me what Facts he had committed; but I would not
let him proceed, for fear I should be called upon as a Witness
against him; and (as I told him) it was too late for him to expect
to be made an Evidence; because John Dyer had got the Start
of him.

Will. Duce: You lie like a Villain as you are, for I never offer'd to
confess any Thing to you, nor desired to be an Evidence; and I
don't know how I should, for I never was concerned in any
Robbery in my Life. And as for Dyer, I never had any Acquain-
tance with him, any farther than as he lodged at my Sister's; I
saw him there now and then. You, Mr. *Evidence*! Let me ask you
one Question! Pray, who was it kiss'd the Prosecutor's Hand at
Parting?
Dyer: Why, it was I.
Duce: I would like to ask the Prosecutor the same Question.
Holms: It was Dyer that made such an Offer; but whether he
really did kiss my Hand or not, I am not certain.
Court to Duce: Your Question has done you no Service. Your
Knowledge of this private Circumstance, which neither *Dyer*
nor *Holms* had mention'd before, is a strong Presumption that
you were present when the Robbery was committed.

After this, Duce and James Butler (whom Wild had also arrested)
were tried for another robbery, with Dyer again the Evidence
against them. Dyer said that Elizabeth Angier had pawned her bed
to raise the money for the pistols to rob with, and then there was
another shouting match in the court. Duce had sent out for a copy
of the January *Sessions Papers* from a nearby bookstall (for there
were no other court records available to him), and these he waved
in the air as he tried to prove that Dyer had already been a per-
jured informer: 'I know nothing of this Robbery, nor of any other!
There is not a greater Villain upon God's Earth than *Jonathan*

Wild; he makes it his Business to swear away honest Men's Lives for the Sake of the Reward, and that's what he gets his Livelihood by. And as for *John Dyer*, it's well known that he has been an Evidence before. Here's the *Sessions Paper* that proves it! And, by the Law of England, no Man is to be twice admitted an Evidence.'

Wild pointed out that in January Dyer had been a voluntary Evidence, not charged with any crime. The court said it knew of no law to say a man could not be an Evidence twice. Butler pleaded guilty but swore Duce was innocent. But the court said that his confession, by which he would be hanged, 'could affect only himself and not William Duce'.

In the afternoon, Dyer tried to swear away the life of Duce's sister, Elizabeth Angier. What had actually happened was that when he had left her brothel for new lodgings, he had found some clothes left there by a previous tenant. He asked Elizabeth to come and take them, and he and Wild now made it seem like a robbery. Butler and Duce (of whom Purney wrote in a typical passage that he 'was born in the 25th Year of his Age and his Crimes were the Occasion of his terminating the World') were hanged and Elizabeth transported.

Humphrey Angier was likewise condemned on evidence that was provably false. One robbery, of Upper-City-Marshal Lewen (Hitchen's superior) may or may not have been true; but the other, of a waggon driven by Edward Herring, was said to have occurred twelve years before. It is odd that no one pointed out that if that were so, then Dyer would have been a boy of eight years old when he held up Mr. Herring's waggon at gunpoint. During an argument over dates, Dyer said he could have remembered more 'punctually' had not his notebook, in which he kept a detailed diary of his crimes, been lost.

> *Court*: What was your Design in keeping such a Journal? Was it, that upon the Perusal of your Robberies, you might the more particularly repent of them?
>
> *Dyer*: No, I thought nothing of Repentence; but I did it to save myself from the Gallows, that I might be the more exact whenever I should have an Opportunity of securing my own Life, by becoming an Evidence against my Companions.

Yet, in the end, Wild cheated Dyer too. Among the Treasury Papers[13] is a Certificate of Payment, dated 27 September 1723, showing how the £40 reward was divided up:

Martin Lewen £8
John Dyer £2
Edward Herring £5
Jonathan Wild £25

Dyer was kept in Newgate for a year and then transported with Will Lock, who had impeached the 'first half' of Carrick's gang, and Jack Sheppard's brother Thomas. They arrived at Annapolis on 27 July 1724, and the Landing Certificate describes Dyer as a 'Hattmaker' of dark complexion, aged twenty-one. He returned in 1727, after Wild's death. He must have obtained a pardon, for with Lewen and Herring he petitioned the Lords Commissioners of the Treasury that the additional £100 reward 'due by His Late Matie's Proclamation of 21 January 1721 for the Apprehending and Convicting of a Highwayman within 5 miles of the Citys of London and Westminster may be paid to the Petrs'.

This document was passed to Anthony Cracherode, H.M. Solicitor for the Treasury (he drew in addition £200 p.a. for perusing newspapers, etc., in search of seditious libel), but it is uncertain that the reward was ever paid. Dyer was hanged in 1729, and left an 'autobiography'. He was careful to omit all references to Jonathan Wild and to any of the more squalid, but historically recorded, episodes in his life, although he claimed that his tract was a true account of all the '*Petty Larcenys*, Fellonies, Burglaries, Housebreakings, Shopliftings, Street and Highway Robberies, Rapes, Cheats *Etc.* . . . wrote by Himself . . . for the Benefit of the Publick, in Order to prevent the Perpetuation of the many Villainies which are daily committed In and About this Town'.

Carrick's gang was now extinct and Jonathan Wild everywhere triumphant. Yet it had been something of a Pyrrhic victory. From the moment he decided to arrest the murderers of the Pensioner, things had begun to go wrong. Evidence had misfired, his gangs had turned against him, and for the first time he had been openly denounced by his victims in court. It must have seemed on several occasions as if his whole system was about to fall apart. As a result, he had been forced to use dangerously crude methods in 'framing' Duce and Angier, and if this had called forth no comment from the Old Bailey judges, it was noticed by the public. Newspapers began to refer not only to the 'renowned', but to the 'scandalous', Jonathan Wild. Worse, in October 1723 his man

Quilt Arnold was arrested over the Martin Bellamy affair, and Arnold's wife transported for shoplifting.

Meanwhile, Edward Burnworth, now twenty years old, had gathered a dozen or so followers round him, including Peter Levee (brother of John 'Junks'), Emmanuel Dickenson (brother of a man in Shaw's gang), and a youth called Kit Leonard, once a member of the gang of William Field and Elizabeth Harris. Although barely eighteen, he had already murdered at least two people.

We have a glimpse of this group through the case of one John Allen, twenty-eight years old. For about six months he had worked as a 'stringer' for the gang, picking pockets at executions. At the hanging of seven of the 'Waltham Blacks' (several others having died in Newgate before being brought to trial) he performed well enough to be allowed to meet the young leader Burnworth and to be elected as a professional. It was an alarming experience for Allen, for '. . . . Pistols were pull'd out, and Proposals made, such as he said, could never have enter'd into his Imagination'. Indeed, the more one reads about men like Burnworth and Leonard, or Wilkinson and others, the more remarkable it becomes that Wild was able to have any kind of control over them at all, let alone keep them in 'Awe'.

Soon the time came, however, when Burnworth needed a scapegoat, and a week later he allowed Peter Levee to impeach Allen to Jonathan Wild. By what Wild said in court, if he was not directly managing the gang, he certainly had some arrangement with Burnworth, for he was well informed of their daily actions:

Mr. *Wasey* (*the man Burnworth and Allen had robbed*) came to me next Morning, and acquainted me with the Manner of his being robb'd, and described the Things he lost, and the Persons who took them. I asked him, if he was capable of knowing the Men again, he said he thought he was; for they robb'd him under a Lamp, by the Light of which he had taken some Notice of them. I told him I did not know but I might be able to give some Account in two or three Days time; for I heard that such Persons as he described had lately furnished themselves with Pistols, as I supposed for some such Purposes. I sent for *Peter Levee*, who came to me readily, for I had given him my *Word and Honour* that he should come and go free, and I always punctually observe my Promises to these Gentlemen, or, otherwise, I could not be serviceable to the Publick. *Levee* being come, I told him it was now his Time to chuse whether he should secure himself, or be hang'd with his Accomplices. Upon which he promised to send me Word when I might have an Opportunity of taking one or both of his Companions, and so I let him go in Safety. He was as good as his Promise, and I took both the Prisoners in his Company, and afterwards, upon offering a Reward of five Guineas, Mr. *Wasey's* Watch was sent to me by a Porter.

This speech has been quoted many times in accounts of Jonathan Wild as an illustration of his method, yet it may be seen what a mixture of truth and falsehood it was. What did he mean, for instance, by saying he took 'both the Prisoners' (i.e. Allen and Burnworth) when in fact only Allen was taken or charged? It seems to have been a slip of the tongue—that is, he took Allen and Burnworth, made his deal and let Burnworth go.

Blueskin Blake was released from Wood Street Compter in June 1724. Wild had apparently stopped paying his allowance of 3s. 6d. a week, but Blueskin managed to find two luckless gardeners who undertook to stand surety against his good behaviour for seven years. Sir John Fryer, an ex-Lord Mayor took the recognizances, and a gentleman who was present asked Sir John how long it might be before they saw Blake again at the Old Bailey. 'Another answered, *About three Sessions*, and he happened to guess right. . . .'[14]

By then, however, the fame of Burnworth and his companions had been overshadowed by the astonishing reputation of a newcomer who had drifted in and out of their gang with a disconcerting casualness—the housebreaker Jack Sheppard.

{ Part III } *Fall*

{ XIX } *Jack Sheppard*

John Sheppard was 5 ft. 4 in. tall, rather thin, with fair hair and a pale face, and he spoke with a slight stammer. He is remembered now as the most famous criminal of the eighteenth century after Dick Turpin. A complete folklore grew round his name even while he was alive and, after his last escape from 'The Castle' in Newgate Tower, he was regarded as a taunting will-o'-the-wisp who in one stroke had shown up the government, the City, and its horrible police system, to be corrupt and ridiculous. Obviously, such a creature could have had no ordinary ancestors, and on 24 October, while he was still at large and an inspiration to all the ballad-singers of the Metropolis, the *Weekly Journal or Saturday's Post* reminded its readers of a man called Sheppard who, in the days of Queen Elizabeth, had been employed out of Newgate by Secretary of State Walsingham to steal some papers from the Spanish ambassador. Sheppard stole the papers easily enough, and took a bag of gold as well; 'at which the Secretary seeming very angry, the Thief gave him to understand that he was out in his Politicks: for if he had left the Gold, the Ambassador would have known it could be no common Thief who had broken open his Cabinet, but now he would never suspect from what Quarter the Robbery came. . . .' And, it was said, our Jack Sheppard was lineally descended from this very man.

In reality, Jack Sheppard was born in Spitalfields on 4 March

1702, and as a child assisted his mother where she worked in the drapery shop of Mr. Kneebone, opposite St. Mary's in the Strand. His father, like Jonathan Wild's, was a carpenter, and his elder brother Thomas soon showed signs of being an irredeemable criminal.

Jack was apprenticed to a carpenter in Drury Lane, where he learned lock-making (and so picking) as a side-line. He had frequent rows with his master, Owen Wood, and added to that person's misery by pilfering from the houses where he was sent to do jobs. He spent his nights hanging about the dives of Lewkenor's Lane, and finally made friends with one of the girls at the 'Black Lion', kept by a button-mould maker called Joseph Hinds, a few doors from 'The Black Boy' where Andrew Wild kept a 'Lock' for street pickpockets. Her name was Elizabeth Lyon. She would seem to have been a large and rather blowsy girl, and she was generally known by her nickname of 'Edgworth Bess'.

Sometime in July 1723, this woman was taken to the St. Giles's Roundhouse for creating a disturbance. Sheppard demanded to see her, and when the Beadle pushed him away, he broke down the door, knocked over the Beadle and carried Bess away in triumph. In August, his brother Thomas was discharged from Newgate after being burnt in the hand, and through him Jack met a group of thieves, most of whom had been in the rank and file of Carrick's gang. One of these was a man called James Sykes, nicknamed 'Hell & Fury'. The person who disposed of the goods stolen by this gang was our friend William Field, who had now opened a 'Lock', or receiving establishment, in the house of Blueskin Blake's mother, in Rosemary Lane, Wapping. Thus it is more than probable that, whether they knew it or not, they lived and worked under the watchful eye of Jonathan Wild, though Sheppard always claimed that he scorned to have anything to do with such a person: 'I was indeed twice at a Thief-Catcher's Levee, and must confess the Man treated me civilly; he complimented me on my Successes, said he heard that I had both an Hand and Head admirably well turn'd to Business, and that I and my Friends should always be welcome to him: But not caring for his Acquaintance, I never troubled him, nor had we any Dealings together.'[1]

Throughout the autumn and winter of 1723-4, Jack Sheppard went robbing with his brother and the rest of the gang, and his specialist skills as carpenter and locksmith made him valuable as a housebreaker. Then in February 1724, Thomas was caught and to save himself impeached his brother and Edgworth Bess. A reward was now obtainable, and 'Hell & Fury' Sykes, meeting Jack in Seven Dials, lured him into Mr. Redgate's alehouse under the pretence of going to cheat two 'Chubbs' ('suckers') at skittles. One of the 'Chubbs' turned out to be a constable whom Sykes had brought for the purpose of arresting Sheppard. By this piece of treachery, 'Hell & Fury' Sykes earned himself a place as a villain both in Harrison Ainsworth's novel, *Jack Sheppard*, and in all the stage melodramas that derived from it. Indeed, it is said[2] that it was during conversations between Ainsworth and Charles Dickens, in which Ainsworth was reading passages from *The Newgate Calendar*, that Dickens was inspired with the name, and above all the character, of his celebrated robber, 'Bill Sikes'. Dickens already knew a burglar called Bill, on whom he drew for technical information, but Bill was rather a gentle and humorous soul. Now, 'Hell & Fury' crystallized perfectly the type of character he wanted.

The curious point about this story, and one that has so far escaped attention, is that the name 'Hell & Fury' did not refer to any particular ferocity on the part of James Sykes, but to his prowess as an athlete. He had been a Running Footman to that most notorious of the Augustan rakes, Philip, Duke of Wharton, but had left his service by 1719. On 16 May, *Applebee's Original Weekly Journal* reported one of his triumphs:

'Sykes, an ex-running Footman to the Duke of Wharton, beat all the Post-Horses between the White Heart Inn, Southwark, and Dover.'

The achievement of a man on foot beating horses from London to Dover is not impossible if it is remembered that the horses had to be loaded, and frequently stopped and changed en route, while Sykes had only to keep up a steady trot. His name, however, would seem to have been given him on an earlier occasion, for on 14 February 1719, the same paper had reported:

'The Duke of Wharton's Running Footman won a race for several hundred guineas. Both of 'em ran with such Fury and Violence that tho' it was but a two Mile Course, they both drop'd down Dead when they came in.'

After leaving the Duke, Sykes became a London chairman, but he was still racing in 1722, as the *London Journal* of 20 January shows:

'William Lovet and the famous James Sykes, "the Hell and Fury Chairman", are to run for 100 Guineas the 31st instant, on Banstead Downs.'

When Sykes became a footpad I do not know, nor have I found any record that he was ever transported or hanged.

Sheppard was put in the St. Giles's Roundhouse, but broke out through the roof on the first night. He was recaptured in May and committed to New Prison. Edgworth Bess came on a visit and found herself incarcerated with him as a result. Within a few days, one of the gang had smuggled in some tools to him, and early on the morning of Whit Monday he breached the wall of his cell and lowered Bess and himself into the yard of the Clerkenwell Bridewell next door. Then he climbed a 22 ft. wall, pulled the heavy Bess up after him, lowered her down again on the other side into the street, and they made their escape.

These two successes made him the hero of the hour amongst his fellow thieves, who now regarded it as an honour to be allowed to go out robbing with him. For his partners he usually chose Burnworth, Blewit or someone from their gang, though he was beginning to prefer to work alone. However, when Blueskin Blake came out of Wood Street Compter in June,* they became partners for a while. He seems to have had a low opinion of just about everybody he knew, and he spoke of them all, later, in cold and sneering terms. Edgworth Bess was the 'sole Author of all his Misfortunes', who by her constant wheedling demands for presents had driven him to crime in the first place; she was incapable of carrying out orders intelligently and was good at nothing but betraying her companions, and 'he cared not what became of her'. As for Blueskin, he 'was never a Master of a Courage or Conduct suitable to our Enterprizes . . . wanting Resolution . . . a worthless Companion, a sorry Thief. . . .'

Meanwhile Jonathan Wild was having worries of his own. On 2 June he petitioned the Court of Aldermen for the Freedom of London.[3] Presumably he was feeling more and more the need for some sort of official recognition of his self-appointed rôle as 'Thief-Taker General', and to become a Freeman was a necessary first step. Perhaps he was hoping to be granted a charter so that he could turn his office into a City Company. The petition reads:

---

* *See page* 203.

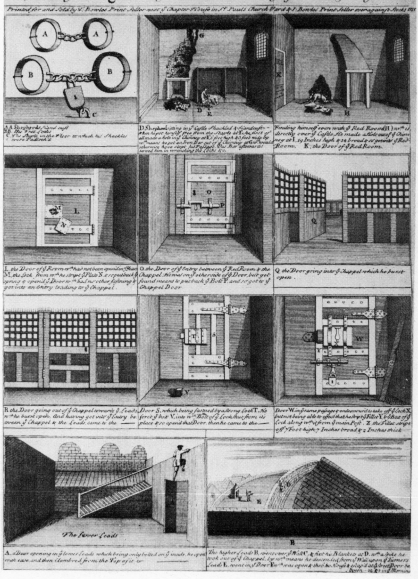

10 A broadsheet showing the stages of Jack Sheppard's last and
greatest escape from Newgate

11 & 12 *Overleaf, Above* Wild's Schedule from the Compter (1712) of
people who owed him money. Obadiah Lemon later became one
of Wild's principal robbers
Below A letter to the Earl of Dartmouth

A Schedule of wtt Money is oweing to me

From Robert Foward — — — —	15: 00: 00
Robt Gilbert — — — —	05: 00: 00
Hediah Lemon — — — —	10: 00: 00
Lucas — — — —	07: 00: 00

Saue all others debt remember being Small —

Jonathan Wilde. —

My Lord

London June 15. 1724

I am Informed by Mr Woolleys man
that your Lordship has lost some things on the road
I humbly beg your Lordship will please to order me a
particular of them yr next post, and I will use all the
Diligence I can to serve your Lordship to the uttmost
of my power, and beg leave to subscribe

Your Lordships

Most obedient & Dutifull
Servt.

Jona. Wilde.

To the Rt. Hon. the Lord Mayor & Court of Aldermen,
The Humble Petition of Jonathan Wild,

SHEWETH:

That your Petitioner has been at great Trouble and Charge in apprehending and Convicting divers Felons for returning from Transportation since October 1720 (the Names of whom are mentioned in the Account hitherto annexed). That your Petitioner has never received any Reward or Gratuity for such his Service. That he is very desirous to become a Freeman of this honourable City, wherefore your Petitioner most humbly prays that Your Honours will (in Consideration of his said Services) be pleased to admit him into the Freedom of this honourable City. And your Petitioner shall ever pray Etc.

JONATHAN WILD

Appended to this was a list of 'Persons apprehended, taken and convicted for returning from transportation, by Jonathan Wild, since October 1720, for which he received no Reward, viz: John Filewood, alias Violet, William Bond, Charles Hinchman, Samuel Whittle, Martin Grey, James Dalton, Robert Godfrey alias Perkins, Old Harry alias Harry Williams, Henry Woodford, John Meffe. Several others have been taken by him, and afterwards sent abroad viz: Moll King, John Jones etc., who were notorious Street Robbers in the City of London.'

The petition was read by the Court of Aldermen, but they seem to have felt that Wild was not quite 'solid' enough as yet to be so honoured, for the entry in the Repertory says:

'Upon reading the Humble Petition of Jonathan Wilde praying that in consideration of his Services done in apprehending and Convicting divers Felons for Returning from Transportacion he Might be admitted into the freedom of this City—the Consideracion thereof is adjourned till another time.'[4]

Two days later (6 June) *Applebee's Original Weekly Journal* reported:

'On Tuesday last, Mr. Jonathan Wild petitioned the Court of Aldermen for a Gratuity, for Detecting Persons returning from Transportation before their Time. And they were pleased to order him a very handsome Sum for that Service. And 'tis hoped that Mr. Wild will double his diligence for the Future.'

There is no record that Wild was ever given the Freedom of

London, and after his death, his petition was held up as a further example of his effrontery. As for the rewards, the payment entry may be found in one of the various City account books, but failing that confirmation there seems to be no reason why they should not have been paid.

On 15 June Wild was to become entangled in another affair that was to end unsatisfactorily. It began as a straightforward business letter to William Legge, 1st Earl of Dartmouth, who from 1710–13 had been Secretary of State:

> My Lord
>   I am informed by Mr. Woolley's man that your Lordship has lost some things on the road I humbly beg Your Lordship will please to order me a particular of them by next post and I will use all the Diligence I can to Serve your Lordship to the uttermost of my power and beg leave to subscribe
>
>   Your Lordships
>   most obedient & Dutifull
>   Serv[t].
>
>   JON[a]: WILDE[5]

The thieves, however, were to prove difficult and the Earl's steward stubborn.

At the same time, it looked as if Carrick's gang, which he had so effectively broken up a year before, was starting a new lease of life with Sheppard or Burnworth as possible leaders. As neither seemed to be particularly keen on working under his direction, this was obviously a growth that would have to be nipped in the bud.

On 12 July, Sheppard and Blueskin broke into Mr. Kneebone's drapery shop in the Strand and removed 108 yards of cloth, two silver spoons and other goods. These they took down to a small warehouse they had rented near the Horse Ferry in Westminster, which was already fairly stocked with goods they had accumulated from other robberies.

The next morning, Mr. Kneebone went to Jonathan Wild and gave him the details, adding that he strongly suspected Jack Sheppard, for he had been warned that Jack had said he was next on the list. This made him especially bitter, for he had always treated Jack very kindly when he had worked at his shop as a boy. What happened next cannot be known for certain, because the stories Wild and Field told in court are not very convincing. Wild said that understanding Sheppard was acquainted with Blueskin and Field, he sent for Field and told him that if he would make 'an ingenuous Confession' he believed he would be able to 'prevail with the Court to admit him as an Evidence. Then *Field* discover'd the Prisoner (*Sheppard*), and gave an Account of how some of the Cloth they stole, was dispos'd of. . . .' It will be noticed that Wild was careful to say not that Field had committed the robbery with Sheppard and Blueskin, but only that he had disposed of the goods, or rather 'some' of the goods. Field himself said that he had committed the robbery, or rather had acted as look-out while Sheppard had cut the bar of the cellar-window and gone inside. For their part, both Sheppard and Blueskin swore to the end that Field had not been present at the robbery, but that they had taken him down to their warehouse in Horse Ferry to show him the goods so that he could price them, and that he had then gone back by night, broken in, stolen the goods and impeached his companions to Jonathan Wild.

What really seems to have happened was this: when Wild heard from Mr. Kneebone that Sheppard was a suspect, he saw that this was the opportunity he had been waiting for, and accordingly sent for William Field. He then instructed Field, who after all had been his agent for years, to find out where the goods were hidden, make an offer for them, and at the same time to find out as many details as he could how the burglary had been done. Then he was to take the goods by night and bring them to him, and together they could work out the details of the story to be told in court. In the event, Sheppard and Blueskin got in touch with Field, which made the job easier, and were only too glad to tell him how they had 'put one over' on the old man, Kneebone.

Meanwhile, however, Sheppard and Blueskin had committed other robberies, two of them on Hampstead Heath. On 19 July they attacked a lady in her coach, but found only 5s., and on the 20th they attacked a drunken attorney-cum-chandler called Pargiter, whom Blueskin knocked into a ditch. The man would have been drowned in the mud, but Sheppard jumped in and held his head up until they could pull him out. The next morning, while Pargiter was exaggerating his sufferings to some farmers and showing them the spot where he had been beaten half to death 'by two burly Soldiers', two actual Grenadiers happened to pass by, and were arrested on Pargiter's identification.

On the night of 22 July, Wild found Edgworth Bess in a brandy shop near Temple Bar, took her down to his office and frightened her into telling him that Sheppard was hiding in the house of Blueskin's mother in Rosemary Lane, Wapping. Next morning, he sent Quilt Arnold down. Arnold burst open the door. Sheppard presented a pistol at his chest, but it flashed in the pan, and he was taken to New Prison. The next day he was brought before Justice Blackerby and, having confessed three robberies, was transferred to Newgate. Mr. Kneebone visited him there and asked him why he had repaid his kindness in this way. Sheppard wept and begged him to use his influence to have the heavy chains and fetters taken off. Mr. Kneebone asked the turnkey to remove them, but the request was refused.

In the meantime, Jack's brother Thomas had been sentenced to transportation.

On 1 August, there was an Instalment of Knights of the Garter at Windsor, and Wild, as he did every year, went down to supervise his men. An enormous amount of jewellery was stolen this year, and Roger Johnson alone was believed to have made off with £3,000 worth, including a necklace belonging to Lady 'C—n' valued at £500. On another evening he succeeded in picking the Prince of Wales's pocket by 'accidentally' tripping him up as he passed through the crowds. It would seem that Roger Johnson had got himself an entrée into court in the first place by bribing one of the Knight-Marshal's men, whom he met in the 'Duke of Gloucester' tavern in Pall Mall (the same that had let its windows at £100 apiece for Marlborough's funeral), with £5 to take him into St. James's Palace and inform the Yeomen Guards that he was some foreign ambassador. Thus he was able to follow the Court to Windsor. However, more far-sighted than most thieves, Johnson gave the jewellery to Wild a piece at a time, so that Wild was forced to pay higher prices for them. Further, it made it extremely difficult for Wild to return the jewellery to the proper owners in a convincing manner, so that by February 1725, when Wild was arrested, the greater part of the goods had still not been found. This was a major reason why 'the Quality', who came flocking to his office in the latter part of August, turned against Wild during the autumn.[6]

According to the *Flying Post* of 11 January 1729, it was at this Instalment that Wild met John Gay. In discussing the 'Origin of the well-known English Opera that gave the Kingdom so much

Diversion last Winter and is now acted by Pigmies' (i.e. *The Beggar's Opera*), the article said that John Gay and a friend went to Windsor for the Instalment and could not find lodgings anywhere in town, until at one tavern, a gentleman, who was alone upstairs awaiting company, sent down word that his room was at their service. After a talk, they found they were in 'Conversation with the genuine Peachum, who discours'd with great Freedom on his Profession, and set it in such a Light, that the poet imagin'd he might work up the incidents of it for the stage. . . .' The story goes on to say that Gay plied Jonathan Wild with wine, and pretended that he and his companion were sharpers belonging to no gang. He met Wild later, and gave him some objects which he pretended to have stolen.

It is the kind of story which could just be true, though it is doubtful if Wild was taken in. What is more probable is that, like many men of his type, he had a secret admiration for writers and poets, especially successful ones, and that when he found himself in company with the famous John Gay, he was unable to control the impulse to boast and talk too much. At the same time, he was canny enough to play along.

Wild returned to London in the second week of August (during which time a saw, a picklock and other instruments of escape had been found in Sheppard's bedding) and a letter dated the 11th shows that he was still having trouble with the Earl of Dartmouth:

To the Right Honble: The Lord Dartmouth
   att Sandall Hall in
     STAFFORDSHIRE,

My Lord,
   Some time Agoe your Lordship Signifyed that you had lost Some writings, which I Endeavoured to discover and after the Reward of 10 Guineas was published, they demanded 20 for themselves, which Your Stewart proposed to pay in part, if he cou'd see all the writings, which were Considerably more than your Lordship at first Seem'd to Mention, and had your Stewart paid all the money down your Lordship undoubtedly wou'd have had them before now, I was upwards of Six pound out of pockett, and I wou'd Still Endeavour to procure them for Your Lordship wou'd you please to order any one Else to me than your Stewart, he allways making so many triffling and

Needless Excuses and putt off's in paying the money and
Expences I have been at. Mr. Wolley's Man James Bidgen was
with me last Sunday and told me that your Lordship wanted to
hear further from me, which is the Occasion of troubling your
Lordship with this, and shou'd your Lordship please to order
Your Commands to be signifyed they shall be faithfully
obeyed by

> Your Lordships
> Most Obedient & Dutifull
> Humble Servant
>
> JONATHAN WILD

That is the last we hear of the matter, though Wild was to write to
the Earl again under very different circumstances.

The next day the Sessions came on at the Old Bailey. The two
Grenadiers who had been arrested on Pargiter's identification
were tried, but as they brought a large number of witnesses—
colonels, majors, captains, a clergyman and others—to prove their
honesty and their innocence, they were acquitted. One, however,
who besides being a Grenadier was a skilled translator of Latin
and Greek and a knowledgeable archaeologist, was ill with gaol
fever, and although the King ordered his personal physician, Dr.
Hans Sloane, to attend him, he died within a fortnight.

Sheppard was then tried for three robberies, acquitted of two
and, after Field and Wild had said their pieces, condemned on the
third. The Court was still at Windsor, and so the Recorder's report
was not dealt with until the night of the 22nd, and the Dead
Warrants did not come down to Newgate until the 30th. That
evening, assisted by Edgworth Bess, another girl from the 'Black
Lion' called Polly Maggot, and a cell-mate called Fowles, Sheppard cut away a bar in the door leading from the Condemned Hold
passage into the Lodge, squeezed through the gap and, covering
himself with a long cloak, walked out of the prison. At that moment,
the turnkeys were all at the other end of the Lodge, round Mrs.
Spurling's Tap, 'concerting Measures for his farther Security'.

Wild found Edgworth Bess next morning and had her committed to Newgate by Sir Francis Forbes. There she was given a
series of purges to make her talk, but it was obvious that she had
no idea where Sheppard was.

He was free for ten days, and on the morning he should have
been hanged (4 September) the *London News* printed a letter

supposedly from him to 'Jack Ketch' (the hangman), signed 'with regards to Mr. Ordinary and Mr. Applebee' (who had already bought the rights to Sheppard's dying speech). In fact Sheppard was in Northampton and did not return to London until the 8th. Wild had gone off to Stourbridge; it was said he had followed a false scent after Sheppard, but it is more likely that he went to Stourbridge, as he did every September, in his armour and with his bodyguard, to supervise the robbing and the thief-taking.

On 10 September, the Keepers of Newgate were told that Sheppard and his partner (a butcher-boy called Page who had followed Sheppard in starry-eyed admiration) were on Finchley Common. A posse of horsemen, with armed men in coaches following behind, were sent, who spread themselves across the common in a line and advanced northwards. They soon spotted the two fugitives and caught them. All accounts agree that Sheppard was 'shock'd with the utmost Fear', 'begg'd them, for God's sake, not to shoot him on the Spot', 'was in a great Agony', 'desired they would let him live as long as he could etc.'

Once back in Newgate he seemed composed and cheerful, and betrayed poor Fowles, the man who had lifted him through the grille in the first place, without a thought. From now on he became the centre of attraction and the newspapers reported daily on his escapade and on his quick-witted cockney humour. Remarks that would have shocked the public had they come from anyone else delighted them when they were made by Sheppard: 'a File is worth all the Bibles in the World'.

On 2 October Blueskin Blake was found by Jonathan Wild, Quilt Arnold and Abraham Mendez Ceixes at a house in St. Giles's. Said Arnold, '. . . going to his Chamber-door, I bid him open it, but he swore he would not, and so I burst it open. He drew a Penknife, and swore he would kill the first Man that came in. "Then I am the first Man!" says I, "and Mr. *Wild* is not far behind, and if you don't deliver your Penknife immediately I'll chop your Arm off!" And he threw the Knife down, and I apprehended him . . .' Mendez said that on the way to Newgate they passed Mr. Kneebone's shop. '"There's the Ken!" said Mr. Wild, and Blake answered, "Say no more of that, Mr. *Wild*, for I know that I am a dead Man! But what I fear is, that I shall afterwards be carried to Surgeon's-hall and anatomized." To which Mr. *Wild* replied, "No, I'll take Care to prevent that, for I'll give you a Coffin."'

On the same day, according to the *British Journal* of 10 October, Joseph Hatfield, the criminal whose career was mentioned in Chapter III because of the light it threw on the history of thief-taking, died in Newgate, where he had been committed at the end of August for 'breaking the House of Mr. Appleby in Charter-house Square'. GD Roll 2432 (Middlesex) confirms that 'Appleby' was John Appleby, but whether or not this was Applebee the publisher is not recorded.

On the morning of the 14th, at about 6.30 a.m., Blake was brought with the other prisoners for trial and put into the Bail Dock. Jonathan Wild was walking about amongst them, holding in his hand a pint of wine. When he came to Simon Jacob (an old member of Carrick's gang) he said, 'I believe you'll not bring £40 this Time. I wish Joe (indicating *Blueskin*) was in your Case, but I'm afraid he's a dead Man: but I'll do my Endeavour to bring you off as a single Felon (i.e. *guilty of simple larceny*).' They were stand-ing 'in the little Yard just within the mid-Gate of the Sessions-House'.[7] Blueskin went up to Wild and said 'Surely you may put in a Word for me as well as another Person?' To which Wild replied 'I believe you must die. I'll send you a good Book or two, and provide you with a Coffin, and you shall not be anatomized.'

After his treatment at Wild's hands over the previous two years, this must have been the last straw. Blake seized Wild round the neck, and tried to cut his throat with a blunt penknife which he pulled from his pocket. A turnkey called Ballard pulled Blake off before he could try again, and three surgeons, Mr. Dobbins, Mr. Marten and Peter Coltheart, who were presumably waiting to give evidence at other trials, ran to the Thief-Taker's assistance. Had Wild not been wearing a 'Muslin Stock twisted in several Plaits round his Neck' and had not the knife been so blunt, Blake would have killed him. The surgeons dressed and sewed up such wound as there was, carried Wild to his coach and ordered him to bed. He was still able to speak, however and, despite the shock, had not lost his sense of humour. It happened that the Rev. Thomas Purney, the Ordinary, had come up from the country (being ill with tuberculosis) for a short visit and to attend the trial of Blueskin Blake. Seeing Wild in this condition, he went over to the coach and begged him to leave such evil company before it was too late. 'Lord!' whispered Jonathan, 'is the Man mad? What occasion would there then be for an Ordinary?'[8]

It is almost needless to say that Blake was condemned to death, but the *British Journal* (24 October) reported that '. . . the said Blueskin being lock'd up after his Tryal in the Bail Dock, together with a Woman Prisoner, till the Jury had brought in their Verdict, had the Audaciousness more than once to attempt Rudeness with her, so as to make her cry out with the utmost Violence, to the Disturbance of the Court.' At the trial Field had added in his evidence that when he had gone to pawn the goods stolen from Mr. Kneebone, Blake had been with him, but had stood 'at a little Distance' from the pawnshop. This was obviously to correct the impression people might form that Field had not stolen the goods from Kneebone but from Sheppard and Blake.

Blake had no remorse at all over cutting Wild's throat. On the contrary, 'the Villain triumph'd afterwards in what he had done, Swearing with many bloody Oaths, that if he had murder'd him, he should have died with Satisfaction, and that his Intention was to have cut off his Head, and thrown it into the Sessions House Yard among the Rabble, and curs'd both his Hand and the Knife for not Executing it Effectually!'

With Wild out of the way and the turnkeys mostly at the Sessions, Jack Sheppard made his escape the very next night (15th), although he was loaded with a huge quantity of irons— chains, fetters, padlocks and bars—which were cemented into the stone floor of 'The Castle'. This was the strongest room in the prison and it was situated half way up the Gate Tower itself. A search of the prison by the dumbfounded gaolers next morning proved that Sheppard had really forced his way up through the rooms of the Gate Tower, breaking down six iron, barred, doors, each one more formidable than the last, several secured on the *far* side with bolts and padlocks, in addition to the door locks, that he had done this without tools or tinderbox, in the total darkness of a moonless night, without being heard, and that having got on to the top of the tower, he went all the way back to his cell to fetch blankets, and with these lowered himself down and somehow reached the roof of a neighbouring house and from thence dropped down into the street. Even nowadays, when we have heard of so many skilled escapes by organized professionals, Sheppard's feat remains one of the most extraordinary of them all. The illustration (*plate 10*) shows very well the size, weight and strength of the doors he broke down, using first his handcuffs and then an iron bar he tore from the Castle chimney to break his way, by touch alone, through the stone surrounding the doors.

Thus he became the most famous man in England. Defoe says it was impossible, the next evening, to find even a porter, for they were all in the alehouses celebrating. Crowds of sightseers blocked Newgate Street, and Sheppard himself listened to ballad-singers improvising verses about his adventure.

Sheppard was out of Newgate for ten days, and he spent most of his time hiding with Kate Cook alias Mackaine and Kate Keys. Kate Cook was an old enemy of Wild's, for she had been a receiver for Elizabeth Harris and her friends in 1721, and so it was natural that she should hide Sheppard. However, he was found on 31 October very drunk in Mr. Campbell's gin-shop opposite the 'Rose and Crown' in Drury Lane. This time he was put into the Middle Stone Room and loaded with 300 lb. of irons.

The rest of his story may be told briefly, for it has been described in detail many times. His cell was constantly crowded with visitors, including a large number of clergymen who came under the pretext of saving his soul ('all Gingerbread Fellows' said Sheppard). His portrait was painted by Sir James Thornhill from a sketch he made in the prison, and it has been said that Hogarth visited him as well; but this idea, for which there is no evidence, is probably based on wishful thinking. He was taken to Westminster Hall for identification by the King's Bench Court, and among the Hardwicke Papers is a letter from the Duke of Newcastle, Secretary of State for the Southern Division, to the Attorney-General's secretary, stating that the King was anxious that this dangerous criminal should be executed without delay. Yet the rumour was going round that the King had it in mind to pardon Sheppard.

At the King's Bench (on 10 November) Sheppard pleaded for his life on the grounds that he had informed against everyone he could think of (the two women, the butcher-boy Page, Edgworth Bess, and Fowles were all waiting to be charged as his accomplices), but when he said that the only help he had received in escaping had come from Almighty God, the implied blasphemy of the remark so outraged the aged Justice Powys that further discussion was impossible. It was too late to include him in the Dead Warrant for the next execution day (tomorrow the 11th) and a special execution was ordered for Monday 16 November. As he left Westminster Hall, the Lord Chancellor, Thomas Parker Earl of Macclesfield, sent for him out of curiosity, and the pair had a short private interview. Outside there were riots. A constable had his leg broken and several people were injured in the crush.

The next day Blueskin was hanged. He lay 'in state' for a few days, and then, as the *Gentleman's York Journal* (23 November) reported:

'The Corpse of Blueskin, lately executed at Tyburn, was interred in a burying ground belonging to St. Andrew's, Holborn, being attended by a great Mob to the Grave.'

Back in his cell, Sheppard continued to admit hundreds of visitors, who were charged 3s. 6d. each by the enthusiastic turn-keys. In the midst of all this crowd, he found time to give the story of his life, for the second time, to 'Applebee's Man', who was probably Daniel Defoe. It was believed, and it was probably true, that Applebee undertook to provide Sheppard with a coffin and a funeral so that his body would not be taken for dissection to Surgeons' Hall. Defoe put into his mouth some noble sentiments regarding Jonathan Wild; and even if Sheppard may have agreed, it is doubtful that he could have expressed himself with such precise, almost pompous, exactitude:

I have often lamented the scandalous Practice of Thief-Catching, as it is call'd, and the publick Manner of offering Rewards for stol'n Goods, in Defyance of two several Acts of Parliament; the Thief-Catcher living sumptuously, and keeping publick Offices of Intelligence; these who forfeit their Lives every Day they breathe, and deserve the Gallows as richly as any of the Thieves, send us as their Representatives to Tyburn once a Month: thus they hang by proxy, while we do it fairly in Person.

At his execution there were violent riots round the gallows after a soldier cut down his body, when it stopped kicking after a quarter-of-an-hour. Unfortunately the mob had not taken the trouble to find out that the hearse-and-four waiting near the gallows had been supplied by Applebee for the express purpose of cheating the surgeons, and so, believing it to belong to the surgeons, they smashed it to matchwood. Again, two parties fought for the body. One was believed to be his gang, who were thought to have arranged a last minute rescue (though after Wild's depredations in the last two years, there was no gang left in London large or organized enough to have carried out such a ticklish enterprise), and the other a group of toughs hired by a club of 'Sporting Gentlemen', who had rented a room nearby and installed a surgeon with hot blankets to resuscitate Sheppard as soon as he was brought in. This three-cornered fight degenerated into a general mêlée, and if Sheppard was alive when he was cut down, he was finished off by being thrown about on the heads of the crowd. His body was taken to the 'Barley Mow' tavern in Long Acre, Covent Garden; but soon a rumour spread that a bailiff had taken it away by a back door to sell to the surgeons, and another mob began to form. They started by throwing bricks at the windows of houses along the street, but soon they were battering down doors with logs, and trying to set fire to the buildings they got inside. A detachment of Foot Guards was called from Savoy Barracks, but they had to fix bayonets before the mob dispersed. At last an unknown gentleman (Applebee?) arranged for the funeral to take place that very night, and Sheppard was buried, attended by a strong military guard, in the grounds of the half-built St. Martin's-in-the-Fields. His body remained there until the plot was dug up in 1866 to make room for the National Gallery.

In December, Jack Sheppard's accomplices were tried. Some, including Edgworth Bess and William Page, were transported; others were fined and imprisoned; a few were acquitted. In *The Trial of Jack Sheppard* Horace Bleakley wondered if Thomas Sheppard ever reached America. He did, though for some reason he seems to have been kept on board ship in the Thames estuary for over six months, having been taken from Newgate on 11 October, and did not reach Annapolis until 25 June 1725, on the same ship as Will Lock.

These events became the subject of a prodigious number of ballads, elegies, epitaphs, sermons, philosophical dialogues, satires and plays.

One of the earliest, called *Newgate's Garland* or *Blueskin's Ballad* came over from Dublin during the last week of November, just in time to be included in a comedy put on at the Theatre Royal, Drury Lane, called *Harlequin Sheppard*. The play was written in great haste by John Thurmond, and Colley Cibber is believed to have had a hand in the production. The play was a flop and was hissed off the stage the first night, mainly because the audience felt Sheppard deserved something better. The only bits that are remembered now are a not very authentic canting song sung by 'Frisky Moll' and written by the actor who played Blueskin, John Harper, and *Blueskin's Ballad*. This is remembered because it is believed to have been written by Jonathan Swift. It is very badly

scanned and the author had got the story wrong, for he thought
Blueskin had actually killed Wild. A few lines will show the
satirical intent of it:

> Ye Fellows of Newgate whose Fingers are nice,
> In Diving in Pockets and Cogging of Dice;
> Ye Sharpers so rich who can buy off the Noose,
> Ye honester Poor Rogues who die in your Shoes,
>> Attend and draw near,
>> Good News you shall hear
> How Honest Wild's Throat was cut from Ear to Ear
> Now Blueskin's sharp Knife has set you at Ease
> And ev'ry Man round me may rob if he please.

. . . .

> Knaves of old to hide Guilt by their cunning Inventions,
> Call Briberies Grants, and plain Robbery Pensions,
> Physicians and Lawyers who take their Degrees,
> To be learned Rogues, call their pilferings fees,
>> Since this happy Day
>> Now ev'ry one may
> Rob (as safe as in Office) upon the High-way,
> For Blueskin's sharp Penknife has set you at Ease,
> And every Man round me may rob if he please.

That indeed is the theme of all the satires inspired by Sheppard:
'Little Villains must submit to Fate, While great ones do enjoy the
World in State', and when a few months later the Earl of Macclesfield was impeached for taking bribes to the tune of £100,000 and
embezzling large amounts of public money (he was fined £30,000,
most of which was paid by the King), the satirists naturally
remembered that interview with Jack Sheppard:

> Since your Curiosity led you so far
> As to send for me to the Chancery Bar,
> To show what a Couple of Rascals we are,
>> Which no Body can deny . . .
> Were your Virtues and mine to be weigh'd in a Scale
> I fear, honest Tom, that thine would prevail,
> For you broke through all Laws while I only broke Jayl,
>> Which no Body can deny. . . .

. . . .

Tho' the Masters were Rascals, that you should swing for't
Would be damnable Hard, for your Lordship in short,
Was no more than the *Jonathan Wild* of the Court,
Which no Body can deny. . . .

Another piece ran:

> Apelles, Alexander drew,
> Ceasar is to Aurelius due,
> Cromwell in Lelys Work does shine
> And Sheppard, Thornhill, lives in thine.

The point of that might have been sharper had the artists named
been more memorable; however, the idea was copied a year later
in a dialogue 'design'd as an Imitation of *Lucian* or *Fontanelle*'
between the ghosts of Jack Sheppard and Julius Ceasar, wherein
Sheppard, who had by then been transformed into a sort of 'Don
Juan', proved that Ceasar was the greater villain. A similar idea
seems to be behind the satirical print *London Raree Shows* (*plate 9*),
which has now lost much of its point because the symbols are so
obscure in their meaning. There was an ostrich (stuffed, I think)
on exhibition at Ludgate Hill in November 1724, and two lion
cubs had recently been born in the menagerie in the Tower. Wild
can be seen on the left by Newgate postern receiving clients,
though what the burning books and globe refer to is difficult to
say. The ostrich may have been intended as Walpole, to show a
man who was willing to swallow anything, but why the lion cubs
should be hanging I have no idea.

Jack Sheppard provided a debating-point for those who
believed that a society in which Ministers of State who swindled
the nation out of millions of pounds were let off with fines, while
poor wretches who stole a shilling were hanged, was unjust and
absurd; and the idea that there was no difference between highwaymen and statesmen remained popular among writers for the
rest of the century: indeed, it became so obvious in Fielding's
novel *Jonathan Wild the Great* that it spoiled the story. Nevertheless,
the charge was unanswerable, and perhaps because it is so
unanswerable people who still hold such sentiments today are
regarded as naïve.

Of all the people involved with Wild, Sheppard is the most
puzzling. It has been said that he became a popular hero not
because of his escapes but because of his small size, dapper

appearance and cool wit: a perfect Cockney Sparrow. Had surly bruisers like Robert Wilkinson or John Malhoney escaped twice from Newgate in that way, would they have had a hundred ballads sung about them, and their portraits under every maid's pillow? Yet, the closer our sources are to the actual events, the more unsympathetic they make Sheppard appear. In the earliest accounts he is seen as a cold, unscrupulous, vengeful guttersnipe, who hurt most the very people who did him the greatest kindnesses. Yet when he betrayed his companions (as his brother had betrayed him), begged for his life and wept in public, or made blasphemous jokes, the public applauded with delighted admiration. His weeping was seen as no more than the device of a cunning rogue, his betrayals as natural political moves, and his blasphemies as proof of an underlying honesty.

Sheppard is an early example of what publicity can do. An 'image', in the modern sense of the word, was created for him by Defoe because his escapes had been truly heroic. With that extraordinary flair for capturing the popular imagination, the author of *Robinson Crusoe* and *Moll Flanders* pulled off another trick, and Jack Sheppard, the diminutive Cockney Hercules, was born.

The failure of *Harlequin Sheppard* only twelve days after Sheppard's death led to the abandonment of a rival production called *The Prison Breaker*, in which the villain, 'Wile', symbolized the evil City government. A number of ideas in this play, including Jack and his two mistresses, and its general atmosphere were used by John Gay when at last he wrote the *Beggar's Opera*. Although the original idea for this is said to have been given to Gay by Swift, I feel certain that it was these events which followed so shortly upon one another—his meeting with Wild, Jack Sheppard's escapes and Wild's own fall a few months later—that put the story together for him.

While *The Beggar's Opera* since its first roaring success has been adapted for every conceivable purpose from light entertainment to revolutionary propaganda, Jack Sheppard was remembered only as one of the more striking characters in the *Newgate Calendar*, until Harrison Ainsworth wrote his famous and very unhistorical romance about him in 1839. This in turn started something of a 'Jack Sheppard' cult in the theatre. In 1839-40, nine dramatized versions of the story were produced in London alone, at the 'Adelphi', 'Sadler's Wells', 'The Surrey', 'The Garrick', Drury

Lane, 'The Pavilion', 'The Queen's', the 'City of London' and 'Queen Victoria's Own Theatre' (the original Old Vic). Several of the people who played Sheppard were women, and thus 'Jack Sheppard' was found to be easily adaptable to music-hall, burlesque and pantomime.

By the end of the century, 'Little Jack Sheppard' (played by a girl), Jonathan Wild, Quilt Arnold, Abraham Mendez, William Field and the rest had become as remote from their originals as Dick Whittington and Ali Baba. It was a *historical* injustice, perhaps, but certainly not a *poetic* one, that Wild's posthumous fame was bound to, and even depended on, Jack Sheppard's. So long as Jack was a standard pantomime hero, Wild remained a standard pantomime villain, and his name was known to everyone in London. He was the great 'Double-Crosser', a figure of fun whose nefarious schemes were foiled again at every exit. His 'business', which included gloves with detachable fingers and a portable snowstorm carried in his snuff-box, which he threw over himself to cool his transports of rage, was suggested by the topics of the day:

> Yet all the while I've a manner and style
> Which I flatter myself must please,
> The things that I say bring Barons to bay
> And Duchesses down to their knees.
> I am ready and smart with my hand on my heart,
> And the agony duly piled;
> In the popular craze of bygone days
> I'm JONATHAN OSCAR WILD!

With the decline of the music-hall, Sheppard and Wild were gradually forgotten for the second time. Jack remained as a vague memory in London folklore because, as 'one of us', he had performed a great, heroic feat, both on stage and in history. What Wild had done in history was not so easy to explain; in fact, no one had ever properly explained it. He receded into the gaslight limbo with Sir Jasper and Sir Montmorency.

May it please Your Lordsp

I doe not doubt but that your Lordship will be surprized at my presumeing to write to you, but I cannot but hope your Lordsp will pardon me for soe doeing, because I am compell'd to seek Protection, by the Violent Prosecution of some Magistrates— (whom I never offended) who have Encouraged severall Notorious Thieves to Swear against mee, and to Quallify them to be Legall Evidences, have procured his Majesties most Gracious Pardon for them, for Crimes for which they have been Condemned,— Tho' when this is done, all they can or dare pretend to swear, Amounts to no more then that they have paid back Goods to me, which they had Stollen, and which I gott restored to the right Owners, and for this my Service, the Mistaken Zeale of those Gentlemen hurries them on to seek my ruine: But if Your Lordship — would be pleased to give me a Letter to such person as you shall Judge proper to hear and redress me, I am Confident that the Designes of my Enemyes will be frustrated, and I thereby at Liberty to Discover Apprehend and Convict — Numbers of Notorious Criminalls, which will be great Service to the Publick, And for which Your Lordship will merite thanks and also the hearty Prayers for your Lordships Long Life and Prosperity, by

March 23. 1724/5

My Lord

Your Lordships most Obedient, and most humble Supplicant & Servt

Jonathan Wild

13 A letter begging the Earl of Dartmouth's protection, written
when Wild was beginning to despair in Newgate

14 Sir William Thomson, the City Recorder, who sentenced so
many of Wild's victims, and finally Wild himself, to death

{ XX } *The Arrest*

The newspaper and pamphlet writers of the early eighteenth century, despite their fondness for ceremony and legal niceties, were not exact when it came to dates and the passage of time. They used such expressions as 'lately', 'soon', 'a while' and 'the late' with the same optimistic vagueness and inconsistency that one finds among the semi-literate poor of Mediterranean countries even today. Because our knowledge of the dates is so imprecise, it is difficult to untangle the complicated and at the end nightmarish events that led to the death of Jonathan Wild. No one who has written an account of them, from the editor of *Select Trials* in 1735 to F. J. Lyons two hundred years later, has made much use of the newspaper reports of the day or even glanced at the actual documents of the case in the sessions records. These throw new light on the affair and reveal a different and more dramatic picture to the one we are familiar with; but, as always happens with new light, the old and simple pattern is confused by new details and unwelcome cross-shadows.

It will be remembered that *c.* 1722 Wild bought a new and larger ship for £500 in which, with Roger Johnson as captain, he sent 'hot' stolen goods to Antwerp, Flushing and Ostend, and that on the return journeys Johnson brought in contraband lace, linen, spirits and 'right Dutch Condoms'. 'H.D.' tells us that Johnson had a warehouse 'within forty Miles of Newington

Butts', and a detail I shall come to in a moment suggests that it was in fact in Southwark. Such places in the east and south of London were not uncommon, and I myself once lived in a house in Butcher Row, Stepney, built *c.* 1704 by a retired sea-captain, which had enormous cellars and a secret passage for smugglers going underground to the Thames. The entrance to the passage can still be seen.

Trade went well for about two years, though there were mishaps and adventures. On one occasion, the ship was blown off course into the Channel and boarded by officers from Dover. Johnson invited them into his cabin for a drink and then, putting his back against the door, covered them with two pistols. He landed them, frightened but unharmed, at Dunkirk and then sailed on for London.[1] The real trouble began when two pieces of Holland linen were lost on a return journey and Johnson stopped the value of them out of the mate's wages. This mate, it happened, was or became friendly with Tom Edwards, the waggon-lay expert and proprietor of the 'Goat' in Long Lane, Smithfields, where Wild used to do much of his business. It was also the place Hitchen described in *The Regulator*. For some reason, Edwards was an enemy of Johnson. The two men informed the Customs House that on such-and-such a date, 'Captain' Roger Johnson would be sailing up the Thames with a cargo of contraband.

The sloop was boarded at Gravesend, 'clamped with the broad R' (*runner*) and Johnson was cast in the Court of Exchequer for £700 damages. A report in the *British Journal* of 6 April 1723, which says that a sloop was boarded at Gravesend by two Land Waiters, Mr. Knight and Mr. Beresford, and seized with a cargo of Flanders lace and Hague whisky, may refer to this incident, but I think it is more likely that it occurred in the first half of 1724.

Edwards then went to a magistrate and procured against Johnson a warrant of arrest on a charge of felony, probably on some information revealed by the smuggling incident.

Edwards had a friend called Butler who kept an alehouse called the 'Black Lion' in the Strand at the corner of Castle Court. Now, Butler had a brother Thomas, who worked for Wild at one time and another and in January 1724 had been indicted of theft and sentenced to transportation.[2] He was kept in Newgate for the April Sessions and indicted of fraud but acquitted. I shall return to his subsequent fate in a moment.

It was when coming out of the 'Black Lion' that Edwards saw

Johnson in the Strand, seized him and carried him back to the alehouse to await a constable. Johnson somehow managed to get word to Wild, who immediately procured a warrant against Edwards from one of his 'own' J.P.s, probably Justice Gwyn Vaughan, who lived round the corner in Southampton Street, and sent a man to rescue Johnson. The surprised Edwards found himself hustled off to the Wood Street Compter.

Edwards sent for help to Mary Wild's aunt, the Newgate Tap woman, Mrs. Spurling. She, as hostile as ever to Jonathan, bailed Edwards out and told him the location of one of Wild's warehouses where, at that moment, a large quantity of stolen goods were 'planted' (which in those days meant 'hidden'). Edwards obtained another warrant, entered the warehouse with a posse, and seized them. Wild, who probably enjoyed this sort of thing, took out an action against Edwards in the name of Roger Johnson, to whom he pretended the goods belonged. He arrested Edwards and had him committed to the Marshalsea, which suggests that the warehouse was in the Southwark area and even at Newington Butts, as 'H.D.' hinted. Thus he turned the tables on Edwards a second time by claiming that Edwards was trying to acquire a quantity of stolen goods in order to dispose of them privately, whilst he, the famous Thief-Taker, was recovering them by law so that they could be returned to their rightful owners. This protected Wild but seriously implicated Johnson, for he was now liable to be charged with theft or receiving of goods to an enormous value.

Edwards, however, was in the Marshalsea for one night only, for Mrs. Spurling bailed him out a second time. Edwards vowed revenge and, over the next weeks, gathered as many 'Informations' against Johnson as he could and started a search for him.

Select Trials says that Edwards searched for Johnson 'a long Time' before he found him after this. 'A long Time' might mean anything from six weeks to two years. The accounts which tell of these events (notably 'H.D.', *Weighley alias Wild* and *Select Trials* despite its phrase 'a long Time') give the impression that they occurred not long before Wild's own arrest, which would mean the summer and autumn of 1724, when Wild was already preoccupied with protecting Johnson after the Windsor robberies, with the Earl of Dartmouth and his steward, with Jack Sheppard and, of course, with 'Blueskin' Blake, but it would exclude the days between 14 October and 1 November, when Wild was lying in bed with his throat cut. For the moment, however, we must return to Thomas Butler.

Among the Middlesex Sessions Papers* for December 1724 is an undated Court Order to William Pitt, Keeper of Newgate, to produce Thomas Butler and show him 'in his usual Habit' to Mr. Bestwick, broker, for identification. Mr. Bestwick's identification, nevertheless, would be valid only in the presence of two Justices of the Peace. Butler, it added, was a returned transportee. On 4 December Butler was indicted of stealing goods, value 12s., from John Wells, and sentenced to transportation.[3]

Meanwhile, there is a second Court Order in the same papers, undated, to William Pitt and 'Bodenham Rews his Turnkey' to attend Hick's Hall on 5 December at three o'clock 'to show why they or one of them refused or *wilfully avoyded* to give accompt unto William William and John Beaver Esq: two of his Mat^ies Justices of the Peace for this County or one of them that Thomas Butler a prisoner in the afd. Gaol had formerly been a prisoner there for felony and was returned from Transportation before the expiration of the term of yeares for which he was transported as being a convict of felony'. It is signed 'Walter'.

Peter Walter was the new Clerk of the Peace who had just succeeded Simon Harcourt, and it would seem that he has written the names of the two J.P.s wrongly. I can find no record of any Justice called 'John', or 'Jonathan' (as it is written on the Middlesex Calendar for February 1725) Beaver, but plenty of documents signed by *Joseph* Beaver. Similarly 'William William' should be William *Wickham*, for so he signed himself and was called on all other documents, except the same Middlesex Calendar for February 1725.

The first puzzle here is that there is no record that Butler *was* transported after April 1724, although he was sentenced to be so. However, with luck he could just have managed the two-way journey in time, as Moll King, John Filewood and others proved. The second is that there is no record of when Butler was committed to Newgate before December 1724, and the earliest mention of him as being in Newgate, apart from the Orders quoted above, seems to be 12 February 1725, when he was bailed out, a point I shall return to later. The third is that Butler, as a prisoner sentenced to transportation, *must* have been in Newgate from at

* Miscellaneous documents relating to the Sessions, not the printed *Sessions Papers* (see *Bibliography IV*).

least 4 December (when he was tried at the Old Bailey) until 12 February. Yet later it was claimed that he was at Wild's house on 24 December, Christmas Eve. On that day, John Tidman, a corn-chandler of Giltspur Street, had his pocket picked in Cheapside, near St. Mary Bow Church and lost a pocket-book containing £116 10s. od. He went to Jonathan Wild's that afternoon. Wild took £50 on account and returned the bank-note, apparently still on the same day. Butler said that he had seen Wild 'committ the Pockett-book to the Flames'⁴ when Tidman was out of the room, though how Butler was out of Newgate is not explained. There are other mysteries about Butler, but I mention this case here because the documents arising from it and related cases seem to bear out what Wild complained of later: that he was being persecuted by certain magistrates, whom he had 'never harmed'. The names of these magistrates are, to name three that appear frequently on the documents against Wild at this time: Joseph Beaver, William Wickham and E. Ridley. Leonard Street is possibly a fourth. He lived at Pallgrave Court, Temple Bar, but I have not been able to discover the addresses of the others. It would appear then that already at the end of November 1724 these three magistrates were trying to build a case against Wild and believed that Thomas Butler was the man they needed for it. It is possible that their informant was Butler's brother at the 'Black Lion' in the Strand, and that the whole thing arose out of the fracas with Johnson. Butler seems to have been the rope in a tug-of-war between them and the Newgate turnkeys who 'wilfully avoyded' to produce him before the Sessions began on 4 December. That would explain why he was not convicted of returning from transportation on the same day, for unless he was identified, he could not be charged. As for the Newgate turnkeys, the reason for their unco-operative behaviour will become clearer in a little while.

Where Roger Johnson was at this time is not known, but his wife of these years, Rosamond, was staying at Jonathan's own house. I mentioned earlier that Roger Johnson, besides running goods to Holland, ran fugitives and immigrants to and fro from Ireland. One of these was a man called Henry Kelley. In July 1724 he had been convicted of trying to pass off as a gold Broad Piece what was really a gilded shilling from the time of Henry VIII.⁵ On 22 January 1725 this Kelley paid a visit to Mrs. Johnson at Wild's house. A little while later an Irish girl called Margaret

Morphew arrived and gave Mary Wild a pair of shoes as a present. In gratitude, Wild suggested that they stole some lace from a shop kept by an old woman and her daughter, who were both 'blind' (which probably meant short-sighted, for Mrs. Statham, as her name was,* seemed to manage all right in the court). They stole the lace while Jonathan waited at the street corner as a look-out. At his house in the Old Bailey, he gave them three guineas and four broad pieces for it. Mrs. Statham consulted Wild in the usual manner and he promised to see what he could do.

Several of the pamphleteers writing after Wild's death assumed that Kelley and Thomas Butler had been accomplices, and that Margaret Morphew, egged on by Kelley and Butler, gave Mary Wild the shoes for the precise purpose of getting on the right side of Jonathan, in the hope that he would put them on to some crime by way of thanks, which would in turn enable them to impeach him of capital felony. 'Remember Filewood!' they said to one another. 'He was betrayed simply because Jonathan wanted the diamond-hilted sword he had stolen at the Opera. Soon it will happen to us!' And so when Wild did put them on to a robbery, he fell for a trick of which he himself had been a master for years. However, I do not think the reality was as neat and poetically just as that.

Then at the beginning of February, Thomas Edwards came across Johnson on the road at Stratford East, arrested him, sent for a constable and took him to the 'Three Crowns' alehouse in the village. One would have thought that by now Edwards had learned his lesson, but while he, the constable and Johnson were drinking at Johnson's expense, a message was again sent to Wild.

Stratford is about five and a half miles from the Old Bailey. Assuming that a rider could make the journey in just over half an hour (for he could hardly gallop once inside Aldgate because of the crowded streets) and that Wild took ten minutes to get swords, guns and horses ready, Johnson must somehow have been able to delay Edwards and the constable for an hour and a quarter.

What Wild did when he arrived with Quilt Arnold and a posse at Stratford is not absolutely clear. Some accounts say that he started a riot in the street and that Johnson escaped in the con-

* From *Select Trials* onwards, the names are given as 'Kelly', 'Murphey' and 'Stetham' On the documents, including the indictments, they are everywhere: Kelley, Morphew (probably pronounced 'Murphey', however) and Statham.

fusion, though it is hard to see how a riot could be started in a sleepy village street. Others say that he attacked Edwards and the constable openly with pistols and rescued him by force. Whatever happened, Johnson got away a second time and fled, with another thief, to Flanders. His gratitude to Wild, however, must have been tempered by the fact that earlier Wild had cold-bloodedly 'framed' him as the owner of the warehouse at Newington Butts and that he was now a wanted man as a result.

Some accounts say that Wild then left London and hid somewhere in the country; *Select Trials* says he absconded for three weeks. 'H.D.' says that it was the indignation caused by the trick he had played over the Newington Butts warehouse that stirred the authorities against him:

A Proceeding so bare-faced and impudent, put certain Persons upon finding out Means of bringing so sturdy a Rogue to Justice; *Jonathan* was threaten'd out loud, which occasion'd a Report all over the Town, that he was fled from Justice; upon which occasion, he published a bullying Advertisement in some of the News Papers, offering a Reward of ten Guineas to any Person who shou'd discover the Author of such a scandalous Report; at the same Time he run into all publick places to shew himself, and let the World see that he was not run away as was reported—Yet, in the midst of all this blustering he was seiz'd and committed to Newgate.

On the morning of 15 February, Mrs. Statham called on Wild at his house in the Old Bailey to ask about her lace. He told her that he was on the track of it and said he would get in touch with her. Shortly afterwards, however, Wild was arrested by Thomas Jones, High Constable of Holborn, and 'the two Willises' (two constables of the Borough). *Select Trials* says this was at his own house. The author of *Lives of the Most Remarkable Criminals* says that Wild was arrested somewhere near Wood Street, and thence taken to the Rose Street Spunging House. 'There I myself saw him, sitting in the Kitchen at the Fire, waiting the Leisure of the Magistrate, who was to examine him.'

A crowd gathered outside. Since the Sheppard and Blueskin affair, popular opinion had turned violently against Jonathan Wild, just as the 'Quality' had begun to look at him askance since his failure to return the jewels stolen at Windsor at about the same time. What a year before might have been a fairly sympathetic mob was now a threatening one. They forced their way into the kitchen and Jonathan, who was unable to walk owing to a sudden attack of gout, argued with them from his chair. The stilted and formal speech which the same author says Wild delivered to them can only be a later reconstruction. Yet it probably gives the gist of what he said, and if one imaginatively puts in the interruptions, repetitions and general pushing and shoving that are always a part of such undignified scenes, one can see the picture quite vividly:

> I wonder, good People, what is it you would see? I am a poor honest Man, who have done all I could do, to serve People when they have had the Misfortune to lose their Goods by the Villainy of Thieves. I have contributed more than any Man living, to bringing the most daring and Notorious Malefactors to Justice. Yet now, by the Malice of my Enemies, you see I am in Custody, and am going before a Magistrate who I hope will do me Justice. Why should you Insult me, therefore? I don't know that I ever injur'd any of you? Let me intreat you, therefore, as you see me Lame in Body and Afflicted in Mind, not to make me more uneasy than I can bear! If I have offended against the Law, it will punish me, but it gives you no right to use me ill, Unheard and Unconvicted.

A coach was brought for him and he was taken to the house of Sir John Fryer.

Sir John, who had been Lord Mayor in 1721 and had attended the trial of Spiggott and Cross, lost all his money in the South Sea Bubble and was now living modestly. He seems to have been an unexceptionable though rather simple man. A notebook of his, the only autobiography to have been written by any Lord Mayor of London, was bought recently by the Guildhall Library. It is not a very exciting document. His main concern is to give thanks to God for his strict upbringing. He was never allowed, he says with relief, to play with 'Loose Children', and he deeply regrets the odd moments he wasted by 'foolish Talking' with his fellow-apprentices. There are a few passages dealing with family matters and minor domestic quarrels. One cannot condemn him for that, but it is a pity that he says not one word about any of the events of these years, when he lived and worked so close to the centre of them, or about any of his contemporaries, who were hardly a dull lot, when he must have had known them so well.

On the day Wild was brought before him, Sir John Fryer was ill and he examined the great criminal sitting up in bed.

Quilt Arnold, the so-called 'Clerk of the Northern Roads', was taken the same day, examined by another magistrate, ex-Lord Mayor Sir Gerard Conyers, and committed, like Wild, to Newgate. *Select Trials* and other writers say that Wild and Arnold were taken together and both examined together by Fryer, but this seems to be contradicted by the London GD roll for February:

'Rem. 14: Jonathan Wilde & Quilt Arnold committed by Sir John Fryer Bart. & Sir Gerard Conyers Knight. Upon an Information on Oath for rescuing one Roger Johnson, a felon Convict, from a Constable who had him in Custody.'

The description of Johnson as a felon convict is odd, for he was not, so far as I can see, at that time convicted of anything. 'H.D.' says that immediately upon Wild's being committed to Newgate, an express letter was sent to Roger Johnson in Flanders, who, with his companion, 'came down to Ostend, and appear'd like Persons of Quality, told the News to all about him, and swore he'd hang both *Jonathan* and the *B*— who calls herself his Wife; so he takes a Packet and hires her for *Dover*: But, as he has not appear'd publickly in *London*, we may very well suppose that the hanging of them was the least Part of his Business.'

Messrs. Beaver, Ridley, Wickham and Street were either waiting at Newgate when Wild arrived or they went there immediately they heard the news, for the Calendar wrapped round the Middlesex GD roll for February (*2434*) says:

'Prisoner No. 31: Jonathan Wilde, Charged in Custody by L. Street, E. Ridley, Jonathan Beaver, William William Esquires upon an Information on oath for feloniously taking 3 Lottery Ticketts from a person unknown and a Bank Note of £50 from another person unknown. Dat. 15 Feb.'

Nothing more is heard of these charges and it looks as if they had been improvised to stop Wild from getting bail. On the same day, or perhaps the next, Peter Levee, the member of Burnworth's gang who had impeached John Allen for Wild, was committed 'on Suspicion of Felony' and ordered to remain in prison.

At first, the newspapers reported the bare fact of Wild's arrest:

'The Famous Jonathan Wild was on Monday committed to Newgate.' (*British Journal* 20 February.)

Then, on the 22nd, *Parker's London Post* said that Wild was charged 'with buying Jewels, knowing them to be stolen at the late Installment at Windsor'. After explaining that Wild had helped Johnson, the thief who had stolen the greater part of the jewels at Windsor, to escape, it added, 'In the Interim, he is pretty secure, and very much afflicted with the Gout, which may in time, by a Receipt from — Ketch Esq: be ('tis thought) effectually cur'd.'

On the 26th, the same paper continued:

'Various are the Opinions about the fam'd Thief-Catcher, as to his Tryal; some say it will be at Chelmsford, others at Burntwood, others here and some elsewhere. . . .'

⁊ XXI ⁊ *Out of a Hat*

The February Sessions began on the 24th. Wild had secured as Defence Counsel Serjeant Baynes and Mr. Kettleby (the same who had unsuccessfully defended the Jacobite conspirator Christopher Layer and was later to defend, successfully, the notorious Wardens the Fleet Prison, Huggins and Bambridge). It must be remembered, of course, that they could argue only on points of law, not on the facts of the crimes with which Wild might be charged. On the 24th, Wild 'enter'd his Prayer to be try'd that Sessions, or bail'd, or discharg'd'. On Friday the 27th, however, he was brought to the Sessions House again and told that none of these requests would be granted. Firstly, an Affidavit from High Constable Jones was read in court which said that there were two persons who had offered to charge Wild with capital crimes. *Select Trials* says *wrongly* that these two were probably Thomas Butler and a man called John Follard (who had been committed for two thefts). Butler, it says, was in Newgate for '*Preaching the Parson*' alias '*the Passing Lay*'. In fact, 'Preaching the Parson' and the 'Passing Lay' were not the same thing,* and Butler was not in Newgate for either of them.

* 'Preaching the Parson' was palming false money while disguised as a clergyman; 'the Passing Lay' was a form of card-sharping, similar to 'hustling' in pool billiards. Success depended on pretending to be less skilful than you really were, and then, your opponents suitably softened, winning everything. One other accomplice was needed.

What happened that morning was that Butler was pardoned of the crime for which he had been sentenced to transportation on 4 December: that is, for stealing 12*s*. from John Wells. His pardon is recorded in the Middlesex GD Book. Butler, nevertheless had another charge to answer, which was that he had stolen three South Sea Bonds from 'Major Lechmere's pockett'.

The *London* Calendar for February says that this was the crime he had been committed to Newgate for in the first place, not the theft from John Wells; but it does not say when. It also says he was to have remained as a 'Prisoner upon Orders' (i.e. remanded until something was decided) but that he was released on bail by Sir John Fryer. His recognizance in the same London GD roll shows that he was released on 12 February. This means that his pardon had already been arranged at least three days *before* Wild was arrested, and not after as all accounts say. It shows that if Wild had not rescued Johnson and been charged with that, he would have been arrested on one of several other charges; but there remains the mystery of where Thomas Butler was between 4 December, when he was sentenced to transportation, and 12 February when he was released from Newgate on bail, and of how he came to be at Wild's house on Christmas Eve. I have carefully checked to see if there were two Thomas Butlers in Newgate at the same time, but there were not.

As for Follard, although all accounts agree he was pardoned along with Butler on the same morning, he could not have been; for he was at Lincoln Fair pretending to be a gentleman of fortune, and no one had yet so much as heard of him.

All these matters were overshadowed by the dramatic entry, for the first time upon the open stage, of the City Recorder, Sir William Thomson. He presented to the Court a 'Warrant of Detainer', which set out in general terms eleven major reasons why Jonathan Wild should be kept in custody. He claimed that every one of the eleven articles was supported by sworn informations and witnesses. Of Jonathan Wild it charged:

I. That for many Years past he had been a Confederate with great Numbers of Highwaymen, Pickpockets, Housebreakers, Shop-lifters, and other Thieves.

II. That he had form'd a Kind of Corporation of Thieves, of which he was the Head or Director, and that notwithstanding his pretended Services, in detecting and prosecuting Offenders, he procured such only to be hang'd as concealed their Booty, or refused to share it with him.

III.   That he divided the Town and Country into so many Districts, and appointed distinct Gangs for each, who regularly accounted with him for their Robberies. That he had also a particular Sett to steal at Churches in Time of Divine Service: And likewise other moving Detachments to attend at Court, on Birth-days, Balls, Etc., and at both Houses of Parliament, Circuits, and County Fairs.

IV.   That the Persons employ'd by him were for the most Part Felons Convict, who had returned from Transportation before the Time, for which they were transported, was expired; and that he made choice of them to be his Agents, because they could not be legal Evidences against him, and because he had it in his Power to take from them what part of the stolen Goods he thought fit, and otherwise use them ill, or hang them as he pleas'd.

V.   That he had from Time to Time supplied such convicted Felons with Money and Cloaths, and lodged them in his own House, the better to conceal them; particularly some, against whom there are now Informations for counterfeiting and diminishing Broad Pieces and Guineas.*

VI.   That he had not only been a Receiver of stolen Goods, as well as of Writings of all Kinds, for near 15 Years past, but had frequently been a Confederate, and robb'd along with the above-mention'd convicted Felons.

VII.   That, in order to carry on these vile Practices, to gain some Credit with the ignorant Multitude, he usually carried a short Silver Staff, as a Badge of Authority from the Government, which he used to produce, when he himself was concern'd in robbing.

VIII.   That he had, under his Care and Direction, several Warehouses for receiving and concealing stolen Goods; and also a Ship for carrying off Jewels, Watches, and other valuable Goods, to Holland, where he had a super-annuated Thief for his Factor.

IX.   That he kept in Pay several Artists to make Alterations, and transform Watches, Seals, Snuff-boxes, Rings, and other

* A coin could be 'diminished' by 'sweating' or 'clipping' 'Sweating' meant shaking gold coins in a bag, collecting the dust rubbed off and making another coin from it. 'Clipping' was the same thing done with a file or clippers.

valuable Things, that they might not be known, several of which he used to present to such Persons as he thought might be of Service to him.

X.   That he seldom or never helped the Owners to the Notes and Papers they had lost, unless he found them able exactly to specify and describe them, and then often insisted on more than half the Value.

XI.   And lastly, it appears that he has often sold human Blood, by procuring false Evidences to swear Persons into Facts they were not guilty of; sometimes to prevent them from being Evidences against himself, and at other Times for the Sake of the great Reward given by the Government.

Wild was sent back to Newgate upon orders and told to be ready for his trial in the April Sessions.

And so it all came out at last. This warrant was the first official recognition of a system of crime, and for that matter crime prevention, that had been progressively refined for a century and a half, always with the connivance, and occasionally with the active support, of City Recorders. It is a pity that the original of this document was not preserved, for by what it contained it was a landmark in the history of crime and of police.

The impression given at the time was that Sir William had learned all this only in the ten days since Wild had been arrested, and had found and sworn his witnesses and drawn up the document in great haste; as such it was reported in the papers after Wild's conviction, in tones of dumbfounded astonishment. Sir William Thomson was praised thereafter by the public and by writers (including Defoe) as being the man who had uncovered and smoked out this hornets' nest of villains more dangerous than had ever been heard of before.

It should be clear by now, I think, that the generally accepted idea of Wild's history—that he continued with great success until the 'Transportation Act' (or 'Jonathan Wild Act') was passed and that he was hanged because he persisted in his folly—is a false one, even though Blackstone believed it. It derived from the early pamphlet writers, including Defoe, and their habit of treating periods of time so vaguely. Besides the countless advertisements for lost property in the newspapers, which prove that the office continued to expand mightily after the Act was passed at the end of 1717 (and this was 1725), we have now, surely, enough examples of his framing prisoners and corrupting witnesses (often not even subtly) during these last eight years to make it incredible that the Recorder did not know perfectly well what was going on. The warrant reads as if it had been carefully prepared over a long period of time. If the Recorder's claim that his charges were supported by informations sworn on oath could be proved untrue, and his cases against Wild consequently defeated, he would have become a laughing-stock. Therefore he must have had real evidence.

Probably, as so often happens, the motives that impelled the Recorder to move against Wild were not, as Defoe says, his humanity and sense of justice, but of another kind altogether. He was not a popular man; he was repeatedly accused of various kinds of corruption (e.g. the Duke of Wharton accused him of tampering with elections, and he still had to live down his defeat at the hands of Lechmere) and all biographies emphasize his greed for office and power. The magistrates who were trying to build one case or another against Wild were all Middlesex, or more exactly Westminster, magistrates. Wild was a resident of London, in the Old Bailey of all places, and as such within the Recorder's provenance. When it became evident that they might actually succeed, it also became evident that he could be accused of negligence if they were allowed to do so. For this reason, he decided to steal their fire and produced his warrant, as it were, out of a hat.

Perhaps then, the Newgate turnkeys did not wilfully avoid sending Butler to Hick's Hall at the beginning of December because Wild was bribing them, but because they were under pressure from Sir William Thomson.

On the same day, the 27th, the *British Journal* published the first of the series of articles by '*Philanthropos*' which I mentioned in the course of Chapter IV. In April the articles were collected, added to, and republished under the author's real name, Bernard de Mandeville, and entitled *An Inquiry into the Cause of the Frequent Executions at Tyburn*. At the end of the first article, the *British Journal* explained that it had been written before Wild had been committed to Newgate, and that the author was attacking not the man but 'the Thing itself, the corresponding with, and transacting Business for Rogues, with other pernicious Practices, which Jonathan was fam'd for when he was at Liberty, and *often made use of by Persons*, that ought, Long ago, to have endeavour'd to punish, than encourag'd what they knew of him.' (*My italics.*)

Like Charles Hitchen before and many others after, de Mande-ville thought that condemned criminals should be kept in solitary confinement after sentence and refused all food and drink except bread and water. This would induce repentance instead of bravado and the 'Mob' would consequently be awed by the solemnity and horror of executions. He recommended also that convicts, instead of being transported to America, should be sold as slaves to the Barbary Moors. Some of his views on people who failed to prosecute through a misguided humaneness, and on those who advertised rewards for the return of stolen goods, were repeated twenty-five years later by Henry Fielding in his *Enquiry*.[1] These articles, and the much-plagiarized pamphlet, were the first study of Wild, and all he stood for, by a serious writer.

On 5 March, *Parker's London Post* reported:

'A Pardon is passed for a Person who is capable of making great Discoveries against Jonathan Wild, and he is to be carried to Winchester to plead the same at the ensuing Assizes.'

This, of course, was Butler. However, five days later Parker corrected himself. The person who was to be sent to Winchester was a man called Rowe; with a Quack Doctor called Johnson he had robbed the Chester Mail (for which they were hanged). The first rumour gave rise to a misunderstanding which was repeated in several of the early biographies of Wild; namely, that Butler had been in Winchester Gaol all this time, where he was being held for cheating a goldsmith's widow of £50. He had fled to Winchester after stealing in the 'Feathers' alehouse in Cheapside (this probably refers to the theft of which Butler was really indicted on 4 December). Then, they go on, High Constable Jones had heard that Butler had offered information against Jonathan Wild and had sent for him to be brought to London. Butler's information was (*a*) that he had seen Wild burn Tidman's pocket-book and (*b*) that he had often been employed to rob the mails and that he used to send bills, bonds and other public securities to Wild via a woman he could produce if need be. Wild always paid her in cash and she paid Tom Butler.

This is such a mixture of truth and untruth that it is hardly worth sorting out. Follard was the man brought from the country. The story of the mails may be true or it may be due to a confusion with Rowe.

Meanwhile other people relevant to this case were being

arrested. The first two were Rosamond Johnson, Roger's wife, and Jane Blin, who may have been one of the French servants Rosamond was supposed to have ('Jeanne' Blin wrongly written). The London Sessions Book for February (Case 28) says that these two women and Jonathan Wild were charged with felony by Susannah Cowell. They were soon released, though why is not recorded, and Rosamond went straight off to Holland. Who Susannah Cowell was I have no idea.

The next was Elizabeth Duce, William Duce's widow. The *Daily Journal* thought she was taken up as an accomplice of Wild's. She may have been, but the Middlesex Calendar for February merely says that she, and our old friend Moll Harvey, were both committed for stealing sheets.

On 5 March there was another incident which was later to take on significance. Susan and Jonathan Price were brought to Newgate on suspicion of robbing the Exchequer. They were committed by Nathaniel Blackerby and Thomas Railston, the father of the Railston who was to assist in the House of Commons Enquiry on the Watch in 1770.

Then, on 6 March, William Field was arrested by Constable Robert Willis (one of the two 'Willises' who arrested Wild). Since his impeachments of all those who had contact with him in earlier days—James Dalton, Wilson, Holmar, Elizabeth Harris *et al.*—his career as an 'affidavit Man' had been crowned by the triumphs of impeaching, first, Sheppard and Blueskin, and then at Kingston three members of a new gang he had joined: Richard Evans, William Elisha and Richard Woodman, all three, it was alleged, on Wild's behalf. Now he was charged with receiving stolen goods found in his custody and with stealing a handkerchief (value 1s.— just enough to hang him) by Abraham Mendez Ceixes. Mendez's recognizance, which was taken by Sir Francis Forbes, is the document by which I discovered Mendez's full name and address, and it is signed by Isaac Mendez Ceixes, Jacob Chaves and Robert Willis.

In the midst of all these comings and goings, Wild, in Newgate, sent for Mrs. Statham on 10 March and returned the lace to her. He insisted that she gave a porter ten guineas, for without the money, he said, the thieves would not have returned the lace. He refused a reward very carefully, however, and asked only for her prayers. All accounts, including *Select Trials*, say that this was his fatal mistake, for it saved Sir William Thomson the trouble of pressing the other charges and allowed him to seize on this one. The documents, however, seem to tell a different story.

The next day, Butler was issued with another recognizance 'on Pain of £100, to appear against Jonathan Wyld for several felonies'. It is signed 'Wm. Wickham'. The Westminster magistrates had no intention of abandoning the race at this stage.

Then Follard was brought to London from Lincoln. *Parker's London Post* reported the event on 29 March:

'We hear a Material Evidence against Mr. Wild, was fetched up last Week from a County Fair in Lincolnshire, who goes by the name of Sir John Pollyard, and was one of Jonathan's Right Hand Men: he is secured in New Prison till his Tryal, when he is either to Hang or be Hang'd.'

The phoney title suggests that it was Follard and not Butler (as *Select Trials* thought) who had been at the 'Passing Lay'. If Follard was taken at a fair, and only the week before, he could not have been in gaol and High Constable Jones could not have known on 27 February that this man was going to inform against Wild. Who then was Jones's second Evidence? I think it was William Field, but my reasons will be better explained when we see what happened between Field and Mendez in April.

Wild must have heard that the King (which is to say, the Privy Council) was arranging to pardon Follard as well as Butler, for on 23 March he wrote to the Earl of Dartmouth again:

May it please your Lordship.

I doe not doubt that your Lordship will be surrprized at my presumeing to write to you, but I cannot but hope your Lordship will pardon me for soe doeing, becuase I am Compell'd to Seek Protection, by the Violent Prosecution of Some Magistrates (whom I never Offended) who have Encouraged severall Notorious Thieves to Swear against me, and to Quallify them to be Legall Evidences, have procured his Majesties Most Gracious Pardon for them, for Crimes for which they have been Condemned, Tho' when this is done, all they can or dare pretend to swear, Amounts to no more than that they have paid back Goods to me, which they had Stollen, and which I gott restored to the right Owners, and for this my Service, the Mistaken zeale of those Gentlemen hurries them on to seek my ruine: But if your Lordship would be pleased to give me a Letter to such person as you shall Judge proper to hear and

redress me, I am confident that the Designes of my Enemyes
will be frustrated, and I thereby at Liberty to Discover Apprehend and Convict Numbers of Notorious Criminalls, which
will be a great Service to the Publick; And for which your
Lordship will merite thanks and also the hearty Prayers for
your Lordships long Life and Prosperity, by

    My Lord
    Your Lordships most Obedient,
    and most humble Supplicant & Servt.
        JONATHAN WILD.

If the letter is in his handwriting, it shows signs of weariness and
exhaustion, for it is thinner and more spidery than that of the
other letters and documents. The tone, like that of his words at
the Spunging House in Rose Street, is of a man bewildered by
unprovoked attack: people were after him, yet he had never
offended a single one of them! His contemporaries put this sort of
thing down to his 'matchless Impudence and Hypocrisy' and they
may have been right. But hypocrisy is never a simple thing and it
is just as likely that during the long struggle with Carrick's gang
from 1722–4, he came to believe in himself, as I have said, as a
public servant; and that when that struggle reached its belated
climax in the Sheppard and 'Blueskin' affair, his near-martyrdom
finally convinced him that as the only effective arm of the law he
was above the law.

His devious character, his lameness, the whining tone of his
letters (with their faint undertone of insolence), and his endless
capacity for treachery and legal tongue-twisting, conjure up the
picture of an evil, bent, sallow-faced, hand-washing, creepy-
crawly, like Uriah Heap; and as such F. J. Lyons portrayed him.
The contemporary documents and accounts show that he was
nothing of the kind. He was stocky, strong, active, his contemporaries were surprised by his physical bravery, and even Defoe
admitted 'he had a Kind of brutal Courage'. He was talkative,
humorous in a dry and cruel way, a hard drinker of wine, and his
personal magnetism is attested by the awe in which the criminals
held him, by the number of women who were his mistresses and,
in some cases, remained loyal to him to the end, and by the way he
captivated the 'Quality'. By 1725 he had two fractures in his skull
and his bald head was covered with silver plates. He had seventeen
wounds in various parts of his body from swords, daggers, and

gun-shots, contracted in the innumerable affrays, set-to's and riots he always seemed to be engaged in. His throat had been cut. He was suffering from some side-effect of syphilis and an incompetent attempt at curing it; on top of all, he had gout, he was in prison and his world had unaccountably started to collapse about his ears. Even if, in the Master Felon's Side of Newgate, he was more comfortable than most prisoners, with a room to himself, a servant or two, freedom to walk up and down the narrow Press Yard all day, and money to buy what he needed, it is not surprising that from the moment he was arrested, 'all his Cunning and Courage forsook him'. For some time now, he had been losing touch with reality.

On 1 April Abraham Mendez Ceixes was committed to the New Prison, as Prisoner No. 86, by Justice Leonard Street, having been charged on oath of William Field with receiving stolen goods.[2] William Field was tried first at the next Sessions (7 April) and acquitted, perhaps because Mendez's evidence was not at that moment to be credited. One cannot prove a negative, of course, and in trying to say what had really happened one must fall back on a guess. The guess that best fits the facts is that Field, now that everybody was trying to get in on the act, decided to join the rush to impeach Wild and made overtures to High Constable Jones. Being so well-known as a liar and a thoroughly bad character, he found that Jones did not, as he had hoped, fall over him in gratitude but, on the contrary, delayed and temporized. Mendez heard of this and trumped up some charges which he hoped would stick: a capital one of privately stealing from the person (himself) to the value of 1s., one of receiving stolen goods (as Field was a known receiver) and two of theft against Sarah Field (who was either William's sister or latest wife) to act as a safeguard; all attested by his brother Isaac and Jacob Chaves. From Newgate, Field sought out one of the Westminster magistrates who were searching for information against Wild and his immediate entourage and found Leonard Street. This is strongly indicated by the fact that neither Mendez nor Field, who were now both residents of the City of London, lived anywhere near Street's district, which was Temple Bar. The normal procedure would have been to have contacted the City magistrate already involved with the case, who was Sir Francis Forbes. Field's case, and all his subsequent cases, are on London Rolls, but Mendez's commitment was to the New Prison and is on a Middlesex Roll.

Whatever Field had to say against Mendez could not have been very much, for there is no record that Mendez was indicted, and he was out by August, when he indicted Field again of receiving stolen goods. This time Field was caught at last, fined ten marks (£6 13s. 4d.) and sentenced to one year in Newgate and to remain until the fine was paid. The final thing which makes me believe that Field was Jones's second intended witness against Wild is a remark the Ordinary of Newgate made in his account of James Dalton, after Dalton was hanged in May 1730. He says that Dalton was once in a gang with '*Fulsome* and *Field* (who were Evidences against *Jonathan Wild* and *Blueskin*)'. Field was not an evidence against Wild, only against Blueskin. But Field *was* an evidence, or tried to be, against Wild's chief assistant Mendez, and he probably told Dalton that he had been, or tried to be, an evidence against the famous Jonathan Wild as well. By the time the Ordinary had written it down the whole tale had become confused.

William Field was indicted again several times in the late 1720s and always acquitted, until he was at last convicted of theft and transported to America. He arrived at Annapolis on the *Forward* galley on 12 June 1730, after a terrible journey in which 32 out of 119 convicts had died on the voyage.[3] That is the last heard of William Field, the notorious betrayer of Jack Sheppard.

Meanwhile on 1 April Mr. Tidman and a Mary Blakesly, of the 'Baptist's Head' in the Old Bailey (which Wild used as an emergency bank), were given recognizances to appear at the next Sessions or 'at the King's Bench next Term' and give evidence about that bank-note of £116 10s. Mary Blakesly's recognizance was taken by Sir John Fryer and Tidman's by 'Joe: Beaver and Wm. Wickham'.

Quilt Arnold appealed for bail again and was refused. His petition, or rather the file copy of it, is signed 'QUILT M. ARNOLD his Mark'.

Then, on the 7th, on the same morning as William Field, John Follard alias Sir John Pollyard was tried on two indictments and found guilty: of stealing a bank-note of £56 4s. 0d. from John Hughes and a gold watch and chain from Robert Hall in Cheapside (again *Select Trials* has this confused). Both indictments are signed by High Constable Jones. Follard was then pardoned and the findings and pardon recorded in the Sessions Book.

Rumours were now circulating in the papers that Wild was so

grave an offender that he was going to be tried at the King's Bench Court, Westminster Hall; but then it was discovered that there were indictments against him this sessions at the Old Bailey, and everyone waited agog.

On the 10th he was brought to stand his trial. The Sessions Book shows that he was to be accused on *two* counts, by Tidman and Butler. There is one indictment only, which sets out the details of the bank-note affair; it is endorsed on the back by Thomas Butler and John Tidman and marked 'BILLA VERA' by the Grand Jury. Probably the two counts are in the same indictment, for it says that Wild not only took the £50 but failed on or after 24 December to apprehend and prosecute the thief. Now these were the *only* charges against Wild this Sessions and there is no hint that Sir William Thomson or anyone else had heard a word about the lace-woman Mrs. Statham. This makes what followed all the more grotesque.

Wild's Counsel began by moving that his trial be deferred until the next, that is May, Session, and read an affidavit by Wild, the purport of which was 'that the last Night he was accidentally informed, that the Grand Jury had found a Bill against him for Felony, but he knew not what Felony, since he had not had Time sufficient to procure his witnesses, without whom he was unable to make his Defence; one of them living near Brentford, and another in Somersetshire.' The Counsel for the Crown opposed this, urging that as he was in custody he should have known that his trial would come on this Sessions and that therefore he should have been prepared for it; that if the single affidavit of a prisoner in such a case might pass, nobody would lack excuses and any trial hereafter might be put off by the same rule; and that he had not so much as named his witnesses, 'and though he says in his Affidavit that he knows not what he's indicted for, yet he swears that these are material witnesses'.

Wild then said that the names of his witnesses were Mr. Hays, at the 'Pack Horse' at Turnham Green, and Mr. Wilson, a clothier in Frome; 'and that, tho' he did not know particularly what he was indicted for, yet he had heard, that it was something about one—*Stetham*. And his Council moved, that the names of the Witnesses might be put into the Affidavit, and that he might swear it over again.'

Parker's London Post (12 April) says that at that moment, someone stood up and said that Mr. Hays at the 'Pack Horse' was 'run away' and might be unable to appear as a witness. The Counsel for the Crown replied sarcastically that though he might fly from his creditors, no one could escape Mr. Wild, the 'Thief-Taker General'.

The Counsel for the Crown then said that while 'Justice would never be deny'd him, he stood entitled to no favours; and that they were not sure that the two Persons, who had pleaded to their Pardons (*Butler and Follard*) would be found at the next Sessions.'

Select Trials says, 'some Gentlemen upon the Bench appearing willing that the Prisoner should be allowed Time 'till the following Sessions, to prepare his Defence, the Court told him, they had no more to say to him. He bow'd and answer'd, *I thank your Lordship, and am very glad of it*'.

Follard and Butler were bound each in a recognizance of £500 to appear at the next Sessions.

Every biography of Jonathan Wild says that as soon as he 'took a reward' (which, technically, he did not do) from Mrs. Statham, the lace-woman, he was doomed, for it could only be a matter of days, or even hours, before the Recorder was told of it. Then the Recorder, with his usual diligence, found the witnesses, sent the indictments up to the Grand Jury and had the case ready for the April Sessions, holding the Tidman and other charges in reserve to be brought up if the first should fail.

There are no documents relating to the Mrs. Statham case which are dated earlier than May. So far as I can see, Henry Kelley, on whose information the case depended, was not arrested until the end of April or early May. Now, the normal procedure was that the Grand Jury sitting in April, which convened a day or two before the other Sessions,* reviewed the indictments for May. In a special case of great importance (e.g. the

---

* Sessions of the Peace dealt with misdemeanours and lesser offences; Sessions of Oyer & Terminer dealt with felonies; Sessions of Gaol Delivery, theoretically, were supposed to clear the gaols (in this case, Newgate) of remaining prisoners. The Old Bailey tried all cases for London, Westminster and Middlesex. There were three juries (one for London, and two for Westminster and Middlesex), but it is not certain if there were two courtrooms. In practice, considerable leeway was allowed regarding which Sessions a prisoner might be tried at. Wild, charged with capital felony, was tried at Sessions of the Peace (which always began at Guildhall and adjourned to the Old Bailey after two days) because he wanted to be tried not earlier than 15 May (see next chapter), which was a Sessions of the Peace day. Such manœuvring cost money, of course.

Hawkins gang, James Shaw or Carrick) they might find a Bill for the current Sessions. But if the April Grand Jury had heard the indictments concerning Mrs. Statham and found them to be 'True', as Wild thought, then they would be listed, together with the names of the witnesses (Statham, Kelley and Morphew), in the April Sessions Book with the other prepared cases, which they are not.

The May Sessions of the Peace were fixed to start on the 11th, and those of Oyer & Terminer and Gaol Delivery on the 13th. Wild was tried, as it happened, on the last day, the 15th. Among the documents of his case is a sheet of parchment called an 'Exemplification'. This was sometimes written out, in Latin, to explain the circumstances of a case whose procedure had been unusual or slightly irregular, as his, apparently was. It says that the Grand Jury, which had convened originally on the 9th, two days before the General Sessions as usual, had to attend a Sessions adjourned from the Guildhall to the Old Bailey on the 13th (there was, presumably, no longer any room at the Guildhall for them to sit in) the same morning as the General Sessions were due to start in the courtroom, for the express purpose of hearing and finding the indictments relating to the prosecution of Wild over his taking a reward from Mrs. Statham. This was a most unusual procedure and was only resorted to in an emergency. In other words, this document, and the dating of the recognizances, indicate that the case had been drawn up in a great hurry and that the Grand Jury had been adjourned especially to deal with it at the last minute.

Therefore, although it is regrettable to have to say so, it was neither the diligence of Sir William Thomson nor the efficiency of his judicial machine (as Defoe and everyone since has believed) that unearthed the evidence to hang Wild, but that, on the contrary, the first they ever heard of Mrs. Statham was from Wild's own mouth.

Wild must have heard a rumour that Butler or someone had got wind of the transaction with the lace-woman. Then, hearing that the April Grand Jury had found a Bill against him (which it had, but it was the Tidman bill) wrongly put two and two together. His instinct, a conditioned reflex almost, was to wrangle and try to be clever as he had always done. He was obviously unaware that he had lost his touch, for he behaved with unbelievable crassness. It is noticeable that the King's Counsel said nothing at this unexpected revelation, though he must have been surprised,

and that he confined himself to a few general remarks about the
fairness of our justice. *The Newgate Calendar* interprets the sudden
willingness of those certain gentlemen on the Bench to give the
prisoner time, after all, to 'prepare his Defence', as proof of their
patience and fair-mindedness. It looks, however, as if they wanted
time themselves to hear more about this 'Stetham'.

Had Wild known the truth, he would surely have preferred to
fight then and there in April. The Tidman indictment, at least
from this point of time, looks so flimsy that it might even have
been an attempt at a 'frame-up'. It is very odd that Wild should
have taken £50 in advance and then returned the bank-note on the
same day, and all this on the very day it was stolen. To be fair,
we do not know if Wild treated bank-notes differently to ordinary
goods, and it is possible that he was desperately pushed for money
(though I cannot imagine why, for he left enough). Then, his
Counsel, who were allowed to argue these points of law, would
soon have discovered that Butler had been pardoned of *one* offence
only, and that he was still charged with stealing bonds from Major
Lechmere. Butler was under sentence of transportation on Christmas Eve, when the transaction took place, and they could have
asked some awkward questions as to why Butler was not in Newgate where he should have been and why he was at Wild's house
instead. They could then have insinuated that Butler had been
brought out of Newgate for identification by the Westminster
magistrates and temporarily released with orders to implicate
Wild in a felony, all of which was illegal. There is a curious sequel
to this, which is that Butler was in fact transported immediately
after the Wild case was over. He arrived at Annapolis, on the
Sukey, on 16 August 1725, with Mary Goldham and Moll Harvey. [4]
Yet he was never indicted for stealing those bonds from Major
Lechmere. If he had been pardoned for the earlier theft (12s. from
Wells), why was he transported? If he was a returned transportee,
he was never indicted of that either, but the Counsel could soon
have proved it and then claimed he was a felon convict and so not
permitted to be an Evidence.

If the Sessions records leave us with some unanswered questions, they do show that the truth about Wild's arrest and trial is
more complicated, and considerably less edifying, than the story
set forth by Defoe, for instance, or *The Newgate Calendar*. The
Middlesex and Westminster magistrates were thrashing about
seizing first one thing and then another. High Constable Jones of

Holborn seems to have acted largely on his own initiative and without consulting them. The City of London magistrates, led by Sir William Thomson, joined the hunt only because they would have looked fools if they had not. The criminals, Edwards, Johnson, the two Butlers, Kelley, Mendez, Field and all the rest, were preoccupied with their own personal fates; sometimes they used the magistrates and sometimes the magistrates used them. I do not wish to attribute too much in this to the old rivalries between the institutions of London, on the one hand, and those of Westminster on the other, but I am certain that once the Middlesex and Westminster magistrates decided to move against Wild, they were spurred on by the desire, aroused perhaps by some dispute too petty to be recorded, to teach Sir William and his followers a lesson in 'diligence'.

What apparently will never be clear is why they decided to move against Wild at all; or why, if they decided to move against him then, which they did with every sign of haste and improvisation, they had not done so at any time during the previous six or seven years. 'H.D.' says that it was only Wild's 'bare-faced and impudent' behaviour over the Edwards and Johnson fracas that opened their eyes for the first time; others that they were under pressure from the 'Quality', after all those jewels had been stolen at Windsor, to do something. This has the negative virtue of saying that the worst sin they were guilty of was inertia. Darker hints are scattered about the pamphlets and newspapers. Some of them may have been no more than scandalous, but none are too far-fetched. Perhaps it was a quarrel between one of them and one of Wild's 'tame' magistrates, such as Vaughan or 'C—n'. Perhaps it was jealousy over Wild's success as a thief-taker after he had broken up first Shaw's gang, then Hawkins's, then Carrick's and finally Sheppard's and Blueskin's, all in Westminster and Middlesex. Perhaps it was a quarrel over the brothel and gaming-house protection-rackets in which so many of them were involved. Perhaps it was that some of them, in collusion with the gangs, were afraid of Wild because he knew too much about them. 'H.D.', in contradiction to what he says earlier, hints at this and so does the *British Journal*. After Wild was condemned, they led him along with hopes of a reprieve to prevent his exposing them, and when at the last minute he saw what was happening and tried to save his life by making disclosures, nobody by then would listen to him The magistrates, who had been 'trembling' lest he should b reprieved, 'because he and they are supposed to be no Strangers to each other's Practices' ('H.D.') were saved. It is true that Butler was packed off to America for no declared reason and with untoward haste. It is true, as well, that Wild's last recorded words, which he said looking round at the shouting, jeering crowds on the way to Tyburn, were 'What a strange Rig they run upon me!' which means 'What a strange trick they play (or played) upon me!' In other words, the tremendous popular indignation was being stirred up for reasons the mob knew nothing about.

The obvious, and what should be the natural, reason is the hardest to believe: which is that they were four untypically honest magistrates who acted on a moral principle, to protect law and justice and eradicate a social evil. For if this were so, one would expect to have heard of some attempt, even if in vain, to reform the abuses Wild so flagrantly embodied; a small pamphlet at least, signed by 'Joe: Beaver' perhaps, or some mention in a charge to the Grand Jury, proposing that thief-takers should now be abolished. Instead, there is silence.

The only visible result of Wild's demise was a sudden and alarming drop in the number of thieves who were 'brought to Justice' each Sessions.

❧ XXII ❧ *The Trial*

In the first week of May the pamphleteers began to circle round like vultures. A 'biography' of the 'Thief-Taker General' had already appeared under the title *An Authentic Narrative of the Parentage, Birth, etc. . . . . of Jonathan Wild* and a pirated edition had been printed in Stamford. Many of its stated facts are wrong but some are right. Wild was interviewed by Defoe, or whoever was 'Applebee's Man'. It does not seem to have been a very long interview, for factual details in Defoe's biography are very brief. Wild seems to have come to an arrangement by which, in lieu of payment, *Applebee's Original Weekly Journal* would publish a list of the criminals Wild had arrested recently. On 8 May the journal printed a short list of ten men who had been hanged for returning from transportation and six men and three women who had been transported again. This was more or less the same list he had put under his petition for the Freedom of London. The journal let it be understood that this list was published only to comply with the wish of a man whose 'Life was in Jeopardy'. However, it promised a longer list in the next issue, due to come out on 15 May.

On 7 May, the trial began at Westminster Hall of Thomas Parker, Earl of Macclesfield, the Lord Chancellor who was accused of taking £100,000 worth of bribes (i.e. about £2,000,000 in modern money) and of general corruption, and while the parallels between this and the cases of wretches like Sheppard and

Wild were obvious, the satirists contained themselves until the case was no longer *sub judice*.

More of Wild's accomplices were being rounded up. First, there was the gang of coiners who had been in trouble after poor Barbara Spencer had been burnt in 1721: Robert Harpham, 'Blind Cooper' the watchmaker, and his wife or housekeeper, Elizabeth Reeve. The terrible example of Barbara Spencer probably explains Elizabeth's actions as reported by the *Daily Journal* on 8 May:

> Yesterday Morning Elizabeth Cooper alias Reeves, the House-keeper and Wife of Blind Cooper, the Coiner of false Money, now in Newgate, was taken by one of His Majesty's Messengers, at a House in a Court in Drury Lane: when she found herself discover'd, she endeavour'd to throw herself out of a window three stories high, but was prevented by the Messenger.

Article V of the Recorder's Warrant of Detainer had said that Wild had harboured people 'against whom there are now Informations' for counterfeiting money. This warrant, of course, was still *sub judice*, and the newspapers had not yet published it. However, by the familiar trick of juxtaposition (which is still very much used today), they gave it to be understood that this gang were connected with Wild. In fact, the trial came on before Wild's, and his name was not so much as mentioned in it. Blind Cooper was found guilty of 'uttering' (i.e. passing off as genuine) false coins, and was sentenced to £100 fine and one year in prison. Elizabeth was not charged. Robert Harpham was less lucky, perhaps because, as I have said, he was not only proved guilty but was brought up in a family of coiners. He was sentenced to death and, in addition, to be drawn to Tyburn on a sledge—which, in the days before metalled roads, was an agonizing torture.

On 7 May *Parker's Penny Post* (as his *London Post* was now renamed) announced:

> We hear that one Elizabeth Doyle, convicted the last Sessions at the Old Bailey, for feloniously returning from Transportation, and who had Sentence of Death passed upon her, but respited being found Pregnant, will shortly be pardon'd, since 'tis supposed she is capable of making far greater Discoveries of

the dark Transactions of Jonathan Wild than any other Persons whatsoever.

On the 10th, the same paper reported:

'John Green, a most notorious Robber, and said to be very deeply engag'd with Jonathan Wild, has also been committed to New Prison & loaded with double Irons.

The *British Journal* (1 and 8 May) said that Roger Johnson's wife, having just returned from Holland, had been arrested at a house in Tyburn Road (now Oxford Street). She was a carrier for a coining gang whose headquarters were in Paradise Row, near Hanover Square. *Parker's Penny Post* (10th) added:

Madam Johnson, the Wife of the famous Roger Johnson, a Burgher of Rotterdam, who is said to have stolen to the Value of about £3,000 at the late Installment at Windsor, has been committed to Clerkenwell Bridewell, where she lives in the most splendid Manner, being (we hear) attended by several Servants, amongst whom is a French Cook.

There is no mention of her on the Clerkenwell Bridwell (or House of Correction) Calendars of these months, but she may in fact have been put into New Prison. Unfortunately, the Calendars for New Prison for April, May and July have been lost, or were never written out; the Keeper, Captain Geary, was notoriously slack in sending his Calendars of prisoners for each Sessions, and the Sessions Books and papers contain many reprimands and £10 fines against him. Therefore, as with Abraham Mendez, it is impossible to say when she was released or why. She and Roger separated, for by 1729 his wife, according to the House of Commons enquiry into the state of the prisons, was called Anne.

Meanwhile, the case against Wild was being reorganized. Henry Kelley was arrested on the information of Butler (but I am not sure which Butler) and on 7 and 8 May recognizances were taken for Margaret Morphew and Mrs. Statham and her daughter. Margaret Morphew, who lived at 'Hay Markett', was bound on pain of imprisonment, and the Stathams on pain of losing £50. It was not written in Latin, as many were, but in English only, and says it was accepted—

Upon Condition that they severally and personally appear and prosecute the Law will Effect and Give Evidence against

Jonathan Wild for felony at yᵉ next Generall Sessions of Oyer and Terminer and Gaol Delivery to beholden for the City of London at Justice Hall in the Old Bailey and not to depart the Court without leave.

Capt. et recognd. 8⁰ die Maÿ Coram   Joe: BEAVER.

On 13 May, the first day of the Sessions, Quilt Arnold was ordered by Joseph Beaver to be sent to the next Assizes in Essex. *Mist's Weekly Journal* (the new name of the *Weekly Journal or Saturday's Post*) of 22 May said that this was on a capital charge, but in the end nothing seems to have come of it.

Wild was still trying one trick or another to postpone or influence the trial. *Parker's Penny Post* (30 April) said that he had attempted to put matters off by a 'Writ of Salivation'. The meaning of this was that the mercury ointment employed to cure syphilis also caused the patient to spit constantly (i.e. 'salivate') until his mouth became so inflamed that he could not speak— until, indeed, his teeth began to fall out. A prisoner suffering this treatment could plead that while he could not speak he could not defend himself and postponements of trials were occasionally granted on this pretext. Wild's writ, however, was thrown out, and his salivation abandoned.

On Thursday, 13 May, he was told that his trial was fixed for the next morning. At no doubt considerable expense he managed through counsel to have the trial postponed until the Saturday, for he knew that Applebee's journal would then be publishing his list of malefactors brought to justice. He was in low spirits, however, and told the others in Newgate Press Yard that he wished Blueskin had made a more effective job of cutting his throat and saved him from all this misery.

On the morning of the 14th, while he was at the Old Bailey arranging the postponement, he went amongst the jurymen and others who were taking the air on the leads in front of the courtroom and gave out printed pamphlets whose purpose was to remind them of the great service he had done his country. Some of these pamphlets were copies of the list to be published by Applebee next day, for he was determined that the jury should read it in good time. It contained the names of seventy-five men and women he had 'discovered, apprehended and convicted', sixty-seven of whom had been hanged and the rest transported. He added a note at the bottom saying that there were other petty felons whose names were 'too tedious' to be inserted, a number of pickpocket-whores whose names he withheld to save the prosecutors from embarrassment, and yet more whose names he could not remember.

> In Regard therefore of the Numbers above convicted, some, that have yet escaped Justice, are endeavouring to take away the Life of the said

> JONATHAN WILD

As the editor of *Select Trials* (who was handed a copy) complained, this list was a source of great confusion for the early pamphleteers, for there were a lot of mistakes and only the vaguest clues as to dating. In Appendix II I have corrected as many errors and supplied as many dates as possible, and have added another twenty-six names, bringing the total to 101. Those who were impeached by others on Wild's instructions would perhaps increase this total by half as much again.

Jonathan Wild was brought to the Bar at last on the morning of Saturday, 15 May 1725. His early biographer 'H.D.' signed himself 'Clerk to Justice R—'; for this reason writers have wondered if 'Justice R—' was Sir Robert Raymond who, on the death of Sir John Pratt in early March, had just been made Lord Chief Justice of the King's Bench, and whether or not the new Chief Justice presided over, or at least attended, Wild's trial. First, if 'H.D.' had meant Lord Raymond, as he now was, he would almost certainly have written 'Clerk to my Lord Chief Justice R—'. Second, the Sessions Books for London and Middlesex, when taken together, give a complete list of who were on the Bench that morning: Sir George Merttins (Lord Mayor), Mr. Justice Fortescue, Mr. Baron Page, Sir William Thomson (Recorder), Serjeant John Raby, Sir Gerrard Conyers, Sir Charles Peers, Sir Peter Delme, Alderman Francis Child, and Alderman Edward Bellamy.

All Wild's efforts to manœuvre and procrastinate did little more than present the prosecution with a chance to set his character in an even worse light than it already was. The King's Counsel began by protesting vigorously against Wild's attempt to influence the jury by handing out his lists amongst them:

> The Jury having taken their Seats, and the Prisoner being brought to the Bar, the Council for the King took notice of the Prisoner's extraordinary Proceeding, in relation to the above-

mention'd Papers. That such Practices were unwarrantable, and not to be suffered in any Court of Justice. This was apparently intended to take off the Credit of the King's Witnesses, and prepossess and influence the Jury. Though, as he believed them to be Men of Integrity, he was under no Apprehensions that it would have such Effect, but that they would give a conscientious Verdict according to Evidence. And that whatever the Prisoner might hope for, from such indirect Management, it was far from making his Cause appear in a more favourable Light. That it was impossible, but that a Man who had trained up and erected a Corporation of Thieves; a Man who had carried on a Trade of Felony for so many Years, and made it his constant Practice to procure Goods that had been lost in any Part of the Town, must have had it in his Power to detect those Felons he was concerned with. And yet, that there was good Reason to believe that (to the great Scandal of Public Justice), he had intimidated many from Reformation, and prevented them from making such Discoveries, as might have been of publick Advantage. That if a strict Enquiry was to be made, after the Motives of his apprehending and convicting those Criminals, named in his List, we might find they were private Interest, old Grudges, or fresh Quarrels, and not the least Regard to Justice, and the Good of his Country.

Wild asked that the witnesses against him be examined apart, which the court granted.

The first indictment against Wild was under the 'Shoplifting Act' (*10 & 11 William III c.* of 1699, by which theft of 5*s.* or over from a shop, etc., was capital) and charged him with privately stealing 50 yards of lace, value £40, from the shop of Catherine Statham in the parish of St. Andrews, Holborn, on 22 January 1725. In his evidence, Henry Kelley described how Wild had put them up to the theft and how they had carried it out with him:

On Friday the 22nd of January last, I went to visit Mrs. *Johnston*, who then lived at the Prisoner's House. Her Husband brought me over from Ireland. I found her at Home, and we drank a Quartern of Gin* together. By and by in comes *Peg Murphey*, with a Pair of brocaded Shoes and Clogs, and makes a Present of them to Madam *Wild*, the Prisoner's Wife. The

* A quarter-pint.

Prisoner was in Company with us at the same Time, and when
we had drunk two or three Quarterns more, *Murphey* and I got
up to go away together. He asked us which Way we were
going? I said, to my Lodging at the Seven Dials.*

'I suppose,' says he, 'you go along Holborn?'

We answered, 'Yes.'

'Why then,' says he, 'I'll tell you what, . . . there's an old
blind Bitch, that keeps a Shop within twenty Yards of Holborn-
bridge, and sells fine Flanders Lace; and her Daughter is as
blind as herself. Now, if you'll take the Trouble of calling upon
her, you may *speak with* a Box of Lace. I'll go along with you,
and show you the Door.'

The court then asked Kelley what was meant by 'speaking-with' a
box of lace.

To speak with a Thing is to steal it. So we agreed, and the
Prisoner, and I and *Murphey*, went together, till we came
within Sight of the Shop, and then he pointed and shewed us
which it was, and, says he, 'Do you go, and I'll wait here, and
bring ye off, if any Disturbance should happen.'

Murphey and I went in, and turned over several Parcels of
Lace, and could not find that which would please us; for it was
our Business to be mighty nice and difficult. This Piece was too
broad, and that was too narrow, and t'other not fine enough.
At last the old Woman stept upstairs to fetch another Piece,
and in the mean Time I took a Tin box of Lace, and gave it to
Murphey, who put it under her Cloak. The old Woman came
down again with another Box, and shewed us several more
Pieces; but we could not agree about the Price, and so we came
away and found the Prisoner where we had left him, and told
him we had *spoke.*

We all went back to his House, where we opened the Box,
and found eleven Pieces in it. He asked us, if we'd have ready
Money, or stay till an Advertisement came out? Stock was
pretty low with us at that Time, and so we chose ready Money,
and he gave us three Guineas, and four Broad Pieces.

'I can't afford to give any more,' says he, 'for she's a hard-
mouth'd old Bitch, and I shall never get above ten Guineas out
of her.'

* *Select Trials* 1742 edn. vol 2, pp 220–8. I have spaced out the paragraphing
to make the transcript of the speeches easier to read

I took the three Guineas and a Crown for my own Share, and *Murphey* had the rest. I was taken up by Means of *Butler*, and so made my Information.

Margaret's Morphew's evidence was the same as Kelley's, except that she said that Kelley took the tin box while the daughter's head was turned aside, and put it under the skirt of his coat before handing it to herself. She also added that Wild said, when he aplogized for giving only three guineas and four broad pieces, 'I can't afford to give any more, for, though I have got some Influence over her, by helping her to Goods two or three Times before, yet I know her to be such a stingy old Bitch, that I shan't get above ten Guineas out of her.'

Two things are noticeable here. If their 'Stock was pretty low', why did they give both a pair of shoes *and* a pair of clogs to Mrs. Wild as a present, when they would surely have sold or pawned them in normal circumstances? Secondly, they both seemed to emphasize the insulting way in which Jonathan had spoken about Mrs. Statham; it looks as if they were trying to incense her against him as much as possible.

Mrs. Statham herself said that she had shown them two or three parcels of lace, 'but they were both so difficult, that nothing I had below would please them. And so, leaving my Daughter in the Shop, I stept up Stairs, and brought down another Box. Well, that would do, but what was the Price? I ask'd them 6*s.* a Yard. No, they would give me four. I told them I could not take it, and so they went out; and, in about 3 Hours afterwards, I mist a Tin-box of Lace, which I valued at £50.'

At this point, the Counsel for the Defence begged leave to observe that according to the evidence, the prisoner could not 'be guilty of this Indictment, because the Indictment sets forth, that HE did privately steal the Lace IN the Shop; when it was certain, that he did not enter the Shop. That he might be guilty of a single (i.e. Clergyable) Felony, in being Accessory before the Fact, or in receiving the Goods afterwards, knowing them to have been stolen; but could not, as they apprehended, be guilty of the capital Offence, except (as the Act directs), it had been inserted in the Indictment, that he did assist, command or hire.'

In other words, if the evidence of Kelley and Morphew was believed, Wild was still shown to be an accessory *before* the fact, a principal in the second degree, and a receiver; but he was indicted only of stealing the goods in the shop, and this he could not have done because he was never in it. In summing up the evidence for the jury, the court said, 'that in other Cases, as in Robberies and Burglaries, an Accessory before the Fact is a Principal. He that stands by, or watches at a Distance, being as guilty, and as liable to the same Punishment, as the very Person who enters the House, or steals Money or Goods; but, as it was not remember'd, that there had yet been any Precedent of the like Construction, being put upon Indictments of this Nature, it remain'd a Matter of Doubt, and therefore in such a Case, it was most elegible to incline to the Side of Mercy.'

In short, an acquittal was recommended. However, Wild was now to be indicted under the Act nicknamed after him—'the Jonathan Wild Act' of 1718 (*4 George I c. 11 ss. 4 & 5*). The indictment reads: '. . . for that, whereas 50 Yards of Lace, Value £40, was privately stolen in the Shop of *Catherine Statham*, by *Persons unknown to the Jurors*, on 22 January 1725, he, the said *Jonathan Wild* afterwards, that is to say, on the 10th of March, in the same Year, feloniously did receive of the said *Catherine*, ten Guineas on Account, and under the colour of helping her to the said Lace again, and did not then, or at any Time since, discover, apprehend, or cause to be apprehended, and prosecute the Felon who stole the said Lace.'

The Court instructed the Clerk to read aloud the relevant part of the Act, beginning, 'And whereas there are divers Persons, who have secret Acquaintance with Felons . . .' which has been quoted in full in Chapter XI. Then Catherine Statham was called to give her account of what happened after the theft.

She said: 'On the 22nd of January last, in the Afternoon, a Box of Lace, which I valued at £50 was stolen out of my Shop. I went the same Night to the Prisoner's House to enquire after it, but not finding him at Home, I advertis'd the Lace I had lost, with a Reward of fifteen Guineas, and no Questions to be ask'd. But, hearing no News of it, I went to the Prisoner's House again, and then I met with him. He desired me to give him a Description of the Persons I suspected, which I did as well as I could. Upon this he promis'd to make Enquiry, and bid me call again in two or three Days; I did so, and then he said he had heard something of my Lace, and expected to hear more in a little Time.

'While we were talking, a Man came in and said, that by what he had learn'd, he believed that one *Kelley*, who had been try'd for putting off gilded Shillings, was concerned in stealing the Lace. I went away, and came again on that Day the Prisoner was apprehended—I think it was the 15th of February. I told him that though I had advertised but fifteen Guineas Reward, I would give twenty, or five and twenty, rather than not have my Lace again.

'"Don't be in such a Hurry, good Woman," says he, "perhaps I may help ye to it for less, and if I can I will. The Persons that have your Lace are gone out of Town: I shall set them a-quarrelling about it, and then I shall get it the cheaper."

'On the 10th of March, he sent me Word, that if I would come to him in Newgate, and bring ten Guineas, in my Pocket, he would help me to my Lace. I went; he desired me to call a Porter, but I telling him I knew not where to find one, he sent out a Person who brought in a Man that appeared to be a Ticket-Porter. The Prisoner gave me a Letter, which he said was sent to him, as a Direction where to go for the Lace; but, as I could not read, I delivered it to the Porter; after which the Prisoner bid me give the Porter ten Guineas, or else, he said, the Persons who had the Lace would not deliver it. I gave the Porter the Money, and he went away, and in a little while returned with a Box sealed up, but it was not the same that I had lost. I opened it, and found all my Lace, except one Piece.

'"Now, Mr. Wild," says I, 'what must I give you for your Trouble?"

'"Not a Farthing, Madam," says he, "not a single Farthing; I don't do these Things for worldly Interest, but for the Benefit of poor People who have met with Misfortunes. As for the piece of Lace that is missing, I would not have ye be uneasy, for I hope to get it for you e'er long; nay, and I don't know, but in a little Time, I may not only help ye to your ten Guineas again, but to the Thief too. And, if I can, much good may it do ye; and, as you are a Widow, and a good Christian, I desire nothing of ye but your Prayers, and for them I shall be thankful. I have a great many Enemies, and God knows what may be the Consequence of this Imprisonment."'

After this, according to *Select Trials*, the following exchange took place:

Prisoner I hope the Court will consider the Service I have done, in convicting a great Number of Criminals. I beg that *Morphew* and *Kelley* may be called in again, and that I may ask them a Question or two.

Court   Let them come in. Now, what is your Question?

Prisoner   Mrs. *Morphew*, I desire to know—

Court   You must not propose your Question to the Witness, but to the Court; and if your Question is proper, the Court will require the Witness to answer it.

Prisoner   I beg your Lordship will ask her, who stole the Lace?

Court   That's not a proper Question, for, as she is upon Oath, we cannot require her to answer any Questions to accuse herself.

Prisoner   She swore upon the first Indictment that—

Court   Whatever she swore upon that Tryal, we cannot take Notice of it upon this, except she was now to swear it over again, which we cannot require her to do.

King's Council   This Indictment is laid for taking Money of *Catherine Statham*, under Pretence of helping her to Goods that had been stolen by Persons UNKNOWN, and the Prisoner would now ask the Witness, 'Who stole those Goods?'

Prisoner   I would ask her if I stole the Lace?

Morphew   No, but he was concern'd with those that did steal it, and he receiv'd it after it was stolen.

To pretend that the persons who had stolen the lace were unknown, when in fact they had openly admitted it only half an hour or so before, was simply a legal manœuvre to prevent Kelley and Morphew from being charged with the theft and to prevent Wild from being able to break down their story and so perhaps dissociate himself from them. It will be noticed that nowhere in this second trial were the thieves positively identified (although Wild's man, according to Mrs. Statham, said he 'believed one Kelley was concerned') and Margaret Morphew said not that Wild was concerned with '*us*' but '*with those that stole it*'.

Wild could have argued, if he had not been silenced, that as the thief had not yet been prosecuted, let alone convicted, then he could not be prosecuted or convicted either. That is obviously what he was aiming at when he asked Margaret Morphew 'Who stole the Lace?'. Sir William Thomson, who had a personal interest in showing that his Act could be made to work, saw this and stopped him by ruling that the question was not a proper one.

Yet this argument was used as a defence later in the century and Strange, Blackstone and the 1795 edition of Hawkins's *Pleas of the Crown* all agree that it was doubtful if a person taking a reward in this way could be prosecuted under this Act *until* the principal felon (or thief) had been convicted. But, of course, Kelley and Morphew could not be punished because the only way they could be brought into court as Evidence was for them to be either not prosecuted at all, or prosecuted, convicted and pardoned, as Butler had been. Having seen that this way was effectively blocked, Wild's counsel tried a little playing with words of their own.

They 'begg'd leave to observe, that as *Morphew* had sworn the Prisoner guilty of a Felony, in being concerned with those who stole the Goods, they presumed that the Act upon which he was now indicted, was never intended to affect him, or any other Felon, but only such Persons as were not Felons themselves, but held a Correspondency with Felons. For as there were old Laws in Force for the Punishment of Felons, it would have been wholly unnecessary, that a new Law should be made to the same Purpose, that is, no Purpose at all. That the very Preamble to the Clause of the Act on which the Prisoner stands indicted, intimates, by a plain Distinction, that the Felons are not in that Place intended.

'The Words are these. "Whereas there are several *Persons* who have secret Acquaintance with *Felons*, and who make it their Business to help Persons to their stolen Goods, and by that Means gain Money between THEM and the FELONS." That, by a Proviso in the said Clause, it could not be supposed, that Felons were then intended, without making Contradictions and Inconsistencies in the Act itself. For the Words are, "Unless such *Person* doth apprehend, or cause to be apprehended, such *Felon* who stole the same, and cause such Felon to be brought to Trial for the same, and give Evidence against him." Suppose now there was but one Person concerned in such a Case, can it ever be thought, that the Legislature intended that this very Person should apprehend himself, bring himself to a Trial, and give Evidence against himself? No, certainly.

'The Council for the Crown reply'd to this Effect, That it was no Absurdity or Contradiction to say, that the Act was intended to affect the Felons; for that a Man's being a Felon did not in any Way hinder him from discovering his Accomplices, if he had any: And, as to the Supposition, that a Felon had no Accomplices, but committed the Felony by himself, it was out of the present Question, and no way relating to the Prisoner's Case, for it was evident, that he had Accomplices, and had not discovered them.

'The Court (*probably Sir William Thomson*) observed farther, that Felons were so far from being excepted in the Act, that it was principally intended against them, for it particularly mentions, "those that make it their Business to help People to stolen Goods". And it was certain, that such Persons must be Receivers of Stolen Goods, knowing them to be stolen, *and such are Felons*. That the Case of the Prisoner came within almost every Circumstance of the Act, it being evident, that *He was the Person who had secret Acquaintance with Felons, who made it his Business to help People to stolen Goods, and by that Means gain'd Money from them, which was divided between him and the Felons, and thereby greatly encouraged such Offenders, and had not apprehended them.* That it was very surprizing Plea for a Man to say "I am more guilty than you are aware of, and therefore I ought to suffer the less"; And that it could never be thought, that the Parliament intended by this Act to excuse a Man meerly because he was a Felon, and more criminal than another.'

The jury acquitted Wild of the first indictment and found him guilty of the second.

Although Messrs. Baynes and Kettleby did not make a very brilliant defence (and there is no knowing what Wild withheld from them), it is almost certain that had the prisoner been anyone else but Wild, or even Wild at an earlier time, he would have got away with it. If the Recorder and others had not been determined to hang him at any cost, they could, and probably would, have held him over for the next Sessions, charged him under the Receiving Act (*5 Anne c. 31*) with being a receiver and an accessory before the fact (which was not always capital) and had him fined, whipped or transported. The fact that Sir William Thomson recommended mercy after hearing the first indictment suggests that he was playing an unpleasant and sadistic game with his prisoner. Perhaps it is a mistake to feel sorry for Wild after all he had done and the callousness with which he had done it; but pity is almost forced on us by the horrible events of the next few days.

As this was the last day of the Sessions, Wild was brought back to the Bar that evening with the other prisoners to hear his sentence. The author of *Lives of the Most Remarkable Criminals* was apparently present:

'. . . he appear'd to be very much dejected, and when the usual

Question was proposed to him: "What have you to say why Judgement of Death should not pass upon you?" he spoke with a very feeble Voice in the following Terms:

'"My Lord, I hope even in the sad Condition in which I stand, I may pretend to some little Merit in Respect to the Service I have done my Country, in delivering it from some of the greatest Pests with which it was ever troubled. My Lord, I have brought many bold and daring Malefactors to just Punishment, even at the Hazard of my own Life, my Body being cover'd with Scars I received in these Undertakings. I presume, my Lord, to say I have done Merit, because at the Time these Things were done, they were esteem'd Meritorious by the Government; and therefore I hope, my Lord, some Compassion may be shown on the Score of those Services. I submit myself wholly to his Majesty's Mercy, and humbly beg a favourable Report of my Case."'

After the hangman had tied their thumbs together with whipcord, the Recorder pronounced sentence of death on Wild, Harpham (the coiner), William Sperry, Robert Standford (two highwaymen) and John Plant (a footpad), and delivered his usual speech. When he came to Wild, he recounted his multiple crimes and recalled that he himself had warned Wild before of the dangers of being a broker for thieves. He then exhorted Wild to make the most of the short time left to him, 'which the Tenderness of the Law of England allows Sinners for Repentence', and hoped he would take this warning even if he had ignored all others. As for that report to the King Wild had asked him to make in favourable terms, he told Wild that he might depend on Justice and ought not to hope for any more.

⸸ XXIII ⸸ *Execution*

Throughout these weeks it had been raining almost daily and the spring had been the wettest that anyone could remember. There were fears of a total failure of crops, and the papers reported that haymakers who had therefore come to London for work were now wandering the streets in a starving condition—indeed several had already starved to death. Public collections for them were raised at the Exchange, and the Duke of Chandos, the wealthiest and most extravagant noble in the kingdom, gave out 150 half-crowns at the door of his London house. Nevertheless, the fate of Jonathan Wild held a prominent place in the news columns.

On 18 May the *Daily Journal* announced:

> The Lace Woman at Holborn Bridge, who convicted Jonathan Wild, is by an Act of Parliament passed in the 6th Year of his Majesty's Reign (*i.e. 6 George I c. 23*) intituled to a Reward of £40 payable in the same Manner as that of convicting a Highwayman.
>
> 'Tis remarkable that in *May* 1717, at the Sessions then held at the Old Bailey, Scull Dean, the former Husband of Jonathan Wild's Wife, did then receive sentence of Death from the Mouth of Sir William Thomson, the Recorder, for Felony and was executed the same Month at Tyburn.

Parker's Penny Post of 26 May says of Mary Wild:

The Wife of Jonathan Wild, the Day after her Husband receiv'd Sentence of Death, a Sunday, hang'd herself, but some one coming into the Room accidentally, cut her down; by which Means she had a Reprieve against her Will.

The Dead Warrants came down on Wednesday the 19th. Only John Plant was reprieved for transportation. Wild must have anticipated as much, for on that day he had written a petition to the King which the next morning Mary Wild 'presented to the Ministers of State Etc.' (*Daily Journal* 22 May). It read:

THE HUMBLE PETITION OF JONATHAN WILD

Humbly Presented to His Majesty, on
Wednesday May the 19th at
His Royal Palace at St. James's

May it please Your Majesty:
'Tis nothing but your Majesty's wonted Goodness and Clemency that could encourage me to sue for your Royal Favour and Pardon, and make me presume so far on the same as to dare to offer this my most Humble Petition to Your Majesty's serene Consideration. For Since Your Majesty has many Times been graciously pleased to spare the Lives of even Traitors themselves I cannot but hope for a Reprieve from so good a Prince whom I can esteem no less than an inexhaustible Fountain of Mercy; wherefore, most Dread and August Sovereign, humbly prostrating myself at your Royal Feet I presume to set forth my wicked and melancholy Circumstances and from your Bounty to seek that Favour which is nowhere else to be found.

I have indeed been a most wicked and notorious Offender, but was never Guilty of or inclin'd to Treasonable Practices or Murder, both of which I ever had in the utmost Detestation and Abhorrence which affords me great Comfort in the midst of my Calamity and Affliction.

I have a sickly Wife loaded with Grief who must inevitably come to the Grave with me if I suffer; or lead a most miserable Life, she being already *non compos Mentis*.

If I receive Your Majesty's Royal Favour of a Reprieve I do firmly resolve to relinquish my wicked Ways and to detest (as far as in me lays) all such who shall persevere therein, as a Testimony of which I have a List ready to show to such whom your Majesty shall appoint to see it, which is all that can be offered by Your Majesty's most dutiful, Loyal, and Obedient Petitioner,

Newgate, May the 19th 1725.

J. WILD.[1]

On 22 May the *Daily Journal* announced that '50 of the Sherriff of Middlesex's Officers, and a proportionable Number of Officers from both the City Compters, are Ordered to attend at Newgate on Monday morning next, with their Javelins etc., to convey Jonathan Wild and the other Malefactors appointed for Death at Tyburn'. *Mist's Weekly Journal* of the same day said:

Jonathan is attended in the Condemn'd Hold by the Rev. Mr. Nicholson, Lecturer of St. Sepulchre's, to prepare him for his approaching Change. He is, as yet, under the greatest Horrors and Agonies of Mind; which, 'tis hop'd, may work a good effect for the short time he has to live, as well upon his wicked Companions as himself.

It may be remembered that in April, two people, Susan and Jonathan Paines, had been arrested on suspicion of robbing the Exchequer. On 24 May the *Daily Post* was referring to this when it said: 'We hear that Jonathan Wyld, in order to obtain a Reprieve, has offer'd to make some Discoveries in Relation to the late Robbery of the Exchequer, about which he hath been examined on Saturday last: whether he is capable of giving any Light into that Affair, we know not; but we are assured, there was no Reprieve for him yesterday in the Evening.'

This gave the Duke of Wharton another chance to bait the government. Lord Chancellor Macclesfield had just been found guilty and fined £30,000 (most of which was paid by the King), and Wharton reminded the public of an earlier scandal, an £8,000,000 deficit in Exchequer accounts which, despite an enquiry, His Grace thought Walpole had never satisfactorily explained. In a sarcastic poem, he pictured Walpole asking Jonathan Wild, his underworld counterpart, to guard the Exchequer from further losses and to find the thieves. Wild answered that a nightly guard would be useless:

From the Night to the Morning, 'tis true all is right,
But who will secure it from Morning till Night?
Quoth *Wild* unto *Walpole*, Make me Undertaker,

I'll soon find the Rogues that robbed th'Exchequer,
I shan't look among those that are us'd to purloining,
But shall, the first, search in the Chapel adjoining.[2]

The *London Journal* of 29 May amplified the story, saying that Wild petitioned for a reprieve for a fortnight or three weeks; 'in which petition he set forth, That he had convicted above 40 malefactors, and received several Wounds and Pistol-shots in the apprehending them: That he could make such Discoveries as would greatly benefit the Publick; and that he could propose Means to prevent, in a great Measure, if not totally suppress, all future Thefts and Robberies. But being examin'd on Saturday, he could offer Nothing material. . . .'

We do not know what discoveries Wild was really trying to make, or what was the list he mentioned in his petition to the King. Was it simply his old list, or had he something sensational to tell about the corrupt activities of magistrates and other officials? If he had, it is not surprising that nobody was interested.

What actually transpired during Wild's last days in Newgate is best told in the Ordinary's account as reprinted in *Select Trials*[3] with additions by the editor. It was published by Purney, but as he was away from London, and as Wild had refused to see anyone except Mr. Nicholson, he must have written it up from notes sent to him.

This Malefactor, after his conviction, affirm'd that he had fasted upwards of four Days, which, together with his Lameness and Indisposition, had render'd him unable to attend the Service of God in the Chapel.

He endeavour'd to convince People, that at *Wolverhampton*, he knew of several Persons that would have proved his Friends, had he thought his Case dangerous, and timely applied to them; But as he carried on the same Practices above a dozen Years, and was now growing old, he could not be made to believe he should suffer at last, for what he had publickly done unpunish'd so long. But he was then told by a Gentleman, that he had artfully evaded the Law, and escaped Justice; which Justice had sometime since overtaken one *Thomson*, who was executed for carrying on such Practices but a very short time. That he ought to have taken Warning when he was first of all committed Prisoner to the Compter, where he should have observed the Misery of vicious People, instead of learning their Ways, and endeavouring to understand them and their Practices, and afterwards associating with them.

He reply'd, That his Business was doing good in recovering lost Goods; that as he had regained Things of great Value for Dukes, Earls, and Lords, he thought he deserved well. That he had apprehended the greatest and most pernicious Robbers the Nation was ever molested by, and had Wounds and Scars still remaining in his Head, Body and Legs.

He appear'd to be very much disorder'd and confused in his Thoughts, which he said was owing to those Wounds, and in particular to two Fractures in his Skull which disorder'd his Brain, tho' cover'd with Silver Plates. He never went to Chapel during the whole Time that he continued under Sentence of Death, saying he was Lame, and unable to support himself on his Legs, and much more unable to go up so far. Another Reason he added was, that certain Enemies of his among the Crowd would not only interrupt his Prayers by pointing, whispering, etc., but would, he believed, insult him and, if they dared, would raise a Tumult; therefore, as he knew that to pray to God without Attention or Regard was worse than wholly to omit Prayers: and as he could not attend his Duty amidst so vast a Crowd as appear'd in the Chapel, he earnestly desired he might not be carried to the Chapel, and accordingly he was not.

Parker's Penny Post of 28 May tells us that as a result, between 300 and 400 people who had paid 8*d.* a head to be admitted into Newgate Chapel that Sunday morning had to wait from 9 a.m. until noon in vain. There was no chaplain, no prisoners, no service. The *Post* says that there was then a 'General Mutiny', and the turnkeys had to parade three other prisoners in front of 'the Mob' to appease them.

Purney (or whoever wrote the account) says that Wild

kept the other Malefactors in Order and Regularity, no Interruption happening either at Prayers or when the Word of God was reading.

The Day before he died, he desired he might receive the Sacrament, at which Time he enquired the Meaning of the Words—'*Cursed is every one that hangeth on a Tree*'. Also concerning the Disposition of the Soul when first separated from the Body, and the local Situation of the other World. . . . '

But he was answer'd, that they were Matters of less actual Moment and Importance than other Things he might employ his Time about: he was advised rather to repent of his Sins, to read and study Christ's Passion, Merits and Attonement, and the infinite Justice as well as unlimited Mercy of Almighty God. He appeared somewhat attentive to the Prayers, especially before he had some expectations of a Reprieve, and after he found all Expectations were vain.

The Evening before he suffered, he enquir'd how the noble Greeks and famous Romans, who slew themselves, came to be so glorious in History, if self-murder be a Crime?

He was desired to consider, that the wisest and most learned Heathens, called Self-Murder Cowardice, in not sustaining the Misfortunes that Providence laid upon human Nature, and that Christianity is much more express against Suicide. He confessed that Self-Murder was Impiety, but his Confession appear'd to be Hypocrisy; for, about two o'clock in the Morning, he endeavoured to prevent his Execution by drinking Laudanum. . . .'

Wild was evidently an inexperienced drug-taker, for he took far too large a dose.

Select Trials says that after taking the liquid laudanum (opium dissolved in alcohol) he grew so drowsy that he could not hold up his head or keep his eyes open at prayers. 'Two of his Fellow-Prisoners, perceiving his Disorder, endeavoured to rouse him: they took him by the Arms, and persuaded him to stand up and walk a little, which (as he was lame of the Gout) he could not do without their Assistance. This Motion awaken'd him a little, and then his Countenance turn'd very pale, he sweated violently, and grew exceedingly faint and sick; soon after which he vomited till he had thrown up the greatest Part of the Laudanum.'

On the morning of the execution was published the broadsheet of *Jonathan Wild's Funeral Procession*. The verse down the middle between the hanging figures (*plate 16*) was reprinted in *Select Trials* and in some of the *Newgate Calendar* editions. It is curious that the line 'While learned Purney makes a pious Prayer' was changed by the time it reached *Select Trials* into 'While Purney sniv'ling, spells a Godly Prayer'. Probably the change was made by the editor himself, for he seems to have had a strong aversion for that particular Ordinary.

The *Daily Journal* added a paragraph at the end of its news column on Monday the 24th:

> The Execution of Jonathan Wild continues fixed for this day, notwithstanding all the artful amusements of his Friends and Accomplices to procure a Respite. We hear he will not be permitted to pass to the Triple Tree in a Coach, but must be carried thither in an open Cart; and we hear that a detachment of Guards will be ordered out, to be assisting to the Magistrates in preserving the Peace.

Samuel Wale, who did the well-known engraving for the *Malefactor's Register* of Wild in the cart on the way to Tyburn, may have been very exact in his background detail, but he certainly did no research for his main subject. It shows Wild in coat, hat and shoes by himself (*plate 17*). In reality, the half-stupefied Jonathan Wild was put between Sperry and Stanford, and he wore a callimanco nightgown, as well, perhaps, as a head-cloth.

As Under Marshal, of course, Charles Hitchen was entitled to ride behind Martin Lewen, at the head of the procession taking his old enemy to the gallows, but whether or not he gave himself this pleasure is not recorded.

The *Daily Journal* (25 May) says:

> . . . the Mob discovered a surprising Satisfaction when they heard that Wild was to suffer, for, at his coming into the Cart at Newgate, they set up the loudest Shouts and Huzzas that ever was heard, which were continued all the way to the place of Execution.

The gentle John Byrom, poet, diarist, and shorthand writer, entered in his diary:

> Yesterday passed by our Gate here the famous Jonathan Wild in a cart between two other malefactors, in a nightgown, without a Hat, with a Book in his Hand, crying.

He was later to elaborate the note into a long and graphic poem. *Parker's Penny Post* (26 May) gives a gruesome picture:

> . . . from thence he was convey'd in a Cart, without a Hat, to Tyburn, in which Passage he seldom look'd off his Book, but through the violent Huzza's of the Mob, calling out *Blewskin!* etc., when he had stopp'd at the Griffin Tavern near Grey's Inn

15 A 'ticket' to Wild's hanging

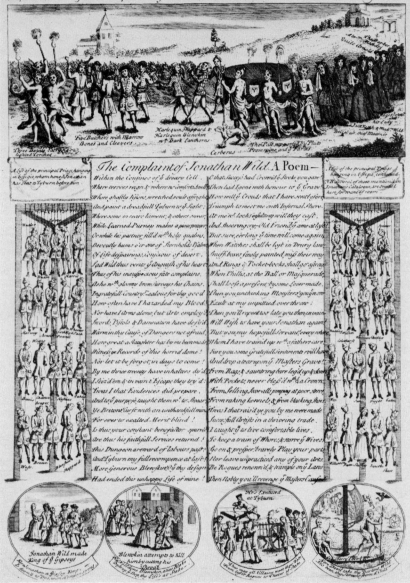

16 A ballad published on the morning of Wild's execution (24 May 1725)

Gate, to drink a Glass of Wine, he said 'What a strange Rig
they run upon me!' The Crowd was greater than ever was
known on such an Occasion, and abundance of Quality and
Gentry's Coaches often block'd up the Road and made a Stop,
while the Populace, as at a Triumph of some General, usher'd
him forward with the loudest Acclamations of Joy, even from
the oldest to the youngest Spectator. . . .

At Holborn, shortly after passing Byrom's gate, Wild's head was
'broke by a Stone thrown from a Window, so that the Blood ran
down him; and other Insults of a barbarous Nature were offer'd
him'. The *London Journal* also had its version:

Never was there a greater Crowd assembled on any Occasion,
than to see this unhappy Person; and so outrageous were the
Mob in their Joy to behold him on the Road to the gallows,
who had been the Cause of sending so many thither; that they
huzza'd him along to the Triple Tree, and shew'd a Temper very
uncommon on such a melancholy Occasion, for they threw
Stones at him; with some of which his head was broke, and the
two Malefactors, Sperry and Sandford, between whom he sate
in the cart, were hurt; Nay, even in his last Lament they did
not cease their Insults. . . .

Captain Smith adds:

I shall hear take Notice, that every execution Day, Jonathan,
being mounted on Horse-Back, he would in great Triumph
ride a little before the Criminals that were going to die, and at
some Taverns in the Way call for half a Pint of Wine, telling the
People about him, with the greatest Joy and Exaltation imaginable, that some of his Children were coming, they were just
behind; So when he went deservedly to be hanged, several
Thieves went a little before the Cart, telling People, their
Father was coming, he's just behind.

Applebee's journal says that the only 'Indulgence he received was,
his not having his Hands tied all the Way'.

Jonathan Wild drank again at the 'White Lion' in St. Giles's,
where he gave some money 'to a Friend in the Cart with him' to
change and pay for the wine, and finally outside James Figg's (the
prizefighter's) house at the 'Oxford Arms', where he had a cool
tankard and some wine.

The Ordinary found the noise and confusion so great at Tyburn that it was almost impossible to say prayers with the criminals. 'The other Malefactors being ready to be turn'd off, and the Executioner telling Jonathan he might take any reasonable Time to prepare himself, he continued sitting in the Cart a little while, but the Mob grew so outrageous at this Indulgence, that they called out incessantly to the Hangman* to do his Office, and threatened to knock him on the Head if he did not immediately perform it. He found Delays were dangerous, and therefore no longer deferr'd to give the Populace the Satisfaction they demanded.'

Applebee's journal said that 'When he was turned off, there was a Universal Shout among the Spectators. As the Cart drew away, his Arms being loose, he happened to catch hold of the Coiner, but was immediately parted from him.' The *Post* elaborated, '. . . he catch'd hold of Harpham's Arm, and slack'd his Rope, till the Executioner (I believe very much against his Will, tho' very dextrously) dispatch'd him; after he was cut down he was convey'd a round about Way, to Surgeon's Hall in a Coach and four Horses, by a Mob who received five shillings per Man for their Service; which was paid at the Cardigan's Head near Charing Cross, where we hear he will not only be Anatomiz'd but his Skin stuff'd and hung up by his Skeleton. . . .

This was the first in a series of ruses and deceptions of which, had Wild lived to know of them, he would certainly have approved. Normally, the mob did all it could to prevent the bodies of criminals from being anatomized, as we have seen many times. Today, however, things were different, and Mary Wild, anticipating some such disturbance, paid for the coach and horses, and for the men to guard it down to the 'Cardigan's Head'. She also paid people to spread the rumour that the coach belonged to the surgeons. The *London Journal* tells us that 'the Body was put into a Coach and Four; and it being given out that it was designed for the Surgeons, the noisy Multitude seem'd easy; by which Means it was carried off, and, we hear, was interr'd on Tuesday night in St. Pancras Church Yard.'

The Parish Register[4] has simply the cryptic entry: '27th. J.W.'

The *London Journal* added that 'the Son of this unhappy Man is now in Town, and, we hear, is preparing for a Journey to Holland, as unable to bear the Reflections that may be cast on him

* Richard Arnet—a prominent guest at Wild's wedding (*see page* 132).

on account of his unfortunate Father; who, 'tis said, left him £300'. *Select Trials* says he was about nineteen years old at this time, and that the magistrates thought it proper to confine him on the execution day; he was of so 'turbulent a Disposition' that it was feared he might cause some 'Mischief among the Mob'. He later sold himself as a servant on the plantations in America.

The *Daily Post* carried a long paragraph about Mary Wild:

> We hear that the Relict of Jonathan Wild is actually contracted to Quilt Arnold, her Husband's Journeyman, and is resolved to marry him at all Hazards; 'Tis remarkable, that this wretched Woman hath had two Husbands and a kinsman executed at Tyburn within these ten years: moreover her Uncle, Mr. Spurling, a turnkey at Newgate, was murdered at the Sessions-house, for which Fact a Man and a Woman were executed before Newgate; so unfortunate hath her Family been. Therefore, what Encouragement a Person of Mr. Arnold's Character hath to venture on her, is yet a Secret.

I have not found out whether or not Mary Wild married Quilt Arnold, and, indeed, this is the last that is heard of her, except that she was dead by 1735. There is a trial of a Mary Wild, who lived in the Old Bailey, in volume 2 of the 1735 edition of *Select Trials,* but if this woman had been either the wife or even a relation of the famous Jonathan, the editor would almost certainly have remarked on it.

Her efforts to ensure that her husband was buried decently were to no avail, for she herself was tricked. On 5 June *Applebee's Original Weekly Journal* reported:

> Yesterday was 7 Night the Body of Jonathan Wild, that was buried in *Pancras Church Yard*, was dug up from the grave and carried off, three or four Days after Interment. The Coffin was afterwards found near Kentish Town. Enquiry is made for the Persons concerned in that inhuman Action, which is Felony by the Law.

Select Trials believed that it was after all the surgeons who had 'thought fit' to remove the body:

> A Hearse and Six was seen waiting about Midnight at the End of *Fig-Lane*, at which Place the empty Coffin was found the next Morning; but what became of the Body is yet a Secret.

What became of the skeleton I shall explain in the next chapter. As to the body, the *Daily Journal* of 15 June contains what is probably the answer:

> Last Sunday Morning there was found upon Whitehall Shore, in St. Margaret's Parish, the Skin, Flesh and Entrails (without any Bones) of a Human Body: the Coroner & Jury that sat upon it, ordered it to be bury'd, which was done on Tuesday last, in the Burying Ground for the Poor, and the Surgeon who attended, gave it as his Opinion, that it could be no other than the Remains of a dissected Body. It was observ'd, that the Skin of the Breast was hairy, from whence People conjecture it to be part of the renowned Jonathan Wild.

{ XXIV } *Aftermath*

> But sure, e'er long, the Time will come again,
> When Watches shall be lost in Drury-Lane;
> Snuff-Boxes, finely painted, miss their Way,
> And Rings, and Pocket-Books shall go astray;
> When *Phillis* at the Ball or Masquerade
> Shall loose a Present from some Lover made:
> Then you—unthinking Monsters!—you that now
> Exult at my unpitied Overthrow,
> Then you'll repent too late: you then in vain,
> Will wish to have your JONATHAN again!
> *The Funeral Procession of Ionathan Wild*[1]

For a while, it seemed as if the prophecy was being fulfilled, for as the *Daily Journal* reported on 5 July 1725:

The Sessions ended last Friday at the Old Bailey, when Elizabeth Roberts, alias Bostock, received Sentence of Death for the Murther of a Pastry Cook in Swithin's Lane. 'Tis remarkable that since the Dissolution of Jonathan Wild, not one Felon has been convicted capitally, which by some is attributed to a Reform amongst the Rogues, and by others to the Want of a proper Person to detect them; but be these Matters as they may, most or all agree, that the giving of Mr. Wild his *Quietus*, was just and absolutely necessary.

A few thieves *were* hanged in 1725 and 1726, but so few in comparison to the droves of the previous years that, as the following paragraph from the *Daily Post* of 5 February 1726 shows, it became a joke:

> Since the Death of Jonathan Wild has been so much lamented for Want of his useful Intelligence, this is to inform the Publick, that his Ghost gives constant Attendance every Night at a certain House in Bury Street; where he resolves all Sorts of Questions. N.B. As his former Business was to discover Robberies committed, he has now the Gift of revealing Rogueries intended.*

The rate of monthly executions did not return to 'normal' for about a year and a half.

At his death, Wild was the subject of more 'Accounts', 'Narratives' and 'Lives'—to say nothing of reams of bad verse of the *Hail rev'rend Tripos, Triple Tree of State!* kind—than any other criminal of the eighteenth century, including Jack Sheppard. Most of the authors, to Defoe's real or pretended disgust, saw Wild's history as providing the chance for a good laugh: yet when it came to pointing the moral Defoe felt was lacking, no one was sure what it was. Some said merely that his wretched state of mind in Newgate should have proved an object-lesson for atheists. A *True Dying Speech* was put out in Dublin, and according to this Jonathan Wild was supposed to have treated the mob to a long, closely-reasoned and grammatically impeccable oration on the existence of God: '. . . I always thought every Religion the Off-spring of the Brain of some Politician, and denied the Existence of that Being, who is the Basis and Foundation of all Religion and Society . . .'.

Had Wild been an educated man he might well have been an agnostic, a cynic or even an atheist. As it was, the questions he asked Mr. Nicholson show that, in common with a large proportion of English people at that time, he had no familiarity with religious teaching at all.

In June, Nathaniel Mist published two articles on 'Wild' (by

---

* It has been suggested that this referred to the impending visit to London of Jonathan Swift, who came to stay in Bury Street, St. James's, on 19 March; but perhaps it refers to Abraham Mendez, who was still apparently, trying to run the Lost Property Office in Bury Street in the City.

whom he meant Walpole), hailing him as a 'great Genius' and model for statesmen. 'Wild' had been too busy for much reading, and his library contained books of a mere practical nature: *The English Rogue, Lives of The Highwaymen, Sessions Papers, Tacitus,* etc. He had often told Mist that he greatly admired a sentence in Farquhar's *The Recruiting Officer*; a magistrate asks a constable what he has to say against a prisoner, and the constable (like Walpole, who despised all idealists in politics) replies, 'Nothing, except that he's an honest Man'. Another favourite quotation of this great man, wrote Mist, was the parental advice: 'Get Money, Son, honestly if you can; but however, get Money.'

How much money *did* Wild earn? According to his own statement to 'H.D.' (if that may be believed) the Lost Property Office alone made a total profit of above £10,000. If we remember that he started taking 5s. deposits in 1716, and that this, allowing an average of two enquiries a day over nine years (subtracting Sundays but adding leap-years), would make £1,410 in deposits alone; that the sum required for the return of goods was never less than half the original value; and that the rewards and gratuities the public 'forced' on him varied between £3 and £400 a time, then £10,000 is not an unreasonable figure. If to this we add £5,000 for goods disposed of in other ways, £5,000 for goods smuggled abroad and £5,000 for goods smuggled in on return journeys, we have £25,000.

Wild claimed that by 1718 he had brought more than sixty 'Rogues to Justice'. That makes £2,400 in State reward money and does not count local rewards (as with the Mrs. Knap affair) which might add, say, another £600. In 1721 the reward was increased to £100 and in 1722 to £140. Between 1718 and 1725 he took perhaps another '60 Rogues' at rewards varying from £40 to £140—let us say thirty at £40 a head and thirty at £140. This makes £5,400, not counting special rewards (as for Wilkinson and Lincoln, the murderers of the Pensioner). We now have a total of £32,800, which might represent £656,000 or $1,540,000 today, tax-free. We cannot assess how much more he got from extortion against thieves in Newgate buying their way out, which may have added several thousand pounds more, to which should be added money levied on bawdy-houses, coiners, forgers and the like, who had to work in more or less fixed premises and so were easy victims. However, against that should be set his expenses in bribes to judges, court-officers, constables and others, shares to his thieves, and hush-money. A further deduction must be made in rewards that had still not been paid to him at his death—perhaps half a dozen. His earnings, therefore, may be averaged out at £25,000, or £500,000 in modern money. By the standards of the gangsters of the twentieth century, this is perhaps not much, but at his time it was unprecedented and a very large sum indeed.

With regard to what happened to Wild's skeleton, we must rely on the word of a Dr. Frederick Fowler, who lived in Windsor in the last century. According to him, the body was dug up by a surgeon named Brand, who had been able to arrange this through his close friendship with one of the Newgate Ordinaries at that time deputizing for Purney (James Griffiths and James Wagstaff). The reverend gentleman presumably went back on his word to Mary Wild that her husband's body would be left in peace. The skeleton and coffin-plate passed from Brand to a well-known Windsor doctor called Thomas; thence to his relative Dr. Rendall, who in turn disposed of his practice and the skeleton to Dr. Fowler. In 1847, following the publicity caused by the Jack Sheppard plays and the discovery of Wild's warehouse in West Street, Fowler presented the skeleton to the Royal College of Surgeons, under cover of the following letter:

Gentlemen, I beg to offer for your acceptance the skeleton of the celebrated Jonathan Wilde, which has been in my possession together with my predecessors upwards of fifty years. The peculiar character of the letters and figures on the coffin-plate that accompanies it, which were in general use at that period, will be an additional proof of the authenticity of the skeleton.

The coffin-plate seems to have been lost, probably in the bombing of 1941. The skeleton now hangs in the Hunterian Museum at the College. The posterior vault of the skull has been cut away, but a few details of the description in the pamphlet prepared by Miss Jessie Dobson, the Museum Recorder, may be of interest: 'The forehead is broad and low, and the face short and square, with prominent malar bones and almost level orbits. The signs of sex are definite. The brow ridges are well developed. . . . There is slight but definite subnasal prognathism. The lower jaw is wide and rounded and the chin broad, but not prominent.' All but one of the teeth were present in the lower jaw, and all in the upper jaw, when he died, at the age of forty-two.[2]

Just and necessary though it might have been, Wild's death taught no lessons, brought no reforms and alleviated no suffering. The offence for which he was hanged, the taking of a reward for returning stolen goods, continued to be common practice for years after, as Henry Fielding's complaints of 1751 bear witness.[3] The old trade of thief-taking and all its evils thrived undeterred. A pamphlet in the Guildhall Library, entitled *A Looking-glass for Informing Constables*[4] relates how bands of these 'Informing Constables', or thief-takers, set upon strangers and broke into houses in order to 'set up' fake crimes and implicate innocent people for the sake of the reward money. Between 1754–6, there were a number of trials at Maidstone, the Old Bailey and the King's Bench, of M'Daniel and 'his Bloody Gang of Thief-Takers alias Thief-Makers'. These had perfected the system of staging pseudo-robberies; an innocent passer-by would see a person being robbed and run to his (or her) assistance. Together they would chase the thief, and with the help of a constable who conveniently came up, arrest him. Then the passer-by would find himself charged with the crime. The robber, the person robbed and the constable all belonged to the same gang. In volume 2 of his *History of English Criminal Law* (p. 339) Professor Radzinowicz gives a list of ten such conspiracies by this gang alone, between 1738 and 1754, to 'frame' people for the sake of the reward money.[5] Several of their victims were hanged, and of course there is no record of how many other successful conspiracies there were by other gangs. Yet, at the trial, the law was unable to decide what crimes, if any, the gang had committed. In the end, after one of the thief-takers had been killed in the pillory by the enraged mob, the Attorney-General waived the prosecutions for what Blackstone describes as 'prudential' reasons. It was not thought advisable to support any move that might discourage or cast into further disrepute the profession of thief-taking.

In 1749 Henry Fielding had founded the 'Bow Street Runners'. His idea owed something to Sir Thomas De Veil, his predecessor at Bow Street, and something even to Jonathan Wild himself. But the 'Runners' were never able to avoid the taint of 'thief-taking' and at the time of the M'Daniel affair, Henry's half-brother and successor, Sir John Fielding, 'The Blind Beak of Bow Street', was at pains to emphasize that *his* men were never guilty of these wicked and bloody practices.

Then in 1816, when the public thought that at last such evils

were things of the past, six constables were tried for exactly the
same offences. These, unlike any of their predecessors back to the
time of Henry VIII, were all hanged.

Meanwhile, Jonathan Wild had become a symbol rather than a
remembered historical person, and this, together with his being
relegated to the part of villain in the Jack Sheppard story,
resulted in his subsequent obscurity. In *The Beggar's Opera*, John
Gay had tried to show that 'Peachum' and 'Lockit' (who was
something of a mixture between Hitchen and Spurling) were really
pillars of the underworld; but his point was missed, for politicians
saw the play only as an attack on themselves, and critics attacked
the play because it showed criminals in a humorous and sympathetic light. Then in 1742-3, Henry Fielding produced his
famous novel, *The History of the Life of the Late Mr. Jonathan Wild
the Great*. It was yet another attack on Robert Walpole, the King's
First Minister, and on statesmen who are called 'Great', and
Fielding chose the name of Wild because, twenty years after the
death of the real Jonathan, it had come to represent total villainy
in all its forms. From such sources as 'H.D.', Mist's articles, and
The Life of the Heroic and Magnanimous Jonathan Wilde he took the
tone of his book and the idea that politicians and thieves are alike,
but little else. Of the real Wild, or the real criminal underworld,
his book tells us hardly anything, whatever its virtues may be as a
satire on 'Great Men'. Perhaps this is not surprising, for Fielding's
knowledge of crime and criminals at that time was probably small.
He was not to become a magistrate in Westminster for another six
years, and his first-hand experience so far amounted to only one
tour of the Wiltshire circuit. Yet it is from Fielding's novel that
Wild's name is most widely remembered today and this, with no
disrespect to Fielding, is a pity.

Of all the satires written on Wild, the most informative is a
remarkable pamphlet in the Guildhall Library called *Jonathan
Wild's Advice to His Successors*,[6] remarkable in that it shows how
property-racketeering in London was being managed during the
first half of the eighteenth century.

'Jonathan Wild' recommends that his successor should, to
avoid the odium attached to the name of 'Thief-Taker', buy himself the position of a Justice of the Peace and rent houses from the
parish (what we would now call the Church Commissioners),
speculative companies and *bona fide* citizens. He should then sub-
let them to suitably chosen people who will turn them into

brothels. Being a Justice he can protect these brothels and raise the rents to any height he pleases.

> There is no Fear of convenient Houses standing empty upon that Account, for those who are in Possession will take Care to make their *Cullys* pay for the extraordinary Charges. Therefore a great Man might be a Bawd without the Reflections of the World, for who should say that a Landlord could help the Vices of his Tenants, or that he is in any Way culpable for suffering such Persons to live in his Houses?

Sober families, unable to cope with the astronomic rents and the gangs of roughs, will be forced to move to more creditable neighbourhoods. When the inevitable disorders break out and such locals as were too poor to move become enraged and start to demonstrate outside the houses, 'forcing the Doors and breaking the Windows', you need not worry, says 'Jonathan Wild', for

> Will it not be in your Power to call for the Assistance of a Detachment of Soldiers on such an Occasion, and, if that won't do, send a few of your *Brave Fellows* with Bludgeons Etc.? I warrant the Mob will soon quit their Purpose. As for the Persons who were in Possession of the House, they have got off, Lord knows how. Then put a Bill upon the Door of the said House, signifying that it is the Property of another Person; and you have no Connection with it, and it will soon blow over!
>
> To drive away all the Dregs of Clamour and Censure, that may yet remain in the Breasts of some Sort of People, soon after come out with some grand Scheme for the Good of the Publick: Let your Puffers be dispers'd in every Company, with Panegyrics on your great Goodness and Philanthropy. Half a Dozen Lines now and then in some Newspapers may be of Service to you, but be sure to let them be well *plaistered* with your extraordinary Care, Diligence, and Publick Spirit.

This is a nearly complete exposition, written out step by step over 200 years ago, of that notorious 'Rachmanism' which caused such dismay and surprise in London in 1963. There have been enough parallels between past and present during the course of this narrative, however, for readers to take their pick without difficulty. The twentieth century has been fairly crowded with Jonathan Wild's successors, for organized crime, corrupt administrations and 'secret' police have provided them with fertile soil.

In England at the time of writing, a promising nursery for a Jonathan Wild of the near future, one might suppose, would be the ever-multiplying commercial 'security' companies. Like Wild, they are successful and, like Wild, they operate in the no-man's-land between the law, crime and private enterprise; and, as in his day, the government is too preoccupied with larger troubles to give them much attention. Within the regular police (and I am speaking not only of England) the safeguards against such a man are more formidable, and some would claim them foolproof.

What would be his personal requisites? Wild had no sensitivity, probably little creative imagination and, morally, he was an oaf. But he did have an abundance of what the eighteenth century called 'Genius'—that is, ingenuity, cunning, resource, energy and that mysterious power we sometimes call 'personal magnetism'. He was able to manipulate the thieves for so long because, I suspect, they felt that he was really on their side, no matter how murderous his behaviour, whereas someone like Lovell was not. Wild's history was a variation on the fable of King Log and King Stork.

If thief-taking was the framework supporting the underworld for three centuries, and played such an important part in the social life of London, why did it receive so little attention from authors and why was the public always in such apparent ignorance about it? Why, for instance, did Defoe, who surely remembered Lovell, write that 'the Life of Jonathan Wild is a perfectly new Scene'? Luke Hutton said that he knew of 'Black Dogs' who had been active for at least thirty years (i.e. since c. 1560) but that their existence was unknown to the public at large. In 1700 Arthur Pepys and his friends were completely out of their depth in the underworld of Lovell, Connelly and their retinue of thieves. In 1718, Hitchen and Wild wrote pamphlets against each other and both assumed, rightly, than the world knew nothing of what was going on. Eight years later, the public was astonished at the revelations about Wild himself, and we can only assume that Defoe, caught in the public enthusiasm like a good journalist, was writing up his story as 'news', and being careful not to offend the City officers again. A quarter of a century later still, the public was equally surprised and outraged when the 'Blood-Money' conspiracies of M'Daniel and his men were uncovered. Each generation, from Luke Hutton's to Sir John Fielding's and after, behaved as if the evil were new to its own time, and was shocked that such unheard-of corruption should flourish under its nose and remain undetected so long.

In this respect, the general public then was probably rather like the general public now. What they knew of crime they learned from what they read, just as we do. Very few people outside the criminal classes ever met a criminal except when they were being robbed, and it is doubtful if any of the writers of pamphlets about the adventures of highwaymen and burglars, etc., had much first-hand knowledge of the underworld. Thus when some notorious case, such as Wild's, exposed the workings of the real underworld to the general gaze, everyone, writers and public alike, were shocked and disturbed, just as we are. In our own age, films and television, even serious documentaries, have not made all that difference because, since the establishment everywhere of what are in all but name national police forces, the professional police-man and the professional criminal have become opposing arche-types in our modern mythology. The intimacy of their ceaseless struggle, and the fact that it is carried on in a region outside or beneath the experience of the layman, gives him the feeling, unwarranted though it may be, that each has more in common with, and so understanding of, the other than either has with the rest of society. It is this feeling that gives the memory of Jonathan's career its disturbing quality. It is not reassuring to know that both organized gangsterdom and that part of the police most directly concerned with it, which we now call the C.I.D., were delivered and nursed by the same man. The ease with which he played his dual rôle is like a warning or a threat, pointing to the time when another moral oaf of genius comes to play the devil with our laws.

Now it only remains to relate what happened to Wild's entour-age of thieves, whores and 'Evidences'.

There is no record that Will Lock, Field, Riddlesdon, Elizabeth Angier, 'Callico Sarah', Moll Harvey, Ruth Arnold, Kate Hacka-bout, Jonathan's son and about thirty others ever returned from Maryland; and therefore either they died on the plantations or bought their freedom, settled down and raised families whose descendants, it is to be hoped, are now thoroughly respectable American citizens. In *The Blind Eye of History* Charles Reith has written that it was transported criminals from Wild's gangs who set up his system on the other side of the Atlantic and so founded organized crime there. The most doubtful part of this theory is that none of the people we have come across in this story would seem to have had the talents for organization and leadership needed for such an undertaking.

The end of Charles Hitchen was sordid and miserable. On 9 April 1727, the Marshal (whom the newspapers described as 'an elderly Man') was seized committing sodomy in a Charing Cross tavern and taken to Newgate. At his trial he brought friends to testify that 'he was a very honest Man, who had taken a World of Pains, and spent a great Deal of Money in *discouraging the Prophaneness, curbing the Vices, and reforming the Manners of the present Age*'.

He was acquitted of sodomy but convicted of the attempt, and sentenced to pay a fine of £20, to stand in the pillory at the end of St. Catherine Street, Strand, for one hour, and to suffer six months' imprisonment.

A 'Sodomite' was always a preferred victim for the terrible London mob, and the pillory was consequently barricaded with carts. The mob, however, were 'very incensed against him', jumped over the carts and, unhindered by the Under-Sheriff's officers, 'used him after their ruff Method, against which he was well provided, having clad himself in Armour to stand their Batteries, which flow'd plentifully upon him, and finding him Armour proof, they tore off his Breeches and Shirt from his Back. . . .' The *Evening Post* adds that 'several Persons struck him on the bare Skin with the end of their Canes', and *Parker's Penny Post* finished the description, 'whereby he appear'd as a tatter'd Scarecrow to fright Owls by Night'. After half an hour, when it seemed that Hitchen might be dying, the Under-Sheriff 'was oblig'd' to take him down.

Hitchen survived his six months in Newgate, however, and was discharged in October. On 31 September, the Court of Aldermen, after so many years, at last took action and dismissed him 'from his Office on Account of being guilty of several notorious practices and having for upwards of six Months past totally neglected the Duty of his Office'. He died shortly after in extreme poverty, and his wife appealed to the court for relief.[7]

Sir William Thomson continued as Recorder until his death in 1739. His career was quite unremarkable, but perhaps he would have been shocked to know that he is remembered now only because he lived at the same time as Jonathan Wild.

In America, Tom Butler disappears from view. Of Follard, or of what his evidence against Wild might have been, I have found no record. Margaret Morphew was hanged on 27 March 1728 for stealing a silver salt-cellar and a silver tea-pot.

After Wild's execution, Henry Kelley went to Roger Johnson and became his servant, Johnson being afraid to refuse him lest he should be betrayed. At this time he was in hiding and working with a coiner called Stone. In the end Kelley did impeach him to Justice Vaughan, and Johnson was sent to Newgate with his father and mother. Perhaps, indeed, this was the occasion, and not an earlier one, Capt. Smith was thinking of when he said that Roger impeached his own mother for coining in order to save himself. Certainly, he bought his way out of the Common Side into the Master's Side, and the New Keeper, Mr. Allen, allowed him the liberty of the Press Yard. However, he and a Henry Fisher, being held for murder, escaped by climbing on to the Press Yard leads and jumping across the narrow street. Thus, by way of Phoenix Yard, they got into the City. Fisher went to Lisbon, and Johnson returned to 'Preaching the Parson'. The enquiry into their escape may be read among the Repertories of the Court of Aldermen and other papers in the Guildhall Records Office.

Eventually Johnson was caught doing his act in Newcastle by two officers of the Poultry Compter. He was double-ironed, and brought all the way back to London chained under a horse's belly. This time he was kept in the worst part of the Common Side, the 'Stone Hold' under the Gate. He was so horrified by the swarms of white lice crawling over his black coat that he became ill and remained so until Allen, bribed, let him out into the ordinary Common Side.

In 1729, Bambridge, the brutal Warden of the Fleet Prison, was committed to Newgate on several charges of murder. During the course of the trials he was visited in Newgate by Lord Chief Justice Eyre, who was at first under the impression that Bambridge was being persecuted. Shortly after this, Eyre was charged with using his enormous influence to try to get Bambridge acquitted (in fact, Bambridge was acquitted). There was a Parliamentary enquiry and the prisoners who had made the accusation were examined. The ringleader was Roger Johnson. The Committee found that Johnson and his fellow-conspirators were merely trying to revenge themselves against the Chief Justice, who had dealt with them at one Sessions or another. Eyre explained that as soon as he became aware of Bambridge's true character, he broke off all contact with him. The man's crimes had been so enormous, he said, that originally he thought they must have been exaggerated by his enemies. On the other hand, *The Life of Roger Johnson* says that when he came into the Common Side, Johnson set up in partnership with a tallow-chandler, running a black-market in spirits. Johnson cheated his partner out of the profits, and the chandler got his own back by denouncing him to the Committee as the leader of a conspiracy. Whatever the truth Johnson was found guilty of leading a conspiracy and sentenced to remain a close prisoner in Newgate during 'the Pleasure of the House'. He stayed in Newgate a long time. In December 1730 he was tried and acquitted of having stolen a wig and thrown snuff in the face of one Mordecai Pitts several years before (*Sessions Papers*, December 1730). He was returned to Newgate on the Master Debtors' Side. Eventually he was given charge of the Tap (presumably after the death of Mrs. Spurling) and became more or less responsible for the discipline of the prison. He used to hold rehearsal trials at which prisoners would have to answer questions likely to be made against them at the Old Bailey. Under his rule, Newgate became quite an orderly place. He severely punished anyone who stole from visitors, saying once to a nervous gentleman who thought he was going to be robbed, 'Damn you, do you think there are any Thieves in *Newgate*?' He discovered the gold which Sarah Malcom, the famous murderess, tried to bring into the gaol, and was released under an amnesty of the Smuggling Act. He became a pawnbroker in Round Court in the Strand, and died on 22 August 1740. By his own wish he was buried in Derbyshire. He was forty-five. In *Jonathan Wild* Fielding portrayed Roger Johnson as an elderly 'ruler' of Newgate whom Wild deposed by trickery.

Edward Burnworth alias Frazier emerged from obscurity after the death of Wild and formed a gang which went robbing in Southwark. In March 1726 they murdered Tom Ball, who was setting himself up as a new thief-taker. They escaped by firing shots over the crowd, and thereafter resolved to murder every person they robbed. Soon, however, alarmed by the 'Hue and Cry' and by Burnworth's ferocious behaviour, the gang began to break up. Some fled abroad. Eventually one of them, Marjoram, was taken and, despite the efforts of the others to kill him, he impeached them to the Lord Mayor. One by one the gang were caught. When Burnworth heard that Quilt Arnold was looking for

17 A well-known print from the *Malefactors' Register*, showing Wild
in the tumbril. Hugh Phillips (*Mid-Georgian London*) has shown that
the spot is Holborn, near Hatton Garden. Nevertheless, Wild
should be in a dressing-gown, hatless, and seated between two
thieves

18 Another version, valuable for its historical details. The Javelin
Men behind the cart, led by the Sheriff's Sergeant, are officers of
the Compter where Wild was once imprisoned. The stout man on
horseback carrying a mace (*l. foreground*) is a City Marshal (the
earliest picture of this officer in existence), whom we could
suppose to be Wild's old enemy, Charles Hitchen. Beside St.
Sepulchre's Church, the Bellman rings his bell and calls out his
exhortation to repentance

him, 'he ventur'd one Night to an Alehouse in the Old Bailey, which Arnold frequented, and, understanding that he was alone in a back Room, he took a loaded Pistol in his Hand, and pushing open the Door, "Damn ye!" says he, to *Arnold*, "What Business have you to do with me? Do you think to set up the Trade of Thief-taking upon your own Account, now your old Master is hang'd? Ye Dog! It would be but tipping ye Justice to blow your Brains out!" Then filling a Glass of Brandy, and putting some Gunpowder into it: "Now, down on your Knees, you Son of a Bitch," adds he, "drink this, and wish it may be your eternal Damnation, if ever you offer to molest me, or any of my Acquaintances!" *Arnold* was forced to comply, and then *Burnworth* knock'd him down, and went clear off.'[8] And that is the last we hear of Quilt M. Arnold.

At length Burnworth was caught. Emmanuel Dickenson, William Blewit and Tom Berry were arrested on board ship at Holland and brought to England under a heavy armed guard. Because their robberies had mainly been in Southwark, the gang were taken in a waggon to Kingston. 'As they past along the Road, they behaved in the most Audacious Manner imaginable, rattling their Irons, laughing, singing, swearing and huzza-ing.' Burnworth refused to plead and, determined to outdo William Spiggott, was pressed for an hour and three minutes under a weight of 3 cwt., 3 qtrs. and 2 lb. After that, he pleaded with the rest, and they were all found guilty.

None of them seemed the least concerned, 'Burnworth diverting himself with drawing Pictures of his Adventures, and the others telling stories of their Pranks.' They made several plans of escape, which included murdering all the keepers in the gaol and setting fire to the town of Kingston, but were taken to Kingston gallows on Wednesday 5 April 1726. Some made short speeches. 'After this they all shook Hands, and kiss'd each other, and a short Time being allow'd for their private Devotions, the Cart drew away, and they were turned off, crying, *Christ have Mercy upon us*!'

Burnworth and Blewit were hung in chains in front of the 'Two Fighting Cocks' tavern in Southwark Mint, and Dickenson and Berry on Kennington Common.

Then in June, an Edward Hartrey, who kept a barbershop in Bolt Court, off Fleet Street, had his pocket picked of his gold watch while he was with Mary Blewit, who had also been the mistress of Dickenson and another member of the gang called

Bowler, in a brothel in King's Head Court, Shoe Lane. He had
been 'a little in for't' (drunk) but when he accused her of taking
his watch, she denied it, 'and up came her Bullies, who beat me,
and maul'd me, and kick'd me down Stairs, and broke my Nose,
and turned me out of Doors, and hustled me up and down a
Parcel of Dark Allies, to prevent me from finding out the House
again; and so they left me in a most lamentable Pickle. I was glad
to get rid of 'em at any rate. . . .' He was able to trace the watch
through a pawnbroker the next day, and found Mary Blewit in her
lodging up two flights of stairs 'in the House of the late *Jonathan
Wild*'.

At her trial in July, Mary was found guilty to the value of 10*d*.
and sentenced to transportation.[9]

One of the witnesses was a Watchman called John Sylvester,
who said that Hartrey was one of his 'Masters', and that he always
took care of his masters and saw them safely home if he should
chance to meet any of them as he beat his rounds.

And so it fell out between 12 and 1 o'Clock on Saturday
Morning, that I see's my Master *Hartrey* come out of a Coach in
Fleet-street, very much fuddled, and who in all the World should
he pop upon, but this very Gentlewoman at the Bar, Madam
Blewit, or *Dickenson*, or *Bowler*, for she was Wife to them all at
the same Time, and the two first of 'em are now a-hanging in
Chains in *St. George's-Fields*. Whether my Master Hartrey
wanted a Whore, or she wanted a Rogue, is neither here nor
there, but they presently laid fast hold of one another and began
to be woundy loving. I found my Master was in Danger, and I
did all I could to get him away from her.

'Hussy,' says I, 'you saucy Brimstone Toad you, what
Business have you with my Master, and be damned to you?
Let him go, or I'll call my Brother Watchman and carry you to
the Round-house directly. And Master,' says I, 'Ah! My dear
Master! come along with me and leave that Hang-in-Chains
Bitch!'—Yes I did call her a Bitch, that I did my Lord, and I
can't deny it. 'She'll certainly pick your Pocket,' says I, 'or
serve you a worse Trick. Come, come, don't expose yourself.'
But all I could say signified nothing, he swore she was a Girl
for his Fancy, and he would go with her in spight of my Blood:
And so they went together, but it had been better for him, if he
had taken his poor Watchman's Advice.

Notes

I *Introduction*

1 *Jonathan Wild, Prince of Robbers* by Frederick J. Lyons (Michael Joseph 1936); an essay in *Twelve Bad Men* (edited by Thomas Seccomb 1894); another in *More Famous Trials* by Lord Birkenhead (1931); *Dictionary of National Biography*; and, of course, Wild receives an important mention in every history of crime. The account in *The Newgate Calendar* series, beginning with the *Bloody Register* of 1764, is a boiled-down version of that in the 1742 edition of *Select Trials*, which itself omits a great deal of information in the earlier 1735 version.

II *In the Compter*

1 *History of Wolverhampton* by G. P. Mander (Wolverhampton C. B. Corporation 1960) pp 111–12. Also *Weighley alias Wild* (1725) p 43.
2 *Weekly Journal or British Gazeteer*, 6 May 1721.
3 Shelf 228—*MSS relating to Insolvent Debtors*.
4 *The Fees of the Sheriff's Court ... Wood Street, Poultry & Ludgate, 1709*. In BM at 11631 bb 100.
5 *House of Commons Journals* vol 21, pp 577–85, Also *Malice Defeated* by Elizabeth Cellier (1680).

III *'The System'*

1 *Song of the Constable*, see *The Elizabethan Underworld* by A. V. Judges (Routledge 1964).

IV *The Founding Fathers*

1 First published 1931; reissued by George Routledge 1964.
2 These letters were a commentary on four articles which had been
   published in the *BJ* from 27 Feb until 27 March, signed
   'Philanthropos', who was in fact the philosopher Bernard de
   Mandeville. Radzinowicz (*History of Criminal Law*, vol 2, p 23,
   n 96) supposes the letters to have been by de Mandeville also.
   Perhaps the names of Arthur Pepys and Francis Harewood might
   establish the author's identity. The four articles were published in
   pamphlet form in mid-April 1725 under the title *An Inquiry into
   the Cause of the Frequent Executions at Tyburn*. It was the first notice
   of Wild taken by an important writer, and its descriptive passages
   have been widely quoted in social histories of the period. It was
   also pirated by authors of guidebooks, etc., until the middle of the
   eighteenth century.
3 *Letters from the Dead to the Living*, 1701. It can be read in Tom
   Brown's *Amusements Serious and Comical* (1927 edn., foreword by
   A. L. Hayward).
4 See *Defoe in the Pillory and Other Studies* by John Robert Moore
   (Indiana University 1939).
5 *Complete History of the Lives of the Most Notorious Highwaymen* by
   Capt. Alexander Smith 1714–19. Republished complete by
   Routledge and Sons, 1933, with foreword by A. L. Hayward.

V 'The Twang'

1 *An Authentic Narrative of Jonathan Wild*. A copy of this, called
   An Authentic History etc. is in Trinity College Library, Dublin.
2 *The Regulator*, p 5.
3 Ibid.
4 *A History of Police and Crime in the City of London* by Donald
   Rumbelow (Macmillan 1970).

VI *The Marshal*

1 Guildhall Records Office: *Journal of Common Council* 57, folio 207b
   (20 Feb 1730). Acknowledgements to Donald Rumbelow for this
   reference.
2 Guild. Rec. Off. MSS 108 5. Sheet 8.
3 Ibid. Sheet 2.

VII *The Protection Racket*

1 Quoted in *Anecdotes of London in the Eighteenth Century* by
   J. P. Malcom (1820).

2 Guild. Rec. Off. *Repertories of the Court of Aldermen,* 117 folio 366
15 Sep 1713; 118 folio 55–6; 118 folio 219.

VIII *Cock Alley*

1 *A True and Genuine Account of . . . Jonathan Wild* by Defoe (?), p 12.
2 *Select Trials at the Old Bailey* (1742 edn.), vol 2, pp 230–1.
3 *The Life of Jonathan Wild* by 'H.D.' (1725), p 15.
4 Guild. Rec. Off. *Rep.* 118 folio 431.

IX *Lost Property Office*

1 *Lives of the Most Remarkable Criminals* (1735), Life of Wild. Republished by Routledge 1927, intro. by A. L. Hayward.

X *Disciplining 'Rebels'*

1 *Select Trials* (1742 edn.) vol 2, pp 268–70.
2 *Ibid.*
3 *Select Trials* (1735 edn.) vol 2, p 107.
4 Noble Collection, C. 42.
5 *Select Trials* (1735 edn.) vol 2, p 93.

XI *The Law Intervenes*

1 Transportation Orders are in the Gaol Delivery Books, at the end
of each Sessions. A number of Transportation Bonds relevant to
Wild's men (e.g. Riddlesdon) are in the Middlesex Records Office,
in Box MJ/SPT/2. Landing Certificates are in Guildhall Records
Office, *Misc. MSS* 57.7. A number of other relevant docs. are in
Small MSS box 38.3.
2 1st edn. 1769, vol 4, p 132.
3 P 57. In BM at 508 b 24. A condensed version is in 16th edn.
(1788) of *Justice of the Peace* by John Burn, vol 3, p 72. Briefly
referred to in *Pleas of the Crown* by William Hyde East (1803), vol
2, p 746, quoting as source Serjeant Forster's *MSS and Select Cases
of Evidence* p. 57. Also referred to in Radzinowicz, op. cit. vol 1,
p 667.
4 *Daily Courant.* Some of these are quoted in *The South Sea
Bubble,* by John Caswell (Cresset Press 1961).
5 *Select Trials* (1742 edn.) vol 1, pp 29–33.

XII *A Paper War*

1 Pepysian Collection, ii, 153.

2 Quoted in *A Compleat Collection of Remarkable Tryals* by 'N.B.' (1718–21) vol 4, pp 193 *ff.* In BM at 518 b 6, 1/2. Also in *Select Trials* (1735 edn.) vol 2, pp 88–97.

3 *Weekly Journal or Saturday's Post* 9 Sep 1721, referring to recapture of John Meffe by Wild.

4 Guild. Rec. Off. *Misc. MSS* Box 57.7—2.

5 *Select Trials* (1735 edn.) vol 2, p 90.

XIII   The 'Double-Cross'

1 The dates of Wild's moves are bedevilled by confusion, due mainly to the mistakes in *Select Trials*. Passages in the 1735 edn. (e.g. vol 2, p 95) were omitted from later editions, and were in any case incorrect. As a result, F. J. Lyons believed that the 'King's Head' was next to the 'Cooper's Arms' (in fact, in Little Old Bailey) and that Wild moved there in 1716. After houses were given numbers in 1777, the 'King's Head' became No. 68 Old Bailey.

2 According to Timbs's *Curiosities of London*.

3 *Common Sense; or The Englishman's Journal*, vol 2, pp 240–5.

4 'H.D.', p 21.

5 *Select Trials* (1724 edn.) vol 1, p 201. *Trial of Charles Johns and James Bradshaw*, May 1722.

6 Quoted in *The Literature of Roguery* by Professor F. W. Chandler (1907), chapter on Wild.

7 *Lives of the Most Remarkable Criminals, v.* Stephen Burnet.

8 *Some Account of London* by Thomas Pennant (3rd edn., 1793), p 180. *Select Trials* (1742 edn.) vol 1, p 148.

9 *Original Letters* by H. Ellis (1825) 1st Series, vol 2, pp 295–303. Also in *Tudor Economic Documents* by R. H. Tawney and Irene Power (Longmans 1951) vol 2, pp 237–9. Original in BM, *Lansdowne MSS*, No. 44, Art. 38.

10 *Daily Journal* 2 Nov 1721.

11 *Daily Journal* 13 March 1722.

12 *Weighley alias Wild*, p 38. For Proclamations, see Radzinowicz, vol 2.

13 *Select Trials* (1742 edn.) vol 1, pp 108–11.

XIV   Jonathan's Circle

1 *An Authentic Narrative . . .'*

2 *History of Elizabeth Mann, the Royal Sovereign,* by Capt. Christopher Johnson (1724). BM at 1418 d 46.

3 Defoe, p 19. *Chronological Register*, p 28, in *Historical Register*, 1717.

4 *Select Trials* (1735 edn.) vol 1, pp 358–9. *Lives of the Most Remarkable Criminals*, pp 437–8.

5 *Select Trials* (1742 edn.) vol 1, p 44.
6 Middx. Rec. Off. GD Book 307/32; Sessions Papers MJ/SPT/2/2.
7 *Select Trials* (1742 edn.) vol 1, p 20; p 122–3 (*Trial of George Nicholas*, Jan 1722).
8 Guild. Rec. Off. *Misc. MSS* 57 7; *Select Trials* (1742 edn.) vol 2, p 266.
9 *London Journal*, 26 Jan 1723.
10 *Weekly Journal or British Gazeteer*, 16 Feb 1723.
11 *Treasury Papers*, vol 32 (2) p 458.
12 Guildhall Library, *Sessions Papers* March 1720; also *Select Trials* (1735 edn.) vol 2, p 102.
13 Guild. Rec. Off. *Misc. MSS* 57 7; *Select Trials* (1742 edn.) vol 3, pp 171–4. For pamphlets on Dalton, see *Bibliog.*
14 *Select Trials* (1735 edn.), vol 1, p 76 *ff*.
15 Middx. GD Rolls 2370–4.
16 *A Descriptive Account of the Old House in West Street* (see *Bibliog.*)
17 *Life of Roger Johnson* in BM at 10825 c 34.
18 *Historical Register*, 1718.
19 In BM at 1094 h 5.

XV *Dividing the Map*

1 Guildhall Library, at A 3 3, No 43. BM at E 927 (4). Reprinted in 1674 as *Francis Jackson's Recantation*.
2 *Select Trials* (1742 edn.) vol 2, p 281.
3 'H.D.', p 33.
4 *The Great Law of Subordination Consider'd*, by Defoe (4 April 1724).
5 *Select Trials* (1735 edn.) vol 1, p 38.
6 *Select Trials* (1735 edn.) vol 2, p 99.
7 *Select Trials* (1735 edn.) vol 2, p 94.

XVI *The Fortunes of Moll Flanders*

1 *Sessions Papers* in BM at 515 1 2 (153), catalogued under *London ii— Civic and Municipal Institutions—Sessions: 'Complete Proceedings on the King's Commission of the Peace, Oyer and Terminer, etc.'*. Also Middx. Rec. Off. Sessions Rolls 1776 and 1824.
2 Middx. Rec. Off. (i) SP Roll 1895 Aug 1697. (ii) SPR 1898 Oct 1697. (iii) GDR 1939 Dec 1699. (iv) SPR 1949 April 1700. (v) SPR 1972 Sep 1701. (vi) SPR 2000 Dec 1702. (vii) SPR 2005 Aug. 1705. (viii) GDR 2135 July 1709. (ix) SPR 2163 Jan 1710. (x) SPR 2183 Jan 1712. (xi) SPR 2205 Feb 1713. SPR—*Sessions of Peace Roll*; GDR—*Gaol Delivery Roll*.
3 Middx. GDR 2370 July 1721, indict. No 40 contains a summary of her 1718 case.
4 *Historical Register*, 8 Dec 1718

5 *Select Trials* (1742 edn.) vol 1, Trial of Sarah Wells, p 312.

6 *Lives of the Most Remarkable Criminals—Life of John Everett*. A pamphlet on Everett in the BM is listed as destroyed in World War II. See also *Select Trials* (1742) vol 2, *Newgate Calendar*, vol 2, and *Hitchin Worthies* by R. L. Hine.

7 Middx. GDR 2370.

8 Guild. Rec. Off. *Misc. MSS* Box 57. 7/5.

9 Middx. GDR 2370, indict. No 11.

10 *Life of Mr. John Stanley*, probably by Rev. Thomas Purney, pub. by John Applebee in December 1723. In BM at 1132 f 32. Of this pamphlet, the editor of *Select Trials* comments sarcastically, 'The Ordinary's Writings are commonly in the Profound Stile, but this Performance is in the Sublime, as you shall see . . .'.

11 *Select Trials* (1735 edn.) vol 1, pp 74–8. Also Middx. Rec. Off. GDR 2370–4, July–October 1721; especially 2370, indictments Nos 5, 8, 9, 10, 11, 13, 23, 24, 40 and 4- (illegible), together with recognizances for Bird, Kinsallaugh, Awbery and Johnson.

12 *Select Trials* (1742 edn.) vol 1, p 65, Trial of R. Hunter and G. Post.

13 *Historical Register*, July 1721.

14 Quoted in this context in *Defoe, His Life and Undiscovered Writings* by William Lee (1869), vol 1, p 355.

15 *An Accurate Description of Newgate* by 'B.L. of Twickenham, Gent.' There is a copy in the Bodleian Library, Oxford, and large selections have been reprinted in *Newgate and the Old Bailey* by W. Eden Hooper (Underwood Press 1935).

XVII *The Science of Gang-Breaking*

1 *Post Boy*, 25 April 1722; also *London Gazette*.

2 At 1851 c 19 (32) under *London ii—Civic and Municipal Institutions—Sessions*. Normally, this would be listed under *Surrey* or *Kingston Assizes* along with other Sessions Papers of that county.

3 Guild. Rec. Off. *Misc. MSS* Box 57 7/2.

4 *Select Trials* (1742 edn.) vol 1, p 93.

5 *A Full, True and Impartial Account of Robberies, etc.* by William Hawkins (but probably written by Richard Burridge, a journalist working for Read's *WJ and British Gazeteer*, who was in repeated trouble for blasphemy). In BM at G 19418 (1).

6 *Select Trials* says 22 Sep and 2 Nov (vol 1, pp 135 and 111), but indictment No 12 in Middx. GDR 2377 confirms date as 2 September.

7 *History of the Lives of Wild, Blueskin, Sheppard etc.* (c. 1725) p 26.

8 Middx. GD Book 308/1. For Wright see *Select Trials* (1735 edn.) vol 1, pp 98–100; *Lives of the Most Remarkable Criminals*; *Life of Jonathan Wild and Modern Highwaymen* by Capt. Alexander Smith.

9 *Daily Journal* 24 April 1722.
10 *Select Trials* (1742 edn.) vol 1, pp 138–9; also *A Full and Impartial Account*, etc., by Ralph Wilson.
11 Middx. GDR 2377 (indict. No 12) and 2380 (Indict. No 8); GD Books 308/1 and 308/7.
12 *Proceedings of the Society of Antiquaries of London*, 1866, 2nd Series, III, p 372: 'Colonel the Hon. Percy Fielding exhibited through B. B. Woodward Esq., F.S.A., a musketoon given by the notorious Jonathan Wilde to Blueskin, and by Sir John Fielding the well-known magistrate to his half-brother Henry Fielding Esq. as shown by the inscriptions upon it. This weapon measured 1 foot 6½ inches in length, and appeared to be of Scotch workmanship.' I shall be most grateful to hear from anyone who knows the present whereabouts of this gun.
13 *London Journal*, 14 and 18 April 1722.

XVIII *A Crack in the Ice*

1 *Select Trials* (1742 edn.) vol 1, pp 260–1, Trials of Wilkinson, Lincoln and Milksop.
2 *St. James's Journal*, 26 July 1722; *Weekly Journal or British Gazeteer*, 28 July 1722; Calendar in Middx. GDR 2393.
3 *Select Trials* (1742 edn.) vol 2, p 165, Account of Joseph Blake.
4 *Select Trials* (1735 edn.), Trial of Simon Jacobs, October 1722. For Lock's stolen Information, see *Select Trials* (1742 edn.) vol 1, p 260.
5 *St. James's Journal*, 5 July 1722.
6 *London Journal*, 22 June 1723; *Select Trials* (1742 edn.) vol 2, p 167, Account of Joseph Blake.
7 *Lives of Six Notorious Street Robbers* (1726). Although this pamphlet is included in several editions or selections of Defoe's works, Professor John Robert Moore does *not* include it in his *Checklist* of Defoe's writings. I have said 'Defoe' here merely for convenience.
8 *Select Trials* (1742 edn.) p 307.
9 Middx. GD Book 308/55.
10 *Life of Wild and Modern Highwaymen* by Capt. Alexander Smith. *Select Trials* (1742 edn.) vol 1, p 269, and vol 2, p 166.
11 *Select Trials* (1742 edn.) vol 1, p 297. Middx. GDR 2398; Middx. GD Book 308/78. The confusion about Oakey which *Select Trials* complains of probably arose because one Richard Oxey in the same gang was tried on the same morning, and the shorthand-writers mixed them.
12 *Select Trials* (1742 edn.) vol 2, p 167, Account of Joseph Blake.
13 *Treasury Papers*, vol ccxlvi, f 86. Reprinted in *Notes and Queries* 6th

Series, vol 8, p 126. The Certificate is signed by Lord Mayor, Sir Gerard Conyers, and Sir William Thomson, Recorder.

14 *Select Trials* (1742 edn.) vol 2, p 167.

XIX Jack Sheppard

1 *A Narrative of all the Robberies . . . of Jack Sheppard.* This was the 'confesson' Sheppard handed to 'Applebee's Man' at the gallows, and authorship has always been supposed to be Defoe's'.

2 *Trial of Jack Sheppard* by Horace Bleackley (*Notable British Trials Series*, Wm. Hodge and Co. 1933). Valuable for its bibliography and its study of the Victorian plays, etc., based on Ainsworth's novel. The best modern account is *The Road to Tyburn* by Christopher Hibbert (Longmans, Green 1957) to which the reader who requires more details about this story is referred.

3 Quoted in *The Times,* 6 May 1841, in an article reporting the discovery of the document among the 'Town Clerk's old records'. Date given as 20 June 1723, and so quoted in *Chambers Book of Days* (vol 1, p 299). F. J. Lyons gives date as 2 January 1724; a pamphlet by Royal College of Surgeons as 2 January 1721; a letter by 'Hirondelle' in *Birmingham Daily Gazette,* 15 June 1883 as 1723 again. I am most grateful, therefore, to Mr. Donald Rumbelow for drawing my attention to the article in *The Times,* and to Miss Betty Masters, of the Guildhall Records Office, for finding the proper entry in the *Repertories of the Court of Aldermen.* The original petition seems now to have disappeared, although 'Hirondelle' said he had seen it in the hands of the City of London authorities in 1883. It was also believed to be among the *Frederick Fowler MSS* in the Library of the Royal College of Surgeons. I should be extremely interested to hear of its present whereabouts.

4 Guild. Rec. Off. Rep. 128, folio 319.

5 Staffordshire County Records Office: D 1778/IV/2. Printed in Historical MSS Commission *13th Report, Appendix IV* (HMC 31).

6 *An Authentic Narrative, Weighley alias Wild,* 'H.D.', *'Life of Parquot'* in *Life of Wild and Modern Highwaymen* by Capt. Alexander Smith, for various fragments of this story, which is further substantiated by newspaper reports of February–April 1725.

7 *Select Trials* (1735 edn.) vol 2, p 105. This detail is not in later editions, and so is misreported in all the *Newgate Calendar/ Malefactor's Register* series.

8 *Lives of Wild, Blueskin, Sheppard etc.* (1725).

XX The Arrest

1 *Life of Roger Johnson* (1740).

2 Middx. GDR 2417.
3 Middx. GDR 2434.
4 *An Authentic Narrative*, p 30; Defoe, p 36; London Sessions Roll for April 1725.
5 *London Journal*, 11 July 1724; *Select Trials* says the coin was Edward VI.

XXI *Out of a Hat*

1 *An Enquiry into the Causes of the Late Increase of Robbers etc.* (1751) reprinted in Heinemann's edition of Fielding's works, 1903, vol 13.
2 Middx. SPR 2441.
3 Guild. Rec. Off. *Misc MSS* Box 57 7/33.
4 Guild. Rec. Off. *Misc MSS* Box 57 7/21c.

XXIII *Execution*

1 BM at 1851 c 10 (39).
2 Quoted in *Philip, Duke of Wharton*, by Lewis Melville (1913). Melville does not date it, but gives the impression that it was written *c.* 1720. I should think, however, that the date I have given above is the more likely, unless there is some conclusive evidence against it.
3 *Select Trials* (1742 edn.) vol 2, pp 284–6. The complete text of Purney's account was republished in *The Political State of Great Britain*, vol 29, pp 507–10. The pamphlet in the BM at 6495 K 7 was probably a forgery, and in any case was destroyed in World War II.
4 Greater London Records Office, County Hall, at P. 90/PAN. 1–3.

XXIV *Aftermath*

1 BM Print Room: *Satirical Prints*, vol 9, No 1751. No 1752 is the *Funeral Ticket*.
2 *Annals of the Royal College of Surgeons of England*, vol 9, November 1951, pp 339–46. Republished as a separate pamphlet. See also an amusing letter sent to Fowler by a phrenologist, who interpreted Wild's character from the skull without knowing the identity. Published in *Weekly Dispatch*, 22 March 1840; quoted in full by F. J. Lyons, p 219.
3 *An Enquiry into the Causes of the late Increase of Robberies.*
4 Guildhall PAM 7318 (1). It is bound with a sermon by Rev. T. Bray at the funeral of a murdered constable, referred to in J. P. Malcolm's *Anecdotes of London* (1820).

5 Joseph Coxe, High Constable of Blackheath, who discovered and
   hunted down the gang, wrote his experiences in *A Faithful
   Narrative of the Wicked and Inhuman Transactions of that Bloody-
   minded Gang of Thief-Takers alias Thief-Makers, Macdaniel, Berry etc.'*.
   In BM at 518 e 20. The story is retold in Patrick Pringle's *The
   Thief-Takers*, a history of the subject which begins with Wild
   (Museum Press).

6 At A 8 6, No 27—in old catal. only. Date is 1758, but that may be
   a late edition. A reprint is bound in with a reprint of 'H.D.', in the
   BM. It is also reprinted in F. J. Lyons.

7 *Select Trials* (1742 edn.) vol 3, pp 74–5; *Evening Post*, 8–11, 15–18
   April, 2 May; *Parker's Penny Post*, 3 May; *London Journal*, 6 May
   1727; Guild. Rec. Off., *Rep.* 131, folio 420; *Journal of Common
   Council*, 57, folio 207b (20 Feb 1730).

8 *Select Trials* (1742 edn.) vol 2, p 353, *Account of Burnworth alias
   Frazier*.

9 *Select Trials* (1743 edn.) vol 3, pp 34–5.

Appendix I

Documents relating to Jonathan Wild in the Wood Street Compter

Under *Shelf 228—MSS Relating to Insolvent Debtors*, there are five documents for Jonathan Wild.

1 A Warrant to the Keeper, dated 25 October 1712, from Sir William Withers (M.P. for London, 1709–15; Lord Mayor, 1707–8; Sheriff, 1701–2; Alderman, Farringdon Ward Within, 1698–1721):

> *London* ss.
> WHEREAS *Jonathan Wilde* hath by *his* Petition set forth unto me, one of Her Majesty's Justices of the Peace of the said *Citty* of *London* that on the Seventh Day of *December*, 1711. was, and hath ever since continued actually a Prisoner for Debt, or Damages in the *Said* —— Prison in the said *Citty* —— and that *hee* is reduced to very great Poverty and Necessities, and become utterly disabled to satisy and pay all *his* Debts to *his* Creditors. And forasmuch as the said Prisoner hath in *his* said Petition prayed to be discharged, by Virtue of a late Act of Parliament, Entituled, *An Act for the Relief of Insolvent Debtors, by obliging their Creditors to accept the utmost Satisfaction they are capable to make, and restoring to them their Liberty.* These are therefore in pursuance of the said Act of Parliament, to require you to bring before Her Majesty's Justices of the Peace at the General Quarter-Sessions of the Peace to be held for the said *Citty* on the *Eighth* Day of *December* next ensuing, by

Ten of the Clock in the *Fore* noon, the Body of *the said Jonathan Wilde* together with the Copy or Copies of the Cause or Causes *hee* is charged with, to the intent that the Oath mentioned in the said Act may be administered to *him* and other Proceedings thereupon made according to the said Act. Given under my Hand and Seal the *Twenty Fifth* of *October*—1712.

WITHERS

2   A schedule of the suits on which Wild was committed to the Compter and still held. The first reads:

'WOOD STREET COMPTER ss. (*to wit*) Jonathan Wild a Prisoner in the Woodstreet Compter yᵉ 13th of March 1709 Dunk Vic (*i.e. while Thomas Dunk was Sheriff—1709 is 1710 in modern dating*): is detained by Action against him at the Suit of Robert Pearson, Case 99s. Entered the 9th March 1709 by Threlkeld Sargt.'

Other debts can be summarized thus: Robert Peacock, 39*s.*, entered by Sargt. Threlkeld; William Smith of 'Blew Ancor Alley White crosse street', 39*s.*, entered 11 March by the plaintiff; Eleanor Roberts of Goswell Street, 39*s.*, entered 13 March by the plaintiff; William Cannon of Gravel Lane, Houndsditch, 39*s.*, 13 March; Elizabeth Lowe, 39*s.*, 17 April; Anne Gibbons of Red Hart Court, Fleet Street, 99*s.*, 12 May; Joseph Hetherington 99*s.*, 5 December 1711. Of these, Cannon, Lowe and Hetherington are crossed out.

3   In Wild's own handwriting:

A Schedule of what monies I owe.

	£	*s.*	*d.*
To Mr. Robert Pearson	04	19	00
To Mr. John Peacock	01	19	00
To Mr. Wm Smith	01	19	00
To Mrs. Elinor Roberts	01	19	00
To Mrs. Elizabeth Harris a bond	12	00	00
To Mr. Wm Wood	07	00	00
To Robert Adams	04	00	00
To Ed: Hillman	03	10	00
To John Shaby	03	10	00
To Samll Shalby	07	00	00
To Eliz Wms	10	00	00
To Wm Smith	03	00	00

JONATHAN WILDE

Theire is Severall other persons I owe Small Debts to, but forgett their Names.

4   Also in Wild's handwriting:
    A Schedule of wht Monies is oweing to me.

	£	s.	d.
From Robert Coward	15	00	00
Robt Gilbert	01	00	00
Obadiah Lemon	10	00	00
Lucus	07	00	00

Severall others wch I cant remember being Small.

JONATHAN WILDE

5   Entries in Sessions Book December 1712, p 15. Wild's pardon was registered in the *London Gazette* on 4–8 November 1712.

Appendix II

Wild's List

This is the list that Wild distributed among the jurymen outside the
Old Bailey court-room on the morning before his trial. It is, I think,
the same as that in *Applebee's Original Weekly Journal* of 15 May 1725
(which I have not seen). The list below is taken from the 1742 edition
of *Select Trials* and contains the names of seventy-five criminals whom
Wild had 'brought to Justice'. It is full of mistakes and inaccuracies.
I have added dates and such corrections as I could, and have numbered
them for convenience.

For Robbery on the Highway—35

1 & 2 '*Edward Spencer* and *Joseph Hutton*, for wounding two Persons
near Fleet Bridge, the Time of the Hard Frost, the Father & Son
named Hoskins, a Gunsmith in the Minories.' (Spencer hanged, 20
Feb 1716; Hutton, 12 March 1716. Their cases were not connected
and neither was the first criminal Wild arrested.)

3–6 '*William White, Thomas Thurland, Timothy Dun,* and *Darville* alias
Chapman, for assaulting *Thomas Middlethwaite* Esq; on the Highway,
with an Intent to rob him & afterwards assaulting (& murdering)
Mrs. *Knapp*, and robbing her Son, and several other Robberies.'
(May–June 1716. Isaac Rag impeached the gang, was sent to Fleet
Bridewell and was afterwards transported with John Filewood.)

7 & 8 '*Footman* alias *Goodman*, and *Thomas Smith*, For robbing Squire *Wetherington* upon *Epping Forest*, of his Watch, Money & Horse.' (March 1716. Wild arrested Goodman after he had escaped from the Bail Dock.)

9 '*Henry Checkley*, for robbing a Gentleman living at *Oxford*, at a Bookseller's, in a Alley, by St. *Paul's Churchyard*, leading to *Paternoster Row*, of his Watch & Pocket-Book, wherein was a Bank Note of considerable Value.' (January 1718. Chickley was impeached, with Joseph Johnson and Dick Berry, by Obadiah Lemon, for robbing in Ave Maria Lane.)

10 & 11 '*John Holmar* and *James Wilson*, for robbing a Sailor, *George Herbert*, in Warwick Lane, of 11 Guineas and a half.' (September 1720. Impeached by William Field.)

12 & 13 '*John Wigley* and *James Reading*, for robbing Mr. *Conyers*, in *Islington*, of a Silver Watch, a Pair of Silver Spurs & some Money.' (August 1721. Reading was hanged for robbing Brownsworth; but for Wild's real motives for arresting Reading, see the text.)

14 '*John Dykes*, for robbing *William Smith*, in *Stepney Fields*, of a Silver Watch, a Silver Pair of Buckles, Coat, Hat, Wig and some Money.' (October 1721. Quite incorrect, for the victim was Charles Wright and the theft of a penknife, value 5s. Impeached by Isaac Drew, and Wild probably looked up the wrong entry in his books, which suggests that Dykes worked for him.)

15 & 16 '*John Easton* and *Thomas Piggot*, for robbing Elizabeth Knowles, of Goods to the Value of 11s.' (March 1722. Impeached by Avery.)

17 & 18 '*William Williams* and *John Thomas*, for robbing *Richard Arnold*, on the Highway, a Baker, in *Spittalfields*.' (A William Williams was transported in July 1720 and re-transported in October 1721, but this may be a different man.)

19 '*Thomas James*, for robbing a Mr. Maud, a Druggist, in the *Strand*, of some Money and a Ring.' (July 1721—*Historical Register*.)

20 & 21 '*Thomas Sinnament* and *William Colthurst*, for robbing Mr. Hearl and others, on Hounslow Heath.' (Sinnamond, 13 February 1719, the day of Wild's wedding; Colthurst, January 1722. They were both of Spiggott's gang.)

22 '*Butler Fox*, for robbing Sir Edward Lawrence.' (March 1722. Actually for robbing Col. Hamilton, but see text for the cause of Wild's mistake.)

23 '*James Shaw* alias *Smith*, alias *Thompson*, for the Murder of Mr.

Potts, Receiver of the Window-lights, taken by others for Robbing, but convicted by me for the Murder.' (January 1722.)

24 '*Jeremiah Rann,* for assaulting and robbing a Clockmaker's Servant of a Clock, who lives in *Lombard-Street.*' (May 1722. Once an assistant of Wild's.)

25 & 26 '*James Lincoln* and *Robert Wilkinson,* for robbing and killing a Pensioner, near *Buckingham-wall.*' (September 1722. Impeached by William Lock.)

27 & 28 '*John Levee* and *Matthew Flood,* for robbing Esquire *Young,* and Col. *Cope,* on the Hampstead Road.' (January 1723. Impeached by Blueskin Blake.)

29 '*Richard Oakey,* for robbing Mr. *Betts,* a Carpenter, near Fig-lane.' (January 1723. Impeached by Blueskin Blake.)

30 & 31 '*James Butler* and *William Duese,* the Prosecutor found out by me, for assaulting and robbing Mr. *Holms,* a Schoolmaster of Chelsea, and at the same Time attack'd my Lady *Chidley*'s Coach, but came off with the Loss of one of their Comrades, whose Name was *Rice.*' (July 1723.)

32 '*Humphrey Angier,* for robbing Martin Lewin, late City-Marshal, near *Highgate.*' (August 1723.)

33 '*John Herrington,* for robbing Dr. Vasey, in Leicester Fields.' (Probably March or April 1724.)

34 '*Edward Joice,* for robbing a Gentlewoman by Exchange Alley, who lives in Mugswell Street. (April 1724, and the gentlewoman was Sarah Wood.)

Wild claims a total of thirty-five. Perhaps he counted Rice.

House-Breaking—22

35 & 36 '*William Rigglesdon* and *Elizabeth Shirley* for breaking into a Dwelling-house, adjoining to the Banquetting-house, *White hall,* and from thence breaking into the Banquetting-house, and stole from the Communion-table a Silver Candlestick.' (September 1714. Wild probably arrested Riddlesdon, who probably impeached Shirley and Parsons, but was not hanged. See text.)

37 & 38 '*William Hoskins* and *John Parrot,* for robbing the Shop of Mr. *Downes,* a Hosier, in the Corner of *Northumberland-Court,* in the *Strand,* of Silk Hose and other Things, to a great Value; and also the Bishop of *Norwich*'s House.' (Robbery in August 1714, trial in February 1715. Robert, not John, Parrot robbed the Bishop, but both were impeached by John Chance.)

39 '*John Fairbone*, for robbing a Brewhouse near *Brick-lane*, in *White-chapple*, of a considerable Sum of Money.' (Probably spring 1715.)

40 & 41 '*John Allen* and *John Chance*, for robbing a Gentleman's House, near Hammersmith Parish, of Goods & wearing Apparel to a great Value.' (June 1715. Chance had already impeached Parrot and Hoskins for Wild; now he was impeached in turn by a fifth member of the gang, for Wild.)

42 & 43 '*Robert Evans* and *John Latherington*, for breaking the House of Major *Harding*, and several of his Neighbours, in *Strutton Grounds*, *Westminster*, of divers Goods of great Value.'

44 '*Samuel West*, for robbing Mr. *Gumbleton's* House, near *New-Exchange* in the *Strand*, of Plate, and other Goods of great Value.'

45 & 46 '*Samuel Davis* and *Thomas Draper*, for robbing a Linnen-Draper's Shop in *Aldersgate Street*, of several Parcels of Goods.' (January 1719. Impeached by John Walker and Will Cryer. All four belonged to Obadiah Lemon's gang, now in a state of dissolution. The draper was Francis Hyam.)

47 '*Henry Browne*, for robbing Mr. *Lambe's* near *Hackney*, and several others in the same Parish, of Goods to a great Value.'

48 '*John Harris*, for robbing the House of *William Taylor* and several other Houses in *Shore-ditch* Parish, of divers Goods to a great Value.' (Hanged 26 October 1720. Impeached by William Field. Husband of Elizabeth Harris, for whom see text.)

49 '*John Wheeler*, for robbing Mr. *Clay's* House, at *Eagam*, of Goods to a great Value.' (Trial 11 October 1719—*Historical Register*.)

50 & 51 '*James Harvey*, and a Person called *Cock-ey'd Jack*, for robbing a Weaver's House in the Park, *Southwark*, of Goods to a great Value.' (3 March 1720. Only Jack was hanged, and Harvey transported. Impeached by Richard Oakey, of Carrick's gang.)

52 '*Arnold Powell*, for robbing a Glass-grinder's House, near *Fleet-bridge*, of Goods to a great Value.' (March 1717. In fact, Powell was hanged not because of, but in spite of, Wild's efforts.)

53 & 54 '*Thomas Eades* and *Thomas Wynne*, for breaking the House of a Shoemaker, near the *Old Mint*, in *Southwark*, and taking Goods to a great Value.' (The pamphlet *Weighley alias Wild* gives date as 1717, but 1723 is more likely. Being a Surrey case, the records are not available. Coupled with these are two called Holmes and Oyston, who may have been the evidences against them.)

55 & 56 '*John Sheppard* and *Joseph Blake*, for breaking the House of Mr. *Kneebone*, a Woolen-draper, near the *New* Church, in the *Strand*, and robbing the same of Goods to a great Value.' (November 1724. Impeached by William Field.)

Returning from Transportation—10

57 *'James Filewood.'* (This should be John Filewood, who was hanged for this in March 1721. James was hanged for a robbery on 31 October 1718, though Wild may have had something to do with it.)

58 *'William Bond.'* (First transp. 19 May 1720. Probably returned 1721.)

59 *'Charles* Hinchman.' (Transp. December 1719. Hanged 21 March 1721 for returning.)

60 *'Samuel Whittle.'*

61 *'Martin Grey.'* (Transp. 19 May 1720. Hanged June 1721 for returning.)

62 'William Holaday.' (His name was John alias James Holliday. Sentenced to transp. with Hinchman on 7 December 1719. Hanged September 1720 for returning. A Joseph Holliday was also transported on Wild's evidence. 'William' probably came into Wild's mind from a well-known character in *Lives of the Highwaymen*.)

63 *'Robert Godfrey alias Perkins.'* (Sentenced. 10 July 1719. Transp. February 1720. Hanged 5 July 1721 for returning.)

64 *'Old Harry alias Henry Williams.'* (Mentioned in *Sessions Papers* for January 1701. Transp. January 1722 with Moll King. Probably hanged 1723.)

65 *'Henry Woodford.'*

66 *'John Meffe.'* (Hanged 1721.)

Transported again after returning from Transportation—9

67 *'John Mason.'* (First. transp. 1718.)

68 *'Edward Catornes.'*

69 *'Sarah Wells.'* (June 1723).

70 *'William Smith.'* (First transp. March 1720. Re-transp. 1721.)

71 *'John Hall.'*

72 *'Thomas Stanton.'*

73 *'James Dalton.'* (Transp. 19 May 1720, then January 1721.)

74 *'Mary King.'* (June 1720, then July 1721, etc.—see text.)

75 *'John Jones.'* (Perhaps May 1721, but it is uncertain which John Jones Wild meant.)

Wild forgot to include the following:

76 John Parsons. (September 1714, for the Banqueting House robbery.)

77   Samuel Cole. (Tried August, hanged October 1718.)

78   Thomas Smith alias Newcomb. (May 1722. A member of Carrick's gang, impeached by William Faulkner, who also appeared as a witness against Wild's ex-assistant, Jeremiah Rand, so there may have been a connection there too.)

79   John Allen. (January 1724. Impeached by Peter Levee of Burnworth's gang.)

There were also those disposed of by indirect means. Some were arrested by Wild, others on Wild's behalf. The total is impossible to guess, but we have records of the following:

80   Hugh Oakley. (October 1717. He escaped the gallows only because the hangman was arrested on the way to Tyburn.)

81   Samuel Lynx. (13 February 1719.)

82   John alias Richard James. (October 1721. Arrested by Wild, impeached by Nathaniel Hawes.)

83   James Wright. (December 1721. Impeached by William Hawkins. Wild gave evidence against him and had arrested him before.)

84   Thomas Milksop. (September 1722. Arrested with Carrick's gang, and impeached, with a man called Ping, by Wilkinson.)

85, 86, 87   Richard Evans, William Elisha, and Richard Woodman. (Hanged at Kingston, probably in autumn of 1724. Impeached by William Field and a man called Push, it was said on Wild's behalf.)

Finally there were those who were transported, or imprisoned, fined, whipped, etc., on Wild's evidence, many of whom were arrested by him as well. We have records of the following:

Joseph Holliday, Thomas Goodram, Charles Hudson, William Dickson, Kate Brown, James Thompson, Margaret Dowdell and Alice Wright, all February 1719; William Robinson, March 1720; Elizabeth Shanks, December 1720; Jeremiah Garraway and Thomas Sly, May 1723; Edward Pawlett and Simon Jacobs, November 1724.

This brings the total to 101. If we were then to allow for all those women whose names Wild omitted for reasons of discretion, all those he forgot, and all those convicted by others on his behalf (e.g. Grantham), a total of 120 or even 150 would seem quite reasonable.

Appendix III

London Gangs referred to in this book

I *Jack Hall's gang*: John Hall, Joseph Hatfield, Arthur Chambers,
Dick Morris, Luke Matthews, Jack Goodwin, alias 'Plump', Stephen
Bunce alias 'Bunch', Dick Low, Moll Raby, Mary Rogers, Martha
Rogers, Simon Rogers, Margaret Yeomans, Magdalene Yeomans,
Mary Yeomans ('Moll Pines'); Richard Yeomans alias Newnham,
Connelly (thief-takers). 1690–1709. See Chapter IV. Refs.: Middx.
GDR 1952, July 1700; GDR 1963, March 1701; SPR 1962; GDR 1966
Apr 1701; GDR 1068 June 1701; SPR 1975 Oct 1701 (Indict. No 4);
SPR 1988, 2000; GDRs 2006, 2056. London Sessions Roll, April 1701
mentions Arthur Chambers, impeached by 'Sam Barber' with 'Severall
Fellonies & Burglaries & burnt in th: fac: & many times in his hands
...'. There are lives of several of these people, and references to
others, in *Lives of the Highwaymen* by Capt. Alexander Smith, and
accounts of Jack Hall, Bunce and Low in *The Newgate Calendar*. Jack
Hall left a 'Memoir' (see *Bibliog.*). Some odd sheets of *Sessions Papers*
in the BM contain further details: at 515 1 2 (153 and 173); 1480 d 21
(16); 1851 c 19 (6), the figures in brackets referring to the sheets in the
albums. The presence of Luke Matthews suggests a continuation of
this gang into Wild's gangs. Yeomans's Landing Certificate is in Guild.
Rec. Off. *Misc. MSS* 57 7/1. Hatfield survived until November 1724
(see Chapters IV and XIX).

II *'The Whitehall Gang'*: William Riddlesdon, John Parsons,

Elizabeth Shirley, John Chance, William Hoskins, Robert Parrot, William Parker (see Chapter VIII).

III   *Obadiah Lemon's gang*: Christopher and William Matthews, Joseph Johnson, Thomas Draper, Samuel Davis, John and William Walker, William Ward, William Cryer, Hugh Oakley, Henry Chickley, Samuel Linn alias Lynx, and John Flanders. There are references to this gang in *The Regulator, A Compleat Collection of Remarkable Tryals,* and *Select Trials* (1735 edn.) vol 2, pp 88–105. (See Chapters IX and XII.)

IV   *Isaac Rag's gang*: William White (see II), Tom Thurland, Jack Chapman alias Darvel, Timothy Dun. Murderers of Mrs. Knap. Rag went to America with John Filewood alias Violet. (See Chapter X.)

V   *William Field's gang*: John and Elizabeth Harris, John and Richard Trantum, Philip Storey, John Holmar, James Wilson, Jonathan Howel alias Johnson, John White, Kit Leonard, Richard and Ruth Grantham, Elizabeth Smith, Mary Taylor, Temperance Walker, Anne Merritt alias Merrick, alias Waldron. Thomas and Elizabeth Glannister, Kathleen Cook alias Mackaine (later protector of Jack Sheppard); through Elizabeth Smith and Mary Taylor, connection with Moll King, Richard Bird, Humphrey Burton, Elizabeth Taylor alias Burton, Sarah Wells alias 'Callico Sarah' and John Everett. Perhaps also Samuel Cole. References to this gang in *Select Trials* (1735 edn.) vol 1, pp 74–80, vol 2, pp 102–4, and under names of persons tried (e.g. Glannister, whom the *British Journal,* 3 Nov 1722, said was 'on crutches, being very old in Years and Vice'). (See Chapters XIV and XVI.)

VI   *Spiggott's gang*: William Spiggott, Thomas Philips alias Cross, Rev. Joseph Lindsey, William Burroughs, William Hayter (or Heater), Thomas Colthurst, William Colthurst and Thomas Sinnamond. The last two are on Wild's list.

VII   *James Shaw's gang*: James Reading, William Barton, John Wigley, William Burridge, Isaac Drew, John Dykes, Joseph Dickenson (elder brother of Emmanuel Dickenson—see X), Richard Norton alias Watkins, Nathaniel Hawes, John alias Richard James, William Wade, alias 'Shuffle' (servant to Benjamin Child the highwayman), Robert Wilkinson, Thomas Milksop (both of whom went to Carrick's gang (see IX). Through Wade, via Robert Simpson, a connection with the Hawkins gang (see VIII). Broken up, largely through efforts of Wild, 1721–2. (See Chapter XVII.)

VIII   *The Hawkins gang*: (1) Ryley, Cummerford, Reeves, Wooldridge, and an Irish officer Capt. Lennard. 1717–18. (2) John and William Hawkins, Ralphson, Pocock (who turned evidence on the rest, about six or eight in all, whose names are not recorded). 1718. (3) The Hawkins brothers, James Wright, Ralph Wilson, Butler Fox, George Simpson (see VII). 1720–2. (See Chapter XVII.)

IX *Carrick's gang*: James Valentine Carrick, John Malhoney, Daniel Carrol, James Lincoln, John and William Casey, Humphrey Angier, Callaghan, Disney—these at least were all Irishmen. Among the English were Robert Wilkinson, Thomas Milksop, William Lock, Matthew Flood, Simon Jacobs alias Joseph Guest, Joseph 'Blueskin' Blake, Edward Pollitt alias Pawlett alias Pollard, Thomas Smith alias Newcombe (hanged May 1722), and Thomas Ping. Then there was a group round Blueskin containing Richard Oakey, John Levee, Peter Levee, Nathaniel Hawes (before he joined Shaw). There was yet another group round Angier consisting of John Dyer, William Duce, Joseph Rice, James Butler. Gang dispersed (mostly hanged) 1722–3, largely through the efforts of Wild. (See Chapter XVIII.) The survivors, Blueskin, Jacobs and Pawlett, drifted together into another gang containing James 'Hell and Fury' Sykes, Grace, Doling, Thomas Sheppard and Jack Sheppard, and used William Field as a receiver (whom they probably met through the fact that Blueskin's mother lived in Wapping, close to Field's family). Blake and Jack Sheppard hanged, Jacobs and Pawlett transported, through the efforts of Wild, assisted by Field. Finally there was a young group round Edward Burnworth alias Frazier: William Blewit (a schoolfellow of Blueskin's and Pawlett's), Peter Levee (again), John Legee alias Large, Thomas Berry alias Teague (these two certainly Irish), John Higgs alias Hicks, Jack Wilson, William Marjoram alias Huggardy. These were still youths, and some children, when Carrick's gang was first arrested in 1722.

X *Edward Burnworth's gang*: same as the last group in IX, plus Jack Barton, Emmanuel Dickenson (see VII), and Kit Leonard (see V). Most of this gang were hanged in 1726, a year after Wild's death. What happened to Leonard I am not certain. He had been with Duce, Dyer and Meads for a time (1723) and is last heard of in Surrey County Gaol (which had just been built in Southwark).

Appendix IV

The Justice House at the Old Bailey

In vol 3 of his *History of London* Walter Besant devoted a chapter to the Old Bailey as it was in the days of Jack Sheppard, Jonathan Wild, *Moll Flanders* and *The Beggar's Opera*. He described the court-room as a high, dark, forbidding place of Dickensian atmosphere, surrounded by echoing corridors. The picture seemed reasonable enough and most writers since have followed him.

Contemporary engravings, however, show something quite different, and it seems to me that the matter is one of unusual interest (if only to the designers of film and stage sets).

The fact that the court *was* open to the air is proved by entries in the Repertories of the Court of Aldermen in the Guildhall Records Office. The first Sessions House was built in 1539, but it was seldom used. The judges preferred to hold the Sessions outside in the garden, and in 1542 a permanent roof was built there to protect them from the rain. This building, and the garden, were destroyed in the Great Fire of 1666 (MSS 149 21, by Dr. Reginald Sharp). In 1668, a new Sessions House was commissioned after two models had been submitted to the Aldermen (Rep. 73, folio 82). Meanwhile, a wooden shed was erected amidst the rubble, and it was in this shed that the famous Claude Duval, for one, was tried and condemned. The new Sessions House was completed in 1673 and is shown in *Plate 3*. The date of this engraving is uncertain, but it may have been drawn by Gaywood and at any time between 1673 and 1720. There is another better-known engraving by John Bowles, drawn probably in 1735, which is not included here as it has been reproduced many times before—though curiously without attracting any comment. Perhaps the reason for this is that the view could be interpreted as a 'cut-away' to reveal the interior. Under the print, by way of caption, is a quotation, unacknowledged, from the 1720 edition of Stow's *Survey of London*, which says: '. . . the Court Room being advanced by Stone Steps from the Ground, with Rails and Bannisters inclosed from the Yard before it. And the *Bail Dock*, which fronts the Court, where the Prisoners are kept until brought to their Tryals, is also inclosed. . . . It standeth backwards, so that it hath no Front towards the Street, only the Gateway leading into the yard before the House . . .'. The precise meaning of all that is difficult to decide on.

On 19 November 1735, a motion was put to the Court of Aldermen to enclose the front of the Sessions House because of the 'Inclemency of the Weather'. The matter was put off several times until December 1736, when George Dance (Clerk of the Works and designer of the Mansion House) was ordered to close up the front with sashes. Thus the court had stood open to the air for sixty-six years. (Reps. 139, folios 20 and 81; 140, folio 80.) During that period the Bench had suffered from the cold but been reasonably protected against stench and the risk of infection. Now they had to suffer both, with little alleviation of the cold. In 1750, sixty people died, including several judges and aldermen, from gaol-fever (a form of typhus) in a single Sessions. Thereafter, the judges used nosegays, and the fumes from a neighbouring vinegar-distillery were piped in to counteract the stink of the prisoners.

Appendix V

Some time after completing this book, while researching another subject altogether, I came across three documents in the Public Records Office that throw a little more light on the Dr. Tilburn affair.

They show that Tilburn was robbed in 1718 by three members of Obadish Lemon's gang, two of them being William Matthews and William Ward, and that Jonathan Wild was a party to the crime in several respects. As related in the narrative, Tilburn applied to Wild, but, for a reason not clearly explained, Ward privately contacted Tilburn and told him the facts. It was then that Tilburn took legal proceedings against Wild, both for the return of his property and to prosecute Wild as an accomplice in the robbery and as a receiver of stolen goods.

The reader may remember that in 1718 Wild had obliged Obadiah Lemon to turn evidence against several members of the gang in order to save his own life, after which Lemon disappears from the records. Lemon's place as an eighteenth-century 'super-grass' was now taken by William Matthews, who, at Wild's instigation, impeached a string of his fellow-thieves in order to escape the gallows. Before Tilburn could bring his actions to court, Wild arrested Ward (among others) and procured Matthews to swear two capital crimes against him: one, the burglary of Mr. Julian Bagley's house in Cripplegate on 24 July 1717, in company with William Matthews, Samuel Linn, David and Alfoy; two, the burglary of Mr. Thomas Lane's house on 12 April 1717, in company with William Matthews only. Ward was tried and convicted at the Old Bailey on 19 January 1719 (i.e. the legal year 1718/19) and condemned to death.

The first document is Ward's petition to the King for a reprieve and transportation, on the grounds that he was 'wholly Innocent of the Fact for wch he is Condemned to Dye', and that he had been convicted 'upon the Bare Evidence of one Wm. Matthews and that out of Reall Mallice on Purpose to take away yor Petitioners Life tho' wrongfully'.

The other two documents are addressed to James Craggs, one of the two Secretaries of State who shared responsibility for home and foreign affairs. The first is a petition similar to the one written to King George I, the second a paper stating the facts of the case, at least as given by Ward. This claims that as a boy Ward had been led into 'base Actions' by such people as Matthews and Wild (spelt 'Wylde'), but, repenting, had turned evidence against them. Although still under 21 years old, he had a wife and two small children who were now destitute. Wild had managed things so cleverly at the Old Bailey that Ward and his fellow-victims had been brought to trial 'on a Surprize', before they had had time to prepare their defence. Dr. Tilburn (spelt 'Tilburge') was especially distressed, for in persuading Ward to turn evidence he had had 'no other vision but ye saving of this poor Unfortunate man's Life'.

Yet his ultimate purpose was to make the Secretary of State aware of what was really going on, and of how Wild, the supposed Regulator of law and order, was in fact the ruler of the criminal underworld, 'for what will not or Cannott such a Villainous person as Wylde Do who has a hundred thieffes at his Comand to swear as he directs them against any person he pleases?'

At this time Craggs was preoccupied by the problems of making a financial killing out of the South Sea Bubble swindle, of which he had been a major perpetrator, and could not be bothered with a trivial matter such as this. The petition of Craggs was ignored, that to the King refused, and Ward was hanged on 13 February 1719. When Tilburn brought his case against Wild in April and May 1719, Wild, as explained on pp. 95–7, extricated himself by means of legal hair-splitting. He had, besides, already hanged Tilburn's witnesses. The reader may remember that William Matthews too fell victim to Wild in 1720.

These papers are at S.P. 35/78/6–10 in the Rolls Room of the Public Records Office at Chancery Lane. The original trial documents in the GLC Records Office are, at the time of writing (September 1986), too fragile to be inspected, but they can be checked against the Old Bailey Sessions Papers for 1718/19 in the Guildhall Library. It is interesting that someone has written *'Wylde'* in the margin beside these trial reports, as well as beside those concerning other victims of his, in a handwriting that is not dissimilar to Wild's own. I wonder to whom this particular set of Sessions Papers originally belonged?

Gerald Howson
1986

Bibliography

As many of the pamphlets have been difficult to unearth, I have put British Museum or Guidhall Library references against items where possible.

I JONATHAN WILD

1 Warrant and Schedules of Jonathan Wild in Wood Street Compter 1712. MSS. Guildhall Records Office, *Shelf 228, MSS Relating to Insolvent Debtors.*
2 *A True Discovery of the Conduct of Receivers and Thief-Takers, In and About the City of London: etc.* by Charles Hitchen (April 1718?). BM 518 L 30.
3 *An Answer to a Late Insolent Libel* . . . Anon. but at instigation of Jonathan Wild (May 1718?). BM 6496 aa 20(1).
Guildhall A 1 2 65s. Guildhall copy printed by T. Warner. Someone has written 'by Jonathan Wild TT' in ink on title page, but it is not Wild's handwriting.
4 *The Regulator: Or a Discovery of Thieves etc.* by *A Prisoner in Newgate* (actually Hitchen) (June 1718). BM 518 e 20(12). Guildhall PAM 5191. An amplification of parts of (2) with names of the miscreants, some lists, and a canting dictionary added.
5 *Petition for the Freedom of City of London* by Wild. 2 June 1724. Entered in Rep. of Court of Aldermen on that date. Quoted in *The Times*, 6 May 1841, and *Chambers's Book of Days*, though both give wrong dates.

6 Three letters from Wild to Earl of Dartmouth in Staffordshire
  County Records Office. D 1778/IV/2. Previously printed in HMC
  13th Report, Appendix IV (HMC 31) pp 496–7.

7 *Newgate's Garland: Or Blueskin's Ballad* (by Swift?). Printed on back
  of *St. James's Post*, 28 Nov 1715, probably because no other sheets
  were available. BM 1876 f 1 (74b), also 515 1 22 (223).

8 *British Journal*, 27 Feb to 27 March 1725. Four articles by
  Philanthropos (Bernard de Mandeville) later expanded into a
  pamphlet *An Inquiry into the Cause of the frequent Executions at
  Tyburn* (April 1725).

9 *An Authentic Narrative of the Parentage, Birth, Education and
  Practices of Jonathan Wild, Citizen and Thief Taker of London, together
  with an Account of his Marriages, Issue etc., with his Effigy.* Sold by A.
  Moor, 6d. April 1725.

10 *An Authentic Narrative of the Life & Actions of Jonathan Wild
   (Citizen and Thief-Taker of London) With the Crimes he stands charg'd
   with, upon a Commitment sign'd by Twelve of His Majesty's Justices of
   the Peace. To which is Prefix'd, His Effigies curiously engraven on a Copper
   Plate, and drawn from the Life by an Eminant Master.* Library of
   Trinity College, Dublin, QQ K 57 No 5. Probably same as (9).

11 *An Authentic History of the Parentage etc. of the Famous Jonathan Wild
   etc.* (Title as (10) with slight variations.) 'Printed from the London
   Copy at Stamford.' 4d. BM 1419 i 25. Text same as (10).

12 *The Ordinary of Newgate's Accounts of the Behaviour of the Prisoners etc.*
   (including Wild's). BM 6495 K 7. Missing from shelf. It was probably
   a forgery. A reprint of the Ordinary's authentic account in *The
   Political State of Great Britain*, vol 29 pp 507–10.

13 *The Funeral Procession of Ionathan Wild*, BM Satirical Prints, vol 9,
   No 1751. No 1752 is the *Funeral Ticket* (May 1725).

14 *Jonathan Wild's Complaint or England's Ingratitude.* A Dublin reprint
   of poem on (13). BM G 121 g 8.

15 *Jonathan Wild's Last Farewell to the World.* A ballad. BM 1872 al (95).

16 *The Whole Proceedings of the Trials of Jonathan Wild etc.* (15 May
   1725). A broadsheet, and definitely not the 'whole Proceedings'.
   On same sheet is mounted '*The Humble Petition for a Reprieve . . .*
   BM 1851 c 10 (39).

17 *The Thief-Taker Taken.* A broadsheet of engravings (adv. *Daily
   Journal*, 20 May 1725.)

18 *The Life of Jonathan Wild, from his Birth to his Death* by 'H.D. Clerk
   to Justice R—'. (29 May and 6 July 1725). BM 1419 i 26. Best of
   the semi-satirical biographies, and many of the anecdotes can be
   found to have been based on truth, even if not very accurate. Was
   published in direct rivalry to (22). John Robert Moore gives this
   to Defoe, as well as the generally-agreed (22). It was published and
   sold by Thomas Warner.

19 *The Life and Glorious Actions of the Most Heroic and Magnanimous Jonathan Wilde, Generalissimo of the Prig-Forces in Great Britain and Ireland. Introduced with the most Memorable Passages in the Lives of his Ancestors etc.* (adv. *Daily Post,* 31 May 1725). Sold by H. Whitbridge, 1*s.* Copy in Trinity College Library, Dublin, QQ K 57 No 4. A curious production, in which some valuable information about the methods of extorting money from debtors used by bailiffs is mixed with utter nonsense, shading from inaccuracy to self-confessed fantasy. It obviously had a considerable influence on Henry Fielding in the composition of *Jonathan Wild.* There is a canting vocabulary of doubtful value, which is nevertheless interesting.

20 *The Life of Jonathan Wilde, Thief-Taker General of Great Britain & Ireland* (1725). Sold by W. Dicey of Northampton. BM 12331 ee 31 (13). Almost identical to (18) but pretends to quote from 'Jonathan's Diary'.

21 *The Life & Actions of Jonathan Wilde* (Gloucester, May or June 1725). BM 10825 aa 18. Missing from shelf. A passage quoted in the *Everyman* edition of Fielding's *Jonathan Wild* is identical to one in (18), and so it is probably the same as (20).

22 *A True & Genuine Account of the Life and Actions of the late Jonathan Wild, Not made up of Fiction and Fable, but taken from his Own Mouth, and collected from PAPERS of his Own Writing.* Printed and sold by John Applebee (8, 10, 12 June 1725). BM C 71 bb 3 (8733). Attributed to Defoe. Frontispiece looks more authentic than the others. However, an advertisement in the *Daily Journal* (which T. Warner printed for Applebee) of 31 May for 'H.D.'s' life (18), also printed by Warner, adds: 'N.B. An Advertisement was published in the name of *Applebee,* giving Notice, that all accounts of this Malefactor are Spurious, except what shall be printed by him: we think fit to advise that this is not published by Applebee, nor were any part of the Materials ever in his Hands; and it will soon be seen which Account is supported by the best Authorities.' Modern reprints in vol 16 of Defoe's *Works* (*Nickerson* 1903), Follett's edition of Fielding's novel (N.Y. 1926), by Alfred A. Knopf (1927), and *Freebooters & Buccaneers* (Dial 1935).

23 *Life of Jonathan Wild* by *Chronicon Newquissimus.* (Ref. *The Roots of Evil* by Edward Cadogan, bibliog.)

24 *Weighley alias Wild, a Poem etc.* by N.P. (July 1725). BM 11716 aa 30. At least has the merit that its author did not steal from anyone else, but many details hopelessly wrong.

25 *The History of the Lives & Actions of Jonathan Wild, Blake, Sheppard etc.* Sold by Edw. Midwinter. F. W. Chandler (*Literature of Roguery*) dates this 1750, but I think June 1725–June 1726 more likely. A mixture of (18) and (22). *Jonathan Wild's Canting Dictionary* at end is

reprint of one in *The Triumph of Wit* by John Shirley. BM 10825 aa 16 (3rd edn.). Guildhall A 1 2 46 (7).

26 *The Memoirs of the Life & Times of the famous Jonathan Wild, together with the History & Lives of Modern Rogues* by Capt. Alexander Smith. Sold by Sam. Briscoe. (July 1726). Pilfered from (10) with additions. Also lives of John Allen, James Wright, John alias Richard James, Jack Sheppard, William Blewit, Ed. Burnworth and William Hawkins's version of the Hawkins gang affair. BM 615 a 28. Guildhall BAY H. 64 (or 0 1 1).

27 *The Life & Villainous Actions of that Notorious Offender, Jonathan Wild.* Sold by T. Catesby. (May 1725–June 1726?). Largely identical to (18). Guildhall A 1 2 No 65.

28 *Select Trials at the Old Bailey*, 1735 edition. (See 80.) Most reliable account so far.

29 *Common Sense; Or the Englishman's Journal*, vol 2, p 240–5. A brief account of Wild written for satirical purposes against Walpole. Periodical founded in 1737 by Lord Chesterfield and Lord Lyttleton.

30 *Jonathan Wild's Advice to His Successors* (1758). A satire on magistrates. Guildhall A 8 6 No 27. Reprinted in 1840 edition of Fielding's novel in BM 10827 aa 52.

31 *The History of the Life and Times of Jonathan Wild ... who exceeded all Mankind hitherto born in villainy, ingratitude, duplicity and fraud: ... with a curious History of his Office for the Recovery of Stolen Property.* Sold by William Cole, 10 Newgate St. (*c.* 1810). There is a coloured frontispiece of Blueskin cutting Wild's throat, in which Wild is dressed, and looks, like George III.

32 *The Life & Death of Jonathan Wild* (*c.* 1820). BM. *Not* in catalogue, but at 1490 pp 58. A digest of (18).

33 *The Life & Death Of Jonathan Wild* (1830). BM 10803 bb 28 (4). Missing from shelf.

34 *The History of the House in West Street.* BM copy destroyed in World War II.

35 *Latest Particulars of the Houses in West Street* (1844). BM 6057 a 22, but missing from shelf.

36 *The Old House in West Street, with illustrations* by W. S. Cotterel (1844). Guildhall PAM 5428. Also in Society of Antiquaries Library.

37 *The Life of ... Jonathan Wild; with an account of all his Villanies* (1830–50?). BM 6495 bb 4 (5).

38 *The Bleeding Phantom, Or Wild in Fetters* (after 1840). One of the *Claude Duval Series.* BM 12706 i 40.

39 *Jonathan Wild, Prince of Robbers* by Frederick J. Lyons (*Michael Joseph* 1936). The only book on Wild to date.

40 *Jonathan Wild, Old Time Ace Receiver* by Edwin T. Woodhall (1937).

In the BM at 6059 aaa 9/20, this is an American 'blood and thunder' for children.

41 Accounts in various books: *The Lives of Twelve Bad Men* edited by Thomas Seccomb (1894), life of Wild by Arthur Vincent (a good study); *More Famous Trials* by Lord Birkenhead (1931)—not to be confused with book of the same title by his father in 1928 (the BM have accidentally acquired two copies of the earlier instead of one of each); *The Blind Eye of History* and *The Police Idea* by Charles Reith, the former spoiled by exaggerated claims for Wild, to whom Reith attributes most of the evils now befallen Western (and Eastern) civilization; *The Roots of Evil* by Edward Cadogan; *The Roots of Evil* and *The Road to Tyburn* by Christopher Hibbert; *Hue & Cry* and *The Thief-Takers* by Patrick Pringle; *The Making of Jonathan Wild* by William Robert Irwin (Columbia U.P. 1941), a study of Fielding's novel, with a valuable bibliography; *Dictionary of National Biography* (one of the best short accounts extant, though now out-dated), and in standard histories of London and histories of crime.

42 *The Newgate Calendar* (1773) (5 vols). BM 6495 c 24–28. Also entitled *Malefactor's Register*. This famous series began with *The Bloody Register* of 1764, although the tradition of books of one to four volumes of collected trials and accounts of criminals seems to have begun with *The Tyburn Calendar* of 1700. *Select Trials* was itself in the tradition, but depended on its own shorthand-writers and on direct transcripts of the *Sessions Papers*. *The Newgate Calendar* was the definitive form, but substituted a plain narrative larded with moralizing for the vivid reportage of *Select Trials*. Thereafter it went into about sixteen editions under various titles. Some, like *The Annals of Newgate*, by the Rev. James Villette, were unacknowledged piratings of *Select Trials*. The title, *Newgate Calendar*, comes from the large 'Newgate Calendars' drawn up each month by the Deputy Keepers of Newgate in preparation for the Sessions, which were wrapped round the other documents.

43 *Notes & Queries*. At the turn of the century, this famous periodical published a number of letters about Jonathan Wild, many by Alfred Robbins. Here are the references: 2nd Series vol 2, p 392; 6th Series vol 8, p 126; 7th Series vol 6, pp 227 and 332; 8th Series, pp 77, 81 and 264; 10th Series vol 8, p 452; 10th Series vol 9, pp 56 and 173; 10th Series vol 11, pp 347 and 435; 10th Series vol 12, p 321; 11th Series vol 2, p 261; 11th Series vol 4, pp 305, 308 and 357; 12th Series vol 2, 2 December 1916; 12th Series vol 3, p 38.

II CONTEMPORARY PAMPHLETS AND TRACTS ON CRIMINALS

44 *Memoirs of the right villainous John Hall* (1708). This famous pamphlet, written in a style rather similar to Ned Ward's, went into several editions, and is still widely quoted because of its description of Newgate and its dictionary of canting terms.

45 *The Whole Life & History of Benjamin Child*. Sold by A. Moor. (1722). BM 518 f 35 and 1415 e 57.

46 *A Narrative of the Life of Benjamin Childe etc*. 'Written by Himself' (1722). Guildhall PAM 8904 (in old catalogue only). A less silly account than (45).

47 *A Full and Impartial Account of . . . Robberies by Hawkins and Simpson* by Ralph Wilson. Sold by J. Peele, 6*d*. (1st edn. 24 May 1722; 4th edn. 29 May—adv. in *Daily Post*). BM 06496 aa 7.

48 *Tyburn Worthies; or The Robberies & Enterprizes of John Hawkins & George Simpson*. Sold by T. Warner (28 May 1722—adv. in *Daily Journal*). One of a series. BM T 1092 (5).

49 Accounts of Hawkins gang by 'E.M.', J. Peale (*not* by Wilson), J. Applebee, T. Sharpe (publisher of *The Freeholder*) and Rev. Thomas Purney. Not in BM.

50 *A Full, True and Impartial Account etc*. by William Hawkins. Sold by Sam. Briscoe, 1*s*. (1st edn. 3 July 1722; 2nd edn. 6 July—*Post Boy*). Probably written by Richard Burridge. BM G 19418 (1). 3rd edn. 1788 at 12612 a 33 (2).

51 *The Thief's Importunity to Christ Upon the Cross*. Supposed to be a sermon by 'John Hawkins A.M.' (i.e. M.A.) delivered in Newgate Chapel before execution. Adv. *Daily Journal*, 21 May 1722.

52 *A Complete & True Account of all the Robberies . . . by James Carrick, John Malhoni, and their Accomplices . . .*'. Sold by J. Peele, 6*d*. (23 July 1722). BM 518 e 20. Seems to be mostly fiction.

53 *Tyburn Worthies*—a number devoted to Carrick, etc. (1722).

54 *Life of Captain John Stanley*. Sold by J. Applebee. (1723). Probably by Thomas Purney and written, as *Select Trials* says, in the 'Sublime' style. Contains a story about Moll King. BM 1132 f 32.

55 *The History of the Remarkable Life of John Sheppard*. Sold by J. Applebee, 1*s*. (three editions: 19 Oct 1724; 26 Oct; 12 Nov). Probably by Defoe. Reprinted in *Trial of Jack Sheppard* by Horace Bleakley (*Notable British Trials Series*, William Hodge and Co. 1933); vol 16 of Defoe's *Works* (*Nickerson* 1903) and *Freebooters & Buccaneers* (Dial 1935).

56 *A Narrative of all the Robberies . . . of Jack Sheppard*. Sold by Applebee. Pretending to be a confession, probably written by Defoe. At the gallows, Sheppard 'gave' the manuscript to

'Applebee's Man' (seven editions : 17 Nov; 18 Nov; 19 Nov; 20 Nov; 21 Nov; 28 Nov; 12 Dec 1724. Also a Dublin edition and a French (*La Vie et les Vols du fameux Jean Sheppard*), 1725.

57 *Authentick Memoirs . . . of John Sheppard*. Sold by Joseph Marshall (1724). Told in form of letters.

58 *The Life & Adventures of Jack Sheppard, executed at Tyburn*. London (1724).

59 *Sheppard in Egypt*, & *A Dialogue between Julius Caesar & Jack Sheppard*, both published in 1724, the latter in *British Journal* (3 Dec.).

60 Three plays : *Harlequin Sheppard* (28 Nov 1724); *The Prison Breaker*; *The Quaker's Opera* (1728).

61 *Epistle from Jack Sheppard to the Late Lord Chancellor of England*, to be sung to the tune of 'Which Nobody Can Deny'.' A broadsheet.

62 *Lives of Six Notorious Robbers* (1726). An account of Burnworth and his gang. Probably by Defoe (though not in J. R. Moore's *Checklist*). Reprinted in vol 16 of Defoe's *Works* and *Freebooters & Buccaneers* (Dial 1935).

63 *An Account of the Lives if Edw. Burnworth alias Frazier, Blewit etc. . . .'.* Sold by J. Roberts (April 1726). BM 6496 aaa 1.

64 *A True & Exact Account of the Lives of Edward Burnworth alias Frazier etc.'* Sold by Applebee, May 1726. Close to, but slightly different from, (63). BM 6496 aa 20 (2).

65 *The Matchless Rogue; Or an Account of Tom Merryman, or Newgate Tom etc.'* Sold by A. Moor. (Jan 1725). BM 1417 e 9.

66 *A Genuine Narrative of all the Street Robberies of James Dalton etc.* With a 'Key to the Canting Language' having a few words not in other dictionaries. This was published while Dalton was in Newgate expecting to be hanged, 1728. However, he was acquitted and not caught again until 1730. BM 1080 m 32 (2). Guildhall A 1 2 No 59 (in old catalogue).

67 *The Life of Martin Bellamy, with an Account of the Several Street-robberies, Burglaries, Forgeries & other Crimes by him committed etc.* 'by Himself'. Sold by John Applebee (1728). BM 1416 c 59. Contains story of his forging Wild's signature on a bank-note. See Chapter XIV.

68 *A Genuine Narrative of the Memorable Life & Actions of John Dyer, who was executed at Tyburn on Friday the 21st Day of November 1729, wrote by himself*. Sold by Applebee and others, 6d. BM 1416 f 56; and 518 f 37. By one of Wild's nastiest 'affidavit men' (see Chapter XVIII), who carefully avoids saying anything about his real life.

69 *A Genuine Narrative of the Memorable Life & Actions of John Everett* (1730). Sold by Applebee. BM 6496 h 2 (3). Missing from shelf, probably destroyed in World War II. The account in *Lives*

of the Most Remarkable Criminals seems to have drawn heavily on this pamphlet, and it is quoted extensively in *Hitchin Worthies* by R. L. Hine. Everett was the bully of 'Callico Sarah' (see Chapter XVI).

70 *Life & Actions of James Dalton etc.* Sold by R. Walker, 1s. (1730). Published after Dalton's execution. BM 615 b 29. Guildhall copy destroyed in World War II

71 *The Life & Actions of John Waller, who made his Exit in the Pillory at the 7 Dials on 13 May 1732; containing all the Villainies . . . swearing Robberies against innocent People, to take away their lives for the Sake of the Rewards granted by Act of Parliament . . .* Sold by W. James, 6d. (1732). BM 518 3 20 (bound in with *The Regulator* and other tracts). Waller's 'Exit' was in fact being torn out of the pillory, trampled and finally dismembered by the mob.

72 *The Life of that Perjur'd Villain, John Waller* (1732). Referred to by F. W. Chandler (*The Literature of Roguery*).

73 *A Full & Particular Account of the Life & Notorious Actions of Roger Johnson.* Sold by C. Cotbett, 6d. (1740). BM 10825 c 34. Says little of Johnson's years with Wild, but a great deal of his life afterwards. One of the better criminal pamphlets. Fielding was doubtless familiar with it, for he used Johnson's name in his novel as a ruler of the prisoners in Newgate. The author also makes the familiar parallel between politicians and thieves.

III BIOGRAPHICAL COLLECTIONS AND TRIAL REPORTS

74 *Complete History of the Lives of the Most Notorious Highwaymen,* by Capt. Alexander Smith. Five editions from 1714 to 1719. Republished complete by Routledge in 1933.

75 *A Compleat Collection of Notable Tryals* by N.B. (1718–21). Precursor of *Select Trials.* BM 518 b 1/2.

76 *A History of the Robberies of all the celebrated Highwaymen to the Year 1722* (adv. July–August 1722). Ref. *Defoe* by W. Lee, vol 1, p 343.

77 *Lives of the Most Notorious Highwaymen* by 'J.W.' 23 July 1722—adv. in *Daily Courant*) 2nd edn. 1724. Contains lives of Benjamin Child (better than in the pamphlets), Carrick and others. BM 6056 pp 44.

78 *An Account of the Lives, Intrigues etc. of Rob Roy, Capt. Stanley, Sally Salisbury & near an 100 more . . .'.* Sold by M. Hothram, 1s. 6d. April 1724.

79 *A History of Executions* (1731). A series in twelve parts sold by Applebee (incl. Dalton, Hackabout, etc.) BM 6495 a 25. This and Guildhall copies destroyed in World War II.

80 *Select Trials at the Sessions House in the Old Bailey.* A 2-vol edn.—adv. in *Post Boy,* 17–19 Jan 1730. Sold by Brotherton and others.

1734–5 edn. (2 vols) sold by J. Wilford, in BM at 6495 aaa 14, though vol 1 seems to be missing. Another copy in Soc. of Antiquaries Library. Several 4-vol editions put out in 1742 by L. Gilliver, Applebee and in Dublin. BM 518 b 6 and 06946 a 25. Guildhall AN 33 1.

81 *A General History of . . . Highwaymen* by Capt. Charles Johnson (1734). Mostly taken from Smith. 1734 edn. with good illustrations in BM C 59 h 1.

82 *Lives of Noted Highwaymen* (1750). Sold by H. Fenwick. BM 1414 e 10

83 *Lives of the Most Remarkable Criminals.* Sold by John Osbourne in 4 vols. Usually dated 1735, but the life of Wild, for instance, is identical with that in (81), while much of (81) was pilfered from Capt. Smith (74). Republished by Routledge in 1927.

84 *Lives of Noted Highwaymen, viz: Du Vall, Atkinson, Rowland etc.* Sold by T. Fenwick. BM 1414 e 10.

85 *A History of Notorious Highwaymen.* Sold by J. Lever. BM 1132 a 57.

86 *A Select and Impartial Account of the most Remarkable Convicts.* Sold by C. Marsh and Applebee (1745–50). Library of Society of Antiquaries.

IV SESSIONS PAPERS

'Sessions Newspapers' would have been a better term. Published after every Sessions; until 1730 in a newspaper format (14 in. × 8½ in.), after that in a smaller (8½ × 6 in.) Until *c.* 1716, the trial reports were very brief, but thereafter the reporters began to include verbatim speeches from the evidence. Thus the *Sessions Papers* became one of the most valuable (and readable) sources of eighteenth century social history we have. Sheets of before 1730 are now very rare. Those in the BM are catalogued under *London ii—Civic and Municipal Institutions—Sessions,* and their full title is *The Complete Proceedings on the King's Commission of the Sessions of the Peace, of Oyer and Terminer, and of Gaol Delivery,* followed by the place. The trial reports in *Select Trials* are usually fuller than those in surviving *Sessions Papers,* but then the originals would have included all the minor cases, which would have made research for this book easier. The presence of the reporters in the Old Bailey court was permitted only in exchange for a fee, and the *Sessions Papers* were regarded as a frankly commercial speculation.

V SESSIONS RECORDS

Those dealing with crimes committed in the City of London and Liberties are kept in the Guildhall Records Office. Those dealing with crimes committed in Westminster or Middlesex are kept at the Middlesex Records Office, 1 Queen Anne's Gate Building, Dartmouth Street, S.W.1. The Middx. records ıre more complicated and may be dealt with first. There are two main categories of documents relevant to our purpose here: Sessions of the Peace Rolls (for misdemeanours and lesser offences); and Gaol Delivery Rolls for all felonies—the Sessions of Oyer and Terminer documents are therefore included in the GD rolls. Each gaol submitted its own SP roll for each sessions— Gatehouse, New Prison, Clerkenwell–Bridewell, etc.—but the GD rolls are for Newgate only, because all prisoners to be tried under Oyer and Terminer and Gaol Delivery *had* to be in Newgate the day before their trials. As we are more concerned with GD rolls, a description of them will suffice for the others: a 'roll' consists of recognizances, bail bonds, jury lists, Grand Jury precepts, coroners' reports (with wavy edges), depositions, bills of indictment, and informations, piled *in that order* (though not all such documents are always present) and wrapped inside the large *Newgate Calendar*. This was a list, in English (the other documents being in abbreviated Latin), of all prisoners committed to Newgate since the last Sessions, together with lists of prisoners 'upon Orders'—that is, awaiting transportation, further punishment, further trial, etc. Because these large parchments were rolled round the other documents, the files have always been called 'Rolls' (which, strictly, they are not). Indictments are numbered according to order of trial, with brief scribbled signs at the top to indicate the outcome of the prisoner's case. Besides the rolls there are Calendar Books of Indictments (useful for finding prisoners' documents), Sessions Books (lists of juries, judges, and cases to be tried, again with notes of the outcome of each case scribbled *above* the names, together with lists of witnesses), and boxes of Sessions Papers (miscellaneous documents dealing with the Sessions, and not to be confused with the printed *Sessions Papers* described above). Finally, the names of witnesses were written on the backs of the indictments, and these, together with the names in the GD Books, have been essential in unravelling the intrigues of Jonathan Wild. The City of London records, being less voluminous, are simpler, the SP and GD rolls being often combined into one. There is, however, no Calendar of Indictments before 1716.

VI GENERAL

It is perhaps hardly necessary to give a list of books dealing with the period as a whole, for excellent bibliographies can be found in standard works on the subject. Many of these are in any case referred to in the text and notes, besides those more special ones, such as Radzinowicz's *History of English Criminal Law*, which have been referred to

repeatedly. A few, however, have been of more than a general use:
Statutes at Large and *Statutes of the Realm*, both essential to this subject;
The Political State of Britain and *The Historical Register* (published by the
Sun Life Insurance Company), two monthly digests of events and news
of the period; The Burney Collection of newspapers in the British
Museum; *Travels in England* by M. Misson, and *Letters from England* by
Baron Muralt, two informative contemporary travel books rich with
social details; Defoe's *Tour Thro' Great Britain*; various seventeenth-
and eighteenth-century dictionaries of cant (e.g. *New Canting Dictionary*,
1725). Among modern works have been: *Mid-Georgian London* by
Hugh Phillips (Collins 1964), a near-encyclopaedia of eighteenth-
century Westminster with superb illustrations; *Hogarth's Graphic
Works* by Ronald Paulson (Yale); *Checklist of Defoe's Writings*, and other
books, by John Robert Moore; *Dictionary of the Underworld* by Eric
Partridge (Routledge); *Anecdotes of London in the 18th-century* by J.P.
Malcom (1820), a quaint book full of out-of-the-way information
and quotations from now lost sources; and finally, *London Life in the
18th-century* by Dorothy George (now available as a *Peregrine Book*).

Index

A NOTE TO READERS

We hope you have enjoyed this Cresset Library edition and would like to take this opportunity to invite you to put forward your suggestions about books that might be included in the series.

The Cresset Library was conceived as a forum for bringing back books that we felt should be widely available in attractively designed and priced paperback editions. The series themes can be loosely described as social, cultural, and intellectual history though, as you can see from the list of published titles at the front of this book, these themes cover a broad range of interest areas.

If you have read or know of books that fall into this category which are no longer available or not available in paperback, please write and tell us about them. Should we publish a book that you have suggested we will send you a free copy upon publication together with three other Cresset Library titles of your choice.

Please address your letter to Claire L'Enfant at:-

> Century Hutchinson
> FREEPOST
> London
> WC2N 4BR

There is no need to stamp your envelope.

We look forward to hearing from you.

THE CRESSET LIBRARY